LANDSCAPES OF THE SACRED

LANDSCAPES
OF THE SACRED

Geography and Narrative
in American Spirituality

Expanded Edition

Belden C. Lane

THE JOHNS HOPKINS UNIVERSITY PRESS
Baltimore and London

© 1988, 2001 Belden C. Lane
All rights reserved. Published 2002
Printed in the United States of America on acid-free paper
9 8 7 6 5 4 3 2 1

Text design by Ellen Whitney

The Johns Hopkins University Press
2715 North Charles Street
Baltimore, Maryland 21218-4363
www.press.jhu.edu

Library of Congress Cataloging-in-Publication Data

Lane, Belden C., 1943–
   Landscapes of the sacred : geography and narrative in American
spirituality / Belden C. Lane—Expanded ed.
      p.   cm.
   Includes bibliographical references.
   ISBN 0-8018-6838-6 (pbk. : alk. paper)
   1. Sacred space—United States—History. 2. Spirituality—United States—
History. 3. United States—Religion. I. Title

BL 2525 .L36 2001
291.3'5'0973—dc21   2001038080

A catalog record for this book is available from the British Library.

Reflections on a Hermeneutics of Landscape

Tell me the landscape in which you live and I will tell you who you are.

—Ortega y Gasset

What we have here is a sacred, mythic geography, the only kind effectually *real*, as opposed to profane geography, the latter being "objective" and as it were abstract and non-essential—the theoretical construction of a space and a world that we do not live in, and therefore do not *know*.

—Mircea Eliade, *Images and Symbols*

Space has a spiritual equivalent and can heal what is divided and burdensome in us.

—Gretel Ehrlich, *The Solace of Open Spaces*

Space is the central fact to man born in America.

—Charles Olson

In the United States there is more space where nobody is than where anybody is. This is what makes America what it is.

—Gertrude Stein, *The Geographical History of America*

We . . . need that wild country . . . even if we never do more than drive to its edge and look in. For it can be . . . a part of the geography of hope.

—Wallace Stegner

Our American land, too, is an artifact. . . . The American artifact incarnates history enormously. It speaks, incessantly babbling myth. We should learn the landscape's language.

—Henry Glassie, *"The Artifact's Place in American Studies"*

A primal desire of man is the imaginative impulse—working under the special conditions of our time . . . to visit strange regions in search of such beauty, awe or terror as the actual world does not supply.

—C. S. Lewis, *Of Other Worlds*

The views of nature held by any people determine all their institutions.

—Ralph Waldo Emerson, *English Traits*

When the Romans sought to punish the Carthaginians for disobedience by razing their city to the ground, citizens of Carthage begged their masters to spare the physical city, its stones and temples, to which no possible guilt could be attached, and instead, if necessary, exterminate the entire population.

—Yi-Fu Tuan, *Topophilia*

What the Mediterranean Sea was to the Greeks, breaking the bond of custom, offering new experiences, calling out new institutions and activities, that, and more, the ever retreating frontier has been to the United States.

—Frederick Jackson Turner

The important determinate of any culture is after all—the spirit of place.

—Lawrence Durrell

Theological reflections on place can no longer ignore that the world of concrete places is full of exiles, displaced peoples, diaspora communities, increasingly inflamed border disputes and the violent struggles by indigenous people and cultural minorities to achieve liberation.

—Philip Sheldrake, *Spaces for the Sacred*

Contents

Preface to the Johns Hopkins Edition

"My wound is geography," writes Southern novelist Pat Conroy. "It is also my anchorage, my port of call."[1] Some wounds—we are grateful to confess—never heal. They grow with us, festering and prodding, reminding us often that the wound is what grants the storyteller his narrative power. Most people, I suspect, can plot a geography of broken places in their lives, pointing to fierce landscapes and threatening terrain they have negotiated alone or with others. Their wound even becomes, sometimes, an anchorage.[2]

As a scholar absorbed in questions of American spirituality and landscape, focusing on actual places and the human experiences of them, I acknowledge that geography has remained for me a wound that refuses to heal, an anchorage that offers balance. The quest for the mystery of place functions as an infirmity of sorts, summoning ever-new forms of diagnosis and methods of treatment. Understanding the incurable attraction of human beings to places they perceive as sacred is an "affliction" I have come to love. I can't get over it.

But the "therapeutic approaches" that I have used through the years in dealing with the subject keep changing. More than a decade ago, when the first edition of this book appeared, my tendency was to emphasize the individual human appropriation of sacred places, focusing more on the spiritualized significance that people attribute to a place than on the place itself as a cultural and phenomenological reality. Influenced by the work of Mircea Eliade, I knew that the enduring identity of a sacred place lies in the stories it bears and the power that these tales exert on the people who repeat them. I am still convinced that this is profoundly important. Yet it can also lend itself to an individualized (even ideological) appropriation of place narratives that quickly strips them of their cultural and material roots in order to serve larger spiritual (or didactic) ends.

In the first writing of this book I had not yet attended enough to a larger critical reflection on place, considering the extent to which sacred sites become a battleground of conflicting claims based on a multitude of cultural voices. Nor had I done enough to analyze the incredible variations of urban as well as rural places, built as well as natural landscapes. In short, the shift from modernity to postmodernity in recent cultural understandings of place had largely been ignored. I have begun to correct that in this new edition.

Over the last fifteen years, there has been enormous interest in matters of spirituality and place. Scholars in religious studies from Robert Orsi to Colleen McDannell have investigated a wide range of devotional sites in popular spirituality—exploring Italian street festivals, shrines to St. Jude, and the function of the Bible in nineteenth-century Victorian homes.[3] Others, like Edward Linenthal, have focused on the religious meanings of public monuments, from the Holocaust Museum in Washington, D.C., to the Oklahoma City memorial for those killed in the bombing of the Murrah Federal Building.[4] In biblical studies, Theodore Hiebert's book *The Yahwist's Landscape* has redefined the way we understand ancient Israelite farmers and their relation to nature and the land.[5] Churches and religious communities have paid more and more attention to architectural space, witnessed for example in the Catholic bishops' statements on environment and worship.[6] Meanwhile, social anthropologists, city planners, and architectural designers have produced shelves after shelves of new books on every possible dimension of place.[7]

This enlarged edition of *Landscapes of the Sacred* is an effort to update its original work in light of this expanded dialogue. At the same time it tries to preserve the narrative style and sense of personal engagement that characterized the first edition. I would still argue that the role of the storyteller is essential in grasping the power that place exerts on the religious imagination. We never exhaust the mystery of a devotional site by simply unraveling the cultural threads from which it is woven. Analyzing a spirituality requires the poet and the theologian as well as the geographer and the cultural historian of religion. The religious perspective of those who perceive a place as sacred is certainly a constitutive part of their seeing, as American studies scholar Rowland Sherrill admits. This is "a fact less attended to these days, but one which adamantly will not go away."[8]

The book, as now arranged, is divided into three parts. The first, Place in American Religious Life, contains a new chapter, "Giving Voice to Place," that balances Eliade's perspective with views on the cultural construction and phenomenological integrity of sites considered sacred. Part Two provides a Geography of American Spiritual Traditions and is drawn unchanged from the first edition. Its chapter on Native American spirituality and place obviously needs the critical cultural awareness I have called for here, but rewriting it would have required another book. Part Three offers a new section on Method and Perspective in Studying American Spirituality and Place, reflecting on the difficult task of defining and analyzing the religious experience of sacred place, especially within the Christian tradition. My hope is that the new book supplies a better introduction to questions both of sacred space and of the emerging academic discipline of spirituality.

University of New Mexico anthropologist Keith Basso tells a story of stringing barbed wire one summer with two Apache cowboys from eastern Colorado. He noticed one of them talking to himself as he worked and soon realized that he was reciting a long list of place-names, punctuated only by occasional spurts of tobacco juice. They were the names of places familiar to him back home: sacred places. Most of them took the form of broken sentences, telling a story, as place-names often do. When asked about this half-conscious habit of listing places—almost as if he were saying a rosary—the Apache cowhand replied that the names were simply good to say. Repeating them was for him almost a way of being there once again.

I can identify with that. My own list of place-names, mumbled unconsciously through the writing of this book, will become apparent in its reading. At different times and in different ways, each has mediated the holy for me. All of us carry inside of ourselves a similar list of places. This book is simply an exercise in trying to help us name them more carefully and consciously.

Working on the book has also required another listing of names—people who have helped make it possible. Henry Tom, executive editor of the Johns Hopkins University Press, is himself keenly interested in issues of religion and place and has provided unwavering support in bringing this book to a second life. I'm also grateful to the editors of journals in which some of these chapters appeared in earlier forms, including the *Christian Century*, the *Way*, the *Christian Spirituality Bulletin*, and *Religion and American Culture*.

I owe many intellectual debts to the cultural historians of religion already mentioned, as well as to my colleague James T. Fisher, at Saint Louis University. In the developing field of spirituality, my most important mentors and friends have been Douglas Burton-

Christie, editor of *Spiritus: A Journal of Christian Spirituality,* and Philip Sheldrake, whose Hulsean Lectures on Sacred Space, at Cambridge University, are just now appearing in print.[9] They, too, know the wound of geography and have been my most esteemed teachers. Doug has been friend and brother to me. Nor can I forget my students, who have helped to shape this manuscript in various ways over the years: Peter Huff, John and Dana Mellis, Judy Eby, RSM, Laura Hobgood-Oster, Paul Myhre, Kevin Hester, Patrick Landewe, and Dennis Durst.

Finally, I wish to thank my wife, Patricia. We have been "home" and "place" to each other all of our lives. Because of her, I warm so readily to the words of a crotchety farmer from Kentucky named Wendell Berry. He knows the restlessness of the American quest for a better place, the ultimate inability of geography to heal, and the deep, deep mystery of home.

> Another place!
> it's enough to grieve me—
> that old dream of going,
> of becoming a better man
> just by getting up and going
> to a better place.[10]

God meets us where we are, in other words. That's all he or I mean to say. But finding ourselves where we are is always the hardest part. For that we need others.

Feastday of George Herbert, poet and priest
February 27, 2001

LANDSCAPES OF THE SACRED

Introduction:
Meaning and Place in
American Spirituality

The top of Kitchen Mesa at Ghost Ranch, New Mexico, is an immense cap of rimrock shorn of any protection from early summer thunderstorms. I climbed it alone one June afternoon, seeking escape from my own words and the teaching I had been doing down below at the Presbyterian Conference Center. I should have been more alert, noticing clouds that were gathering to the north. But the storm was on me before I could flee the mesa and find shelter. Cowering in a crevice of rock beside what was left of an old piñon tree, I protected my head from hailstones and began counting the shortening seconds between lightning flashes and thunderclaps. Suddenly there was no interval between light and sound, only instant terror and the smell of ozone filling the air, followed by the surprise of still being alive.

If I had come to northern New Mexico to meet God in a desert seminar, I ended up getting more than I bargained for—a long hour huddled in freezing rain without proper gear, fears of hypothermia as well as lightning strike, and the long embarrassment of a well-crafted lesson in stupidity. These were as much a part of my "experience of God" in leaving the mesa that afternoon as the memory of random patches of sun eventually breaking through the clouds onto the valley below.

Like many others, I have come to love Ghost Ranch, considering it a sacred place of sorts. Even Georgia O'Keeffe, not ordinarily inclined to religious language, felt the same way. Of her love for Pedernal, the mountain on the horizon south of the ranch, she used to say that if she painted it enough God might give it to her. Identifying the sacred character of a place, however, involves much more than gathering the random accounts of its individual spiritual encounters, significant as these may be. To experience a place as

3

sacred is to participate, knowingly or unknowingly, in a whole history of cultural tensions and conflicting claims, even ecological shifts in the terrain itself.

Located on the northern edge of the eighteenth-century Piedre Lumbre Land Grant region, Ghost Ranch has through the years been fought over by Spanish settlers, raiding parties of Comanches and Utes, the U.S. Forest Service, and land developers of various sorts. In 1966, nearby Echo Amphitheater was seized and occupied by local Hispanos laying claim to the "commons" that were said to have been guaranteed in the original land grants. Some of them proclaimed a free republic, seeking independence from the United States.

As a bioregion, the land including Ghost Ranch has suffered severe devegetation due to overgrazing by livestock, especially sheep, since the nineteenth century. This, in turn, has brought flooding and gullying, which eventually led to the construction of the Abiquiu Dam in the 1960's, putting 14,000 acres of the beautiful Chama River Valley under water. Recreation now threatens to destroy much of what is left.[1] Such is the wider history of experience that shapes the reality of a "sacred place" like Ghost Ranch. To ignore this part of the story is to betray the dignity of the land itself and to silence the voices of those who have lived upon it and made it their own. Sacred places generate political polarities, just as does the practice of any authentic spirituality.

At the same time, sacred places also participate in the entire array of sensory exchanges that play across the land, reaching far beyond the impact of human influence alone. The motion of wind through the limbs of a juniper tree in a red rock canyon, the long-tailed magpie that leaves seeds of a distant wildflower in its droppings beside a small arroyo, the shifting of rock in a fissure caused by water erosion—these, too, are a part of the dynamic reciprocity that makes up the ambient character of any desert monastery or roadside shrine. Michael Taussig, in his *Mimesis and Alterity*, would suggest that the human understanding of the meaning of a place emerges out of the process of an imitation of all the "differences" that we discern there. We mimic (in language and action) the full range of sounds, movements, and other sensory perceptions that come to us from the more-than-human world.[2] Only in this way do we begin to make sense of it. The place, in other words, demands its own integrity, its own participation in what it "becomes," its own voice. A sacred place is necessarily more than a construction of the human imagination alone.

One of my concerns in the revision of this book, as I take part in the scholarly discourse about the mystery and meaning of place, is to steer a difficult course between the Scylla of the constructivists and the Charybdis of the essentialists. Those who rightly insist on the cultural construction of all placed experience too often ignore the web of interconnectedness that extends deeply into the natural world. On the other hand, those who would emphasize the autonomous, even magical qualities of places that reveal the sacred too easily disregard the social, economic, and political forces that inevitably determine negotiations about their use.

All this raises questions about precisely what we mean when we speak of a place as sacred. How do we understand the interplay of cultural, religious, and ecological forces that constitute the identity of a given site? I remember feeling the pull of these tensions when, shortly after the first appearance of this book, I participated in a panel discussion at the American Academy of Religion. John Sears's *Sacred Places: Pilgrimage Sites in Nineteenth-Century America* (Oxford, 1989) and Ed Linenthal's *Sacred Ground: Americans and Their Battle-fields* (Champaign, Ill., 1991) had also just been published, and the three of us were invited to reflect together on our work. In the lively discussion that followed, some of the people present wanted to set my book over against theirs. They saw Sears and Linenthal as minimizing the "sacredness" of place, reducing it to a matter of cultural forces, while they perceived my book as defending the unique, irreducibly *religious* character of sacred place as religious people experienced it.

I was uncomfortable with too simple a dichotomy between religion and culture, as if one could locate a religious experience of place that was not thoroughly embedded in its cultural milieu. So I didn't know where to situate myself in the midst of this larger debate. On the one hand, I did not want to be co-opted by the "supernaturalist folk," those anxious to identify sacred places on the basis of their inherently sacral character. I balked at the idea of geographical Shrouds of Turin, places that could be used to prove or authenticate genuine religious experiences of the Other, dotting the landscape. And yet I was not comfortable with an exclusively cultural-studies approach either. For me the contested character of sacred places did not exhaust their fullness of meaning. It was not enough to define a holy site as one that people were willing to fight over.

I valued my colleagues' approach in looking at sacred place from the *outside*, as a thoroughgoing cultural construction of reality. This was an important corrective to my own exploration of the same phenomenon from the *inside*, as intimately perceived by the people making claims to its multiple uses and symbolic meanings. But I could not limit the study of place to a complex system of cultural interactions alone. What fascinated me most was the messiness, ambiguity, and mystery of people's deeply personal experience of place, as this works its way through the cultural grid that they inevitably bring to it. That's why this book begins as it does, with an examination of the innermost human experience of place. The construction of personal and communal identity is invariably related to primal spatial categories. Who we are, in other words, is inseparably a part of where we are.

As Gabriel Marcel expressed it, "An individual is not distinct from his place; he is that place."[3] Cultural geographer Yi-Fu Tuan used the word *topophilia* to describe the attachment we often feel for particular places.[4] This may range from the affinity some have for mountainous terrain or the cityscape of large urban centers to the pilgrimage one makes to a particular *loca religiosa* at Mecca, Kyoto, Benares, or the Holy Sepulcher.[5] John K. Wright spoke of the emotional bonds between humans and their earth in terms of *geopiety*. This sacral relation to the earth involves a reciprocity between person and place. As one has been nurtured by the soil and ambience of a given locale, one learns—in turn—to revere the site that has become the anchor of memory.[6] This attachment to place is prevalent in the history of religious experience and is found among various traditions of American spirituality as well.

What Rudolf Otto described as the *mysterium tremendum*, the profoundly disturbing encounter of the holy as "other," is inevitably associated with the particularity of place. The Buddha reached enlightenment, choosing the life of the bodhisattva, under the Bo Tree—the Immovable Spot near Gaya on the floodplain of the Ganges. Moses was instructed to take off his shoes so as to respect the holy ground on which he stood before the burning bush on Mount Horeb. Muhammad first heard the reciting voice of the angel Gabriel in the lonely cave on Mount Hira outside Mecca. Even amid the celebrated rootlessness of American culture, the phenomenon is still observed. The chapel at Valley Forge is a civil pantheon built on hallowed soil. The hill, Cumorah, in Palmyra, New York, is the sacred link of Mormons to an ancient past. Native Americans of the Pacific Northwest still refer to Mount Rainier as Tahoma, "The

Mountain That Was God." Human beings are invariably driven to ground their religious experience in the palpable reality of space.

One way of grasping the importance of this connection is to observe the sense of alienation that prevails when it is lost. Of all twentieth-century philosophers, Martin Heidegger wrote most persuasively of the rampant estrangement from place that is prevalent in contemporary culture. Men and women experience the loss of a place that might give them an "existential foothold" or "dwelling" in the world.[7] Heidegger insisted that "'place' places man in such a way that it reveals the external bonds of his existence and at the same time the depths of his freedom and reality. . . . 'Place' is the house of Being."[8] For Heidegger, a "person" is a *Dasein*, literally translated as a "being there." A person by definition, then, is one who is "placed," one who is "there." Yet despite this longing for anchored existence, a feeling of displacement is today the persistent experience of "the homeless mind." Sam Keen has argued that "the disappearance of a sense of place, of the significance of particular spaces and locations, is one of the deplorable characteristics of our time."[9]

Personal identity is fixed for us by the feel of our own bodies, the naming of the places we occupy, and the environmental objects that beset our landscape. But the effects of modernity, the impact of the technological society, and the various sea changes in our manner of travel and communication have all tended to separate us in the last century from the three-dimensional realities of our world. We feel out of touch, without a place. The impulse of postmodernity has been to recover what was lost. Psychologist Paul Tournier observes that a recurring theme in the dreams of contemporary men and women is that of the seat that cannot be found—the anxiety that one feels in seeking his or her appropriate place at a meeting, on a plane, at a formal banquet."[10]

In short, it is the nature of human beings that they cannot get enough of place. "To be rooted," wrote Simone Weil, "is perhaps the most important and least recognized need of the human soul."[11] If deprived of a sufficient sense of placement in our world, we proceed even to make up places with the power of our own imagination. Soren Kierkegaard, for example, was prevented as a child from playing outside with other children, cut off from the places of normal maturation. But his father made up for the loss by taking him periodically on imaginary trips to the seacoast, to castles in Spain, to the streets of great cities where the father's voice would be drowned out by passing carriages, where a cake lady would sell them goodies surpassing anything the boy had ever tasted in actual life.[12] His desperate need was for a series of fixed points by which he could know his position in the world. In the absence of such secure moorings in the natural environment, the psyche will necessarily demand visionary places of its own: Atlantis, Lilliput, Cibola, Disneyland, and Middle Earth. The human imagination has ever reached—both sublimely and pathetically—for a geography that gives meaning to existence.[13]

As a child, Walt Disney lived for a while in the small north-central Missouri town of Marceline. Years later he would memorialize its downtown area in the stylized Main Street U.S.A. that leads to Sleeping Beauty's Castle at the entrance to Disneyland in southern California. "Main Street," of course, is a wholly artificial place that hardly resembles any actual small town in America.[14] Yet in the fantasy environment of the Disney theme park, it represents the epitome of village life in an imagined American past.

In something of a double irony, over the last couple of years the town of Marceline, Missouri, has tried to capitalize on the reputation of its favorite son, applying for federal grants that would allow it to reconstruct its small business district after the pattern of Main Street in Disneyland. If art imitated life in the first case, this seems a curious case of life imitating art in the second. Yet it exemplifies the longing that people have to be situated in an idealized place that expresses the symbolic life they imagine themselves living. It also epitomizes the growing tendency toward what sociologist Mark Gottdiener calls the "theming of America." Increasingly, we organize the built environment in a symbolic way that reflects the media world of television, commercial advertising, films, music, and fashion.[15] As an exercise in environmental design, the whole Disney phenomenon evinces what one landscape planner describes as an "architecture of reassurance."[16] And yet, in a sense, reassurance is what we hope to discover in all of our places. However we conceive of the multifarious environments we build, and to whatever extent they appear contrived or unpretending, they inevitably define our individual and communal identity.

The human's persistent effort to anchor meaning in place expresses itself in endless variations. It is particularly evident, for example, in personal narratives of religious experience. Knowing God, like falling in love or living through a near-death experience, is inescapably contextual. All "limit experiences" cause us to gather up every thread of meaning from the contexts in which they occur. In our memories of such events, we return first to the place "where it happened." That's why Augustine, in his *Confessions*, remembered so clearly the place in the garden where he heard, at the time of his conversion, the children's voices calling "take and read." That's why the teachings of the desert fathers would be incomprehensible apart from the Egyptian desert, or Julian's revelations apart from her cell at Norwich, or even Martin Luther King's prophetic call for justice apart from the streets of Montgomery and Birmingham. That's why Luther happened to remember that it was on the privy in the monastery at Wittenberg where he was struck in 1512 by the freeing words of justification by faith in Romans 1:17. Norman O. Brown, in a tour de force of psychoanalytic interpretation, has argued that the particular site was one of no little consequence.[17] Whatever hermeneutical framework one brings to the question, however, meaningful experience is always "placed" experience. The sceptic need only consider Karl Marx's celebrated seat near the reference shelves in the reading room of the British Museum. It became the preeminent seed-place of revolution in our time.

As obvious as all this may seem, it still is an insight too often overlooked in the history of spirituality. The study of religious experience has frequently tended to dis-*place* the phenomena it has observed, abstracting an experience from its specific context and cataloging a whole theoretical spectrum of religious affections. Adolphe Tanquerey's *The Spiritual Life* is a classic expression of this approach at its best.[18] While its pattern of classification had significant value, it unfortunately lent the study of spirituality a certain rarefied, unsubstantial quality. Similarly, the tendency to focus attention on extraordinary, mystical experience alone serves to remove spirituality still further from the phenomenal world.

Many factors have conspired to give spirituality a sense of vague airiness. On the level of popular culture, a gnostic interest in "spiritual techniques" and gifted gurus has been part of a restless search for spiritual experience in general, while some—leery of all esoteric enthusiasms—have discounted the notion of spirituality altogether. As a result, Josef Sudbrack can speak of the "banality . . . the anaemic unreality which is almost always connected with the word 'spirituality'" in common usage.[19]

Both the word and the subject deserve better than this. The need, then, is for greater clarity in what we mean by the word and a more adequate methodology for analysis of the subject. Otherwise spirituality will remain the amorphous "glob" area that it appears to so many to be.[20] Spirituality must be defined in such a way as not to exclude the palpable context of one's lived experience of the holy. Theology may at times be free to explore ideas more abstractly, from the perspective of eternity, but spirituality is necessarily tied to the particular. Carolyn Osiek rightly suggests that spirituality is "the experience, reflection and articulation of the assumptions and consequences of religious faith as it is lived in a concrete situation."[21] Its study will be drawn instinctively to the manner in which one's lived experience of faith is rooted in time, space, and culture.

William James defined religion as one's "total reaction upon life." He sought as comprehensive a definition as possible, so as to emphasize the way religion influences the whole of one's experience. It constitutes, he said, "that curious sense of the whole residual cosmos as an everlasting presence, intimate or alien, terrible or amusing, lovable or odious, which in some way everyone possesses."[22] Spirituality is especially concerned with addressing this givenness of one's particular grasp, in time and space, of an enduring presence. The subsequent question—of the methodology employed in pursuing such a study—is one that largely occupies this book.

My own background is that of the church historian interested particularly in the history of spirituality. But involvement in a graduate American Studies program over many years has disrupted all neat categories and blurred the lines between disciplines that I once thought fixed. Rather than setting up camp exclusively within any one of the disciplines of history, theology, or cultural studies, therefore, I have found myself somewhere in between—preoccupied with the question of "placement" itself.

What does it mean to experience the holy within the context of a spatially fixed reality? The question serves as a nexus for bringing together a number of intriguing, though disparate, areas of research—the work of Yi-Fu Tuan and J. B. Jackson in cultural geography, philosophical reflections on "placed" existence by Heidegger and Edward Casey, and studies of sacred space by scholars in religious studies from Mircea Eliade to Robert Orsi. Research in the history of spirituality can be enriched immensely by such provocative interdisciplinarity. A spirituality focused on lived experience necessarily draws widely on the behavioral sciences in its effort to describe the human appropriation of the holy. For Christians, the powerful impulse of the incarnation demands nothing less.

The more seriously one takes the particularity and substance of any placed experience of the sacred, the more he or she is drawn to a unity that encompasses them all. Sir Edwyn Hoskyns was aware of this essential paradox when he wrote that "at the supreme point, at Jerusalem where the Lord was crucified, the *whole world*—please notice, the whole world—comes back to us in all its vigorous energy, shining with the reflected glory of the God who made it and us.[23] Christian faith is drawn, said Gerard Manley Hopkins, to "all things counter, original, spare, strange." In the specific and concrete— even the grotesque—it returns always, through Christ, to the holy.

Beyond the need for interdisciplinary insight is the deeper, even more difficult question of language. How can spiritual experience be examined and described without either abstracting it entirely from the emotions and ambience of the original encounter, or simply repeating the naked event in the nonreflective immediacy of the placed moment? Either way, the experience remains ultimately inaccessible to the observer. The language of objective analysis is too abstract, on the one hand, and the language of engaged participation may be too impenetrable, on the other. The only alternative, perhaps, is to borrow the poet's third eye. The poetic language of metaphor and suggestion—the gloved hand that touches lightly but true—has always been the medium best used to describe a sense of place and one's experience of it. The most gifted travel writers— from Lawrence Durrell to Peter Matthiessen—have all performed the impossible task of affording entry to the landscape and consciousness of another world. The same holds true of theologians, as well—especially those plotting the varied geographies of the divine-human encounter.

This present work, therefore, is an effort to employ a wider methodology and a richer range of language in the study of the history of spirituality. To that end, the first chapter suggests an approach to understanding a phenomenology of sacred space, as a way of grasping the meaning of religious experience as "placed" experience. The second chapter offers a more critical reflection on the study of place, asking how larger cultural, political, and ecological questions are inevitably involved. These are followed by chapters devoted to specific traditions in American spirituality, each of them examined from the angle of their particular geography of knowledge or spatial construction of reality. None of this is entirely adequate, however, in getting at the deeper, more personal dimensions of apprehending the sacred through the ambience of a given place.

Interspersed between chapters in parts one and two, therefore, is a series of short poetic and impressionistic pieces that lend more imaginative entry to the landscapes of the holy. These "mythic landscapes" reflect the need to interpret the experience of place with the lyric sensitivity of a Willa Cather or a Charles Kuralt. Adrian Ivakhiv's recent study of traditional and New Age pilgrims seeking the power of the sacred at Glastonbury and Sedona offers an example of the sensitivity to religious experience (balanced by cultural analysis) that I aspire to myself.[24]

The third part of the book attends to questions of methodology, probing some of the recurring problems that arise in the study of religion and place in American culture. Chapter eight, for example, attends to questions about the restless mobility of American life, the cultural differentiation between space and place, and the Platonic rejection of placed experience in the history of Western spirituality. Chapter nine uses Jonathan Edwards's image of the spider as a way of discussing interdisciplinary approaches to the academic study of spirituality. Finally, chapter ten explores the tension between place and placelessness in the kataphatic and apophatic traditions of Christian spirituality, asking about the way places are constructed and deconstructed in the human imagination.

Henry Miller may have been right, after all, when he said that "our destination is never a place, but rather a new way of looking at things." To be able to recognize the place of our encounter with God and to know it as if for the first time is to be twice blessed—to "be there" in all the gathered immediacy that human dwelling in the divine presence makes fully possible. St. Francis found himself returning all of his life to the Portiuncula, that tiny abandoned church down the hill from Assisi. The rolling Apennines, the red poppies in the fields, the extraordinary light of Umbria itself—all drew him to the place. But it was ultimately a new way of seeing, more than the place seen, that marked the spirituality of this thirteenth-century troubadour. He regularly discerned wonder in what others viewed with scorn. His insight would turn us back to all the places that we might once have found plain and abandoned. Indeed, such is the goal, finally, of any geography of the spirit.

PART 1 | Place in American Religious Life

On her way to New York by train to sell some of her stories during the Second World War, Eudora Welty remembers, "Once, when my train came to one of those inexplicable stops in open country, this happened: Out there was spread around us a long, high valley, a green peaceful stretch of Tennessee with distant farmhouses and, threading off toward planted fields, a little foot path. It was sunset. Presently, without a word, a soldier sitting opposite me rose and stepped off the halted train. He hadn't spoken to anybody for the whole day and now, taking nothing with him and not stopping to put on his cap, he just left us. We saw him walking right away from the track, into the green valley, making a long shadow and never looking back. The train in time proceeded, and as we left him back there in the landscape, I felt us going out of sight for him, diminishing and soon to be forgotten."

—Eudora Welty, *One Writer's Beginnings*

(a) A sacred place constitutes a break in the homogeneity of space; (b) This break is symbolized by an opening by which passage from one cosmic region to another is made possible (from heaven to earth and vice versa; from earth to the underworld); (c) Communication with heaven is expressed by one or another of certain images, all of which refer to the *axis mundi*: pillar (cf. the *universalis columna*), ladder (cf. Jacob's ladder), mountain, tree, vine, etc.; (d) Around this cosmic axis lies the world (= our world), hence the axis is located "in the middle," at the "navel of the earth"; it is the Center of the World.

—Mircea Eliade, *The Sacred and the Profane*

A native thinker makes the penetrating comment that "All sacred things must have their place." It could even be said that being in their place is what makes them sacred for if they were taken out of their place, even in thought, the entire order of the universe would be destroyed. Sacred objects therefore contribute to the maintenance of order in the universe by occupying the places allocated to them.

—Claude Levi-Strauss, *The Savage Mind*

1 | Axioms for the Study of Sacred Place

*"Once in his life a man [or woman] ought to concentrate his
mind upon the remembered earth. He ought to give himself up
to a particular landscape in his experience; to look at it
from as many angles as he can, to wonder upon it, to dwell upon it.
He ought to imagine that he touches it with his hands at every season and
listens to the sounds
that are made upon it.
He ought to imagine the creatures there and all the faintest
motions of the wind. He ought to recollect the glare
of the moon and the colors of the dawn and dusk."[1]*

Above all else, sacred place is "storied place." Particular locales
come to be recognized as sacred because of the stories that are told about
them. The oldest stories, it would seem, are all tales about places—favorite hunting grounds painted inside paleolithic caves, Gilgamesh seeking the land beyond the sun, the body of the Egyptian pharaoh bound
for the underworld, Abraham headed toward Canaan. The places become valued in proportion to the number and power of stories that are
attached to them. In Wales, for example, there are five hundred place-
names that begin with the preface "llan" (meaning enclosure, holy place,
or church), and ending with a storied description of the site.[2] The longest of these is the village of **Llanfairpwllgwyngyllgogerychwyrn-
drobwllllantysiliogogogoch** on the island of Anglesei in northern Wales.
Commonly referred to as "Llanfair P.G.," the fifty-eight-letter name refers to "The Church of St. Mary's by the Pool near the White Hazel
Trees beside the Whirlpool Rapids and the Church of St. Tysilio near
the Red Caves." Each place in the name is, in turn, shrouded with stories of saints and beasts that reach back into the collective memory of
the people who dwell there. Without exception, the sacred place is the
place rich in story.

The best way to introduce the study of sacred place in American

15

spirituality, therefore, may be to share a particular place-tale in which one's encounter with the holy is inseparably related to the place itself. From such a narrative we can go on to draw certain axioms helpful in the further exploration of religious experience and its relation to place. This book will provide an abundance of such tales, drawn from a wide variety of spiritual traditions. But since part of the concern in this study is to observe the personal dimension of one's "placed" experience of the sacred, it may be best here to offer a story of my own.

For several years now I've been accustomed to making periodic retreats to Pere Marquette State Park, along the Illinois and Mississippi Rivers north of St. Louis. My attachment to the place has grown proportionately to the stories I'm able to tell of it—tales of eagles sighted along the bluffs, the scream of a wildcat heard in the dark of night, the memory of problems resolved through hours of sitting beside running water. I have come to love this place.

Curiously, however, my pilgrimages there are marked by a recurrent pattern that somehow seems characteristically American. Exhausted by too many uninterrupted months of saying "yes" to everything, I finally escape in desperate loneliness to the river and woods, there (as I always hope) to rediscover God in some grand and mystic encounter. In the heartland of America, along the banks of the Mighty River, in close proximity to the navel of the earth, I seek out the holy in unexpurgated splendor. But, of course, it never quite works out as well as I had hoped. The cabin never bursts into blazing light as I pray on my knees before an open breviary. Cloven tongues of fire never descend as I walk the bluffs above the river, searching for mystery. Instead, I find myself predictably faced with the same fretful anxieties I had hoped a change of place might mend. The serpent invariably comes crawling back into the garden with me. God's presence remains elusive, try as I may to see it materialized in the Waldens and Tinker Creeks of my own experience. In short, I expect too much of the place.

Each time, on arriving at the river, I want to find God immediately—I want direct access, I want power and preternatural wonder. I'll listen to the sound of squirrels and birds, expecting God's voice to echo in the rustle of every stirring leaf. I'll stalk God, as it were, along all the trails above the lodge. And usually, after at least twenty hours into the trip, I'll finally realize there's going to be nothing there but trees and clouds and distant river after all. I find myself left with dead leaves and a thin line of geese flying over the western sky. Yet it is at this precise moment, where I give up looking for the burning bush, that my retreat usually begins.

The Clearing in the Woods

It happened this way on one such occasion.[3] Toward dusk, I was weary of walking all day—having come once again to abandon hope of finding Yahweh in every leaf and bush. This time, at least, God would not be caught. I would drag the bag and snare back empty, no trophies to mount. It was time to head back to the cabin before dark, as I passed by a less-traveled path going in the opposite direction. I traced it quickly along a ridge until it came to a wooded end. By then the sun lay heavy and red through the trees. I knew I should press on home. But beyond a fallen tree I noticed a small clearing covered with leaves, dimly lit and inviting. There was nothing numinous about the place; I had been there before. Yet somehow it seemed at that time a good place to be still and to wait. I had been driven all day in a fevered search for wonder. This place, however, invited one's acceptance of it for its own sake alone. So I stood leaning against the fallen tree and remained quiet, thinking whimsically of Annie Dillard's great tenacity at waiting for muskrats.

I don't know how long I waited, getting used to the untroubled sounds of the trees and distant birds, the occasional movement of chipmunks in the leaves. But suddenly I heard something in the brush to my right. The sound was different from the others, heavier. I knew it was made by something more conscious than the smaller creatures around. I felt not only its weight but also its consciousness—its frightening likeness to myself. A person, I thought, or a dog. Then I saw it. For some time I thought it was a large dog, or some animal I couldn't name. (As I think of it now, the lack of a name was what formed so much of the mystery I felt.) It was a deer, a young doe, I think.

Staying perfectly still, I breathed as lightly as possible, my warm breath nevertheless smoking around my face in the cold air. Gradually, the deer made its way right into the clearing where I had been waiting. In fact, she reached the very point where I had first been looking to meet something long moments before, when suddenly she saw me. She stopped fast, stamping her right front hoof, moving her head up and down, then from side to side, studying me intently. She wagged her white tail fiercely and seemed to gaze through me with those large, dark eyes. For a moment she jumped back into the brush, but I waited, and soon she came back out, eyeing me carefully but walking on in the direction she had been heading. Down the slope to water, no doubt. I watched until she disappeared.

A simple, utterly peaceful and mysterious meeting it had been. The uncanny thing was that I had been invited to the place, I had felt the deer (I felt some presence) in the clearing a good ten or fifteen minutes *before* she came. I somehow *knew* that if I just were still and waited, there would be a meeting. It was a gift, and a strange conclusion to the whole day's experience. Having spent the day searching for mana, for mystic voices, a luminous encounter with the Other, I met simply a deer. Walking back home, toward the vanishing red sunset, with honking geese passing high overhead, I felt an enormous joy.

The pastoral idyll has been a common form of the place-tale in the history of American myth. My own simple story fits this larger pattern—with its idealized flight to a redemptive wilderness, a renewed innocence never quite realized but always sought, a quest for the holy that is fulfilled finally in accepting the ordinary. My experience was not unlike that of young Ike McCaslin in William Faulkner's story, "The Bear." He, too, had longed to see the mystery which so often evaded his grasp—the great elusive bear, Old Ben. It was only as he abandoned his gun, his watch and compass (all his tools for mastering mystery), that he was able at last to enter his own clearing in the woods where the meeting occurred.

> . . . tireless, eager, without doubt or dread, panting a little above the strong rapid little hammer of his heart, [he emerged] suddenly into a little glade and the wilderness coalesced. It rushed, soundless, and solidified—the tree, the bush, the compass and the watch glinting where a ray of sunlight touched them. Then he saw the bear. It did not emerge, appear: it was just there, immobile, fixed in the green and windless noon's hot dappling, not as big as he had dreamed it but as big as he had expected, bigger, dimensionless against the dappled obscurity, looking at him. Then it moved. It crossed the glade without haste, walking for an instant into the sun's full glare and out of it, and stopped again and looked back at him across one shoulder. Then it was gone.[4]

The momentary, ambiguous encounter with that which is smaller than one dreams, yet larger than one expects. It is the experience of Natty Bumppo, the Deerslayer, facing his first Iroquois warrior in the clearing of another woods. It is the quintessential meeting of an American Adam, fallen and cast from Eden, with what he has lost, with what he has despaired of ever finding again. Martin Buber knew that "all real living is meeting," and Faulkner, like Cooper, knew that the *place* of meeting serves always as the trigger of memory, the occasion for hope.

The clearing in the woods forms the palpable context around which the story will grow. It is the remembered place that excites and directs the mythic imagination in its effort to understand the inarticulate and ambivalent experience of meeting.

Out of such a narrative as this, we can suggest four different rules or "axioms" which are able to guide the student of American spirituality in seeking to understand the character of sacred space. These are basic, self-evident principles that underlie the way by which landscape is molded in the religious imagination.[5] They are phenomenological categories, describing how places are perceived in the process of mythogenesis. The first such axiom is that *sacred place is not chosen, it chooses*. Only after abandoning the frantic search for an *axis mundi* on the slopes above the Mississippi, was I unexpectedly "found" by the clearing in the woods. I perceived it as a place quietly seeking me out, whispering beyond all my previous, conscious efforts to locate and fix the place of power. Sacred place, therefore, is a construction of the imagination that affirms the independence of the holy. God chooses to reveal himself only where he wills.

A second axiom asserts that *sacred place is ordinary place, ritually made extraordinary*. The *loca sacra* is frequently found to be surprisingly unremarkable, esteemed because of neither its sublime setting nor its functional importance in the life of the community. It becomes recognized as sacred because of certain ritual acts that are performed there, setting it apart as unique. In the case of my own story, for example, the undistinguished clearing in the woods was made memorable by the ritual act of silence which I had assumed there. The discipline of waiting had the effect of sanctifying the site in my memory.

A third axiom would insist that *sacred place can be tred upon without being entered*. Its recognition is existentially, not ontologically discerned. The identification of sacred place is thus intimately related to states of consciousness. I had criss-crossed all of the bluffs above the river several times in the past, but it was only on this occasion, from this given perception, that I saw the clearing as distinct and holy ground.

A final axiom suggests that *the impulse of sacred place is both centripetal and centrifugal, local and universal*. One is recurrently driven to a quest for centeredness—a focus on the particular place of divine encounter— and then at other times driven out from that center with an awareness that God is never confined to a single locale. I find myself caught in a curious cycle of movement between my office in St. Louis and the clearing in the woods. There are several "river places," in fact, that periodically draw me away from my broken attentiveness to life as usual. Yet none of them are able to guarantee the continued presence of the holy, and each time that they operate at their best they force me back to God's diffused presence in the world.

The Mythic Power of Sacred Place

Having disclosed the four principles to be explored in this chapter, we can begin systematically to think through their implications—asking how the category of sacred place illuminates the study of American spirituality in general. "Tell me the landscape in which you live and I will tell you who you are," declared Jose Ortega y Gasset.[6] By this he implied that place not only has a way of molding personality, but it serves also as an anchor of human existence. Landscape is a connector of the soul with Being. Yet this is true only selectively. Not every place seems equally adept at communicating the fullness of being. Even before Cro-Magnon artists began inscribing their sacral paintings on the subterranean walls of the caves at *Les Trois Freres* in southern France, numinous power had been associated with particular places set apart from all others. Joseph Campbell asserts that "the idea of a sacred place where the walls and laws of the temporal world may dissolve to reveal a wonder is apparently as old as the human race."[7] But what is it about a place that causes it to be recognized as sacred? Why is one cave chosen for painting and not another? Why were Puritans drawn to the desolate landscape of New England winters, when balmier lands lay further south? What was it in the "Burned-Over District" of western New York that occasioned such phenomenal outbursts of religious enthusiasm in the early nineteenth century?

"For religious man," says Mircea Eliade, "space is not homogeneous; he experiences interruptions, breaks in it; some parts of space are qualitatively different from others."[8] It is as if the human psyche were continually feeling along the surface of a great rock face, in search of the slightest fissure, a discontinuity that might afford entry beyond the rock to a numinal reality which both underlay and transcended the stone facade. The sacred place becomes the point at which the wondrous power of the divine could be seen breaking into the world's alleged ordinariness. As a result, that fixed point becomes the center of the world, the navel of the earth or *axis mundi* by which passage can be obtained to the cosmic region beyond, from where all meaning derives. Here the *real* could unveil itself in space.[9]

This emphasis on the initiative being taken by the holy in revealing itself is seen in the first axiom already mentioned—that sacred place ultimately is not chosen, it chooses. Its identification as sacred is never essentially one of individual or even communal recognition. One never decides that "this" will be a sacred place—because of the beautiful view or the proximity to the village or the number of people who pass that way. "In actual fact, the place is never 'chosen' by man," says Eliade. "It is merely discovered by him; in other words, the sacred place in some way or another reveals itself to him."[10] Richard Rubenstein, speaking to architects involved with the design of religious buildings, once cautioned that "the sacred cannot be constructed. It makes itself. . . . Men can never deliberately create sacred precincts."[11] Ultimately the holy exists entirely apart from any human control. It demands its own freedom to choose.

This is an angle of vision admittedly foreign to the consciousness of the modern, positivist mind. We aren't accustomed to attributing intent or cognizance to inanimate locations in the environment. Yet the worldview of the ancient Near East readily accepted such an idea. When the biblical Job spoke of the man who has gone to his death, he said that "he returns no more to his house, *nor does his place know him* any more" (Job 7:10).[12] This is more than quaint poetic expression. It is an awareness that place may be itself possessed of power and life. In the village of Minahassa on the island of Celebes in Indonesia there lies a sanctuary of sacred stones which forms the "salvation and strength" of that place. Under these stones certain planks are said to be buried which represent the song notes of birds first heard at the ancient founding of the village. Curiously the stones are known as "the callers" because of the power they are said to possess in mystically calling back native villagers who may have wandered to distant lands.[13] Some cultures even speak of people dying who stray too far from the life-sustaining strength of the native landscape. Peter Matthiessen observes how the Ona Indians of Argentina, now extinct, were unable to tolerate relocation from their native soil, dying off within weeks of their forced removal.[14]

In the religion of Australian Aborigines there is the belief that the very power of conception is located in the features of the natural environment. A mother's pregnancy occurs as her body is entered by a spirit child hidden in a rock or plant near where she had been at the moment of conception. Hence, this location or particular object will later become the personal emblem (or totem) of the infant when it is born. In this way,

> Individuals are tied to the earth and derive their identities from specific items in the landscape. Sometimes Aborigines point to various marks on their bodies (for instance, warts or patches of different skin color) as being the same as the marks on the rocks where the spirit children entered their mothers' womb.[15]

Place has thus become, in this instance, determinative of one's very existence—choosing the individual long before he or she is able to respond with a conscious choice of her own.

This essentially shamanistic understanding of the determinative power of nature has been extensively studied by anthropologists.[16] Carlos Castaneda popularized the notion in his description of the Yaqui Indian sorcerer Don Juan's lessons on places of power and the means by which they can be sought out.[17] In this view of the world, the landscape is extravagantly peopled with spirits and contact with their numinal power is obtained, in part, by physical proximity to their *loca sacra*. One therefore learns to respect, even fear, the dangerous force that pervades that place, observing carefully the "gestures of approach" required in coming to it.[18] Much care will be taken particularly in distinguishing hallowed from unhallowed ground, lest one intrude upon the sphere of malevolent, evil spirits as well as those that are beneficent. As late as the nineteenth century in northeastern Scotland, for example, it was not uncommon for farmers to set aside small plots of ground as secretly consecrated to the devil. Known as "Clootie's Croft" or the "Goodman's Field," this area was walled off and left unplanted, with the hope that the powers of darkness might be content to remain safely there.[19] In this manner, a cautious balance could be obtained among the various cosmic forces pervading the terrain.

Now this entire notion of a richly sacralized landscape may seem utterly inimical to the mainstream of the Judeo-Christian tradition. In the Hebrew scriptures, the "high places" of Canaanite worship were consistently destroyed by the righteous and the groves of Baal laid waste (2 Kgs 23:8; Dt 16:21–22). These sacred places, marked usually by a central pillar or tree that afforded access to the numinous world, were uniformly rejected by the Deuteronomic tradition and its heirs. Max Weber spoke of this insistent rejection of pagan animism to have resulted in a "disenchantment" of the world within the western mind, a freeing of nature from its intense religious associations. Mircea Eliade observes:

> It was the prophets, the apostles, and their successors the missionaries who convinced the western world that a rock (which certain people have considered to be sacred) was only a rock, that the planets and the stars were only cosmic *objects*—that is to say, that they were not (and could not be) either gods or angels or demons.[20]

This effort to deconsecrate the world, dispelling its sacral aura, would make possible a new relationship to nature, essentially secular and open to technological manipulation.[21] But in the process of lending impulse to the rise of western science, it would destroy almost entirely any notion of sacred space.

In much of Jewish and Christian theology the freedom of a transcendent God of history has regularly been contrasted with the false and earthbound deities of fertility and soil. God has been removed from the particularity of place, extracted from the natural environment. Hence, the tendency in western civilization has been toward the triumph of history over nature, time over space, male dominance over female dependence, and technical mastery of the land over a gentle reverence for life. In this artificial schema, God has often been viewed as a Lord of times but not of places—involved in mighty acts but not so much in the quiet energies of creation. The result has been a rampant secularization of nature and activism of spirit in western life, leaving us exhausted in our mastery of a world stripped of magic and mystery.[22]

What, then, asks Eliade, are the possibilities of a "demystification in reverse"—an effort to recapture the mystery of divine presence today, though without returning to a pre-critical naivete with its "enchanted enclosure of consciousness."[23] How can one develop a legitimate theology of place—being able to recognize once again the shekinah glory of a God we thought altogether driven from the world? And how is this done without resorting to a syrupy nature mysticism which dissolves all boundaries between God, the world, and our human response? In short, is it possible to recover the power of sacred space for those today who have forgotten hierophanies and all signs of the sacred? Not out of a regret for lost groves on the slopes of Shechem, but because of hope for a renewed sense of being placed in mystery. Crucial here is Paul Ricoeur's conception of the hermeneutical circle by which one moves from an original naivete, with its easy immediacy of belief, through a necessary process of criticism and demythologization to a "second-naivete" by which wonder is restored, chastened of its earlier confusion and credulity. He insists that "the dissolution of the myth as explanation is the necessary way to the restoration of the myth as symbol."[24] This is the recovery of myth in all its power and awe, while retaining the insistent demands of intellectual objectivity. It means that the concept of sacred space will be owned as truly mythic. Places *can* be formative of our very being as humans, rooting us at the deepest levels of mystery and meaning.

Our study of sacral geography will have to recognize that one's symbolic participation in a place of mythic significance is never totally available to scrutiny. The aborigine's relation to his totem stone, like the devout Roman Catholic's attraction to the shrine at Lourdes, cannot finally be reduced entirely to anthropological categories of scientific explanation. This is because, in the most basic sense, myth that is understood is no longer myth. That which we analyze with thorough objectivity—turning into psychology, history, or social geography—has ceased to exercise any formative power upon us. "When a civilization begins to reinterpret its mythology in this way," says Joseph Campbell, "the life goes out of it, temples become museums. . . . The living images become only remote facts of a distant time or sky."[25] If our study, therefore, is to be life-giving (as this intends to do) it is necessary to suggest that holy places *can* partake of mystery. They essentially are not chosen, but they choose—as the Divine Majesty may encounter us through them.

Yet, at the same time, this openness to myth can never be removed from critical judgment. We need to avoid especially the tendency to canonize the primitive, to celebrate with nostalgia the naked encounter with cosmic power once found in the high places and sacred groves of yore. In this world come of age in the twentieth century, half of us have abandoned all hope of awed wonder in the world, while the other half tried frantically to rediscover a lost magic. "We doused the burning bush and cannot rekindle it; we are lighting matches in vain under every green tree," says Annie Dillard.[26] The effort to see life as a vivid series of burning bushes—a movement of ever-increasing intensity from one numinous encounter to the next—is not only spiritually exhausting; it also misses the profound truth that most often the holy appears in the commonplace routines and incongruities of human experience. This is why Jonathan Z. Smith offers an important caveat to the work of Mircea Eliade and others who tend to focus primarily on the extraordinary, exotic categories of experience, removed from everyday modes of thought.[27] The study of spirituality has to engage not only the exotic, but the mundane categories of existence as well—bringing them all under the most rigorous scrutiny.

Sacred place, we have said, seems to have an unaccountable identity distinct and separate from those who move in and through it. Indeed, it appears that, from one point of view, place creates people. But it is equally the case, from another point of view, that people create place. We form significant locales out of our memories, our relationships with others, a whole network of associations sacred and profane. "The overriding meaning of the landscape is social," argues David Sopher.[28] The hermeneutical circle, therefore, demands our applying all the categories of scientific investigation—from behavioral geography to material culture research—as well as the most rigorous attention to biblical and dogmatic sources. Any thorough experience of sacred space will have to follow this deliberate pattern of mystery, demystification, and the subsequent reawakening of wonder. Only then will we grasp the full significance of the *genius loci*, the spirit of the place where God is met.

The Recognition of Ordinary Places as Holy

A second axiom observes that sacred place is very often *ordinary* place, ritually set apart to become extraordinary. Its holiness resides not in certain inherent marks of external significance or obvious distinction. It is, instead, only *declared* to be different, heterogeneous, discontinuous from the commonness of the surrounding terrain. The particular site may not at all be readily discerned by the uninitiated eye. The prophet Micah, for example, recognized Bethlehem Ephrathah, a singularly undistinguished place ("you who are little among the clans of Judah") as the geographical source of the Davidic kingdom (Mi 5:2). The Christian mythos will later emphasize still further the startling paradox that the messianic hope derives from this very town of inconsequence (Mt 2:5–6) and that Jesus himself is raised in unillustrious Nazareth, outside the mainstream of Israelite life (Jn 1:46).

This curious phenomenon of the sacred place as ostensibly unexceptional can be seen to cut across all periods and cultures. It is not the stunningly beautiful isle of Mykonos in the Aegean Sea, but the rocky, barren island of Delos nearby which is holy—the sacred birthplace of Apollo. The most sacred mountain of the Himalayas is not the towering Everest, nor any of the fourteen peaks which exceed 26,000 feet in height, but instead the less imposing Mount Kailas, sacred to Hindus and Buddhists as the throne of Shiva and mandala of perfect bliss. Repeatedly in the economy of salvation, what is almost prosaic and commonplace is chosen as the site of divine blessing. Yathrib under Muhammad would change to Medina—an undistinguished town reconsecrated as "The City." "Lost-town," as it was disparagingly known in the seventeenth century, would grow into the holy city of Boston revered by Cotton Mather as an "outcast Zion," a stone originally cast aside by the builders, only later to become the chief cornerstone.[29] Similarly, the village of Commerce, Illinois would be transformed into Nauvoo under Mormon blessing and a neglected site on the Wabash River renamed Harmony by the followers of George Rapp. In each case, the ordinary would be reconsecrated as the holy. Mircea Eliade notes that the most primitive of all sacred places known in the history of religions is the archetypal, simple landscape of stones, water, and trees.[30] This scene of markedly ordinary simplicity, like that found in the classical age of Chinese landscape painting, constitutes a microcosm of the world as a whole—its representation of the holy molded more by subtlety than by noteworthiness.

Illustrations from the American landscape document the same principle. One of the mountains most sacred to Native Americans in the southwest is Mount Cuchama, an obscure and scrubby slope on the California-Mexico border.[31] Similarly Death Valley, seldom valued for anything more than its tales of misfortune and blundered survival, was curiously known by the Spanish as *La Palma de la Mano de Dios*, the palm of God's hand. Here the place of abandonment strangely became the site of encountered majesty. And Thoreau took great delight in celebrating the commonness of Walden Pond, even while seeing it to be marked by a certain cosmic comprehensibility. Referring to the alleged limits of his rounded experience in the world, he remarked that he had traveled extensively throughout the wide expanses of Concord township. The Transcendentalist doctrine of correspondence allowed him to recognize threads of the fabric of the whole of reality woven through the common woods and farmland along the Concord River.[32] At work here, then, is the process by which universality is frozen in microcosm, the holy transfigured in the ordinary.

Modern consciousness may balk at this idea because of the highly aesthetic expectations that we bring to the conception of any place of inherent importance. The heritage of Romanticism since the late eighteenth century has conditioned us to expect the holy place to be marked by excessive beauty and grandeur, or at least by idiosyncratic fascination. Albert Bierstadt's grand vistas of the Rocky Mountains became a model for nineteenth-century American landscape painters, depicting the sublime as the monumental.[33] Perhaps the American mind tends always to project the sacred landscape onto a canvas of monumental proportions. The Grand Canyon, the vast prairie, the panoramic Pacific seacoast—these are the broad strokes by which we conceive the geography of transcendence. The subtlety of the miniscule and austerely simple Japanese garden, therefore, may be lost on us altogether. Characteristically American, for example, is the fact that the sculptured grounds of *Seiwa-en* in the Missouri Botanical Garden at St. Louis are often described as "the largest Japanese garden in the world"—a deeply revealing contradiction in terms. The American national measure of landscape is inevitably the monumental.[34]

Yet the tendency to exaggerate or hyperbolize the wonder and preeminence of a given site is also itself characteristic of the human response to sacred space. The ordinary is projected beyond first appearances so as to be seen as the *extraordinary*. The topography of Jerusalem, for instance, is singularly unpronounced. Standing only 2,500 feet above sea level, it is neither the highest point in Israel nor even in the immediate vicinity. But this particular topographical point has been revered for thousands of years as the cosmic hub of the universe. "The Center of the World is there," wrote a twelfth-century pilgrim. "There, on the day of the summer solstice, the light of the Sun falls perpendicularly from Heaven."[35] Midrash Tanhuma had declared much earlier:

> Just as the navel is found at the center of the world . . . Jerusalem is at the center of the land of Israel, the Temple is at the center of Jerusalem, the Holy of Holies is at the center of the Temple, the Ark is at the center of the Holy of Holies and the Foundation Stone is in front of the Ark, which spot is the foundation of the world.[36]

This stone of foundation, venerated at the Dome of the Rock in Jerusalem today, is richly elaborated in the mythos of Jews, Christians, and Muslims alike. Here Isaac was bound for sacrifice, the veil over the stone was rent at Jesus' death, Muhammad ascended to heaven from this point on his mystical "night journey." Deriving mystical power from this *axis mundi*, the whole of Jerusalem is seen to be imbued with mystery. Ancient legends said that all the winds of the world converged from this given point, that "any spittle found in Jerusalem may be deemed free from uncleanness," and that "even the gossip of those who lived in the land of Israel is *Torah*."[37]

This same tendency to hyperbole can be found vividly in the early colonial experience of New England. Indeed, it becomes the taproot of the later tradition of the American tall tale. Easily secularized, later to be spun in story-form around countless campfires, it nevertheless was originally lodged in the early American mythology of a New World. The language of Canaan, the metaphors of biblical geography, became the Puritans' primary means of planting themselves mythically in a New Israel, a New Jerusalem far from the fleshpots of Egypt beyond the sea.[38] Here the very landscape itself could exude the aroma of divine blessing. "A breath of New England's clear air," said one early observer, "was more nourishing and intoxicating than Old England's ale. Here partridges grew so heavy they couldn't fly, turkeys were the size of sheep, mosquitoes as large as birds."[39] These initial exaggerations of paradise were often written as promotional material to attract new colonists. They would soon be qualified, however, as the actual settlers of New England found a different reality, subject to an altogether different mythos. One chastened reporter would eventually write back to his readers in England:

I will not tell you that you may smell the corn fields before
you see the land; neither must men think that corn doth grow
naturally, (or on trees,) nor will the deer come when they are
called, or stand still and look on a man until he shoot him, not
knowing a man from a beast; nor the fish leap into the kettle,
nor on the dry land, neither are they so plentiful, that you may
dip them up in baskets, nor take cod in nets to make a voyage
[being pulled through the water by the great fish], which is no
truer than that the fowls will present themselves to you with
spits through them.[40]

This had been the language of embellishment and fancy. Yet the
continued repetition of these early tales would exhibit a longing for the
discovery of the holy and extraordinary in the midst of all that might be
considered common. The same quest for a mythical sense of empowered
space continues today—if retained only in the private, unrecognized
dreams of the modern individual, ostensibly stripped of myth. Joseph
Campbell insists that "the latest incarnation of Oedipus, the continued
romance of Beauty and the Beast, stand this afternoon on the corner of
Forty-second Street and Fifth Avenue, waiting for the traffic light to
change."[41]

The application of the concept of sacred space to modern, technological society may at first seem anomalous. We tend to associate the
sacralization of place with "primitive cultures" or at least with pre-in-
dustrial societies where the pastoral landscape is conceived exclusively
as the abode of the holy. If we imagine sacred places within the heart of
great cities, we usually think only of grand cathedrals or sculpted city
parks. Yet the axiom that sacred place is often very common place ritually made extraordinary would insist that manufactured as well as natural places can function in this way.

David Stein, a member of the Chicago Catholic Worker Community, writes of a place under the intersection of Halsted Street and Chicago Avenue as one that had functioned for him as sacred and life-
giving. Identifying with people living on the streets of Chicago, he had
camped for several months in the passageway under that intersection,
along the tracks of the Northwestern Railroad. He slept on a bed of flattened cardboard boxes, watching the sun come up on a summer morning
over the Chicago Tribune printing plant nearby. He said that what sold
him on the spot was the presence of a stubby cottonwood tree near the
tracks—one that had been cut down by railroad workers years before
but had stubbornly refused to die. Knowing the cottonwood to be sacred to the Plains Indians, David Stein chose the tree as his totem and

lived out his months in that place, thanking God, as he said, "for being privileged to live amid such exquisite beauty."[42]

Sacred place is not at all necessarily pastoral and rural in character—something to be sharply distinguished from the fabricated spaces of an urban landscape. It is, after all, a function of the religious imagination, not a quality inherent in the locale as such. That is why Americans fascinated by the power of new machines in the late nineteenth century could speak with religious fervor of standing in the presence of a huge electrical generator. Henry Adams, at the Great Exposition of 1900 in Paris, walked into the gallery of machines and stood before a forty-foot dynamo, seeing it almost to project a moral force, a sense of infinity. "Before the end," he said, "one began to pray to it; inherited instinct taught the natural expression of man before silent and infinite force."[43] He understood the space created by the force of such a great machine to exercise far more power on the American imagination than the force of the Virgin, for example, still felt at a holy site such as Lourdes. The sacred place, in short, takes root in that which may form the substance of our daily lives, but is transformed by the imagination to that which is awe-inspiring and grand.

The Paradox of Being Present to Place

A third axiom, closely related to the first two, concerns the means by which entrance is made into the place of numinal presence. It affirms that simply moving into an allegedly sacred place does not necessarily make one present to it. One can *be* there and yet *not* be there at the same time. Being bodily present is never identical with the fullness of being to which humans can be open in time and space. This is a basic paradox of existence. Being fully open to the world, says Heidegger, is a matter of "dwelling" in a place so as to unite the four essential facets of true human existence—earth, sky, gods, and men.[44] Yet our being so often estranged from place means that we tragically are able to occupy the space without actually "dwelling" within it as place.[45] Hence, even though we stand on the inaccessible ground of the holy, we may never yet have been brought into any relationship to it. What, in the possibilities of being, could have become a Thou-place for us has remained an It-place, shorn of any bond of union.[46] Gertrude Stein once said of Oakland, California, that "once you get there, you find there's no there there." This caustic reflection on the monotonous and lackluster quality of suburban California life can refer also to the experience of all moderns in being estranged from place in general—finding "no there there."

What, then, are the mechanisms for gaining entry to the full existential presence of the place that may become for us sacred? What do writers mean, for that matter, when they speak of a particular spirit of place or *genius loci*, as if one could distinguish its peculiar guardian spirit?[47] Lawrence Durrell argues that "the important determinant of any culture is after all—the spirit of place."[48] But what are the avenues of access to such a phenomenon? Is this entirely a mystical-poetic insight, or does it find parallels in our common human experience of recognizing the enduring texture of the familiar—discerning there more than we had first expected to find? Perhaps the process of "making strange" that to which one has become habitually accustomed—viewing it in a different perspective so as to enter it anew—can be seen as the most important manner by which meaning is continually renewed in any community.[49] This is as true of place as it is of any other mythic conception.

The folkways of all cultures involve rituals of initiation, gestures of approach, and certain life passages that allow one to enter a familiar place in an altogether new way—as if for the first time. Crossing the threshold of a house after being married involves entering that space in a wholly new manner, even as going into a hospital becomes an entirely different experience when one enters as a patient instead of as a visitor. In each case, the space which had previously been neutral, demanding no involvement, suddenly becomes a place impingent upon one's existence. In a similar way, Isaiah had been accustomed to passing through the temple in Jerusalem all of his life, when unexpectedly in the year that King Uzziah died he "saw the Lord there, sitting upon a throne, high and lifted up." The very foundations of the thresholds shook and the house was filled with smoke (Is 6:1–4). The overly-familiar sanctuary had suddenly become for him a new place of dread and wonder. This is the deeply human experience, described so well in T. S. Eliot's conclusion to "Little Gidding"—the experience of being surprised by place, the very place thought ordinary.

> We shall not cease from exploration
> And the end of all our exploring
> Will be to arrive where we started
> And know the place for the first time.[50]

Poet Wendell Berry speaks with Buddhist simplicity of the difficulty, however, of completing in experience this circle of discovery. In an essay entitled "An Entrance to the Woods," he describes a trip made one weekend to a forest near his home in Lexington, Kentucky. Leaving work and driving hard over interstate highways for an hour or more, he finally arrived in the woods. But he sensed also that he had not yet arrived. Restless and uneasy as he unpacked the car, uncomfortable in the intense silence of the forest, his body was telling him that "people can't change places as rapidly as their bodies can be transported." Having come there by freeway, his mind was not yet as fully there as if he had come by the crookeder and slower state roads. He could set it down as a maxim, in fact—"the faster we go . . . the longer it takes to bring the mind to a stop in the presence of anything." It was only the next morning, therefore, as he lay in the sun on a large outcropping of stone for a long, quiet hour that he began to enter the place for the first time. In his slow forgetting, there was also an *anamnesis*, a deep remembering. Only then could he remark, "As I leave the bare expanse of the rock and go in under the trees again, I am aware that I move in the landscape as one of its details." The occupation of space has thus become for him a matter of "dwelling"—an entry inviting passage to the fullness of being.[51]

What are the possibilities of examining this renewed openness to one's customary place or places as a means of understanding and ordering a given religious experience? An example may be found in a geographical structural analysis of Charles Finney's famous narrative of conversion in the early nineteenth century. At the age of twenty-nine, while still practicing law in the town of Adams, New York, Finney experienced a phenomenal religious encounter on Wednesday, October 10, 1821. This he recounts in great detail in his *Memoirs*, using a succession of ordinary places and their renewed significance as the means by which he orders his memory of the experience. All of these were common places that he frequented daily—the road that led to the village, a piece of woods through which he was in the habit of walking, and the law office that he shared with Judge Benjamin Wright. Specifically he remembers stopping that morning in the middle of the road where an "inward voice seemed to arrest" him. In the woods he later overcomes his reluctance to pray—determining not to leave until he has given his heart to God. And in the office alone that night (before a smoldering fire) he feels the Holy Spirit descend upon him "like a wave of electricity."[52] Each place was familiar and yet new. The movement through the day from road to woods to road to office was a movement from anxious conviction, to release from guilt, to quiet peace, and, at last, ecstatic joy. The marks of the ordinary landscape and the progression of spiritual experiences were inseparably interrelated in his mind. A symbolic analysis of the road, the site in the woods, and the law office might offer still further insight into the "placed" character of the entire event. Finney's reading of law under Judge Wright, for example, is crucial to understanding the later union of Calvinist and perfectionist themes in his spirituality. But the point made here is that religious experience is invariably "placed" experience and that those places are frequently the most ordinary ones entered anew with awe.

One last concern, with respect to this principle of gaining access to the place of meaning, is to remember that various religious traditions differ as to the mechanism by which a holy place derives and replenishes its own power. The Place of Emergence near the southwest corner of Colorado is inherently sacred to the Navajo because it was here that the first humans emerged from the depths of the earth at creation. Hence, a primary means of renewing that sacred power is through the use of a sweat lodge or ritual sandpainting which reenacts in the ceremonial hogan the event of original empowerment. To a large extent, power is inherent to the place itself. By contrast, in the Hebrew scriptures entry to a sacred place is always a matter of one's dynamic and ethical relationship to Yahweh alone. There is no unchangeable quality of holiness seen to reside statically in any given place. The site is not revered because of what it is in itself. In itself it is just a location. While the Jews did adopt certain categories of mythical space, therefore, they were ultimately uncomfortable with the notion of primeval power being permanently possessed by a given locale. Their God was continually calling them, not back to a mythical *Urzeit* when particular sites were set apart as sacred, but forward to a new spatial reality, discovered in prophetic faithfulness to Yahweh. "The Old Testament's understanding of space," says Brevard Childs, "was eschatological, not mythical. It looked to the future, not to the past."[53] In this sense, therefore, openness to the particular place of God is, first of all, an openness to the God of all places.

A Tension Between the Local and the Universal

A fourth and final axiom is that sacred space always possesses a double impulse—a movement which is at once centripetal and centrifugal, a pulling in and a pushing out from a center, a tendency alternately toward localization and universalization. The idea hinges on yet another essential paradox that human existence is an ever-renewed tension between exile and home. There is always the desire of the settled to be unsettled and the unsettled to be settled. On the one hand, the psalmist will cry out from Babylon, "If I forget you, O Jerusalem, let my right hand wither! Let my tongue cleave to the roof of my mouth" (Ps 137:5–6). The holy city is the center to which all memory and meaning are bound. But on the other hand, Jesus can resist being engaged in an ar-

OUT OF EGYPT
INTO
CANAAN.
"Out of Darkness into His marvelous Light."
WHERE ART THOU?

This Map is designed to show the routes of Israel and spiritual states illustrated by events occurring in them. It should be carefully studied in connection with the reading of the book.

The effort to plot the course of the spiritual life in geographical and metaphorical terms is illustrated in this nineteenth-century devotional book by Martin W. Knapp, entitled *Out of Egypt into Canaan; or Lessons in Spiritual Geography* (Cincinnati: Cranston & Stowe, 1888).

gument with the woman at the well over the precise place where worship should occur. It can be localized neither at Jerusalem nor Mount Gerizim, he insists. "But the hour is coming, and now is, when the true worshipers will worship the Father in spirit and truth" (Jn 4:23). This is the spiritual transcendence of all particular places, under the stimulus of a catholic sense of the divine presence located throughout the *oekumene* or inhabited world.

The tension is one that exists in every religious tradition. In Islam, the pilgrimage to Mecca (the *Hajj*), made at least once in one's life, forms one of the five pillars of the faith. Entry into the Great Mosque and the site of the Kaa'ba lends access to the unique presence of Allah. Yet a twelfth-century Sufi mystic, al-Hallaj, could affirm the universal, spiritual character of the *Hajj*—asserting that it could even be undertaken in one's own room, because the true sanctuary lay only within the heart.[54] The religious impulse periodically moves both toward and away from the center point where contact with the holy is made.

Recognizing, on the one hand, the centripetal attraction that sacred place often exerts, Walter Brueggemann claims that "land is a central, if not *the central theme* of biblical faith." The Hebrew conception of God's mighty acts in history never occurs in a sense of spaceless time. Salvation is always rooted in the movement forward or back to the land. As a result, there is a "preoccupation of the Bible for placement."[55] In scripture, a distressing anxiety is attributed to the experience of landlessness and rootlessness. The people of Israel restlessly move through the wilderness of Sinai under the leadership of a God who tabernacles with them, but they are always en route, on the way somewhere, enduring the journey because of the hope of arrival. The lure of sacred space, therefore, is strongest among those who are homeless, alienated, estranged. Being separated from the geographical source of renewed being, they sense a discontinuity in existence. Oscar Handlin, describing the archetypal experience of the Eastern European immigrant to American soil in the late nineteenth century, observed a similar pattern.

> 'I was born in such a village in such a parish'—so the peasant invariably began the account of himself. Thereby he indicated the importance of the village in his being; this was the fixed point by which he knew his position in the world and his relationship with all humanity.[56]

Human existence is heavily dependent upon such fixed points; they enable one to "dwell" in the world with meaning. When that experience of being rooted in the land is lost, however, a deep sense of *anomie* results. Harvey Cox relates the experience of a woman who survived the Nazi destruction of the tiny village of Lidice in Czechoslovakia. Reinhard Heydrich, deputy chief of the Gestapo, had been assassinated there in the spring of 1942 and, in reprisal, the Germans determined to obliterate even the memory of the place. After exterminating all the villagers they could find, Cox says:

> They burned the village completely, destroyed all the trees and foliage and plowed up the ground. Significantly they demanded that on all maps of Czechoslovakia the town of Lidice must be erased. The woman survivor confessed to me that despite the loss of her husband and the extended separation from her children, the most shocking blow of all was to return to the crest of the hill overlooking Lidice at the end of the war—and to find nothing there, not even ruins.[57]

This is the feeling of void, even dread, that results from the deprivation of place. It underlies the psalmist's plaintive cry, "How shall we sing the Lord's song in a strange land?" (Ps 137:4). The place which functions as sacred will always draw the pilgrim inexorably toward its center.

Yet, on the other hand, there is also a sense in which sacred space involves a centrifugal impulse, *away* from a center which may have become fixed and constricting—as if the holy were presumed to be located only in a single contracted place. When in later years the Delphic oracle degenerated into arrogant presumption, the restriction of Apollo to the slopes of Mount Parnassus became increasingly questioned by the ancient Greeks. When Yahweh's presence was perfunctorily assumed to fill the temple, the prophets called for a universalized conception of covenant identity. "Our lives," says Brueggemann, "are set between expulsion and anticipation, of losing and expecting, of being uprooted and rerooted, of being dislocated because of impertinence and being relocated in trust."[58] We long to be placed in the land of the holy, but on gaining possession of the sanctuary we come quickly to presume upon its guaranteed mystery—only then to be driven from it in search of yet another place, another center of meaning.

This frequent tendency to restrict the activity of the sacred to those precincts narrowly defined by religious custom is often the object of prophetic critique in any religious tradition. Joseph Campbell tells of an ancient Hindu sannyasin or holy man, who—while lying down to rest by the hallowed Ganges—propped his feet upon a venerated lingam, the revered symbol of Shiva. His feet were resting on this sacred phallus when a priest passing by asked how he dared so to profane the holy site.

"Good sir," he replied, "I am sorry; but will you kindly take my feet and place them where there is no such sacred lingam." The offended priest roughly grasped the man's ankles and moved his feet first to the right, then to the left, but—to his amazement—every place the feet touched a new phallus sprang from the ground. Finally he understood that this was no ordinary pilgrim and that the holy can never be confined to selected places, even those most revered by religious custom. The recognition of a localized presence of the divine and yet the subsequent refusal to limit that presence to guarded enclaves is a common tension in the study of social and religious geography.[59]

J. B. Jackson, one of the founding figures in the scientific study of American landscape, once offered a telling illustration of this axiom in his analysis of the spatial changes evoked by the Great Awakening in the eighteenth century. He saw this first movement of revivalism in America to have reoriented the previous organization of space in New England, establishing "a new vernacular landscape."[60] Before 1730, the structure of American ecclesiastical space had been centripetal and hierarchical. Attention focused exclusively on the parish context, seating in the church was arranged to indicate social status, and services were held only in the proper place at the proper time. But with the advent of popular, itinerant preachers like George Whitefield, the notion of territoriality—"the idea that the church or congregation was firmly identified with a legally defined, consecrated space: the parish"—came into serious question. Under the freedom of the revival spirit, services could be held outside or even in private houses. The outpouring of God's grace might be felt anywhere and—indeed—by anyone. Provincial ties to the narrowness of place were, therefore, weakened in favor of uncircumscribed freedom. Revivalism would continue to foster a centrifugal impulse as Methodist circuit riders and camp meeting exhorters moved across the frontier in the next century. God would thereby increasingly be found in a spatial world democratically conceived.[61] Given this perspective, many of the subsequent tensions between Old Lights and New Lights, Old School and New School can be viewed in spatial/geographic categories—contrasting conceptions of sacred space as centripetal or centrifugal.

■ ■ ■ ■ ■ ■ ■ ■ ■ ■ ■ ■ ■ ■ ■ ■ ■

These four axioms for the study of sacred place suggest a richer perspective from which the variety of American religious experience can be understood. They each underscore the important role that is played by the phenomenon of place in the function of the religious imagination. They demonstrate that the human spirit is inexorably drawn to the appeal of place, whether real or imaginary. Landscape, after all, is a constructed reality—a form which is given to nature by a particular human perception. The geography of religion, therefore, must necessarily attend to fantastic as well as earthbound places. The two are frequently intertwined, caught as they are in the same tenacious web of imagination. Take, for example, the famous pilgrimage observed each year near the city of Allahabad, two hundred miles southeast of Delhi, India. Known as the *Allahabad Triveni*, the event celebrates the convergence of three rivers at this site—the Ganga, the Yamuna, and the Saraswati. Only the first two rivers, however, can be found on any map of the subcontinent of India. The third one is an invisible, mythical river, unseen except to those who enter its waters by faith. Yet the Saraswati, of course, is the river which most captures the imagination. It is the one about which most of the stories are told. Sacred place, as "storied place," will always function in this manner. Those who study it will be driven simultaneously to cartography and poetic insight, to geographics and narrative—to that fine, fragile nexus where myth and *terra firma* intersect.

2 | Giving Voice to Place: Three Models for Understanding American Sacred Space

Ten miles east of Bighorn Canyon in northern Wyoming, you start to climb up out of the desert heat toward Medicine Mountain, looming in the distant haze. At this point Highway 14A begins a steep seven-mile ascent, along a 10 percent grade, rising ever higher into sweet clover and green meadows, spruce trees and lodgepole pines. Staying in first or second gear the whole way up, your engine still overheats by the time you have reached the crest. But if you follow the small National Forest sign off to the left near the summit and walk another mile and a half after parking the car, you come to what seems to be the top of the world: the Great Medicine Wheel, high in the Big Horn Mountains, an ancient eighty-foot-diameter circle of rocks with a cairn in the center and twenty-eight spokes radiating out to the rim.

From above the tree line at almost 10,000 feet, looking out onto thousands of acres of tree-covered peaks to the north, it is readily apparent, even to the most cynical traveler, that this remote site has functioned for centuries as a sacred place. It is a location given to astral observation, the invocation of the gods, deep reflection on the riddle of being. But what constitutes a "sacred place"? How are earth and sky joined here? By an otherworldly mystery piercing through the land itself? By the cultural construction of a rock pattern imposed by human invention? By the interplay of human and more-than-human influences in a place where blue sky and green earth seem to invite an intersubjective awareness on the part of every possible participant? All these are aspects of the subtle appeal exercised on the human imagination by the places that we often are tempted to call holy.

Chapter one focused on the individual experience of place, asking how its mystery becomes operative in the religious life; this chapter explores a range of current scholarly approaches to the study of sacred space. It deals with larger cultural questions, probes the work of contemporary philosophers attending to the phenomenology of place, and offers a critical perspective that balances (without denying) the more personal emphasis of the previous chapter. Taken together, these two initial chapters investigate both interior and exterior (existential and cultural) dimensions of the analysis of places identified as sacred in the American experience.

A curious transformation of consciousness occurs when "an ordinary place" like this—a mere dot on the map, such as this one particular site in Bighorn National Forest—becomes gradually (or perhaps even suddenly) a place of extraordinary significance. On Medicine Mountain I found myself wondering again about the process by which this happens, drawn so immediately as I was into the compelling mystery of the place. What allows a site initially known to us as *topos*—a mere location, a measurable, quantifiable point, neutral and indifferent—to become a place available to us as *chora*—an energizing force, suggestive to the imagination, drawing intimate connections to everything else in our lives?[1]

These two Greek words for place—*topos* and *chora*—were emphasized by Aristotle and Plato, respectively, in the ancient world. Aristotle understood place (as *topos*) to be a point no different from any other point, an inert container exerting no particular influence on the creatures or objects within it.[2] Topographical maps and global positioning systems are preoccupied, after this pattern, with precise elevations and fixed contour lines, being able to pinpoint exactly one's location on the globe. By contrast, Plato preferred to speak of place as the wet-nurse, suckler and feeder of all things.[3] His fascination was with the capacity of a place to resonate to the immediacies of human experience. Place as *chora* carries its own energy and power, summoning its participants to a common dance, to the "choreography" most appropriate to their life together.

Participation in deliberate ritual activity is what invariably occasions the transition from experiencing a place as *topos* to encountering that same place as *chora*. For most people in the United States, for instance, a McDonald's restaurant offers a classic example of *topos*, a place without any distinctive sense of presence. "If you've seen one of them, you've seen them all." But if you have proposed to someone you love in a particular McDonald's restaurant or experienced a life-changing conversation in another, that *topos* suddenly becomes a *chora*, intimately a part of your life.

My own experience of Medicine Wheel in north central Wyoming, first known to me as an indiscriminate spot in the *Rand McNally Road Atlas*, began with the slow and impressive approach up Highway 14A. It involved my wife and me camping for the night within the shadow of its mountain ridge, adjusting to the cool, clear air moving over distant patches of July snow, walking sunwise around the wheel the next morning, and attending to offerings left there by First Nations people. There were two deer hooves linked by a leather thong; bundles of sage or tobacco tied in pieces of red, black, white, and yellow cloth; a turtle shell bound with crossed sticks of cottonwood; a peeled banana and three Bing cherries—gifts left as prayers for family and friends in need, as atonement for offenses to Mother Earth. Material objects of this sort invariably focus one's attention, recalling gifts left at the foot of the Vietnam Memorial wall or prayer flags whipping in the wind at a Tibetan shrine in the Himalayas.

Half anticipating some peculiar experience of the holy in walking around the circle myself, I saw nothing unusual—only a woman I noticed on the opposite side of the wheel as I made my way halfway around it. She stood facing my way, looking toward me but seemingly so deeply entranced by something in the middle distance between us that I wondered what she saw that I had missed. Her rapt attention to some mystery in turn captured me. Few people had come to the wheel that morning. I had not noticed this woman before. But the circle joined us in that brief moment, making us part of a connectedness that the entire place seemed to share—as if endless sky, weather-beaten trees, sweet grass, and offerings were all joined to the perimeter of this rock-strewn spider web around which we moved. Indeed, the "web lines" of white stone—fanning out from the center—could have been cast by Spider Woman, the creator figure in Tewa and Navajo tales who draws everything into community.

There was nothing particularly "numinous" about this experience, only a deep sense of being connected in a single moment to everything present. By a strange twist of perception, in fact, I suddenly recognized the woman across the circle as my *wife*—the only figure in the landscape that I might have taken for granted, the one to whom I am sacramentally bound more than any other, the one whom I had married thirty-one years ago that very week. This unexpected experience of connectedness (shared with every detail of the built and natural landscape) became an integral part of my own perception of the place as "sacred." From a traditional native perspective, one might say the place had played tricks on me, jog-ging my perception.[4]

Moments like these, when we glimpse what seems most famil-iar to us with wholly new eyes, remind us that time—like place—is also experienced in multiple dimensions. There are two Greek words for time that parallel the two Greek words for place. Time as *chronos* is perceived as the repetitive ticking of the clock, every second precisely equal to the next. But time as *kairos* is an unrepeatable moment when events of great significance come to be gathered in the life of an individual or a people. To experience oneself simulta-neously in a situation of *chora* and a moment of *kairos* is truly to encounter wonder.[5]

In the poststructuralist world of academic discourse, however, there are no readily available categories for acknowledging and in-terpreting such experience. To speak of my personal (and highly idiosyncratic) awareness of connectedness-to-the-earth as part of a larger interpretation of Medicine Wheel as sacred place seems to endorse a pietist reading of landscape—turning a culturally formed terrain into a privatized "soulscape."[6] Moreover, to suggest that the connection was initiated as much by the *place* as by myself sounds magical and naive. In poststructuralist thinking, nature is essentially a projection of human language, a social construction of a particular cultural perspective. Scholarly discourse about sacred place often lacks any basis for appreciating the traditional native conviction that nature "talks back," that it *participates* in the experience humans have of it.[7]

If we say that language can do no more than that and exclude the voices of the natural world (failing to honor it as a participant in the creation of meaning), the most transformative narratives of places that are deeply significant to us are rendered meaningless. When John Muir speaks of being part of the very flow of rock and river in Yosemite, we dismiss his prose as the exercise of an overwrought imagination.[8] When Gary Snyder writes of merging with the Cas-cade Range of the Pacific Northwest, "the blue mountains walking out to put another coin in the parking meter" as he moves through his day, we attribute his passion to a Buddhist eccentricity or a poet's playfulness with language.[9] Yet the stories most people tell of their own experiences of place as "sacred" almost inevitably honor the participation of the whole environment. Contemporary nature writ-ers, like Terry Tempest Williams and Richard Nelson, typify such sensitivity to the presence of place.

When I ask students in a course I teach on religion and nature to write about a place profoundly meaningful to them, they hardly ever speak of miraculous encounters. Nor do they make claims for the inherent spiritual powers of a given site. Yet they often *do* suggest that their experience was not simply inside their heads but was somehow *shared* in a particular moment by everything around them. They speak with poetic intensity of a childhood memory—of an apricot tree, for example, with the yellowed rope of an old swing hanging from it, clouds overhead and dead leaves underfoot—as if to evoke the depth dimension of an experience that "had" *them* as much as they could be said to have "had" *it*.

What I am asking in this chapter is how we can give voice to place, recovering a sense of the highly embodied and imaginative way that the natural environment participates with us in the creation of meaning and the mystery of experience. How do we attend to the intricate operations of the "mind" (and body) that often accompany a vivid—perhaps even "sacred"—experience of place?[10]

How, also, do we bring critical analysis to bear on the interpretation of such experiences, even wildly diverse experiences, of the same place? Medicine Wheel, Wyoming, attracts not only tourists and researchers like myself, but Native Americans from sixty-nine different tribes bringing liturgies of celebration and lament, New Age enthusiasts searching for vortex points of electromagnetic energy, and artists and naturalists drawn to the delicate wildflowers found on its windswept slopes, as well. The mix of voices vying for rights of interpretation is staggering. In weighing and evaluating each one, how do we also allow the place itself to participate in the process? How do we move, as Paul Ricoeur might suggest, from a first naivete (that perceives place as wholly magical) through a hermeneutics of suspicion (that remains critical of all authoritative claims) to a second naivete (that rediscovers wonder in the deepening of discourse)?[11] That is the question that most engages me.

Three Approaches to Understanding the Medicine Wheel as Sacred Place

Scholarship devoted to the definition and description of sacred place has developed in three directions over the last thirty years, offering three different ways of interpreting the intimately personal (and transcendent) experience of place as *chora*.[12] In the effort to define what constitutes a sacred place, we can speak of ontological, cultural, and phenomenological approaches, each of them coming at the question of place from very different philosophical and method-ological starting points.

The ontological approach, exemplified by historians of religion like Mircea Eliade, began with field research among indigenous peoples, asking how place and time were understood in the earliest mythic tales of tribal wisdom. From this perspective, a sacred place is radically set apart from everything profane; it is a site recognized as manifesting its own inherent, chthonic power and numinosity. It is a place of hierophany, where supernatural forces have invaded the ordinary.[13]

This approach had the advantage of perceiving the dynamics of sacred place from "within," as it were, understanding its magical power to captivate the aboriginal imagination. It described the ex-perience of believers, those participating in mystery. Its disadvan-tage, however, was its failure to recognize that sacred and profane, religion and culture, are inevitably *overlapping* dimensions of human experience. The "sacred" never appears as full-blown transcendent reality, wholly removed from cultural influences.

Therefore, the cultural approach to the understanding of sacred place, exemplified by cultural historians of religion like David Chidester and Edward Linenthal, reacted to this older perspective. Formed by their own work on the social analysis of racial tensions and disputes over public monuments, they disclaimed the notion that sacred places inherently possess an intentionality and power drawn from within or beyond themselves. They insisted, instead, that every human attribution of sacrality is always a social construc-tion of reality. Places in themselves are void of any intrinsic mean-ing, "open to unlimited claims and counter-claims on [their] signifi-cance." Hence, they emphasized the conflictive character of sacred sites as central to their identification. A sacred place is most readily defined, culturally at least, as a site over which conflicting parties disagree—a place about which people are willing to fight and even die.

The considerable advantage of this approach is that it anchors the analysis of sacred place within the critical discourse of social science methodology. It keeps religion from being perceived solely as a matter of transcendent experience wholly separate from the rest of culture. It is able to identify the play of ideology and various cultural agendas hidden within religious claims upon place.[14] As important as this is, however, the social and cultural analysis of sacred place has a tendency also to discount the significance of "place" itself. It views sites as neutral and indifferent objects, pulled this way or that by conflicting parties. If the cultural studies approach has brought religion back down to earth (in its insistence on the social construction of all human experience), it fails to recognize place itself as a participant in the formation of that experience.

The phenomenological approach, therefore, began to emerge as a way of giving voice to yet another participant in the process of perceiving and experiencing sacred places. To the operations of the esoteric power of the divine in setting apart the place from everything around it and the function of conflicting cultural values in the human claiming and defending of the site was now added a concern to listen to the place itself, to recognize its own topography and material character as suggesting affordances or offerings of their own.

Ecological thinkers like James Gibson and Edward Casey, molded by the philosophical tradition of phenomenology, began suggesting that places themselves participate in the perception that is made of them. They began calling people's attention to the intersubjectivity that exists between the human and more-than-human world, stressing the importance of embodiment in the human experience of place. To be fully present to any locale is to recognize the reciprocity involved in touching and being touched by its particular array of rocks, trees, animals, and geographical features. Given this reciprocity, in fact, one may even have to speak of the place as perceiving *itself* through us.

This perspective urges that we take into account the integrity of the place in interpreting the way in which any particular site is to be perceived as sacred. Left to itself, however, it is inadequate in providing a full understanding of how the transcendent and the cultural come together in identifying the presence of the holy, failing to address theological and sociological dimensions of that reality. It quickly becomes apparent, therefore, that to a certain extent all three of these approaches are necessary in grasping the diverse character of any particular sacred place.

This surely is the case with respect to Medicine Wheel, Wyoming, the example with which I began. Ontological, cultural, and phenomenological perspectives all come into play as various communities reflect on its assorted meanings. Some speak of the place as inherently powerful, because of supernormal forces associated with its placement. Claims of contact with the Great Spirit and the earth's wisdom are made by Sioux, Crow, and Cheyenne peoples who have engaged in vision quests there. Others say the site gains its power from anomalies in the earth's electrical system that create unusual energy channels.[15] Archaeoastronomers have discerned a particular alignment of the wheel with respect to the rising sun at the summer solstice and dawn-rising stars like Aldebaran in the constellation Taurus.[16]

From a cultural studies perspective, the great Medicine Wheel is clearly a cultural artifact, an engineered design taking shape between the twelfth and seventeenth centuries. As a human construct, it exists in visible conflict with other cultural and religious purposes associated with the place. The primitive spell of the immediate terrain, for example, is broken by the huge white sphere on the mountain's crest nearby—an air traffic control tower erected by the FAA. A tall chain-link fence surrounds the wheel itself, keeping tourists and non–Native American visitors from "desecrating" the site. Forest Service guides working there request that nonnative visitors not touch any of the offerings or leave any of their own. This is unquestionably a contested site, subject to a considerable variety of conflicting claims.[17]

From a phenomenological point of view, finally, the Medicine Wheel atop Medicine Mountain offers an environment filled with interconnecting surfaces, constantly inviting mutual response. Furry marmots chirp like birds among the rocks, golden eagles rise on thermal currents of desert air, humans pass on the long uphill walk toward the wheel (drawn to slow and quiet reflection by the thinness of the air and the sense of endless horizon). Wind and sun assume new relationships to plant and animal life at that altitude. Sky takes on new texture. In the reciprocal interchange that occurs there "between the living intentions of any animal and the dynamic affordances of its world," the psyche seems to become "a property of the ecosystem as a whole."[18] The place presents itself as more than merely the sum of its parts.

Each of these perspectives, then, is important in seeking a multidimensional understanding of how a sacred place functions within the human imagination. They provide three different procedures for discerning, if not "measuring," the way meaning is put together in relation to any given site. They necessarily argue and contend with each other, speaking respectively for the presence of the sacred, the operations of culture, and the particularities of place. Yet no deep and incisive reading of sacred space is possible apart from the multifaceted conversation they provoke. Taken together, they form a dance-like exchange that is essential to the holistic perception of the way any manifestation of the holy is perceived in space. The purpose of this chapter is to reconsider them individually and to argue for their usefulness as mutually self-correcting tools.

Beyond Eliade: Primitivism and the Magic of Place

The most primordial response of the human spirit in reacting to a place associated with deep mystery is to set it apart from everything else "mundane." Circles are drawn, sharp distinctions made, temple walls erected. As Eliade insisted, "Every sacred space implies a hierophany, an irruption of the sacred that results in detaching a territory from the surrounding cosmic milieu and making it qualitatively different."[19] Shoes are removed, hats taken off (or put on), conversation changes (or ceases altogether). The place is ritually cordoned off as inherently dissimilar from its surroundings.

D. H. Lawrence freely acknowledged the classical idea of the *genius loci* of a place, a "subtle magnetic or vital influence inherent in every specific locality," its spirit of place. Yet he also knew that some places evince such a spirit far more than others, whether or not due to "polarity with particular stars or some vital effluence" he did not know. Still he claimed they spoke a "universal mystic language."[20] Similarly, Carl Jung described certain places as possessing an "autonomous numinosity." From atop the adobe buildings at Taos Pueblo in northern New Mexico, looking toward the 12,000-foot mountains beyond, he was profoundly moved, finding "the air filled with a secret known only to the communicants" of the place. He said it gave him an inkling of what Eleusis must have meant to people 2,500 years ago.[21]

The sacred place, in this way of thinking, is wholly infused with a sense of extranormal power. Whether this is conceived as coming from deep-laid resources in the earth's own mystery or intervening forces from without, the result is that devotees of the place recognize it as structurally, ontologically different. For them it pulses with an energy not found in the surrounding terrain—an energy that might, however, require supersensitive, even shamanic, awareness to detect. Winifred Gallagher and James Swan report on a wide spectrum of paranormal phenomena connected with sites allegedly sacred. These vary from ley lines and vortex centers to energy fields and crop circles. They attract a curious range of investigators, including those measuring electromagnetic fields and negative air-ion emissions, alongside UFO buffs and New Age travelers in quest of "power places."[22]

The stunning red rock country of Sedona, Arizona, for example, is a magnet for many of these sorts of seekers. One finds Jeep tours of vortex sites, Medicine Wheel gatherings led by Native American teacher Sun Bear, psychics and channelers of various kinds, people seeking contact with extraterrestrial life on huge formations like Bell Rock south of town along Highway 179. Spiritual tourism forms a crucial part of the local economy in such a place. Travelers come there because of the mysterious attraction of the terrain.

Other places of this sort may be more particularly associated with healing properties, some of them claimed by indigenous peoples and traditional Roman Catholics alike. The brown adobe chapel of El Santuario de Chimayo in a small village north of Santa Fe has often been described as the "Lourdes of America," a place where people continue to come for miraculous healing. It stands near a dozen huge cottonwood trees beside the Santa Cruz River flowing down from the Sangre de Cristo Mountains. Indian legends recall an ancient shrine there, where smoke and hot water once belched forth from the earth. The Spanish Catholic presence on the site goes back at least to 1805, when a miraculous cult associated with the healing qualities of sacred earth was introduced from the town of Equipulas in Guatemala. Believers spoke of seeing a bright light coming from the ground there at Chimayo and digging up a crucifix of the Black Christ buried near the river.[23]

That crucifix still hangs today on the wall behind the altar of the small chapel. It is a tiny church, yet it contains the whispered prayers of thousands who have come there through the years. On my first visit, I found it difficult to sit in silence over to the side on one of the wooden pews. It was as if the walls continued to echo the agonized cries of endless numbers of pilgrims who had journeyed there. The only other place I have felt the atmosphere so abuzz with the anguish of stored lament was the Wailing Wall in the Old City of Jerusalem. There are sites, it seems, where the very rock itself has absorbed human pain.

Adjoining the nave of this chapel at Chimayo is a small sacristy filled with a veritable museum of cultural artifacts associated with Spanish Catholic spirituality. Multiple statues of Our Lady of Guadalupe and Santo Niño, the child Jesus, are dressed in doll clothes, with slips of paper pinned to them bearing requests for prayer. Abandoned crutches and prosthetic devices hang from the walls with testimonial letters speaking of experiences of healing. Even more impressive is a small chamber in the rear where a hole in the concrete floor (*el posito*) reaches down to the earth below. Here the devout can kneel to take a handful of holy dirt to use in anointing and praying for the sick. To the faithful, the healing power of Christ and that of the earth itself are indistinguishable here at the sacred place.

Such a place obviously functions as a cultural palimpsest, on which many cultural patterns have been written and erased through the years. Yet it also fits well with Eliade's conception of the irruptive, heterogeneous character of a site deliberately set apart as holy. These two perspectives continually wrestle with each other. Jonathan Z. Smith, Eliade's successor at the University of Chicago, has been critical of his mentor's work, rejecting the notion that sacred places always have to evince a unique, epiphanic quality different from everything else. Frequently, he urges, holy sites have a way of sliding in and out of the profane and common places around them. One has to resist, therefore, turning religion into "an extraordinary, exotic category of experience which escapes everyday modes of thought."[24] Religion isn't always a matter of otherworldly transcendence. It continually sets up camp in the ordinary.

Take the "sacred dirt," for instance, that is found replenished every morning in the *posito* at the rear of the sacristy at Chimayo. No one denies that sand from a nearby stream has been brought in, by someone on the chapel staff, to refill the hole. "Holy dirt" drawn from the sacred place is simply ordinary dirt brought in from outside. Far from being a repudiation of the religious character of the site, however, this is but another way of saying that the sacred inevitably extends itself into the profane. The two are never wholly separated in religious practice.

Another way of putting this is to insist, with Jonathan Smith (as opposed to Eliade), that sacred places are not always located at the "center," carefully differentiated from everything on the fringe.[25] Indeed, the periphery often becomes the locus of the holy. Victor Turner emphasized the place of pilgrimage, for example, as a liminal place—not marking the central structure of a community's life but found over on the edge, where new things may happen that very much *question* the center.[26] The official Roman Catholic Church, for instance, will often distance itself from extraordinary claims of irregular religious experience made at places like Chimayo and other sites of ethnic popular devotion.[27] The sacred place, therefore, has the potential of being as disruptive as it is integrative. It can blur distinctions between the sacred and the profane as well as fortify those distinctions. To demand that the *locus religiosus* is ever (and only) the *axis mundi*, located at the center and separated from all profane attachments, is simply not possible.

Contested Places: Sociological and
Legal Efforts to Define the Sacred

With scholars increasingly criticizing Eliade's notion of a sacred shrine "as emanating directly from the matrix of an animated landscape," the study of holy sites has come to be perceived more as "a field of social relations" and "a realm of competing discourses." John Eade and Michael Sallnow have spoken of a shift from a place-centered to a person-centered understanding of sacredness. They have defined a pilgrimage shrine as providing "a ritual space for the expression of a diversity of perceptions and meanings which the *pilgrims themselves* bring to the shrine and impose upon it. As such, the cult can contain within itself a plethora of religious discourses."[28]

Instead of Eliade's timeless, ahistorical approach to the sacred as inherent in the place itself, they have adopted a Durkheimian approach that attributes the meanings of a place to the various political and religious, national and regional, ethnic and class backgrounds of its people. A place can become anything its patrons conceive it to be. Indeed, the principal quality of a holy site becomes its capacity to accommodate a wide diversity of meanings and practices. This means that the study of sacred places focuses ever more specifically on their contested character, attending to the conflicting discourses continually staking claim and counterclaim to their efficacy and control.

Edward Linenthal's work on public memorials and their function in American religious and cultural life exemplifies the profound importance of this attentiveness to the play of discordant languages. In his study of American battlefield sites—from the Alamo to the USS *Arizona* Memorial at Pearl Harbor—he describes a rhetoric of veneration, defilement, and redefinition that operates in each case.[29] The Daughters of the Republic of Texas and living-history reenactment groups in San Antonio speak a language of patriotic reverence in remembering the self-sacrifice of the heroes of 1836. Veterans groups at Pearl Harbor give similar honor to the 1,177 crew members who died when their ship was sunk one early December morning in 1941, reinforcing that "day of infamy's" lesson in preparedness.

Yet dissident voices can also be heard in both of these places. Chicano Catholics have criticized the misuse of the Alamo as a symbol of Anglo-American superiority and Mexican defeat.[30] In the early 1980's members of the Maoist Revolutionary Communist Party raised a red flag on the site, protesting its role as a symbol of oppression. The Ku Klux Klan responded the following year by offering to "protect" the Alamo against communist threat. At Pearl Harbor, various groups have reacted to the "desecration" of the memorial by the presence of Japanese tourists and the effort of the National Park Service to remember Japanese airmen who died there. Irresolvable tensions are intrinsic to such places, as contending discourses pull them in every direction.

Sacred places are inevitably *more* than any one of their competing claimants might want to make of them. From a sociological perspective, they function not only as a battleground of warring voices but also as a way of nesting religious and nonreligious concerns within each other. For some people, the Grotto of Our Lady of Lourdes down the hill from the chapel on the University of Notre Dame campus has as much to do with college football as with the Virgin Mary and the memory of a girl named Bernadette in nineteenth-century France. In the fall of 1985, it caught on fire when students lit more than 1,500 candles the night before an important game against the University of Michigan. The "Touchdown Jesus" pictured in the Eastern Icon above the entrance to Hesburgh Library is not the only symbol of how gridiron and Catholic devotion stand in creative tension at the school of the Fighting Irish.[31]

One finds the same principle at work in the shrine of Ermita de la Caridad on Biscayne Bay in Miami, a site of Catholic Marian devotion where anti-Castro Cuban-American politics are interwoven with the Virgin's protection of refugees journeying across the dangerous waters of the Straits of Florida. A vast mural on the wall behind the altar portrays Hispanic heroes of faith through the history of the New World, yet pilgrims who come there interpret each of its narratives according to their own particular mixture of folk Catholicism, Santería, and Cuban nationalist sentiment.[32] The ritual life of a religious community and the political self-identification of Cuban exiles operate simultaneously alongside each other.

In some cases, "sacred sites" are able to function wholly apart from any institutionalized religious structure or any dominant cultural pattern of civil religion. What matters most in defining such places as "holy" is the presence of ritual activity and symbolic meaning, as well as a language that claims vigorous ownership of the site. One finds an interesting example in a streetside shrine on Main Street in downtown Tucson, Arizona. Near the barrios on the west side, it is known by the locals as *El Tiradito*, which means "the little cast-away one." The term refers to a young sheepherder who was murdered by his father-in-law near that site in the 1920's, supposedly because he had had an affair with his wife's mother.

It is a bizarre story, but for many years people in that area have been leaving petitions and lighting candles there along a wall at the rear of a vacant lot.[33] They have, in effect, attributed saintly status to a common sinner, bypassing entirely the canonization authority of the Roman Catholic Church in setting up a shrine without religious sanction. Miracles have even been claimed there, even though the church hierarchy wants nothing to do with the shrine, discouraging its religious use in every possible way. When the site was threatened with destruction by a proposed freeway in the early 1970's, people in the area organized themselves in defense of what they identified as a powerful symbol of Hispanic identity and *communidad*. The fight to protect the shrine eventually led to its becoming an official historic landmark. Once again, it is often the contested character of a place that most signifies its sacral quality.

Where this finally becomes most apparent is in particular cases that have appeared before federal courts, arguing (poignantly, if not successfully) for the protection of Native American sacred sites.[34] In the case of *Badoni v. Higginson* in 1980, the Navajo Medicine Men's Association protested the desecration of Rainbow Natural Bridge in southern Utah.[35] For centuries the area around this natural sandstone arch had been a remote site where Navajo gods were thought to perform protective and rain-giving functions for generations of Navajo singers. But with the damming of Glen Canyon and the formation of Lake Powell in 1963, tour boats could now bring tourists right up to its edge.

The First Nations people complained that many of their shrines had been flooded and that tourists were profaning the bridge itself with noise, litter, beer drinking, and actual defacement. The United States District Court ruled, however, that the Navajos had no property rights there and that access to the place depended on the principle of "highest use." Since the dam forming the lake served the "higher" values of flood control, irrigation, electrical power, and public recreation, the Indians' claim to a religious place could be ignored.

In another case (*Wilson v. Block*, 1983), the Navajo and Hopi sought to stop a massive development of the Arizona Snow Bowl ski area on the San Francisco Peaks, north of Flagstaff. For generations the Navajo had revered this site as one of the four sacred mountains surrounding their homeland. They regularly gathered soil there to put in medicine bundles that provide sacred power for healing ceremonies. The Hopi cherished the same site because of the honored Kachinas—spirit beings who send them rain and snow to sustain the villages below—who live on these peaks for half of every year. Again the Native Americans lost, because they could not (or would not) point to a particular site in the mountains where sacred power was concentrated and because the court ruled that preventing ski runs there would be an "unconstitutional establishment of religion."[36]

These cases and others like them raise a number of issues about the way sacred places are defined—whether they have to be carefully demarcated from everything else around them, the extent to which secrecy may be an intrinsic part of a site's ability to function as sacred, even how the "narrative rights" to a place may be as important religiously as property rights. Each of these concerns points up the importance of meticulous anthropological and sociological analysis in the study of sacred places.

Beyond Cognitivism: Phenomenology and the Recovery of Place

I have argued so far that sites perceived as holy *do* seem, from a believer's point of view, to draw people by the invasive, thaumaturgical power of their mystery. It was this sense of wonder that never ceased to fix the imagination of Mircea Eliade. But from the perspective of cultural analysis, these same places seem, at their core, to constitute "a religious void."[37] They can be made to represent practically anything one chooses. Admittedly, each of these approaches captures an important aspect of the interior and exterior dynamics of how sacred places are perceived and defined. But neither of them alone is wholly adequate. A sacred place is not simply a unique site magically "possessed" by chthonic forces. Nor is it a topographical wax nose that can be culturally twisted into *anything* one makes of it.[38] A difficulty with both approaches is that the perceiver largely ignores the actual particularities of the place itself. It becomes a blank slate on which divine or human meanings are arbitrarily inscribed—by means of luminous revelation on the one hand or cultural construction on the other.

A third perspective, therefore, is necessary in taking the place itself into account as it is perceived in the richly interactive way that all deep knowing requires. Philosophers who address the question of place from a background in phenomenology remind us that perception of landscape is never a purely cognitive process. We distort the world and our relation to it when we imagine the environment as merely an external container filled with neutral objects to which we (or God) may capriciously attach meaning.[39] We reduce the world and its places to fabrications of the mind, to nothing more than the interior exercise of human subjects operating on a neutral and insensate environment that remains entirely separate from us. As a result, we never escape the rigid dualism of subject and object, mind and matter, culture and nature that has characterized (and limited) so much of the history of Western thought. Phenomenologist Edmund Husserl criticized this assumption of "pure objectivity" because it lets humans so easily *explain* the world without ever attending to their own *participation* in it.[40]

By contrast, ecological psychologists and philosophers like James Gibson, Tim Ingold, and Edward S. Casey insist that all human perception of landscape is relentlessly interactive. "We are enmeshed within webs of environmental relations."[41] Our embodied presence demands that we cannot know the world without also being actively engaged in it. To relate most fully to any given terrain, according to David Abram, is to respect its role as "sentient subject" as well as our own role as "sensible object."[42] Gibson, for example, speaks of the world as offering us (and other animals) numerous "affordances" as we move through it: fundamental possibilities of the physical environment that propose meanings of their own, independently of what we make of them.[43]

A flat surface of rock about knee high "affords" humans a place for sitting. Trees and crevices afford other animals possibilities for climbing or resting. A stone lying on the sand isn't purely a "neutral object": "A crab may have concealed itself beneath it; a thrush may have used it to break open snail shells; an angry human may have picked it up to hurl at an adversary." All of these possibilities—the crab's use of it as a shell, the thrush's use of it as an anvil, the human's use of it as a missile—lie within the "subjective universe" of the stone's own presence in the world.[44] Whatever is made of it, therefore, becomes a matter of reciprocal interaction between the stone itself and all the other participants within its environment.

One's actual embodied experience in encountering a place perceived as sacred is crucial, then, to the sense of magic or awe that one finally attributes to it. The place is "known" only to the extent that we participate in the various affordances it offers, responding to the striking geographical features it projects, adjusting to its changing visual, auditory, olfactory, and kinesthetic qualities. An evocative landscape, possessed of unanswered questions about its physiographical and social history, seems to call for certain kinds of interpretation.[45] Husserl used the word *intersubjectivity* in describing this process of reciprocal perception. Discerning the full significance of a site necessarily involves attending to the place's own contribution to its meaning.

French philosopher Maurice Merleau-Ponty pointedly emphasized the importance of our bodies in the interactive exchange by which perception occurs. We relate to the world in far more than purely cognitive ways. Our bodies are not simply a cage or repository of the mind. They move through an environment as "part" of it, actively engaged in perceiving and being perceived.[46] Merleau-Ponty declared: "As I contemplate the blue of the sky I am not set over against it as an acosmic subject; I do not possess it in thought, or spread out towards it some idea of blue such as might reveal the secret of it, I abandon myself to it and plunge into this mystery, it 'thinks itself within me,' I am the sky itself as it is drawn together and unified, and as it begins to exist for itself; my consciousness is saturated with this limitless blue. . . ."[47] Phenomenologically speaking, the world *beyond* us is also deeply *before* us. We speak "for," "to," and "with" it in a way that demands the total investment of ourselves.

My first experience of the Vietnam Veterans Memorial in Washington, D.C., taught me this in a vivid way several years ago. Initially my approach to the site was solely academic; I wanted to take slides of a place that many people had described as "holy." I quickly recognized it as fitting many of the criteria of sacredness. It is readily perceivable as different, set apart from all the other places on the Mall, functioning almost as a counterpoint to the neighboring shrines of American civil religion. People, especially of my generation, do not have to be told to be silent as they walk through the trees and across the grass to where a wall of black granite rises from the earth. The ground itself seems to cry out with the silent voices of the dead.

The site is also a deeply contested one, as the history of its design and final completion reveals. Veterans who had been through the Tet Offensive in 1968 and others who had raged against the war during the Democratic National Convention in Chicago that same year obviously perceived (and still perceive) the memorial in extremely different ways. Bearded veterans at tables on the edge of the Mall recall today the heroism of the fallen. Others lament the failures of a misbegotten war, as Abe Lincoln gazes from his stone seat nearby onto an America he once described as God's "*almost* chosen people."[48]

As I walked slowly along the wall, with its 58,000 names, I was drawn physically by the surfaces, shapes, and artifacts that make up the ambience of the place. It was impossible not to be touched by the mementos left at the foot of the wall by family members and friends of the dead: a small vase of flowers, a pomegranate signifying love, a cap from someone's infantry unit, a handwritten note reading, "Mike, I still miss your face, your laugh, your dancing eyes. Love, Mary Beth." The stark form of the wall (in its long V-shape) seemed to afford little more than slight shelter—as if from incoming fire on the other side. Its polished black surface starkly reflected my own image, broken by endless rows of etched names. The surroundings receded into distant trees with bronze statues of men shouldering automatic weapons and women bending over the dying. The very ground out of which the wall abruptly rose seemed capable of absorbing all the blood and memory anyone could pour into it.

My body responded to all of this, even as I reminded myself that I had not been personally involved in the Vietnam War and knew no one who had been killed in it. I was about to leave the wall, in fact, when I noticed people over to the side looking up names of the dead in books provided for that purpose. (The names on the wall are not listed alphabetically but according to the date of a given person's death.) Out of curiosity, I wandered over to one of the books and looked up my own family name, finding no one I knew. Then I thought of high school classmates who might have served in the war and, for some reason, the name of Pete Lantz came to mind.

I had not been in touch with Pete Lantz for twenty-five years, but we had been close friends back at Colonial High School in Orlando, Florida. If I had ever returned for a class reunion, he would have been one of the people I would have wanted to see. Not knowing exactly why, I looked in the book to see if there were any Lantzes, perhaps someone related to Pete. These words suddenly took my breath away: "Lt. Peter J. Lantz, born September 17, 1943, died November 23, 1967. Orlando, Florida. Panel 31E, row 71." I could not believe it. Walking to section thirty-one on the east wing of the wall, I traced down to the seventy-first line with my fingers and touched the name of my friend. I sat on the ground before it and cried like a baby—grieving over a friend I had let slide into a forgotten past, coming to realize that I had been involved in the Vietnam War after all, much more intimately than I had ever known. The place became sacred for me in a way I had never expected.

I don't know how to explain this. What was it that made me think of Pete Lantz in that moment before leaving? Had the name jumped off the wall at me earlier as I had walked by it, speaking to my body as part of the total sensory input received in moving through that space? Something more than cognitive, beyond cultural construction occurred in my experience there. I felt called by the place, entering into something of its mystery in a profoundly embodied, interactive way. Whatever happened there, the insights of Merleau-Ponty, David Abram, and Edward Casey seem to be as helpful as any in trying to explain it.[49]

When Casey talks about the manner in which an embodied subject actively perceives a landscape, he mentions six different "moments of Nature" that are intrinsic to any exchange occurring between the two:

1.   The surrounding "ambient array" is what encircles or distinguishes the place (such as a low-lying valley, a large inland lake, or a mall running from the Lincoln Memorial to the U.S. Capitol).

2.   The "sensuous surface" is what stands out on one's first encounter of the place (its colors, shapes, textures, etc.).

3.   The "things" are physical entities that are profiled on the sensuous surface (particular rocks, trees, or other objects— even inscribed names—that draw one's attention).

4.   The "ground" is the underside extension of the sensuous surface, anchoring the site in the depths of the earth.

5.   The "arc" refers to that which fades from explicit presentation on the edges of the scene, a receding band of land or sea that also serves to hold everything in view.

6.   The "atmosphere," finally, is what embodies the "emotional tonality" or "mood" of a place, what makes us aware of the landscape as "itself containing feeling."[50]

Each of these was present in my experience at the wall, operative in that built landscape as much as in a natural one. The six "leading traits" or "features of being," as Casey also describes them, help to clarify the various ways by which a place comes to impose itself on our consciousness.

The sacred site speaks, then, with its own voice, even as that voice is heard by thoroughly culturally conditioned ears. Furthermore, the individual's perception of the numinous or wholly Other in connection with a site is inescapably mediated by culture and place. The joining of these three terms—place, culture, sacredness—allows us to recognize what it is that attracts people to some of the most peripheral places traditionally understood as sacred—places so remote that few human beings have ever had the opportunity of seeing them. An ancient pictograph site deep within the Maze district of Canyonlands National Park in southern Utah offers a case in point, showing how the play of Casey's "moments" can engage the human with the more-than-human world in a strangely insistent way. The Maze is entered either by an extensive float trip down the Colorado River or a punishing sixty-mile drive through twisting canyons, followed by a rock-climbing descent nearly five hundred feet into the depths of the Maze itself. There are few places in North America more isolated.[51]

But were you to venture up one of its winding ravines, on a south-facing cliff you would discover a work of religious art as astounding (and ancient) as anything on this continent. "Harvest Scene" is the name given to the series of pictographs left there by a mysterious Barrier Canyon people some 2,000 years ago. The figures painted on the rock in red ocher appear to be Spirit Beings summoned by a people who knew well the fragility of life in a desolate place. One sacred figure holds an Indian rice plant in a large hand, seeming to offer the gift of life. Other elongated figures with horns on their heads stand nearby like guardians spreading protection over the place. These are haunting presences, particularly as seen by moonlight in the dead of night.

Photographs of the site do not begin to convey its mystery. Your immediate encounter with the place involves a combination of truly intersubjective moments in which neither perceiver nor perceived is wholly passive. Your first impression is one of being trapped at the end of the earth in a dry canyon carved by the distant memory of water. Slickrock winds its way along meanders traced by the forgotten music of swirling streams. The silence of the place is unnerving. That distracting echo you occasionally hear is but the sound of blood pumping through your own temples. But if you are patient, you become gradually attentive to the way aging juniper trees speak to the rock, how wind whispers along canyon walls and morning sunlight dances on yucca plants and Mormon tea. You flinch, startled, as Raven, the Trickster, comes out of nowhere, soaring overhead with the audible, rhythmic beating of feathers on air. You begin slowly to move through the place as part of its own distinctive pattern.

This is the sensitivity to landscape and its myriad occasions for human entry that have fascinated nature writers from Barry Lopez and Paul Shepard to Mary Oliver and Pattiann Rogers. Douglas Burton-Christie probes this literature with an eye to asking about the "spirituality" it evinces, the way meaning emerges as a co-construction of human and more-than-human sensibilities.[52] Emerging from these writers is the recognition that the human role in completing the task of jointly perceiving a given landscape is to tell its story, to weave a narrative that embraces the energies of land and sky in suggesting common meanings only discovered together.

Keith Basso's ethnographic work among the western Apache in Arizona shows how the cultural appropriation of a particular landscape allows a people to view the land as carrying its own stories. Sacred places become bearers of moral and communal values as stories of particular Apache experiences are connected to the topographical features of distinctive places. A site called "Line of White Rocks Extends Up and Out," for example, harbors the memory of a girl who once disobeyed her grandmother and was bitten there by a rattlesnake as a result of her carelessness. Elders in the community need only point to the site in order to suggest the narrative *or* recite the narrative in order to suggest the site. As a result, the place, the story, and the moral demands of communal life all become interchangeable realities, each one able to signify the other. Claims of place, culture, and sacredness are thoroughly interconnected.[53]

The Gifts of the Poet and Lyric Geographer

How does one chart the uneven topography of the contemporary study of American sacred places? It ranges over so many different methodological and philosophical points of view that consensus is impossible, even if desired. I have argued, though, that critical/scientific and personal/humanistic approaches are both necessary in appreciating the interchange of divine, human, and more-than-human influences operating on any site a community considers sacred. Clifford Geertz's call for "blurred genres" may nowhere be more important than here, in the holistic effort to understand the attractions of place.[54] The interdisciplinary sensitivities of both the social scientist and the poet of inner and outer landscapes are not options in this work. They are mandatory.

W. G. Hoskins, the great English geographer, once proclaimed that "poets make the best topographers."[55] He was referring to the need for a creative and imaginative plotting of the cultural landscape in discerning the power that place exercises on a people. Whether his maxim holds true probably depends on the context in which one applies it. If you are using a U.S. Coast and Geodetic Survey map to make your way backpacking and fishing through the Wind River Range of the Wyoming Rockies, you do not want a poet to have taken the vectors on which your map is drawn. You want that chart to be as precise and accurate as possible. But if you are asking about the "gathered meanings" of the land through which you move—found in the stories of native peoples and others who have dwelt there for years—the last person to ask may be a clerk at a government mapping office. The techniques one employs in mapping territory must be appropriate to the kind of terrain one studies.

The gifts of the poet are most particularly appropriate, even imperative, in the task of defining and describing "sacred" terrain. It is the poet who recognizes the intricate play of social and natural forces that join to constitute a place as *chora*. The poet knows that the human experience of the sacred is awash in the particularity of things, the sensuous surfaces and ambient array of details that make possible any sense of dwelling in the presence of mystery. While we may *know* this in our bodies, our scholarly language about place has little capacity for recognizing or expressing it. We analyze sacred place from *above* (as a medium through which sublime powers move) or from the *outside* (as a commodity over which contending parties fight), but we seldom consider it from *within* (as a milieu in which all living beings are interactive subjects). The poet, therefore, helps us overcome the problem of the isolated, abstract interpreter, the one who remains cut off from his or her own richly embodied experience of place.

The poet also reminds us that sacred places are, first of all, "storied" places—elaborately woven together on a cultural loom that joins every detail of the landscape within a given community of memory. If we omit the storied experience of the place (the shared subjectivity of its human and more-than-human participants), we lose the power it exercises on the imagination. Tales of extranormal energies breaking into the ordinary are sometimes a part of the human experience of the sacred. So are stories in which a keen perception of the ordinary is deemed sacred in itself. In either case, the stories are shaped and told within a ritual process over which the poet often presides.

In opening language to all its astounding possibilities, the poet subversively loosens control over the process of interpretation. He or she gives voice to place in recognizing that language itself is not an exclusively human property. Language arises from the very flesh of the world around us. It is more than a creation of abstract human reason. It resonates in the highly expressive patterns of birdsong, in the howling of winds, the rustling of branches and chattering of brooks. Our conventional use of language to denote fixed meaning is but a derivative of that primal reality.[56] When nature speaks, Heidegger insists, it does so with a highly textured and poetic voice. Its primordiality "leaps toward us from the things themselves in an elemental way."[57]

Until we begin to grasp this, the process of interpretation remains a purely cognitive exercise. We perceive places as fabrications of the mind. We dismiss narratives of vivid participation—like my own at Medicine Wheel, Wyoming—as an interpreter's private, romantic construction of place rather than (in some intriguing way) as the *place's* construction of the interpreter. Encountering the sacred, as poets and prophets insist, frequently involves the undermining of the certainties by which we live (even as interpreters), forcing us into new paradigms of interpretation.

Poets are those who mediate between alternative worlds of discourse, inviting the crossing of boundaries from one side to the other. Ordinary social constructions of daily life and passing moments of extraordinary mystery are, in truth, continuously intersecting realities in human experience. The one often slides into the other.[58] Sacred places return us to the ordinary as often as common places disclose for us the underside of wonder. God, after all, is in the details. To stand at the sacred place is to participate in a poetic consciousness that glimpses the woman (the other) on the opposite side of the wheel in the turning of one's life. To walk the perimeter of a circle of common stones laid out to form twenty-eight spokes is to echo the twenty-eight days of the lunar cycle, the twenty-eight ribs of the buffalo, and the twenty-eight poles in a Sun Dance lodge. Each of these represents a common earth-wisdom close to the life of northern Plains Indians, close to the living earth itself. The holy is invariably akin to the prosaic and mundane, interconnecting the whole of life.

Methods of interpretation, therefore, have to be able to address every dimension of one's perception of the sacred. My particular encounter of mystery at Medicine Wheel, Wyoming, was deeply embedded in the interwoven threads of culture. It raised specific social questions about ownership and privacy, the ecological protection of the site (even from tourists like myself), the role of the National Park Service and the FAA in relation to native peoples there, and the whole complicated history of cultural overlays on the land. At the same time, it involved my body and mind in a tangled interaction with all the other living voices arising from the surrounding land and sky. I was a participant in something beyond my capacity for language, almost as if the place, in all its particularities, wanted to speak itself through me.

Finally, there was even a sense in which these questions of ownership, privacy, and connectedness were also turned back onto my own experience, as if God were inviting me to reconnect to family, to fresh political and ecological responsibilities, to a renewed valuing of quotidian gifts in general. Sacred places do that. Our study of them, accordingly, requires an openness to every aspect of the process.

PART 2 | The Geography of American Spiritual Traditions

The beavers had to go and build another goddamned dam on the Colorado. Not satisfied with the enormous silt trap and evaporation tank called Lake Mead (back of Boulder Dam) they have created another even bigger, even more destructive, in Glen Canyon. This reservoir of stagnant water will not irrigate a single square foot of land or supply water for a single village; its only justification is the generation of cash through electricity for the indirect subsidy of various real estate speculators. . . . I was one of the lucky few who saw Glen Canyon before it was drowned. In fact I saw only a part of it but enough to realize that here was an Eden, a portion of the earth's original paradise.

—Edward Abbey, *Desert Solitaire: A Season in the Wilderness*

A sacred place is not merely a meaningful place; it is a powerful place because it is appropriated, possessed, and owned. . . . Sacred space is inevitably contested space, a site of negotiated contests over the legitimate ownership of sacred symbols. As Michel Foucault insisted, "space is fundamental in any exercise of power" . . . A sacred space is not merely discovered, or founded, or constructed; it is claimed, owned, and operated by people advancing specific interests. . . . Sacred space is inevitably entangled with the entrepreneurial, the social, the political, and other "profane" forces. In fact, a space or place is often experienced as most sacred by those who perceive it at risk of being desecrated by the very forces—economic, social, and political—that made its consecration possible in the first place.

—David Chidester and Edward T. Linenthal,
American Sacred Space

Until recently, the phenomenology of city religions was not a specific field of scholarly inquiry. The very idea of "city religion" struck many as an oxymoron. . . . Mircea Eliade, the great historian of religions and a lifelong resident of cities himself, argued that what passed for religion in contemporary Western urban settings were degraded and impotent "survivals" of real religiosity, which necessarily existed in intimate and ongoing connection to the rhythms and revelations of the sacred in nature. . . . A romantic sensibility akin to Eliade's is more likely to identify mountaintops and ocean beaches as places evocative of religious feelings than street corners and the basements of housing projects.

—Robert A. Orsi, *Gods of the City:*
Religion and the American Urban Landscape

Mythic Landscapes:
The Ordinary as
Mask of the Holy

Experience may be akin to what Dorothy Day once said of property: the more common it becomes, the more holy it is.[1] Writers like Wendell Berry, Annie Dillard, and Lewis Thomas all speak of the most ordinary things, yet find in a weasel's stare, a swollen river, a snail's strange life something far more than ordinary. How does one learn to see with their eyes? Whence comes that double magic of recognizing the ordinary as extraordinary and the extraordinary as ordinary? Standing knee-deep in miracles myself, I often glimpse only a world of profane commonness. The turn of focus that brings the holy into view seldom occurs.

This is a book concerned with ordinary landscapes, seen—with the eyes of faith—in binary vision. Spanish Catholics in the early seventeenth century gazed on Death Valley and saw, like anyone else, only rock-strewn sand with heat waves hovering over the horizon. Yet, by a metaphorical twist of insight, they also discovered in that lifeless terrain the very "palm of God's hand." The Seneca Iroquois traveled often to a large hill at the head of Canandaigua Lake in Western New York. Unremarkable in any outward way, they nevertheless saw it to be the great Ur-Stone of their people, the primitive place of emergence where life began. Shaker believers in Hancock, Massachusetts, took their visitors on tours of the Round Barn, a fine stone structure built in 1826. They demonstrated dances at their rectangular meeting house and offered vegetables grown in gardens laid out according to a four-square plan. But in looking on these common geometric forms, the believers also discerned the lineaments of a grander pattern corresponding to the heavenly sphere above. In each case—Spanish Catholic, Seneca, Shaker— the landscape was read in multiple ways, the ordinary valued simply for what it was and yet also seen to occasion an entree to something more.

In Christian thought, the one great practical truth of the incarna-

65

tion is that the ordinary is no longer at all what it appears. Common things, common actions, common relationships are all granted new definition because the holy has once and for all become ordinary in Jesus Christ. G. K. Chesterton's Father Brown became the uncannily clever detective that he was simply because he knew this truth. While others were always ready to evoke the occult and supernatural in their efforts to explain the most difficult crimes, it was this balding and unassuming Catholic priest who invariably solved the mystery by means of the most everyday, commonplace observations. As a believer in the incarnation, he really could not do otherwise. Having become accustomed to expecting the holy in the undistinguished form of human flesh, he now looked upon every ordinary detail with more than usual attention. What struck him as conventional and natural, seen with his eye for the peculiarly "normal," impressed others—ironically—as miraculous. Similarly, Dietrich Bonhoeffer sought a this-worldly Christianity, knowing Christ to be the center even of that which fails to recognize him as such. Christianity is simply the process whereby men and women are restored to normal humanity, reclaiming everyday existence. "The Christian is not a *homo religiosus*, but a man, pure and simple, just as Jesus was man," Bonhoeffer states.[2] "Human beings fully alive!" shouted Irenaeus. "Such is the glory of God."

Why do theologians so often lack this ability to consecrate the normal and natural? They too readily abandon the field, letting the poets celebrate the creation they leave unpraised. Part of the problem is that theologians find it hard to escape the rigid dualism of sacred and profane, subject and object, nature and supernature. Poets, on the other hand, can more easily think beyond such limits—reaching, as they do, for mythic wholeness. Yet theirs can be the tendency toward a shallow monism in which God, the world and the self rollick in a syrupy nature mysticism. How does one learn to esteem the commonplace without resorting to apotheosis? The theologian at last is driven to listen with the poet's ear for the muted and unremarkable mystery of the cosmos.

Canoeing down the Red River Gorge in Kentucky, Wendell Berry paddled past wild flowers pasted with reckless splendor on the banks. He followed the current into the quiet water of a deep pool and sat in the long silence. There, in a single moment of Zen awareness, he became present to himself and to the space he had entered. "Ahead . . . a leaf falls from high up in a long gentle fall. In the water its reflection rises perfectly to meet it."[3] Such an absurdly simple and yet strangely profound observation. Had I sat for hours in the same canoe, watching many leaves fall into the silent current, I might never have connected those three things—the descending leaf, the joining reflection, and the moment in which they precisely met. Although I know with Martin Buber that "all real living is meeting," I seldom make myself fully present to those occasions when the ordinary whispers of the holy.

What I lack is a hermeneutic for the interpretation of ordinary landscapes. There is too little subtlety in my own reading of the world in which I live. It remains dense and opaque. Others see more clearly the possible realities hidden within the commonplace, because they attend more carefully to the commonplace itself. "All visible objects, man, are but as pasteboard masks," said Captain Ahab in Melville's *Moby Dick*.[4] They point sacramentally to mysteries far beyond themselves. Ahab's own fixation was on the great white whale as the mask of some "inscrutable malice," sinewing the whole. Melville's vision was a fixed, haunting gaze into the heart of darkness, but he knew the power of masks, the ability of the ordinary to evoke the numinous.

It was Martin Luther who explored the other side of that idea of the holy—its *fascinans* as well as its *tremendum*. He insisted that God's naked, awful majesty could never be pursued directly. In order to shield human beings from the unapproachable light of God's glory, God always remains hidden, veiled by a mask (*larva*). Though not seen face to face, this God is yet encountered with a striking immediacy in the *larvae Dei*—the created marvels of God's hand, the bread and wine at Mass, even the twisted mystery of one's own self as created being. They all "contain Christ," himself the veiled and incarnate God. Of course, they form only a "dark glass" at best. None of them can be read with clarity. They serve to tantalize, to intrigue, to lead always beyond themselves. Yet, because of Christ, all ordinary things assume new importance. They are masks of the holy: not sterile occasions for rationally inferring the existence and attributes of God, but vivid, if broken, means by which God as Mother of creation comes to meet us.[5]

Many of the spiritual traditions discussed in this book perceive the American landscape, both in its rural and urban forms, as a kind of mask of the holy. They understand it simultaneously to hide and reveal certain aspects of the splendor, grace or terror of the divine. Native Americans, Puritans, and Shakers have all approached the world with a hermeneutical lens by which the mask's power could be recognized and appropriated. They have seen their environment to offer some measure of correspondence to the alternative world of the sacred. It was not that they sought to lift the veil and gaze directly into the face of the Ineffable. Still less was it a pantheistic immanentalism, imagining the sacred to be wholly subsumed under species of Mountain Laurel and Queen Anne's

Lace. It was rather a conviction that the world, in the eyes of imagination and faith, functions as icon. It mythically incorporates in its evocative power the utterly transcendent reality to which it dimly points.

Pablo Picasso was fascinated all his life with the vitality and mystery of the ceremonial masks used by primitive peoples. Exotic African masks unaccountably appeared on the faces of women in his painting of "Les Demoiselles d'Avignon," that masterwork which inaugurated the modern art of the twentieth century. In his paintings, he wanted to find the mask that gave life, the mask that opened new possibilities in the very act of concealing the old. He longed "to paint something that, in defiance of the secular, spiritually exorcised conditions of modern life, would not just challenge, but actually invest the viewer with its iconic power—the lost power of the mask."[6] The vision became an obsession in his old age. He furiously covered canvases with paint, searching for that combination of color, form, and primitive simplicity that might lend access to the mystery always beyond his reach. "I must absolutely find the mask," he died crying. He sought the same energy that Kwakuitl woodcutters in Western Canada hoped to contain in the brightly painted visages they carved. They invariably chiseled ritual masks out of a living tree, taking an axe to the trunk only after the effigy had been made complete. In this way, the power of the tree's own life could be contained within the mask. One of the deepest impulses of the human spirit is to find the mask that invests with power and life.

The implications of this notion of the holy as masked in the ordinary are often drawn out more convincingly by artists and storytellers than by theologians. Metaphor, with all its multivalent concreteness, may be ultimately the most faithful servant of truth. It masks as it also opens one to life. It is said, for example, that a man once came from a great distance to study under Rabbi Shneur Zalman, the founder of the Lubavitcher Hasidim. This great rebbe had himself pushed upward the heights of mystical knowledge through his studies with the celebrated Maggid of Mezritch. Only the brilliant Gaon of Vilna exceeded his ability in memorizing and arguing Talmud. In the balance of spiritual and intellectual insight the man was without peer. To this distinguished tzaddik, therefore, came the distant visitor. On learning of his quest, the villagers of Ladi all asked with pride if he wanted first to hear their great rabbi read Talmud or to hear him pray. Neither, he said. He wanted only to watch him cut bread or tie his shoes. The villagers were stunned as the visitor simply observed the rabbi sitting absently in thought in the light of the afternoon sun, and then went away edified.

One begins to suspect that the contemplation of any ordinary thing, made extraordinary by attention and love, can become an occasion for glimpsing the profound. Lewis Thomas finds hope for the human species in the accumulative intelligence of termites, the thrush in his backyard, and a protozoan named *Myxotricha paradoxa*. He simply attends with the eye of a biologist to what passes beneath our senses every day.[7] G. K. Chesterton once suggested that "it is a good exercise, in empty or ugly hours of the day, to look at anything, the coal-scuttle or the bookcase, and think how happy one could be to have brought it out of the sinking ship onto the solitary island."[8] Such an exercise can be no small aid in attaching true value to the most commonplace of things around us.

Yet most of us balk at the sharp paradox of God's mysterious presence in the world. On the one hand, the ordinary reaches out to be noticed: it cries for recognition. The holy makes itself obvious in every turning leaf. Shug Avery, in Alice Walker's novel *The Color Purple*, says, "Everything want to be loved. . . . You ever notice that trees do everything to git attention we do, except walk?"[9] How, then, can we so readily overlook the presence of the sacred? It is because, on the other hand, the ordinary also conceals—by the very fact of its ordinariness. It anesthetizes the mind with its dull predictability. Saturation perception takes over, turning what we see all of the time into what we don't actually see at all.

This paradox of seeing and not seeing discloses the central nature of metaphor and mask alike. It is something which bewilders or disguises in the very process of revealing and making known. That is why the notion of "mask" is so appropriate to the mystery of the divine presence. A mask *identifies* the character represented, as in ancient Greek and Roman drama, but it *hides* identity as well. It is this juxtaposition of the familiar and the strange that grants a metaphor its power to engage the imagination. Understanding the ordinary as a mask of the holy, therefore, is a way of maintaining a metaphorical tension between similar and dissimilar things.[10] The mask is never able to contain or consume the holy, yet neither can the holy be known apart from the mask. Both must be kept in tension. We live in equivocality like fish in the sea. But our discursive minds seldom rest content with metaphor. We seek its resolution in a single dimension of clarity. We are uneasy with ambiguity. In a course I teach on storytelling and theological method, the hardest task is to persuade students that the story itself, with all of its intense and colorful imprecision, *is* the truth.

Our tendency is to seek the holy directly, apart from any mask or ambiguity—through what Luther criticized as a *theology of glory*. In other words, we want to possess the sacred without owning the ordinary. Trying to grasp heaven in all of its naked majesty, we denigrate the sign, the mask. We lift up its edges in order to gaze first-hand on the glory it shades. As a result, inevitably we look *beyond* everything without seeing it for what it is. We scoff at the commonplace in the process of reaching for a grandeur we're convinced it lacks. Ironically, in doing so we miss both. The sacred in its naked glory completely eludes us, while we contemptuously pass by the subtlety of the mask itself. The trick is to be able to see the holy both in and through the mask, even as the archaeologist traces back the various layers of writing on an ancient palimpsest or as the artist explores an old canvas to discern the effect known as pentimento. Lillian Hellman offers a vivid description of the latter:

> Old paint on canvas, as it ages, sometimes becomes transparent. When that happens it is possible, in some pictures, to see the original lines; a tree will show through a woman's dress, a child makes way for a dog, a large boat is no longer on an open sea. That is called pentimento because the painter "repented," changed his mind. Perhaps it would be as well to say that the old conception, replaced by a later choice, is a way of seeing and then seeing again.[11]

It is this simultaneity of vision which the mask, with all of its multivalence, makes possible. I see with greatest depth that which I observe from different perspectives at the same time.

There's a deep intrigue in the double seeing, as well as in the anonymity, that a mask affords. Whether we think of All Hallow's Eve, the white face of clowning and mime, or the masquerading heroes of primitive mythology, the appeal of the mask is profound. Take, for example, the rituals surrounding the use of masks in Native American religion. The subtle dynamic of the mask as at once revealing and concealing the holy is powerfully exemplified in Hopi initiation rites in Arizona. There children between the ages of seven and ten are introduced to the cult and mystery of the kachina masks. Prior to this time, the children have always considered the kachina figures to be magical beings bearing gifts or frightening them with numinous wonder. They have never dreamed that the faces of the dancing figures are anything less than the visage of the sacred itself. But in the process of initiation they suddenly are shown the kachina figures *without* their masks. They discover, to their dismay, that the figures have been their own male relatives all along. The masks carried by them appear to be mere false faces of carved wood. This is a keenly liminal experience for the initiates, brought as they are to the very threshold of formal religious life. It is marked by confusion, disenchantment, and rich new insight—all at the same time. One must not think that the child's experience is merely one of disillusionment. On the contrary, says Sam Gill, what the Hopi child discovers is that things are much more than what they appear. The child is put into a position to learn "what is perhaps the most important lesson in his or her entire religious life: that a spiritual reality is conjoined with, and stands behind, the physical reality."[12]

I sometimes ask myself if I, with my own neat Cartesian distinctions, have begun to learn as much. Am I able to accept the holy, without taking offense at receiving it through the commonplace? Indeed, can I discern my own relatives—my wife and children—as themselves masks of the holy for me? Luther insisted that the freedom of Christians is realized in our becoming Christs to each other.[13] In wearing *that* mask, putting on that reality, we discover in each other the presence of more than what appears. We are set free from despising ourselves and all the trivial details of our lives. Suddenly they become masks of the Lord Christ, calling us through them to an intense focus of attention and love.

This tenacious insistence on life—an ability to attend unremittingly to the particular—is what I find especially compelling in Annie Dillard's writings. Her opening essay in *Teaching a Stone to Talk* describes a meeting she once had with a weasel in the woods near Tinker Creek. They surprised each other beneath a tree one afternoon and stood stupified in each other's presence for a full half-minute. It was as if their eyes had locked and someone had thrown away the key, Dillard writes.[14] The experience led her later to read further about such animals and to learn that weasels are known for the tenacity of their grip. Their teeth, like those of English bulldogs, are able to lock, once they bite down on something. In fact, an eagle was once found in the wilds with the dried skull of a weasel still anchored to its neck. Apparently, the weasel had struck the eagle in a desperate attempt for food. Missing the jugular vein, the teeth had sunk into the cartilage of the neck as the eagle flew off with its attacker in tow. Gradually the eagle then ate what it could of the animal dangling limply like a pennant from its throat. A grisly story, this—full of fervid, sanguine ordinariness. Yet Annie Dillard asks herself, can I sink *my* teeth into life with such tenacity—even if it means in the end being borne aloft as dried bones hanging from an eagle's underside? That's the only way worth living. "You must go at your life with a broadax," she says in *Holy the Firm*. And she's exactly right. The created detail of all of God's world cries out for merciless attention.

According to the mystical tradition of Pseudo-Dionysius, the seraphs are the highest of nine choirs of angels. They are borne of a stream of fire flowing from under the throne of the Almighty. Being all wings, they perpetually move toward God, rapt in praise and crying, "Holy, Holy, Holy . . . " Yet it is said that they can sing only the first "Holy" before the great intensity of their love ignites them into flames, returning them to the stream of fire from which they are replaced by others.[15] Of such intensity is the fire that belongs to Annie Dillard. It is the wondrous delight that invites each of us to the contemplation of everything common, an invitation to gaze stealthily on that which would dissolve us into flames if viewed firsthand. The seeds of faith are always sown on the fertile landscapes of the commonplace. At the end, then, I'm driven—like the aged Lear—to own what I have denied so long. To the once-scorned Cordelia, Lear uttered a last eloquent cry for prosaic mystery:

> So we'll live,
> And pray, and sing, and tell old tales, and laugh
> At gilded butterflies, and hear poor rogues
> Talk of court news; and we'll talk with them too—
> Who loses and who wins; who's in, who's out—
> And take upon's the mystery of things
> As if we were God's spies. . . . [16]

Take upon us the mystery of things, indeed. It lies there masked in ordinariness, whispering the splendor of a God whose name remains *Deus Incarnatus*. I discover it all: Wendell Berry's falling leaf, the rabbi's quiet pose, the mask carved from living tree, the Hopi kachina and eagle's flight. In each case, Dorothy Day proves right: the more common it is, the more holy it becomes.

"Split the stick and there is Jesus," said the ancient Gospel of Thomas, knowing the ordinary to be fraught with wonder. The dictum is only partly true. Theologians rightly caution against any simplistic Gnostic gazing at the naked sign. The stick reveals its fullness only because of the emptied Christ. Otherwise a stick is a stick is a stick. The mask, therefore, is not the holy; it only suggests access to the holy. Neither the stick, nor the falling leaf, nor the wonder of my own children ever reveals the fully formed face of Christ. The masks remain masks. Yet the poetic insight still holds true—Christ *is* the center. My eyes strain to discern the reality behind what I see. "Split the stick and there is Jesus; lift the stone and one finds the Lord."[17]

3 | Seeking a Sacred Center: Places and Themes in Native American Spirituality

"If there exists such a thing as a spirit-of-place, imbuing each of the continental masses of the world with its own unique and ineradicable sense of rhythm, mood, and character, and if there exists an indigenous form of faith deriving from it, then it is to the Indian we must look for that expression of life's meaning which alone differentiates America from Europe, Africa, and Asia."[1]

Sleeping Ute Mountain lies in quiet dignity at the southwestern corner of Colorado very near the center of the earth (by the reckoning of any number of tribes). In the shadow of its memory the Ute peoples long ago celebrated the Bear Dance, pursued buffalo hunts in the fall of each year, and endured the Indian Wars of the 1880's. Not so long ago a small child often stood beside her mother, watching the evening sun fall between the folded arms of that great stone figure, remembering the promise that one day he might yet awake to lead his people to new power and life. The child was Maria José Hobday, today a Franciscan sister who still remembers clearly the words her mother spoke as they stood before the purple silhouette of that slumbering peak. "Take this beauty into your heart," she urged, "learn it. Some day you will only be able to see this with the eyes of your heart. Then it will be important for you to have the beauty inside you. Memorize the land."[2] In that moment the mother spoke a wisdom deeper than she knew. The most sacred place to us is invariably that which has been internalized—constituted as an inner beauty, remembered into a being richer even than it had been in reality. We know all the most meaningful places only in retrospect. The sacred center is thus essentially a non-geographical entity, a created thing, ultimately an illusion,[3] yet, paradoxically, also a place more real than real. The most important places are always so. "It is not down in any map," Melville said of the site where the Great White Whale had once been found; "true places never are."[4]

The interpenetration of "true places" and particular sites charted

73

by map coordinates is a matter of keen interest in Native American spirituality. Encountering God at the sacred center of one's being is the goal of all worship, yet entering that center involves a union of both interior and exterior states. To "memorize the land" is to adhere both existentially and physically to the center of all that is holy. Hence, a passion for placement is basic to Indian thought. As Sam Gill suggests:

> The symbolic language of place—the set of symbols that gives the people of a culture orientation in space and time—is pervasive in Native American cultures. . . . We find in many Native American cultures that landscapes, villages, ceremonial grounds, ceremonial lodges, and common homes replicate the form and process of the cosmos.[5]

This careful attention to the nuances and interchanges of mythical and geographical place can offer important insights to the character of Native American spirituality in general. The present chapter, therefore, will make use of five representative places, sacred to as many different Indian traditions, as a way of introducing five themes common to Native American piety as a whole. Admittedly, such an effort to characterize the broad sweep of Amerindian spirituality, even under the specialized rubric of sacred space, is an exercise in presumption, if not futility. There *is* no typical American Indian experience, given a history dating back hundreds of years and scanning over a thousand separate and highly-developed Native American cultures.[6] All we can do is to offer a pastiche or jumbled medley that suggests an ambience more than it describes any particular tribal tradition—yet, in the process, may still be true to the larger spirit and vision of Native American life.

Mythic Correspondence and the Place of Emergence

The Navajo have never lived far from the place or the story of their creation as a people. Proximity to the four corners (formed by the nexus of the states of New Mexico, Arizona, Utah, and Colorado) and repetition of the tales pertaining to the emergence of the first peoples in that region have long characterized the Navajo experience. Their children will hear the story sung in chants around evening campfires or whispered in the night as the moon rising in the east shines through the door of the hogan where they sleep. The hogan is an appropriate place to hear these mythic tales of earth's beginnings, for the hogan itself is sacred—symbolizing home, the center of power, the universe in microcosm. Its shape is that of the broken circle, a single door opening always to the east—the direction of the golden sun, of wisdom, of the road to life. The circle or sacred hoop is a symbolic form revered in almost every Native American tradition. "Everything the power of the World does is done in a circle," said Black Elk.[7] Indeed, at the genesis of humankind, a ceremonial hogan—its circle embracing the whole of what would be—was built on the rim of the Place of Emergence by First Man and First Woman.

The ancient myths tell of a series of worlds (four or more) that had long existed below the level of present life on earth. In the fullness of primeval time, certain cosmic figures began an upward journey which brought them into the world as we know it. They emerged from their underground origin at a place which continues to serve as a vertical *axis mundi*, the location where contact with numinous power is still made. This Place of Emergence functions very importantly in the ritual and narrative life of the people, but it can be plotted on maps as well, some say. Trout Lake in the San Juan Mountains of southwestern Colorado has been occasionally suggested as its site. Others point to Island Lake in the nearby La Plata Range or even Window Rock, the site of the Navajo Reservation headquarters northwest of Gallup today.[8] Some of the oldest tales speak of this place as the Mountain-Around-Which-Moving-Was-Done. But outside of their dreams, no one knows precisely where to pinpoint creation's center. Somewhere near the four corners—that's close enough. More important is that the place is mythically reconstructed in every ceremonial hogan or sweat-lodge where the ritual of creation is still rehearsed today.

The sacred art of sandpainting, for example, makes careful use of the circle shape as it depicts the archetypal events and figures of creation, bringing the person for whom the painting is done within proximity to the healing power of the Emergence Place itself. Clean riverbed sand is first spread on the floor of the hogan and colored pigments, ground with sand, sprinkled on top in the form of mythic persons and cosmic designs. The individual needing healing or spiritual rejuvenation is then invited to sit in the middle of this sand-strewn mandala, facing through the broken circle to the door on the east. Chants will be sung inviting to that place the same holy figures who were present at creation and grains of sand from their painted effigies may even be applied to the body of the one seeking wholeness. The entire ritual is an intriguing duplication in miniature of a redemption accomplished *in illo tempore*, at the beginning of time. Ancient legend has it that First Man and First Woman constructed a primeval sand painting of their own in the hogan initially built on their emergence from below. There they drew the shapes of all forms of life that would be created on the earth and scattered the sands in exuberant fecundity.[9] The hogan floor where the sands are spread today is, therefore, a locale rich in power. Indeed, the Navajo word for sandpainting (*'iikaah*) means "the place where the gods come and go."[10] Seated on the sand, looking out onto the road to life, one senses his having fallen into a distant, clouded mystery—only to reemerge with new life at the very center where power had always dwelt.

Being properly "placed" with respect to the holy, therefore, is a concern central to Indian piety. "All sacred things must have their place," Claude Levi-Strauss noted. "Being in their place is what makes them sacred. If taken out of their place, even in thought, the entire order of the universe would be destroyed."[11] In Navajo ceremonial life one of the most difficult tasks expected of a hero is that of ascending a high mountain (in the vicinity of the four corners) and being asked to discern and name every holy place which could be seen from that height.[12] There are many sacred mountains in this terrain, but the holiest of all (seen far beyond the horizon in mystic insight) are the four directional Holy Mountains planted at the time of emergence. These include Mount Taylor to the south, Mount Humphrey to the west, a peak known as Mountain Sheep to the north (perhaps Hesperus Peak), and the Black-belted-one to the east (perhaps Wheeler Peak). These form the perimeter of the Navajo world.[13] Soil from each of their summits is collected for use in a mountain soil bundle, an article of great power which may be applied to various parts of the body when prayer for healing is made.[14] Again the numinous power attributed to these sacred peaks has its source in their connection to the events of creation which occurred at their center. The landscape is embedded with mystery because of its proximity to the source of life's beginnings. The trained Navajo hero thus sees more than the mesas, buttes, dry canyons, and twisted riverbeds observed by the casual seer. He recognizes as well another geography of transcendence that exists in, with, and under the painted desert itself.

This is a concept deeply rooted in the very ancient philosophical notion of correspondence—the idea that the visible world is a "double" of some prior, cosmic counterpart, deriving its energy from that hidden, metaphysical connection. It's a doctrine as old as history, polished by Plato, rehearsed by Philo of Alexandria, and carried on in the mysteries of Kabbalah. In ancient Egypt and Babylonia, the Nile, Tigris and Euphrates rivers (and the huge cities along them) were all seen to be modeled after cosmic rivers and sacred cities not apparent to the eye.[15] Similarly, when the Navajo shaman looks out over the horizon from the four corners, he sees, as it were, two worlds. As if a cosmic, plastic over-

PLACES SACRED TO THE NAVAJO, HOPI, APACHE, UTE, AND ZUNI INDIANS

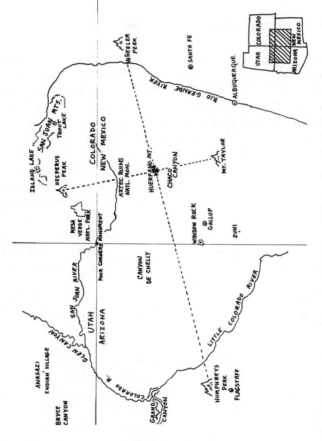

Charted here, alongside the ruins of pre-Columbian cliff dwellers, are various sites considered by tribes of the Southwest to be the Middle Place of the world or their Place of Emergence. At the intersection of the coordinates of four sacred mountains lies the mythical mountain, Mt. Huerfano, understood as the center of the earth, seen only by the eyes of the spirit.

lay could be superimposed on the Rand-McNally map of the Southwest picked up at the Shell station outside Farmington. In this unified view of the world there is no distinction whatever between sacred and profane. The ordinary carries within it the latent power of its heavenly double. Reality conceived in this manner, therefore, is always open to "emergence"—to the inbreaking of mystery at the place where the navel of the earth is met.[16]

The Golden Earth as Middle Place

Francisco Vasquez de Coronado, carrying the Spanish flag and clad in silver armor, marched with three hundred troops into the Zuni village of Hawikuh in the hot July of 1540. He had come with hopes of fulfilling a dream as old as the Middle Ages and as recent as current rumor—a dream that seven sumptuous cities of gold could be found in the hinterland of this unexplored and unexpended land. He was quickly disappointed, however, finding no precious metals there at all—only Zuni sandstone and a few pieces of turquoise. His eyes traveled over the variegated flaxen colors of the nearby cliffs, the yellow corn growing along the muddy river, and the village's sun-baked adobe in the gilded afternoon light, and he saw nothing. The Zuni love of the golden earth as a richness in its own right was an appreciation lost entirely on the sensibilities of a hard-bitten treasure hunter like Coronado. Frantically he pressed on further west, then east, ever in search of New World gold in the fabulous seven cities of Cibola.[17]

The Zunis, however, knew that he had passed over a far greater treasure than he could have imagined. For, according to their most hallowed myths, the seven villages of Cibola were situated at the earth's Middle Place—a location where they entered most fully into relationship with the land itself. Here the earth was gold enough. Time before time, when the world was still young and the Zunis had newly emerged from beneath the ground, they had moved from site to site in search of an appropriate place to settle. They finally had summoned the water-strider, a great mythic spider and cosmic ally who stretched out his legs toward the distant oceans, revealing the Middle Place as that point directly beneath his heart. There the middle town was built, with six others nearby, each at the points where the spider's legs had touched. There still today the single pueblo of Zuni stands on the banks of the Zuni River in western New Mexico near the Continental Divide. The place even remains golden in its possession of the ocherous earth, and ancient chants still say that the rest of the world depends on this place for its fertility—"when it rains at Zuni it rains all over the earth."[18]

This attachment to the soil as a nurturing source forms another theme central to much of Native American spirituality. To reverence the earth with the whole of one's senses is a posture highly prized in Amerindian theology, rooted as it is in the sensate and concrete world. This is a foundational theology Thomas Aquinas would have approved. He, too, was convinced that *asensuality* is a vice, the rejection of one's senses too often leading to sacrilege.[19] An example of the particular affinity of Native Americans to the red soil on which they dwelt is found in a reflection by Chief Luther Standing Bear of the Lakota Sioux:

> The Lakota was a true naturalist—a lover of nature. He loved the earth and all things of the earth, the attachment growing with age. The old people came literally to love the soil and they sat or reclined on the ground with a feeling of being close to a mothering power. It was good for the skin to touch the earth and the old people like to remove their moccasins and walk with bare feet on the sacred earth.[20]

One's relation to the soil, therefore, is a means of making subtle connection with the holy. Yet such is an appreciation that grows only with sustained proximity to the land. Jonathan Z. Smith recalls an experience in his college years that contrasts this reverence for the clayey sod with the fetish for cleanliness found in our dominant white, urban-American culture.[21] Working for a dairy farmer one summer, he noticed with interest how his boss always scrubbed his hands carefully before leaving the house early each morning. But then, immediately outside the front door, he would stoop down to rub his hands in the dust before beginning the day. Smith couldn't understand the absurd consistency with which the farmer carried out this daily ritual. "Don't you city boys understand anything?" the boss finally responded, with all the confidence of one accustomed to life at the Middle Place. "Inside the house it's dirt; outside, it's earth. You must take it off inside to eat and be with your family. You must put it on outside to work and be with the animals." This is not a distinction between sacred and profane, but between two forms of sacral experience. In each case the tactile sensation of removing and applying dust serves as a means of access to something profound. Hence, when Moses and Joshua were told to take their shoes from their feet, so as to touch the holy ground on which they stood, the symbolic gesture was more than one of respect and fear (Ex 3:5; Jos 5:15). It also signaled an occasion for receiving the divine presence with the fullness of their senses.

This intimacy of the Native American with the land may be seen as part of a larger "participation mystique," said by Lucian Levy-Bruhl to be characteristic of pre-modern cultures. A consciousness of oneness with the world is especially prevalent in the Amerindian notion that all creatures are possessed of language—the two-leggeds, the four-leggeds, the wings of the air, and all green things that live.[22] All of creation lifts its voice in praise. A Stoney Indian from Canada named Walking Buffalo once asked:

> Did you know that trees talk? Well they do. They talk to each other, and they'll talk to you if you listen. Trouble is, white people don't listen. They never learned to listen to the Indians so I don't suppose they'll listen to other voices in nature. But I have learned a lot from trees: sometimes about the weather, sometimes about animals, sometimes about the Great Spirit.[23]

The cottonwood, for example, is a tree particularly sacred to many Indian peoples in the West. Always chosen by the Sioux for use in the Sun Dance ceremony, this tree is regarded as holy because it can grow where most others cannot. Furthermore, the rustling of its leaves even in the slightest breeze is said to form a continuous prayer to *Wakan-Tanka*, the Great Spirit. There is a unity shared here by all those beings whose life is knit to the land and its ways. That's why the Plains Indians spoke of the Buffalo as a people and the Northwest Indians saw the Salmon as a people. In each case their lives were intertwined, connected at the Middle Place where the earth blossoms in shades of gold, blue, white, and black—the colors of the four corners, the colors of life's varied and changing seasons.[24]

If one were to drive a hundred miles west of Albuquerque, up into the hills of Cibola National Forest, toward Bluewater Lake, the ancient hunting lands of the Zuni would soon come into view. This is a terrain which gives frequent birth to compelling tales, and a Zuni initiation narrative from this locale may finally offer the most direct access to this notion of intimate participation in the life of the earth and its creatures. The earth knows that story often speaks where explicit discourse is but dumb. In the ancient regions of Cibola, so the story goes, a young Zuni brave once prepared for his first deer hunt—rehearsing carefully the warrior's ways of listening, walking, and releasing his bowstring. But most of all he studied the ritual acts involved in singing the deer to himself, learning the sacred song of promise and offering which united his own intention with that of the deer. This song offered to the animal the possibility of changing its being, inviting the deer to give its life so *he* and his family might have life. In return, the song promised that the hunter would hang long red prayer streamers from a tree in the deer's honor and would offer sacrifice to the Great Spirit in his memory. He sang all this so that the deer would come even to *relish* his arrows, freely offering its life to him.

Starting out early one morning, with his friend and tutor, the cunning Coyote, the boy began tracking through the light snow of a box canyon in the area west of Bluewater Lake. Coyote told him that whenever the deer sighted them, he would slip off to run ahead, cutting the animal off at the canyon's upper rim. Meanwhile the boy would follow softly, singing his song of promise and offering. As it happened, the young hunter—in his excitement—forgot some of the words, stumbling poorly through his song. The buck, listening up ahead, heard him falter and thought that young hunters sometimes *also* forget their payments, their sacrifice on the deer's behalf. So the animal raced on over the rocks to higher ground. Giving determined chase, the boy this time did better as he sang with all his attentiveness the haunting chant. Gradually boy and deer were joined in a hesitant dance as they worked their way, in flight and pursuit, up the canyon floor.

The deer finally slowed and listened, as the song worked its way deeply into his hearing. "I could die contentedly if I only *knew* he would remember and offer sacrifice," the deer thought. " . . . But who can be sure?" Once more he turned to flee, though this time his way was blocked by Coyote. At last the great, eight-point buck, filling the air with energy and the smell of musk, turned to charge at the young hunter. The boy nervously drew and shot, but the arrow missed, glancing off the antlers. Fortunately the deer missed, too. But he turned to charge a second time. Only this time the arrow found its mark—sinking to the feathers in the massive breast of that charging beast. The buck staggered and almost fell. The boy—filled with feelings of fear, regret, necessity—ran to the deer. In his excitement he thought only of what came next in the choreographed ballet of this ceremonial hunt. But the deer was still very much alive and struggled to rise again, even as the boy had run to embrace the fallen animal and blurt out the appropriate words, "I give thanks, my brother, this day to have drunk your sacred wind of life." Coyote had yelled to stay back and shoot again. But, as the buck thrashed his antlers, the boy dodged their points to press his face against the animal's neck and speak his holy words. Caught up in this odd, tortured wrestling, the boy was close enough to breathe the deer's life breath, to be covered with his blood. And the deer, seeing the boy so anxious to fulfill his duties, knew at last that he *would* remember to offer sacrifice. With release, a sense of peace, even tranquil submission, the great animal then relaxed and relinquished his spirit to the boy's clutching arms. In that moment, the young brave, the great beast, and the ground which absorbed their common blood, were all made one—at the Middle Place, the place where life is drawn from earth and given back again.[25]

The Sweat Lodge as a Place of Vision

A third representative place, able to summarize yet another aspect of Native American spirituality, is a symbolic locale—one artificially set apart for effecting contact with the sacred. This may be a place not previously recognized as holy at all, but designed instead to invite the holy to it. Such is the ceremonial hogan of the Navajo already mentioned. Another example is the Pueblo kiva, its underground chamber soliciting the presence of totemic spirits, as the initiate descends the ladder to its womb-like enclosure. A similar function is served by the sweat lodge of the Sioux and other Plains Indians or the tipi where the all-night ceremony of the Peyote Cult is held. In each instance, the symbolic place of divine encounter is the confined and dark place of visionary insight. It is a black hole with fire at its center where the sacred imagination takes flight on beating wings. Amerindian consciousness will attach far greater significance than most white Americans to the images that come through induced dreams. "Sometimes dreams are wiser than waking," urged Black Elk.[26] Where the Enlightened mind, secure in its Cartesian, Newtonian universe, will dismiss all visionary experience as hopelessly subjective, the Amerindian worldview will readily celebrate such inspired openings onto the landscape of correspondence.[27] Yet, at every point, it will test and condition this visionary encounter by the most careful attention to ritual, tradition, and the proper observance of place. The Sioux rites of purification and lament—each having the reception of visions as a major goal—can provide excellent examples of this structured context in which dreams are sought.

Imagine on the slopes of Bear Butte Mountain near the Black Hills, or along the White River region of South Dakota—between the Badlands and Pine Ridge Reservation—a campsite set apart from ordinary and common uses.[28] Willow saplings have been forced into the ground and tied with thongs to make a crude circular framework over which heavy buffalo robes can be thrown. The enclosed space is maybe six feet in diameter, enough room for four or five people to crouch around a central pit dug in the center. Olive-green leaves of sage have been spread in a circle on the ground, the sweet-pungent odor filling the air. A short earth-packed path runs ten paces out from the single door of the hut, facing east. It ends in a small mound where a fire has been set to heat stones for the ceremony. All preparations have been made with care, for here in the sweat lodge of the Sioux the sacred rite of purification (*Inipi*) will soon be observed. This is a sacramental act repeated frequently in an individual's life, especially on occasions when spiritual direction is needed for important decisions. In this hut the spirits of all living things are brought together—the purifying qualities of fire, water, earth, and sage all joining to give new life and new vision to those who enter the place's mystery.

Imagine, therefore, yourself bending over to enter the small enclosure, walking with others sun-wise around the interior circle, then sitting on the scattered, fragrant sage. Expectation is heavy in the air. Tobacco is offered to the six directions (east, south, west, north, up and down) as prayers rise like incense. A pipe is passed, the smoke both inhaled and rubbed over one's body even as the divine spirit is seen to pervade all things—within and without. Then rocks from the sacred fire are passed in and placed in the pit. Heat instantly fills the small space. The door is covered. There is no longer light, only intense darkness, and then steam—blinding, seering steam—as ice cold water is poured onto red-hot rocks. In that moment, sky and earth meet. Grandfather and Grandmother. The presence of God. Your head is buried between your knees, your mind screaming to escape, as your lungs gasp for air but breathe only fire. You know that you can always cry out, *Mitakuye oyasin*, "All my relatives!" if the heat becomes too severe; someone will throw open the flap and you will live again. But you remain silent, not knowing entirely why. You become all the scorching pain that you feel, until after several minutes (which seem hours), the flap is finally opened and the world is remade with air, light, and a mind that thinks again. Soon the cycle will be repeated (four times in all)—each time with more steam, as the white breath of the Great Spirit absorbs the whole of what you are. Nothing exists but sage, fire, water, rock. You have lost names for all these things, though perhaps you also find new names that seem wiser than old. At last, when it finally no longer matters, your body emerges from the sweat lodge, half-hearing the leader's words, "May we be as children newly born." You walk slowly, moving and seeing as if for the first time—your life given back with breathless wonder, your mind still filled with blackness . . . and a vision inarticulate.[29]

This is the search for insight that the Sioux peoples associate with the sweat lodge as sacred place. It forms a fertile landscape for dreams. Still other visions may be received in the Sun Dance ceremony, also performed in a specially-constructed lodge. Blowing on a shrill whistle of eagle-bone, the exhausted dancer—attached by cord and wooden skewer to the cottonwood pole at the center of the world—may suddenly see a rider coming in at a dead run between the white flags. He wipes the sweat from his eyes and looks again with anxious fear. But the dread horseman still comes—a single feather in his hair, the chest of his huge gray horse wet and heaving with breath, its thundering hooves never touching the ground. The dancer is stiff with terror as the rider charges on to touch him with his lance, then suddenly disappear. With relief, joy, he falls to the ground, freed at last from the dance, gifted with a vision that will bring life. It is an image later to be repeated often in his dreams—a vision and healing touch he will never forget.[30] On another occasion, a young teenage boy may be taken to a distant hilltop to spend four days and nights alone without food, taking part in his first vision quest. He goes with a boy's name and hopes to return a man, scanning the sky for the peculiar flight of a hawk or eagle, sifting the east night wind for voices, holding close the sacred pipe which links him to a tradition he seeks to make his own. From the Ghost Dance of the 1890's, with its millennial visions of a renewed land, to the Peyote songs and hallucinogenic images of the Native American Church today, the expectation that God speaks through dream is as real as that of Joseph in ancient Egypt or John on Patmos.[31]

I discovered this more fully two years ago on meeting Kevin Locke, a Lakota Sioux storyteller from South Dakota. He also performs traditional dances, especially the Hoop Dance with its use of twenty-eight separate, colored rings. These are symbolic of the earth's circle, the lunar cycle, even the mystery of woman's ovulation. The dance is one of enormous life and power. To the insistent beat of a drum, he gradually links the various hoops into enchanted and wondrous patterns. Intertwined on his arms and legs, one recognizes the birth of flowers and cloud formations, the floating wings of an eagle, the movement of a butterfly. At one point he even binds the unwieldy hoops into a massive sphere around his torso and throws it up over his head, like a morning sun cast into the pale-blue sky. But more moving even than the dance is his story of how it became his gift. He said a very old Indian by the name of Goodbear, living on Pine Ridge Reservation, had once told him he would teach him this dance before he died. It was very difficult and would take at least four sessions to learn, but Kevin Locke listened well as they began the work together. Unfortunately, however, Goodbear became ill and died before they could go beyond that first lesson. Locke despaired of ever learning the dance. But he declares to this day—with dumbfounded amazement—that Goodbear later came to him in his dreams to complete carefully the instructions he had begun before his death. One has only to see the dance to know the story to be true. There is numinous power in its movement—a flow and rhythm borne along by the strength of dream. I remember now its mimed patterns of the holy and wish myself to hear the old grandfather's voice in the quiet passing of the night.

Stories at the Place of the Stone

The Finger Lakes District of Western New York is known today for its wineries and rolling hills, a land rich in soil and history alike. This once was the proud land of the Iroquois, its five nations spread from the Adirondacks to the Alleghenies. The westernmost tribe of the Iroquois League was the Seneca, "Keepers of the Western Door," a people who worked the black earth west from Seneca Lake to the shores of Lake Erie. Their name, from the Algonquin word "O-sin-in-ka," means "People of the Stone."[32] Rock-hard they were, heirs to the rugged stories of an ancient past and zealous to preserve their memory. Long before paper and quill, they chiseled legends onto the faces of stone cliffs, like the Indians who scratched petroglyph sea-monsters on the rocks of Vancouver Island or Algonquin thunderbirds along the Susquehanna River.[33] These were tales written only in nouns—hunters, arrows, running deer. They lacked the verbs of experience to give them life. But these were supplied by the oral tradition—stories that carried on the identity of a people. These People of the Stone trace their lineage to a particular rock of foundation—a primal site and Ur-Stone usually located at the head of Canandaigua Lake. There a great hill marks the place where the Senecas first emerged from the earth Mother themselves.[34] There too, it is said, the first stories ever heard were whispered from a crevice in the great, smooth rock. The Storytelling Stone, therefore, offers a fourth representative locale and theme in Amerindian spirituality—the language of story as the language of faith.

"Stories are central to the Native American way of understanding and passing on spiritual values," says Mary Hobday.[35] This is largely because metaphor, the irreducible substance of story, makes such frequent use of concrete, earthy images to define the ephemeral and obscure. Native American spirituality refuses ever to be very far removed from the context of ordinary "placed" experience. While drawn to visionary insight and the wisdom of dreams, it returns continually to the place of the stone—finding the plain and commonplace to speak in concert with the transmundane. Stories are prized because of their unique capacity to enhance the experience of rootedness to place. Area legends and aetiological tales especially attach themselves to places and place-names, as if giving voice to the speechless stones of memory lying there. Every locale bears its peculiar tales, particularly those with Indian names. A whole sub-literature encompasses the matter—from Von Engeln and Urquhart's *Story Key to Geographical Names* to John Rydjord's *Indian Place-Names*, a study focused on Kansas alone.[36]

The Seneca tale of the origin of stories is the place then to begin. It tells of an orphan boy named Poyeshaon, sent for the first time into the deep woods to hunt. For several days he did well, bringing back a string of birds each evening for his foster mother to cook. But one day, venturing farther into the forest than he had gone before, he found in a clearing a great rock, its high, flattened top inviting seated contemplation. No sooner had he scaled the stone, however, than he heard it speak, offering to tell him stories, a magic of which he had never heard. "What does it mean to 'tell stories'?" the boy asked—a question, of course, no teller, even a stone, has ever been able to resist. Stories echoed from the depths of the stone for the rest of the day, as Poyeshaon, spellbound by its craft, listened until long after night had fallen. He returned home with only a bird or two on his string, leaving the others as payment to the stone, in exchange for its tales.

Unable to resist the rock's enchantment, he came back to the clearing the next day, and the next as well. When the mother became suspicious of his being gone so long and bringing back so little, she sent another boy to spy on Poyeshaon. But the day simply ended with *two* boys atop the stone, both transfixed by the tales. Soon there were four, and eventually the mother herself and the whole village crowding around the stone as it spun its tales. There were stories of an ancient Seneca past, a prior world filled with little people and giants, even a creation account including the role of Sky-Woman and the origin of the colorful false faces used in ceremonial dances.[37] To hear their own stories told back to them was more important even than food. They learned that a people always live by tales and bread. Without either one they starve. The time finally came when the stone no longer spoke, when others had to carry on the tradition of storytelling themselves. But the hill east of Canandaigua Lake is still there, and if it is indeed the ancient site, it may still whisper threads of narrative to those willing to teach a stone to talk.

A large part of the appeal of story in Native American spirituality is the oral quality of the sound itself. In traditional oral cultures, sound has always carried a peculiar force, not readily grasped by those most influenced by the visual medium of writing. From ancient Hindu mantras to the drum languages of certain African tribes, sound has been able to generate that sense of *mysterium tremendum* which Rudolph Otto saw to be the essence of the Holy. There is power in the voice, deriving—as it does—from the physical interiority of the speaker. Sound is an agent of inwardness and mystery. It provokes and disturbs.[38] The Keeper of the Talking Sticks or tribal storyteller, therefore, does far more than simply entertain. He or she functions as custodian of a sacred fire, searching the collective memory of a people, evoking the presence of hallowed ancestors.

N. Scott Momaday, writing so poignantly out of the context of his Kiowa past, describes the struggle he had one night in trying to finish his book, *The Way to Rainy Mountain*. He wanted to write about an old woman he had met in Oklahoma years before. Her name was Ko-sahn. Remembering how she had spoken and sung to him that hot summer afternoon as if in a dream, he longed to recover the experience. But the words lay dead on the page. He was caught in the distance that writing always places between experience and memory. But then, he says:

> My eyes fell upon the name Ko-sahn. And all at once every-thing seemed suddenly to refer to that name. The name seemed to humanize the whole complexity of language. All at once, absolutely, I had the sense of the magic of words and of names. Ko-sahn, I said, and I said again KO-SAHN.
> Then it was that that ancient, one-eyed woman Ko-sahn stepped out of the language and stood before me on the page. I was amazed.[39]

Evoked by the power of the spoken name, she talked of their meeting long ago, of her sense of being as old as her people, and of his need to trust his hearing of her in that moment. "You see," she said, "I have existence, whole being, in your imagination. . . . If I am not here in this room, grandson, then surely neither are you." This is the sacred power of storytelling at its best—the verbal repetition of names that are able to call into being an entire tradition. It involves a collective remembering or *anamnesis* that makes the listener immediately present to the past in all of its fullness.

The discomfiture that white Americans of European consciousness experience when they enter the world of Amerindian spirituality is one rooted not simply in the difference between a magical and mechanical worldview. It may be grounded even more in the difference between oral and written means of perception. In an oral culture, patterns of communication and thought alike are marked by a high degree of im-mediacy and spontaneity, due to the ephemeral nature of sound. The process of maintaining reality is thus highly participatory—something grasped only in the continual recital and reception of what matters most. In the oral tradition, therefore, life is marked by all the effervescence of the passing word. But consequently, oral cultures struggle with the problem of permanency—not being able readily to record (in writing) what is learned. Nor do they possess the same capacity for distance and reflectiveness that writing can lend to experience. Neither orality nor literacy is inherently "better," of course—only very different and complementary ways of conceiving reality. But an oral spirituality can never fully be appreciated by means of literate categories alone.

Joseph Cahill of the University of Alberta offers an intriguing example of the problems and possibilities that arise in the study of spirituality when these two traditions of orality and literacy engage each other. He tells of an opportunity that once was his to participate in a rare ritual practiced among certain tribes in British Columbia. He was told beforehand that it was an entirely oral event and that no one should try to write anything during the ceremony. Yet as he became involved in the experience, he was so deeply moved by what he witnessed that he felt compelled to make a few notes so as not to forget what occurred. Being a creature of linear, visual consciousness, he found it hard to rely on the oral story's power to remember itself in him. He was constrained to preserve it in writing. As he surreptitiously tried to put his pen to paper, however, he found that he could not move his fingers, no matter how hard he tried. It was as if some strange force stayed his hand. At the same moment, the Indian leader of the ritual, whose back was turned to him, said that he could feel someone trying to write and that this should not be done. Cahill says that if he had never before been a believer in the oral tradition, this would have made him one.[40] Yet the importance of the story lies less in its numinous display of shamanic power than in its elucidation of the immediacy and vitality of oral experience. To be moved by story is to abandon oneself to its life-changing impact, not simply to remember its details as data filed for later analysis. A spirituality rooted in story, therefore, will demand the fullness of oral understanding.

Silence Under the Arctic Ice

Fifteen hundred miles north of Winnipeg, Manitoba, long after the world should have ended, it seems, one enters the treeless, gloomy terrain of the tundra. Here the Netsilik Eskimos, another tribe of native peoples, track the sea and follow caribou trails between Pelly Bay and Queen Maud's Sea. Their life is tenuous, held together by strict taboos, shamanic tales, and large amounts of silence. Here we find a fifth and last dimension of Native American piety—its recognition that silence may be the most appropriate response to God's lean and austere pres-

ence in the world. A stark economy is as characteristic of Eskimo life
and language as it is of Arctic topography. Anthropologist Edmund
Carpenter describes the harsh land found north of the Arctic Circle.

> [It] ranges from great glistening, coloured cliffs to flatlands
> that roll away, mile after empty mile, featureless and undif-
> ferentiated, save for quiet inland pools that blue-spangle its
> monotonous expanse. The wind seems never to stop. It is a
> hard land, with few extras.[41]

In this landscape where survival is always in question, one lives continually on the fierce and quiet edge of starvation. Very little vegetation grows in the few short weeks between winters each year, so
life is drawn from seal, whale, and fish, wolf and caribou. Life is
strangely preserved in the taking of life. Of necessity, nature here
is red in tooth and claw.

A Pelly Bay Eskimo hunches motionless for hours over a seal's
breathing hole in the ice. Only through incredibly sustained silence will
he bring home food by the end of the day. He watches carefully a feather
of swan's down that has been suspended over the hole. When the least
rush of wind stirs the feather he knows a seal has surfaced for air and he
thrusts his harpoon into the hole. In this manner, he patiently trains in
silence to snare a prey he never sees. A spiritual exercise is this, perhaps
ultimately not unlike prayer. Other hunters will resort to more grisly
means of finding game. Tightly-coiled strips of razor-sharp whalebone
are embedded in frozen balls of blubber. These may be swallowed
whole by unsuspecting wolves, who then are tracked until the lumps
thaw and the coil springs open, splitting the animal's stomach and bringing painful death. At other times, sharpened splinters of caribou bone
are set in ice and smeared with fat. As a wolf licks at the bait, it slashes
its tongue. Stirred then even more by the taste of fresh blood, it keeps
licking until at last it bleeds to death.[42] This is an austere, grim existence—the severity of its life matched by the cold, clean-edged beauty
of its land. It fits none of the polite, simplistic patterns I use to make
sense of the world. I imagine with horror the hunter watching in placid
silence as the animal's life is deftly snared. But what seems to be the
calculated, uncaring theft of life is actually a carefully-ordered balance
in a very fragile world. Being entirely dependent for one's existence on
taking the life of other beings, the Eskimo is necessarily related to the
game he seeks in a particular, spiritual way. The hunter must exercise
respect as well as wit, or the animals will not willingly present themselves as sacrifice.[43]

This is where taboos must painstakingly be observed. The Netsilik Eskimos speak of a Sea Spirit named Nuliajuk, the Mother of all animals and all life, living in the depths of the sea. She releases or withholds sea animals according to the way humans have observed the sacredness of life. When the taboos are not kept, the Eskimo shaman may have to perform his greatest feat—that of visiting Nuliajuk far below the ice at the bottom of the sea, stroking her hair, and appealing to her for release of the animals.[44] She loves them because they all have been made, in the distance of mythic time, from the flesh of her own body. Nuliajuk had originally been an Indian girl unjustly rejected and thrown into the sea by her family. When she tried to grab the edge of their raft, they even cut off her fingers. The finger joints then began to swim, turning into seals and fish, and she herself sank to the Arctic's depth, becoming its spirit of life. There in silence she still seeks harmony in the interdependence of all human and animal life. Alaskan Eskimos will appease her still further in their annual Bladder Festival, a time when seal bladders (thought to contain the animals' souls) are ceremonially returned to the sea. There they will report on how well they were treated by humans and experience rebirth to yet another life.

Scarcity, balance, a haunting silence—all these are marks of the Eskimo way in the world. It is for most of us a disturbing existence, disconcertingly closer to the awareness of life's dependence upon death than our meat-processing plants and grocery stores generally allow. We live many stages removed from the sharp edge of survival. But what enigma of life and death do the Inuit, the Eskimo people, find on the bleak, frozen tundra? How is God met in that awful silence? Peter Freuchen speaks of the notorious kayak sickness that sometimes afflicts Arctic hunters on the quiet sea. It may serve as metaphor of that strained absence of meaning humans often feel in the face of inexplicable mystery.

> The Greenland fjords are peculiar for the spells of completely quiet weather, when there is not enough wind to blow out a match and the water is like a sheet of glass. The kayak hunter must sit in his boat without stirring a finger so as not to scare the shy seals away. . . . The sun, low in the sky, sends a glare into his eyes, and the landscape around moves into the realm of the unreal. The reflex from the mirror-like water hypnotizes him, he seems to be unable to move, and all of a sudden it is as if he were floating in a bottomless void, sinking, sinking, sinking. . . . Horror-

stricken he tries to stir, to cry out, but he cannot, he is completely paralyzed. He just falls and falls.[45]

This is a terrifying, numinal silence. The *via negativa* and dark night of the soul. Encountering God *in extremis*—at the poles of earth's bitter ends, in the face of life's fragility, I only can be dumb.

But there is another, gentler silence that Native American faith extols. It knows that sometimes words may speak most clearly in their absence. This is a silence of choice—a simple decision not to clutter one's conversation with an endless flow of chatter. In Amerindian cultures, people tend to be much more comfortable with silence than Americans in general. They are able to sit at ease in each other's presence without speaking for long periods of time. The Hindus speak of such quiet communion as receiving one's *darshan*, absorbing the unspoken presence of a nobler spirit. From this point of view, silence is by no means the stark "emptiness" that modern communications media may seem to suggest. It offers a generous, imaginative border around the few words that one chooses to speak. Silence, then, is not absence, but a different form of presence, a subtler expression of meaning. One needs only training to be alert to what it says. Sherlock Holmes, having a keen interest in Native Americans himself, was a master of such subtlety. In a case recorded in his *Memoirs*, there seemed to be absolutely no clue whatever to a particular crime. But the sleuth of Baker Street drew the inspector's attention to "the curious incident of the dog in the night-time." "The dog did *nothing* in the night-time!" retorted the inspector. "That was the curious incident," replied Holmes.[46] Only the one actively attuned to silence, so as to discern its meanings, is likely to hear what is said in the middle of the night.

Silence in the gradual passage from night to day is especially valued in some native traditions. The Hoopa Indians of the West Coast have a practice of rising slowly from sleep and beginning the day with silence. They tell their children that they ought not to jump out of bed before their shadows have had time to return. During the night, they suggest, one's shadow may wander out to explore the world that it cannot touch during the day—bound then, as it is, to the person to whom it clings. Traveling at night on its own, however, the shadow may be reluctant to return home by dawn, so one may have to pause to "hum" her shadow home. Everyone has a particular hum known only to her shadow alone, and the shadow is solemnly obliged to come when called. So the day should always begin in this fashion. One is never ready for the day to start until time has been taken to sing the song of one's shadow.[47] Time for silent reflection thus forms the context in which one meaningfully dwells in the world.

■ ■ ■ ■ ■ ■ ■ ■ ■ ■ ■ ■ ■ ■ ■ ■

Five places, five themes in Native American spirituality. They suggest only the barest outline of a geography too vast to comprehend. Yet the concrete, "placed" character of the land may offer finally the most accessible means of attempting the impossible task of summarizing the Indian approach to the holy. How does one enter the distinctive, alternative world of Amerindian consciousness? On the one hand, it's so easy to discount any possibility of understanding at all. To look with jaded, critical eyes at the primitive Indian mentality was once even a mark of scholarship. One reads that, in the sixteenth century, Hopi Indians sprinkled lines of sacred cornmeal as a first defense against the *conquistadores*.[48] Such quaint naivete seems absurd to the modern mind. We know too well the commanding superiority of Spanish sword and musketry. We know also what seems to be the inexorable triumph of technology, force, and critical insight throughout Western history. But what we don't know—and have only begun to learn painfully in this bloody century—is that large dimensions of our humanity are denied by the very loss of what Native Americans have sought all along to maintain. A sense of transcendence, a love of the earth, a renewed vision, a story worth telling, silence in the presence of mystery—all these are aspects of the American Indian quest for a fuller humanity. The reductionist attempt to discount such ideas as lingering vestiges of a pre-scientific age may ultimately endanger our own survival.

But, on the other hand, in one's attempt nostalgically to preserve Indian sensitivity, it's also easy to romanticize the Native American experience. This was the tradition of the Noble Savage school in the eighteenth and nineteenth centuries. Its approach was reflected in elegant portraits of Indian figures, painted to look like Roman patricians of the second century. With the books of Carlos Castaneda and the concern for mind-expansion in the 1960's and 1970's, the more recent tendency has been to extol the American Indians as turned-on precursors of a post-modern explosion in consciousness. Ultimately this sort of pop appreciation may hermeneutically be no different from the opposite, reductionist approach of those who reject all notions of primitive, cosmic power. In either case the resulting interpretation is simply a mirror of the observer's own *a priori* point of view. The dream of a "paleolithic revival," in which all the rudiments of a magical universe would again be restored, is just as impossible as the positivist effort to drive all mystery from the world. We are inextricably caught today between criticism and wonder, forced at once in both directions, and finally—beyond both—to a second naivete in which myth is reborn in clarity of vision.

Novelist William Carlos Williams struggled frantically to grasp the compelling mystique of Native American wisdom, growing as it does from the rich, dark earth.

> The land! don't you feel it? Doesn't it make you want to go out and lift dead Indians tenderly from their graves, to steal from them—as if it must be clinging even to their corpses—some authenticity, that which—[49]

He ran out of words, being unable to describe what white Americans have sometimes sensed, more often feared, and never fully understood in the Amerindian attachment to the land. Perhaps giving it specific expression in concrete representative places, recognized as sacred, will offer a path to critical understanding, if not also a pointer to that elusive "authenticity" of which Williams wrote. The human psyche, after all, still seeks a sacred center. With ear close to the ground, it listens, waits, believes. It dares to hope that what Walt Whitman wrote is finally true: "To her children the words of the eloquent dumb great mother never fail."[50]

Mythic Landscapes:
The Mountain That Was God

We departed Seattle that morning in an old, borrowed Toyota truck, anxious to leave Interstate-5 for the smaller state road that winds its way to the National Forest on Mount Rainier. It was mid-May, two weeks from my fortieth birthday; and I was going to the Mountain. We set out with no sense of spiritual pilgrimage, simply longing to see something of the Cascade Range, and especially that slope shrouded in cloud and mystery against the southern sky. A British navigator, George Vancouver, had sailed the Washington coast in 1792, presumptuously naming this grand volcanic peak after an admiral in the Royal Navy. But Native Americans of the Pacific Northwest had always known its true name—Tahoma, "The Mountain That Was God." N. Scott Momaday insists that some names are "old and original in the mind, like the beat of rain on the river."[1] In a world shorn of magic, they still carry power. At 14,408 feet, this great mountain named Tahoma looms high above Puget Sound. On a clear day, the icefields of its twenty-seven glaciers give way to lower alpine meadows, recklessly scattered in late spring with wild flowers and lakes. Further down, heavy forests of tall conifers encircle the peak on all sides, like silent guardians of a sacred presence.

Our approach was from the northeast, taking the road toward White River. But our progress was slow. As the trees got larger, we stopped more and more often—to study waterfalls trickling down distant slopes, to listen to melted snow rushing over rocks, to breathe the air made almost palpable by its clarity. Travelers in Nepal often describe the heightened color contrasts and the seeming eradication of distances noticed in the rarefied air of the Himalayas.[2] But the same phenomenon occurs on Mount Rainier, and other slopes as well. In this air, space becomes telescoped and intensified. The simple act of being present assumes here a sense of gathered immediacy. We were aware of this as we stopped for lunch—cheese and bread shared on the rocks of an overlook near the road. Suddenly this world of out-sized grandeur was alive with tiny life. Birds and chipmunks, fed well by previous pilgrims, fluttered to outstretched arms and ate bread from our fingertips. Protected by Park Service laws and the stately presence of the peak itself, they behaved as all animals might once have done in a long-forgotten past. Their universe, wet and green, was filled with mosses of all shades, boulders washed by rain, huge cedars and hemlocks. And towering above them all—a mere fingertip away—was, as the clouds briefly opened, the brilliant sun on the dome of the mountain we had come to see.

Driving on toward White River we found the road closed, for winter was still very much alive at 5,000 feet. So we took the chance of continuing on around the mountain by lower roads, hoping to get a better view from the southern approach where the road ends at Paradise Valley. But in mid-May Paradise lay more than twenty feet under snow, with fog so dense that the lights of cars peered suddenly and eerily through the gloom. We might as well have been at Amundsen-Scott Station, Antarctica—so complete was the sense of strained isolation. Rangers at the visitors' center there said they hadn't seen full daylight for three weeks. We left quickly, welcoming the sun and trees as we descended again to the road going west, following it to complete our circle of the mountain's girth.

Leaving the slopes of Rainier that afternoon was not easy. Having, without intending it, circled the peak in sunwise fashion—following the clockwise pattern of movement sacred to Native Americans—we had "entered" the place and it was reluctant to let us go. When we stopped one last time in the late afternoon, my wife sat by the car in silence as I wandered slowly into the dark trees nearby. The rain forest there was unusually lush and inviting—the colors of lichen, fern, and Douglas fir ranging from bright emerald to deep turquoise. I took off shoes and socks, letting my feet sink into the cold, marshy greenness of the moss that enveloped the forest floor. Everything was intensely quiet. One could almost hear the roar of growth itself—water being heaved up a hundred feet through the phloem fibers in the trunks of trees, oxygen relentlessly pumped through the stomata of fir leaves and moss blades, a symphony of seedlings insistently extending new roots into the soil below. I, too, was washed in the wetness of this wild, inexorable life.

I wanted to give thanks for the day and all of the places it had offered—to leave something there as a gift, an appreciation of what the mountain had been for me. But I realized suddenly how deep my human poverty was. I had nothing to leave—nothing of value to give back in thankfulness for what I'd received. The thought occurred that, if nothing else, I could leave my coat. But precious little substance would its artificial fibers ever give back to the soil. With pain I knew myself hollow and naked before those great trees. But suddenly came the absurd and happy thought that I could leave my blessing, if nothing else. This, at least, was in my power, and perhaps was gift enough. So in a kind of crazed delight, I turned in circles to lay my hands on little trees, giving them blessings—that they might grow to be like their great mothers and fathers, reaching with arched splendor for the sun above. From one seedling to another I raced, dispensing grace with all the fervor of a daft and moonstruck priest. It seemed I had tapped some hidden reservoir of boundless blessing that overflowed from the spirit of the place, the *genius loci* of Tahoma—The Mountain That Was God. Father, Son, and Holy Spirit sang a gloriously redundant *Te Deum* through every leaf and branch.

I remember the day as one of the most graced and gifted of my life. Perhaps such experiences are universal—duplicated in the perception of far more devout pilgrims in Chinese monasteries along the slopes of Mount Omei, at the ancient oracle of Delphi on Parnassus, in the slow ascent of others up Mount Fujiyama in Japan. The holy mountain is one of the most ancient and appealing of all sacred sites—from the thunderous cliffs of Sinai to the Delectable Mountains of Bunyan's dream. What is this attraction that mountains exert on the human psyche? What symbolic connections root our bodies and minds to the landscape of earth itself? From China and West Africa to North America there are mythic tales that describe the earth as a cosmic pattern of our own physical form. According to this image, "the earth is the human body writ large."[3] Mountains and rocks make up its backbone and flesh, water the blood running through its veins, trees and grass its hair, and clouds the breath of its inner life. Touching the earth, therefore, becomes a way of entering more fully the deeper mystery of ourselves and God—as if some vast correspondence linked our being to the mountain's distant silhouette.

Mountains have always absorbed the imagination in one way or another, suggesting patterns beyond themselves. Geologists speak of two great bands of mountainous activity on earth. The Pacific belt, containing most of the world's active volcanoes, is known as the "Rim of Fire." It circles the Pacific Ocean, moving north from the Andes to the High Sierras, Cascades, and Alaskan Range, out across the Aleutian Islands, and down through Kamchatka to Japan and New Zealand. The other, more complex Eurasian belt majestically rises from the sea near Indonesia and curves westward through the Himalayas to the Caucasus, then

on through the Alps to the Pyrenees.[4] It is as if the earth's own backbone
were exposed in these vast ranges, the largest mountains standing like
chakras along which immense waves of energy pass. Mountains have
power—however one perceives it. The High Sierras drove John Muir
crazy with wonder.

For me, the experience of Tahoma was so rich because it came, as
in Dante's *Divine Comedy*, "midway on the journey of my life," when I
found myself "within a forest dark," on the way toward a distant, but
seven-story mountain. It was for me an inadvertent pilgrimage, though
such pilgrimages may sometimes be the best of all. The layered meaning
of the event grew clearer only later as I read with delight of another's
pilgrimage around another mountain. Anagarika Govinda recounts his
own experience as a Buddhist pilgrim in Tibet in his fascinating book,
The Way of the White Clouds. There, in the land of the snow leopard,
where prayer flags whip in the wind and native sherpas slowly trek the
high passes north from Katmandu, there is a mountain silence that invites reflection on all the passages of one's life. Particularly he describes
the *parikrama*, that most sacred pilgrimage that encircles Mount Kailas,
recognized throughout Asia as the holiest mountain in all the world.
This unclimbed, hallowed Himalayan peak—located on the "Roof of
the World"—has long been sacred to the ancient civilizations of India
and China. Its icy summit, in the perfect shape of a Buddhist stupa, is
still uncharted by surveyors—22,028 haunting feet of *terra incognita*.
Flowing out from its slopes, in the four cardinal directions, are four
great rivers—the Indus, Ganges, Sutlej, and Brahmaputra. They form
a vast mandala around which the pilgrim walks in a two- or three-day
circumambulation.

"He who performs the *parikrama* . . . with a perfectly devoted and
concentrated mind," says Lama Govinda, "goes through a full cycle of
life and death."[5] This holy mountain, with its sun- and crescent-moon-
shaped lakes at the southern foot, occasions the symbolic union of male
and female, light and shadow, the successive hard and yielding movements of one's life. From these sacred lakes, the pilgrims pass, as if in
the full vigor of youth, through the red valley of Amitabha on the
west—a sculptured canyon of high, ornate ledges. Then, making the
long ascent toward the northern pass of Dolma at 18,000 feet, they enter
the dark and threatening portals of death. Between these boulders, if
they listen to their hearts, they know well the terrors of the Great Void.
But finally, as they continue down the east side through the green valley
of Aksobya, life is renewed once more in silver streams and alpine
grasses. At last, in the completed circle of the peak, the pilgrims have

entered a pattern grander even than that traced by their feet. They know the psalmist's truth that "God's holy mountain, beautiful in elevation, is the joy of all the earth" (Ps 48:1–2).[6]

Now Mount Rainier is not Kailas, nor is this inadvertent, middle-aged pilgrim a Tibetan sage. I encountered no sudden rending of the sky in my own unintentional circling of the peak that spring day, yet there was a quiet sense of passage nonetheless. From the threatening gloom of "Paradise" to the renewed life symbolized by the seedlings growing on the final slope in the afternoon sun, I knew the place for the first time and knew it, too, as home. It lingers yet in imagination and fragment of dream, the abode where mountains finally reach their greatest height.

What is this inner need we humans have for the mountain seen within? In cultures around the world, there are tales of mythical mountains assuming far more grandeur than any found on map or chart. Mount Meru, for Tibetan Buddhists, is greater yet than lofty Kailas— 80,000 miles high, reaching to the corners of the earth. Yet its coordinates are those of the spirit alone, plotted by a cartography Ptolemy never knew. In New Mexico, the Navaho and Taos Indians speak of *El Huerfano* ("the orphan"), a lordly pinnacle that marks the center of their universe. Also known as the Encircled Mountain or the Mountain-Around-Which-Moving-Was-Done, it is a peak of sacred metaphor, seen chiefly in one's dreams.[7] Even Thoreau, who wrote with joy of Mount Katahdin, Mount Washington, and other New England peaks, said that the grandest mountain he ever had climbed was the one just east of Concord. But travelers to Walden Pond all know that no peak lies on the low, flat floodplain east of Concord. This mountain is one he climbed only in his dreams. Over twenty times he made the same ascent—through the thick, dark woods at the mountain's foot to the grand and awful summit, revealing every detail of Concord village far below.[8]

This is the mountain of undiscovered self that Carl Jung described and the cosmic mountain found by Mircea Eliade as a pattern in mythologies around the world.[9] It lies brooding in the unconscious mind, like the image of Devil's Tower that transfixed the American imagination in the film *Close Encounters of the Third Kind*. An ancient emanation, it formed the last apocalyptic vision of the Apostle John, who spoke of being carried to a great, high mountain and shown the holy city Jerusalem coming down out of heaven (Rev 21:10). It is the mount of all transfigurations, the peak of divine love described by John of the Cross in *The Ascent of Mount Carmel*, the seven mountains of Thomas Merton's thirst for God. Indeed, this is the God who was Israel's Rock (Ps 78:35), a living stone (1 Pet 2:4), the Mount which "followed" after those it sought—even that Rock, Christ (1 Cor 10:4).[10] I know its mirrored grandeur in every lesser peak. It is the white stone with a new name written on it, known only to those who receive it (Rev 2:17). So seek the craggy peak in all the dreams, on all the maps, through every circled quest, but finally call it by its rightful name. Call the mount Tahoma, "The Mountain That Was God."

4 | Baroque Spirituality in New Spain and New France

By the end of the 16th century circumstances favored the emergence of a new style. The Catholic Church, countering the inroads of the Reformation, utilized art as a vehicle to heighten its own appeal. It projected a conscious art program in the form of a dynamic, emotional, realistic, space-creating, and even sensuous style, since known as baroque.[1]

The coming of Spanish and French Catholics to the New World in the sixteenth and seventeenth centuries was paralleled by an unprecedented outburst of spiritual energy at the time back in Old Spain and Old France. This was the age of the great traditions in Jesuit and Carmelite spirituality, on the one hand, and of the flourishing and ebullient school of French spirituality, on the other. Ignatius Loyola, Teresa of Avila, and John of the Cross would be followed by Vincent de Paul, Francis de Sales, and Pierre de Berulle. But the overflow of this spirit into the western hemisphere can best be summarized in the experience of a lesser-known figure, Marie of the Incarnation, the first woman missionary to the New World.

Shortly after Christmas in 1634, this young French Ursuline nun, still cloistered in the convent at Tours, had an uncommonly vivid dream in which her future apostolate was revealed. She spoke of entering in her dream into a place of great beauty, "a majestic and vast country, full of mountains, of valleys, and of thick mists." There she saw a little church of white marble, with the Blessed Virgin seated on its pinnacle, the Child Jesus in her lap. The Holy Mother turned toward her and smiled in invitation. Later, in mystical prayer, Marie would hear clearly the words, "It is Canada that I have shown you; there you must go to make a home for Jesus and Mary." Such was Marie of the Incarnation's extraordinary first encounter of America. Six years later, on finally arriving in Quebec, she would recognize those very mountains and valleys that had been engraved upon her mind.[2] This story speaks of the psychic and mythical power which the New World could exert upon the Old. For over a century, the ambiguity of America had exercised the European imagination. Some thought of the American natives as descendants of the Ten Lost Tribes of Israel. Others anticipated entry into the New World to signal the advent of a Third Age of the Holy Spirit, promised by many since Joachim of Flora in the twelfth century. Attempts would always be made to understand the New World as completing the unfinished dreams and stories of the Old. America, especially in the 1630's, was the nexus for an infinite cluster of dreams. But more concretely this particular vision offers an important occasion for observing the transition of an existent spirituality from its original landscape to an altogether new land and space.

The historical roots of Roman Catholic spirituality in what would later become the United States can be traced to three distinct sources, each differing in national origin as well as geographical point of entry. The Spanish missionary advance came first, moving up from New Spain along the southern rim of the continent. It covered a span of time ranging from the proto-martyrdom of Fray Juan de Padilla in New Mexico in 1542 to the founding of St. Augustine, Florida in 1565. It stretched from the entry of Eusebio Kino into Pimeria Alta (in Sonora, Mexico and southern Arizona) in 1687 to Junipero Serra's establishment of the Carmel Mission in 1770. In addition to numerous baptisms, uprisings, and subsequent suppression of indigenous peoples by the Spanish authorities, this Hispanic missionary effort resulted in the increased use of the horse and growth of Spanish wheat, the denunciation of Indian slavery, the rise of a not-insignificant religious folk art and lore, and the architectural simplicity of the Spanish mission. But ultimately its influence was not felt beyond the southern rim itself, tied as it was to the economic and political fortunes of the Spanish Empire in the New World. The contiguous relation of church and state proved both the genius and the *bête noire* of Spanish American Catholicism. The *conquistadores'* unquenchable quest for gold continually compromised the missionaries' pursuit of spiritual conquest.

Much of the same may be true, *mutatis mutandis*, of the French missionary advance, making its way down from Canada along the midwestern lake and river systems in the seventeenth century. Following French fur trappers, early Jesuits joined the Recollet missionaries who had first come to the St. Lawrence valley in 1615. Isaac Jogues made his way into Iroquois territory as far as Lake Superior in 1641 and by 1673 Père Marquette had traveled with Joliet as far down the Mississippi as the Arkansas River. But the French effort at civilizing and Christianizing the Amerindians of the Northeast proved ultimately even less successful than that of the Spanish in the Southwest. By the fall of Quebec in 1759 (in the French and Indian War), it was clear that the triumph of the *fleur-de-lis* in America would be short-lived. A few French place-names and scattered enclaves of old French culture are all that remain along the Mississippi. The rootstock of American Catholic life and spirituality, therefore, would grow from a third source—the influence of English settlers following Lord Calvert to Maryland after 1633. There, along the mid-Atlantic seaboard, Catholic piety would finally be firmly engrained into the American landscape.[3]

This is the way histories of the American Catholic Church have tended quickly to dispense with the significance of the early Spanish and French settlements. Yet the story is far from complete when it comes to the impact of those traditions on the formation of Catholic spirituality. The fabric of American Catholic piety is woven through with various sensual and artistic images, dimensions of Marian devotion, an identification with the poor, and certain Jansenist tendencies that all can be traced in part to the influence of New Spain and New France. In examining more closely these traditions of Spanish and French spirituality in colonial America, the concern here will be to ask about the images of culture and geography which these people brought in their minds from Europe. These cognitive maps of reality, subjected to the influence of the new terrain found in the Sonora desert or on the shores of Lake Huron, would form the living context of the American Catholic encounter with God. In each case, therefore, the intersection of faith and geography in the old world can be identified, examples of New World spirituality set against this background as it responds to its own milieu, and specific conceptions of Christ and the Virgin traced in the folk art and devotion of the respective churches. Underlying this approach is the insistence that one's spirituality never takes form in a spatial or temporal vacuum. Discovering God is an experience no less culturally-conditioned than any other human encounter.

Spanish Temperament and Suffering: Philip II in the Age of Counter-Reform

What certain—if tenuous—relations, therefore, can be drawn between Spanish geography and Spanish spirituality? Drawing generalizations about national temperament from climate and topography is often a parlor exercise given more to chauvinism than to science. The garrulous English spar at their dour Scots neighbors while carefree Italians scoff at the rigor of transalpine Germans. Scholars in the nineteenth century were similarly inclined to draw simplistic connections between geography and the history of ideas, as when Ernst Renan understood the desert environment inevitably to incline the mind to monotheism. Erich Isaac has rightly cautioned against this tendency toward the "etiological fallacy."[4] Nevertheless, we know Ortega y Gasset to have been right when he said, "Tell me the landscape in which you live and I will tell you who you are." Environment definitely conditions one's perception of reality, even as perception conditions and alters environment. The entire spatial and cultural context of Spain in the Golden Age will be an important background against which to consider the character of Spanish spirituality as it comes to the Americas. *El siglo de oro*, the grand century in Spanish civilization and faith alike, extended from the last years of Charles V through the reign of Philip IV, reaching its height in the late sixteenth century under Philip II. This was the age of El Greco and Velazquez in art, Lope de Vega and Cervantes in letters, and the solemn splendor of Counter-Reformation architecture and music. Spanish mysticism flourished in every form, from the Teresan-Johannine school of Carmelite spirituality to the various excesses of illuminati and *alumbrados*. Everywhere Spain was alive with an intensity of faith and creative expression.

Emperor Philip II summarized in his person most of the values of this Counter-Reformation. An austere man, given to personal asceticism, he was married for a while to Mary Tudor—"Bloody Mary" as she was known to English Protestants, a woman equally austere and serious herself. A stern supporter of the Inquisition, Philip once said, "I would prefer not to reign at all than to reign over heretics."[5] In short, there was more than a little Castilian austerity coursing through the veins of this uncompromising Spanish monarch. The man was in many ways a reflection of the landscape itself. Spain has been described as a great, rugged castle rising from the sea. Mountains all around its edges surround the vast central tableland of Castile. This interior plateau, making up sixty percent of the peninsula, is an arid and desolate place—largely without trees, its soil eroded by rains. "This is the part of Spain that gives the country its stern character, stoic endurance to pain and suffering, its vitality and its bareness."[6]

This is the landscape which bred half of the thirty-some saints of the Counter-Reformation era. "A land of saints and boulders" it has been called. Here the air is sharp and clear, blistering in summer, bitterly cold in winter. A Castilian proverb speaks of "nine months of winter and three of hell." The result is a people fiercely engaged with life, zealous of their independence and proud of their language. That resolute spirit is captured in the famous oath taken by the people of Aragon to their King:

> We, who are as good as you, swear to you, who are no better
> than we, to accept you as our King and Sovereign Lord, pro-
> vided you observe all our statutes and laws; and if you don't,
> we don't.[7]

This same stern, independent character can also be seen in the stoic acceptance of pain that fascinated people in the national sport of bull-fight-
ing, not to mention the tortures of the Inquisition dramatized in the
sixteenth-century *autos-da-fe*. The Spanish temperament was curiously
drawn to this hidden mystery of suffering, even as it bordered at times
on the regions of sado-masochism.

When Philip II built a new capital in Madrid, this same theme of
austere suffering would even mark its architecture. El Escorial, the vast
monastery and mausoleum built for his dead father Charles V, also
served as royal residence and court. Constructed of hard, unyielding
yellow granite, with clear, plain lines, it resembles a military barracks
or prison in its unostentatious majesty.[8] The design is that of a huge
quadrangle with intersecting quadrants, after the form of a massive
gridiron. The symbolic reference is to the martyrdom of St. Lawrence,
on whose feast day—August 10—Philip had been successful in defeat-
ing French forces at St. Quentin in 1557. St. Lawrence had been mar-
tyred by the Romans in the third century, slowly burned to death over
a fire on a huge gridiron. According to the legends of the saints, he sto-
ically declared half-way through his torture that he was done on one side
and they could turn him over. The story would have appealed to Philip's
own taste for grim and unyielding endurance.

The emperor's architectural masterpiece soon was filled with the
best work of sixteenth-century artists. El Greco, for one—the Cretan
expatriate attracted to Spain by the possibility of a commission to work
at El Escorial—painted in a mystical style that uniquely summarized the
longings of the Counter-Reformation. His ethereal, elongated figures
seem caught up in an ecstatic suffering as they yearn to ascend heav-
enward. In their austere beauty, they agonize with unconcealed joy—
engrossed as they are in the process of turning pain into eternity.

If the mystery of pain torturously transformed into glory can be
seen in the landscape and art of Counter-Reformation Spain, it is read
still more clearly in the spiritual writers of that age. Ignatius Loyola, the
Basque knight groomed at the court of Ferdinand and Isabella, embodied the principle in his paradigmatic experience at Pamplona. Cruelly
wounded in the legs by cannon fire in his courageous effort against the
French, he watched in silence with hands clenched as the doctors later
broke and reset one of his limbs. The injury was so severe that a piece

of bone protruding through the skin had to be sawn off. Yet through it all—being stretched on the rack, fever and infection—the inexorable cavalier endured the anguish, finding in his casual, recuperative reading of a book of saints still nobler possibilities for devotion and self-denial. Ignatius eventually proceeded to Montserrat where he hung up his sword and did vigil at the Lady Chapel there, preparing for a knightly vocation he had never dared imagine. His Company of Jesus would become a religious order based on military severity. Indeed, the *Spiritual Exercises* themselves are arranged so as to move from rigorous self-reproach to heavenly joy, from the sorrowful to the joyful mysteries.[9]

The pattern is one that Teresa of Avila would realize still more profoundly in the highest reaches of mystical experience. Teresa of the sparkling dark eyes and joyful mien—who once prayed, "From frowning saints, good Lord, deliver us"—had introduced a fervent new seriousness to the Carmelite order of which she was part. She organized a reformed, "discalced" community of nuns—those going without shoes in obedience to the poverty of Christ. Her own union of intense suffering and joyous ecstasy is best expressed in her *Autobiography* and in Bernini's masterful sculpture for the Cornaro Chapel in Rome. Reading her *Autobiography*, one discerns how much the deepest numinal experiences are for her associated with physical pain. She writes:

> The soul doesn't strive for the pain of this wound caused by the Lord's absence, but at times an arrow is thrust into the deepest and most living recesses of the heart in such a way that the soul doesn't know what has happened or what it wants. . . . You can't exaggerate or describe the way in which God wounds the soul and the extreme pain this wound produces, for it causes the soul to forget itself. Yet this pain is so delightful that there is no other pleasure in life that gives greater happiness. The soul would always want, as I said, to be dying of this sickness.[10]

This erotic, almost voluptuous, ecstasy is frozen in white marble by Bernini's chisel. As the cherub withdraws the pointed shaft, the saint's head is thrown back in rapturous agony. Here the intoxicating transport of encountering God is shown to be humanity's grandest gift—even as it comes through the physical sensibility of the human creature. Freudian explanations of sublimated sexual desire are not wholly unwarranted here, and yet the phenomenon is equally a part of the very culture and landscape of sixteenth-century Spain. A passion for twisting impoverished pain into radiance cuts a swath across the whole of Spanish consciousness in this era. In 1542, while Teresa recovered from paralysis at the Convent of the Incarnation in Avila, the infant John of the Cross would suffer malnutrition in a nearby village as his widowed mother barely survived on a weaver's wage. Thirty years later, while El Greco was preparing to paint his celebrated "Martyrdom of St. Maurice" in Toledo, John of the Cross would be confined to a stone-walled cell in the monastery of the same town famous for its fine-hammered blades. There he was beaten and exposed to the cold by leaders of his own religious order who resisted his reforms. He spoke of his jailers, however, as his "great benefactors," for it was here that he wrote his *Spiritual Canticle*, learning the love of God to be mediated through the dark night of the soul. All across the bare and jagged *sierras* or *monts* of Castile, often shorn of vegetation other than thyme or other small shrubs, this land of saints and boulders offered a poignant setting for the growth of Counter-Reformation spirituality.[11]

Poverty and Pain in
Spanish-American Spirituality

As this same spirituality is transferred to the landscape of New Spain in the years following Cortes and the Conquest, it assumes a flavor still more closely related to the earth and the people who work it.[12] A look at the contour of the land and the popular piety of New Spain may offer a case in point. While the American Southwest and Sonoran zone have relatively little desert terrain in the strictest sense, the prevalence of hot cactus and yucca plains lends a sense of physical austerity to the region. Ross Calvin says of the New Mexican landscape:

> Over a great deal of the country no plants thrive without special adaptation, and the grotesque appearance and general thorniness among them, as well as an unusual abundance of predacious types of birds and animals, indicate that here competition for life is fiercer and the penalty for incompetence more fatal than elsewhere.[13]

Aridity is the dominant climatic factor in this land where jack rabbits race through juniper and prickly pear, where tangy-red *chiles colorades* hang drying on adobe walls. It is a landscape, in short, which invites meditation on the limit-experiences of life.

Consequently, it is here that a rich folk tradition in Spanish-American spirituality would emerge—a tradition drawing heavily upon the theme of endured suffering and its power to elicit divine compassion.

The folk art of the *retablo*, a simple icon painted on a piece of sawn pine, covered with gesso, pictured most often the sorrowing Mother (*Nuestra Señora de los Dolores*) or *Santo Niño de Atocha*, the holy child of Spanish legend who miraculously delivered bread and drink to starving prisoners.[14] Carved *bultos*, often ornate statues of the Virgin or saints made from the cottonwood root and covered with clothes and jewelry, again portrayed the *Mater Dolorosa* or the scourged Christ, crowned with thorns. These were frequently maintained in individual homes and used regularly in church processions, especially during Lent and Holy Week. Some life-sized *bultos* of the suffering Christ were constructed with hinged shoulders so as to be hung from a cross carried through the streets. Others were painted with brightly-colored wounds and the blue skin of death, human hair pasted to the body. Thomas Steele even describes one with an opening in its back through which a life-like "heart" could be grasped and made to palpitate, to the awed gaze of the faithful.[15] It was this fascination with the passion of Christ which consumed the Spanish-American imagination.

The tradition may take its most vivid form in the somber piety of the Penitentes, the lay religious order known as *La Cofradia de Nuestro Padre Jesus Nazareno* (the Confraternity of Our Father Jesus of Nazareth). During Holy Week these anonymous, black-hooded penitents, walking to the strange notes of a piper's flute, carried crosses and lashed themselves with leather whips, emulating the sufferings of Christ to the highest degree. Traditional *alabados* or folk-hymns were sung in Spanish as these flagellants wound their way through the village streets. One of the brothers, secretly chosen by lot, was even tied to a full-sized cross and left there hanging until he fainted.[16] Such excesses could be characteristic of the extremity of Baroque piety. But the drama was also one deeply rooted in certain strains of Franciscan piety (the stigmata of Francis himself), in the earlier passion plays and theatrical performances conducted in Mexico for and by the common people, and in the profound experience of crucifixion with which the poor lived out their lives.[17] Perhaps also it evinced an austere spirituality torn from the dry and naked earth itself.

Desert has always exerted a haunting effect upon the American imagination. Henry Nash Smith asked what it was that drew Americans as late as the mid-nineteenth century to the fabulous notion of a Great American Desert.[18] Journalists at the time popularized a vast inhabitable wasteland stretching some three hundred miles east from the Rockies, even when contemporary observers knew it didn't exist. What inexorable need is there in the American consciousness for immeasurable empty spaces in the midst of our experience? Does the inner psy-

Through the opening in the back of this life-size wooden crucifix, the heart of Jesus could be made to palpitate by the person carrying it in a penitential procession. Gift of the Historical Museum of New Mexico to the Museum of International Folk Art, a unit of the Museum of New Mexico, Santa Fe. Photo by Blair Clark. Used by permission.

cho-topography of all humans require the moral equivalent of the desert—a place for the shadow, the unknown, the area of painful growth? The Rev. Tom Marshfield's desert sermon in John Updike's novel *A Month of Sundays* offers an ancient, if not thoroughly American view of the barren wilderness as scene of redemption. For Marshfield, the desert of the Southwest is a metaphor of his own personal emptiness and longing for life. He speaks of the mesquite plant that sends taproots a hundred feet into the ground, searching for any moisture it can find, or the strange adaptations of the horned toad or kangaroo rat, animals which never drink water but absorb whatever humidity they can from the air itself.[19]

Yet in this solemn arena where life and death dance side by side, the proximity of God is never lost on the imagination. The Spanish spoke, without mockery, of Death Valley in southeastern California and Nevada as *La Palma de la Mano de Dios*, the hollow of God's hand. The drama of sweat and survival, captivity and deliverance, crucifixion and resurrection is all played out on this landscape of dry lake beds and barren rock. Alice Corbin Henderson described perfectly the geographical setting from which the Penitentes drew life as she once sat in the late afternoon of a New Mexican summer.

> Meanwhile, the sun sinking at our backs had turned the cliffs across the valley into splendid cathedral shapes of rose and saffron beauty—a beauty that is touched here in this country with a sometimes terrible sense of eternity, loneliness, and futility. For all the gay laughter of youth on the hillside, the stark parable of the Crucifixion is close to the country's soul. It eats into the heart, this terror; and it is not difficult to imagine how the early Franciscans felt, as they gazed upon this terrible afternoon light on bare mesa and peak, and felt the thorns of this eternal loneliness pressing into their souls. Actual mortification of the flesh is perhaps less poignant.[20]

The early Franciscans—as well as Jesuits, Dominicans, and secular priests—who came to New Spain were as hardy as the land which they had left and as scabrous as that to which they had come. They soon identified not only with the mineral-stained ridges and mesas in the region of the Rio Grande, but also with the Indian and Mestizo farmers and shepherds who worked most closely to the earth. One of the earliest such missionaries was Bartolomé de Las Casas, the first priest to be ordained in the New World. His father was a merchant who had accompanied Columbus on his second voyage. Initially Las Casas fell into the pattern common to most *encomenderos*, those Spanish colonists who received a tract of Indian territory with its natives to be held in virtual slavery. But as he reflected on the misery and servitude of the people in Cuba, as he witnessed the massacre of thousands on the neighboring island of Espanola, Casas underwent a religious conversion, seeing himself to have been—in the words of Ecclesiasticus—"one who offers sacrifice from the possessions of the poor."[21] As a result, he began speaking out against colonial policy throughout the whole of New Spain. Making some fourteen trips across the Atlantic to the Spanish Court, lobbying for Indian rights, he was primarily responsible for the New Laws of 1542–43, which provided the Indians relief from the *encomienda* system. He rejoiced when *Sublimis Deus*, the papal bull of 1537, prohibited Indian slavery in the colonies. When at the age of seventy he assumed the role of bishop in the small and poor Mexican diocese of Chiapa, he met understandably with stormy hostility from the local Spanish authorities. But his determination was as hard as the rocks of the Sierra Madres seen from his residence in Ciudad Real.[22] That same adamantine spirit would be shown later in his famous controversy with Juan de Sepulveda over the alleged inferiority and barbarity of New World savages.[23] Bartolomé de Las Casas remained all his life a stubborn champion of *los pobres de la tierra*, the disinherited of the earth.

He initiated a tradition carried on by Peter Claver (1580–1654), the Spanish Jesuit who worked with African slaves in Cartegena, Colombia. Serving as doctor, priest, and advocate, he met the slave ships at the docks, converting some 300,000 souls as he ministered to their distress. One can almost put it down as a principle that identification with the sufferings of the people would become characteristic of Spanish-American saints. This is particularly seen in the figures that appear in the Mexican folk *retablos*. San Benito de Palermo, known as St. Benedict the Black, was a sixteenth-century son of slaves who joined the Franciscans and became a saint prized especially in Spain and Portugal. He became the patron of Negro slaves in the Americas, but was valued throughout Mexico for his protection against smallpox. Another interesting phenomenon in this popular folk art is the prevalence of numerous Black Christs in Mexico and Guatemala. The Indians could readily identify with the sufferings and dark color of *El Christo Negro*. Indeed, a still more frequent *retablo* figure was *El Señor de Los Trabajos de Puebla*, Our Lord of Hardships, a Christ figure who took on himself the drudgery and pain of the common folk.[24] Hence, when Padre Kino made his historic trip north from Mexico City to Pimeria Alta, beginning his missionary work there in 1678, he carried rolled up in his saddle bag a Mexican painting of *Nuestra Señora de los Dolores* to use in the founding of his new mission. He knew that the Pima Indians to whom he came would—like himself— relate readily to the Lady who sorrowed for all the sons and daughters of the earth.[25]

Mexican-American spirituality is, of course, incomplete without reference to Our Lady of Guadalupe—an apparition of the Virgin in 1531 that summarizes the heart of Hispanic piety throughout New Spain. According to the story, an Indian peasant named Juan Diego, from the village of Tolpetlac near Mexico City, was on his way to Mass early on the morning of December 9, when he passed a hill formerly consecrated to the Aztec goddess Tonantzin. There he beheld a woman in brilliant light who identified herself as the Virgin Mary and, speaking in his native tongue Nahuatl, promised her help if the people would build a church on that hill. He protested that she should send someone more noble and influential than himself, but the Virgin insisted that the task was his. As he came to the bishop, the word of an unlettered peasant was indeed doubted, as he had feared. But he returned later with evidence in the form of roses given him by the Lady, wrapped in his cape or *tilma*. Suddenly when the *tilma* opened and the roses fell to the floor, a stunning image of the Holy Mother appeared on the inside of the cloth, and a powerful legend was born. The tale speaks poignantly to the identification of the Virgin with those peasants who draw their name and sustenance from the *pais*, the land itself. In the Spanish-Mexican context, the Virgin is very often *Nuestra Señora de los Pobres de la Tierra*, Our Lady of the Poor People of the Earth. This is uniquely the case with *La Morenita*, the "Little Dark One," as the Guadalupe Virgin is affectionately called by the people. The figure on Juan Diego's *tilma* is not that of an elegant European Señora, but has all the markings of an Indian maiden nourished by the soil of Mexico itself.[26]

The adaptation of indigenous Mexican imagery by Spanish Catholicism is particularly seen in the way the Virgin of Guadalupe came to displace the earlier Aztec Tonatzin. The former goddess of earth, moon, and fertility was one of terrifying visage, wearing a necklace of human hands and hearts, addicted to blood. Her symbols were those of the moon and the serpent, both images of eternal return. Distant and removed from the people, this goddess was replaced there on the hill of Tepeyac by the gentle maiden of Guadalupe, the "serpent crusher" as the word implies. Pictured most often as standing triumphantly on a moon-shaped sphere, she both incorporates and transcends the mythic imagery of her predecessor. A popular ballad or *corrido* sung to guitar accompaniment in the small villages of Mexico today is one that celebrates the Indian virgin, "Our Country's Guiding Star."

> And to this day we hymn her
> Guardian of our soil;
> In every Mexican breast she reigns
> Queen of all our toil.[27]

This folk piety of New Spain, as it developed from the sixteenth to the eighteenth centuries, was a Baroque spirituality, given to all the swirling excess and extravagance that ensued in Western art and thought following the stately restraint of the Renaissance. In Spain itself the movement would reach its grandest expression in the art of José Churriguera (1650–1725). Even the term "baroque" may derive from the Spanish word *barrueco*, a large irregularly-shaped pearl. Such grandiosity and irregularity would frequently characterize this spirituality as it dwelt on the fathomless sufferings of Christ and the saints. After all, says a Spanish proverb, the world ends at the foot of one's sick bed. Suffering has a way of absorbing all of one's system of meaning. Fascination with pain, therefore, could easily lend itself to aberration as well as pathos. One bereft friar, for example, who came to Mexico shortly after Cortes, was said to have spoken no Indian language, traveling instead with large paintings of heaven, hell, and purgatory by which he taught the eternal mysteries. He even illustrated the horrors of hell with a portable oven in which he roasted live cats and dogs.[28] This was the extravagant temper of the *auto-da-fe* gone wild. Fortunately it found infrequent expression in the Mexican-American setting.

More often there were friars, like Junipero Serra (1713–1784), who walked the length of New Spain, from Yucatan to the Monterey Peninsula with a swollen leg, covered with sores—identifying more with the pain of the people than his own. Following the apostolic pattern of 1 Peter 4:13, he thought suffering should be shared, not inflicted. His was a spirituality that gloried in the mystery of incarnation—the manner in which shared poverty and pain could lead to exaltation. Hence, when he asked a blacksmith along the way to apply hot tar to his wounds, after the remedy commonly used for lame pack mules, this Franciscan was perhaps celebrating the dignity of mules as much as he was diminishing his body, his own "brother ass."[29] Spanish Catholic spirituality, at its best, sought always to move from the enigma of pained existence to the consecration of what often is scorned as common. It drew its strength in no small part from the subtle austerity of the land and the people who work it.

The French Temperament of Resplendence: Louis XIV and the Age of Absolutism

The entry of the French into the New World came a full century after that of the Spanish, but it too was accompanied by a dazzling age of cultural and religious efflorescence back on the native soil of France. The seventeenth century, begun by the French in America with the founding of Quebec by Champlain in 1608, was *Le Grand Siecle*—the splendid century of Pascal and Descartes, Bossuet and Vincent de Paul, Moliere and Racine. The celebrated French School of Spirituality had its beginnings in this century under Pierre de Bérulle. The classical spirit with its aristocratic refinement found expression in the dignified prose of La Rochefoucauld. But towering above the century, lending his name to an age, was the grandest of monarchs ruling by divine right— Louis XIV, *Le Roi du Soleil*, the Sun King (1638–1715). Like the sun itself, he stood at the center of a solar system of French culture and influence. The new cosmology of Copernicus suited perfectly the cult of majesty that Louis XIV fostered at Versailles. The Polish astronomer had written, "The sun, as if sitting on a royal throne, governs the family of stars which move around it," and the French King would live out that cosmic design in metaphor. The life of Louis XIV, during his fifty-four year reign, was a great ordered pageant, surfeited with luxury. At 8:00 a.m. every morning a cloud of two or three hundred attendants flocked into the royal bedchamber for the *lever du roi*. "The Master of the Wardrobe pulled off the King's nightshirt by the right sleeve, and the First Valet of the Wardrobe pulled it by the left sleeve." Other select favorites then handed the King the various parts of his jewel-studded apparel of ermine and purple.[30] During the day he would consult with his nine hundred individual secretaries, each dealing with a narrowly-defined task, and then spend the evening in elegant *divertissements* and *plaisirs*. Finally at 10:00 p.m. the choreographed ballet of the King's toilet would occur in reverse at the *coucher du roi*, the highest honor at this time being that of holding the royal candlestick. It was a garish age of the theatrical, when absolute majesty and nobly-rendered obedience held the French imagination enthralled.

The architects of royal absolutism in seventeenth-century France had been Cardinals Richelieu and Mazarin, serving as ministers under Louis XIII and his son. But it was Bossuet, the Dauphin's tutor, who helped him to develop most clearly his theory of divine right monarchy. In his *Memoirs*, Louis XIV would later write:

> The One who has given the King to the people has willed that they respect him . . . that whoever is born a royal subject must obey without questioning (*sans discernement*). . . . There is no maxim more firmly established by Christianity than this humble submission of the subjects to the one placed over them.[31]

This royal claim of divine approbation expresses a culmination of centralized authority that had been nourished for centuries by a number of factors, including even the convergence of rivers in the Paris Basin of northern France. It is a theme that would find keen expression in the grand air of seventeenth-century French spirituality, with its exalted and regal imagery of Christ and the Virgin Mother. Hence, political, topographical, and ecclesiastical determinants are all inextricably interlaced as one tries to define most clearly the texture of the French spiritual tradition in this era. A reverence for unbounded majesty connected many diverse currents in French life and thought. From the architecture of Versailles to Marguerite de Beaune's cult of the Child King, the trappings of royal absolutism were tied to images of the the divine.

Much of this can be observed in the physical environment which formed a gilded stage for the pageantry of the King. If Louis XIV had never said the words, "*L'état, c'est moi*," it would have been unnecessary; his palace at Versailles said it for him. "I am the state," declared the stunning splendor of this vast chateau—with its elegant salons and Hall of Mirrors, its 10,000 employees, absorbing as it did sixty percent of the national revenue. Versailles became the symbolic center of the realm, drawing on the prestige that Paris had enjoyed for centuries as the hub of riverways and valley routes throughout the northern basin. "On the green map of France, writes Lawrence Durrell, "the rivers curve outwards like the veins on a tobacco-leaf."[32] Traditionally whoever controlled the four great river-kingdoms of France controlled the realm.

The imagery of the French King as master of rivers was an ancient and important one. Thus, it was with conscious symbolism that Louis XIV made the Seine do obeisance to his new palace, when in 1682 the huge and intricate *Machine de Marly* began conveying water from the nearby river to Versailles. He even constructed a new bridge, the Pont Royal, over the Seine in Paris, ordered a canal connecting the Atlantic with the Mediterranean, and scattered statues of river gods and nymphs throughout the fountains and pools surrounding the Versailles chateau. This is the symbolism of royal majesty always prevalent in riverine civilizations, from Egypt to Mesopotamia.[33] The Pharaoh's mystical power had lain largely in his ability to predict the flooding of the Nile, a science involving the careful reading of high and low water marks. With typical royal immodesty, Queen Semiramis of Assyria had inscribed on her tomb the words: "I constrained the mighty river to flow according to my will and led its waters to fertilize lands that had before been barren."[34] In this same tradition, Louis XIV tried to make even French geography subservient to his glory.[35]

Against this backdrop, the French School of Spirituality can be seen, not so much to have lent direct support to the King's cult of majesty, as to have breathed the same air of sovereign grandeur that pulsed through the art and politics of the whole age. Its principal leaders—from Bérulle and Vincent de Paul to Francis de Sales and John Eudes—had little or no connection whatever to the royal court, but they delineated their religious experience within a cultural and linguistic milieu which inevitably conditioned the metaphors they would use for the holy. All of French spirituality, for example, had "a constant anxious care to exalt God over all else," with a corresponding concern for self-abnegation in the presence of such majesty.[36] Pierre de Bérulle observed that while Copernicus' notion of the sun as the center of the universe might be highly suspect in the science of astronomy, it nevertheless had its uses in the science of salvation. For him, the immovable sun was a grand metaphor of God the Center, of "Him Who is Very Light, the Splendour of the Father, the Living Sun of the universe."[37] It is this insistent theocentrism that Henri Bremond sees to be the soul of the French School and, in the intellectual climate of seventeenth-century France, this exaltation of the divine would necessarily assume the aura of royal sovereignty. Bremond concludes:

> So they are all—Condren, Olier, Eudes, down to the least mystic of the Oratorian writers—profoundly, and as if by nature, theocentric. Thence comes their particular prestige, their *grand air* of religion. If, as in the physical world, there could be shades of rank in the spiritual, I should be ready to affirm that the French School confers on all its members patents of nobility.[38]

This is a spirituality that thrived on images of hierarchical authority, whether these were defined as heavenly, royal, or sacerdotal. A brief glance at even the titles of spiritual works in this era indicates the prevalence of the motif. Bérulle wrote on *Les Grandeurs de Jesus* (1623) and popularized a vow of servitude to Jesus and Mary. John Eudes discussed

The Life and Kingdom of Jesus in the Christian Soul while, at the same time, Oratorian Guillaume Gibieuf wrote on *The Life and Glories of the Most Holy Virgin* (1637). Jean-Jacques Olier, founder of the Sulpicians and author of *The Contemplation of the Kingdom*, especially emphasized Mary as *Le Reine du clergé*, having her pictured on the frontispiece of his writings as crowned and seated on a throne, a scepter in her right hand, surrounded by her nobility, the bishops and priests. He even commissioned a painting by Le Brun of the "Triumph of the Virgin at the Council of Ephesus," showing her received into glory as *Theotokos*, the mother of God, and crowned by her Divine Spouse.[39] In this French setting, the Holy Mother will most always appear as *Notre Dame Reine du Ciel*, Our Lady Queen of Heaven—an image much more lofty and triumphant than that of the Spanish *Nuestra Señora de los Pobres de la Tierra*.

The twin themes of exaltation and self-abasement echo continually through the writings of the French School. Vows of servitude and formulas rehearsing one's submission to the Kingly glory of heaven filled the devotional literature of the time. Typical of the prayers of adoration or "elevations" in this age of absolutism is John Eudes' prayer to the Virgin Mary:

> Mother of grace and mercy, I choose you for the Mother of my soul. . . . I accept and recognize you as my sovereign, and in this position I give you all the power over my soul and my life that is possible under God. O holy Virgin, regard me as something that belongs to you, and by your goodness treat me as the subject of your authority.[40]

Perhaps the most telling example of this association of Jesus and Mary with the Kingly aura of majesty can be seen in the cult of the Child King advanced by the Carmelite nun, Marguerite de Beaune (1619–1648). In 1637 when King Louis XIII and the queen were hoping for a child and heir to the throne, Sister Marguerite of the Blessed Sacrament received a revelation that the queen was indeed with child. This promise, she said, had been disclosed to her by the Child Jesus himself. Thus, when the royal heir—the future Louis XIV—was born the following year, Marguerite placed a commemorative crown on the statue of the Holy Child Jesus which she had long revered. Devotion to the "Little King of Glory" flourished in this period, becoming at times saccharine and syrupy. Popular art also portrayed the newly born *Dauphin* being presented by angels to the Queen of Heaven, her own Child King held in her left arm.[41] From his birth, therefore, the Sun King would be accustomed to the highest associations of majesty.

At work here, in the popular imagination, was the impulse of totalism—a longing for absolute devotion to that which deserved the whole of one's self. It was a spirituality of abandonment, even of excess, as it was borne along by the Baroque spirit of its age. Excess and exaggeration may be the primary characteristics of the Baroque style—with its gold-gilted swirling columns in architecture, its great emotion in the music of Bach and Handel. Similarly, French piety rang all the changes on the exalted imagery of the divine. Jansenism and Quietism simply emerged as natural extremes of this Augustinian effort to magnify the sovereignty of God over all miserable human effort.

Majesty and Abnegation
in French-American Spirituality

This same sense of majesty and some of the same excess in devotion would also be carried to New France. Both are seen in the extraordinary life of Marie of the Incarnation (1599–1672), the Ursuline teacher of Indian children who came to Quebec in 1639, drawn by the vision of the Virgin she had received while still in Tours. In fact, the Queen of France, Anne of Austria, had taken keen interest in this missionary enterprise, receiving at her royal quarters in Saint-Germain the nuns who were about to depart for America. Mother Marie was even brought to the crib of the year-old *Dauphin* and granted a glimpse of the future Louis XIV. A devotion to the Virgin as Queen of Heaven, no doubt ornamented by this memory of the French Queen's own gracious reception, would characterize Marie's piety all of her life. After the fire which destroyed the Ursulines' convent in Quebec in 1650, she spoke of placing the care of the rebuilt structure into the hands of "our most worthy Mother and Superior." "We did this," she said, "with great solemnity, rendering her our homage and acknowledging her as our first and principal superior."[42] Not long after her death, a wood carving of the Virgin as *Reine du Ciel et de la Terre* would be placed in prominence at the cathedral church of Bishop Saint-Vallier in Quebec. Dressed in an exquisite ermine cloak and crowned in majesty, the statue would express all the glory paid by French devotion to the Holy Mother.[43]

Similar representations of the Virgin would later be found at Cap-de-la-Madeleine, up the St. Lawrence River from Quebec. There the shrine of Our Lady of the Holy Rosary, with its statue of the Virgin enthroned—wearing a crown of jewels and gold—is still frequented today.[44] A deep sense of traveling the waterways and tributaries of the St.

Our Lady of the Cape, Queen of the Rosary. This French Canadian statue of Mary Queen of Heaven is in the Basilica of Notre-Dame-du-Cap in the southern Quebec town of Cap-de-la-Madeleine. It is located on one of the oldest church sites in Canada, dating back to 1662. The statue is said to have miraculously opened its eyes on June 22, 1888, and has since become the most visited Marian shrine in North America. Used by permission of Franciscan Press and the Notre-Dame-du-Cap Shrine.

Lawrence under the aegis of the Holy Virgin characterized the French missionaries in general. Père Marquette took care daily to place his trip with Joliet under the special protection of the Blessed Virgin Immaculate, promising in 1673 to give to the Great River (the Mississippi) the name *La Conception*, if they actually found it.[45]

The counterpart of this emphasis on the grandeur of the Holy Trinity and the Virgin herself would be a typically seventeenth-century French emphasis upon self-abnegation. Marie of the Incarnation spoke of herself as "an abject and vile creature in the presence of so great a majesty." In her own sight she was "the lowest, most debased, and most contemptible person in the whole world."[46] This abasement of oneself in proportion to the degree of God's excellence was largely representative of the French School. Under the influence of Jansenism it could become a scrupulous, even self-abusive effort continually to question the dispositions of the soul.

Jansenism, as an offshoot of Counter-Reformation intensity, appeared similar to Calvinism—with its harsh views of predestination and total depravity. But its pessimistic asceticism and otherworldly character gave it a cast more severe than anything in Geneva. This was the party of the excessively devout in seventeenth-century France.[47] Warmly debated is the extent and the means by which this austere spirit of Jansenism would later make its impact on American Catholicism. Many would trace the connection through the Irish Church—especially as Augustinian, if not actually Jansenist theologians, expelled from France after the Revolution, taught at the Irish Seminary in Maynooth, training priests for service in America.[48] But it may be unfair to blame the moralistic rigor of American Catholicism on "Irish Jansenism" alone.[49] The Seminary of St. Sulpice in Paris, formed by Olier with a special eye to training priests for America, also brought to this country the stern motifs of French Sulpician spirituality—with its emphasis on total renunciation of self. But whatever the combination of Irish and French, Jansenist and non-Jansenist sources, they would all lend to American Catholic spirituality a certain obsessive severity, an extreme emphasis on mortification, a tendency to focus on sins of the flesh, and even an exaggerated respect for the clergy. Contemporary Catholic novels—from Mary Gordon's *Final Payments* to John R. Power's *The Last Catholic in America*—poignantly express some of the traumas derived from this lingering heritage.

Early Canadian examples of this French spirit of stern abnegation can be found not only in Marie of the Incarnation, but in the Jesuit martyr, Isaac Jogues (1607–1646), and the Indian convert, Catherine Tegahkouita (1656–1680). Writing to a friend in France in 1640, Mother

Marie expressed the zeal for martyrdom that marked many of the French missionaries at that time. She mentions a Father Poncet who was rumored to have been captured by the Iroquois, "and perhaps eaten already." "It is possible that we shall have a martyr in his person," she adds, "which will cause great jealousy to the others, who sigh incessantly after this high grace."[50] At another time she relates a grisly story of the brutal crucifixion of a three-year-old child by the Mohawks, only to add that anyone would naturally envy the fortunate death of this holy infant.[51] Such was the impulse to self-denial that led her to bloody scourgings of her own body, to the use of a hair shirt, and the mixing of wormwood in her food lest she take any pleasure in eating. This is the same austerity seen in the conversion and holy death of Catherine Tegahkouita (*Kateri Tekakwitha*), the Mohawk maiden who in 1676 joined the Christian Indian village at La Prairie de la Madeleine. In many ways her newly-adopted French Christianity combined with the physical rigors of her Iroquois background to produce the most severe mortification of the flesh.

> Sometimes she walked barefooted on the ice and snow, till she lost all feeling. Sometimes she strewed her couch with thorns. She rolled for three days in succession on branches of thorns, which deeply pierced into her flesh, causing inexplicable pain. Another time she burned her feet, as is done to prisoners, wishing thus to give herself the stamp and mark of a slave of Christ. . . . [52]

A similar sanguinary appeal is found in the gruesome accounts of the martyrdoms suffered by early French missionaries at the hands of antagonistic Indians. At the shrine of the North American Martyrs in Auriesville, New York today, the stories are still told of Jesuit saints like Jogues, Lalemant, Brébeuf, and others. Indeed, the captivity narrative is one of the earliest genres in all of American literature. From Isaac Jogues and Mrs. Mary Rowlandson to the tales collected by Cotton Mather and later fictionalized captivity accounts in the eighteenth century, the experience of being held captive by Indians would long grip the American imagination. The account of Père Jogues' experience is in many ways paradigmatic of the lot. In 1642 he was first captured by Mohawks, as he and a number of Huron companions were traveling down from the St. Lawrence into what is now upstate New York.[53] Jogues describes the fury and violence with which they were attacked by the traditional enemies of the Hurons:

> When I began to breathe again, those who had not struck me, approaching, violently tore out my finger-nails; and then biting, one after another, the ends of my two forefingers, destitute of their nails, caused me the sharpest pain—grinding and crushing them as if between two stones, even to the extent of causing splinters or little bones to protrude.[54]

This was only the beginning of an incredible experience of being tortured and held captive for over a year until he finally escaped into Dutch territory and made his way back to France. There the devout Jesuit and his mangled hands were the object of intense fascination, even by the Queen who received him with reverence. A special dispensation was obtained so that he might celebrate Mass, despite his disfigured limbs. But what most excited those French (and American) listeners to his tale was the fact that he would go back to the very Indians who had tortured him, finally to be put to death by them, receiving the martyr's crown in 1646.

The story of Isaac Jogues is one that continues an ancient, pre-Constantinian tradition in the Church, yet it also remains distinctive of the French-American spiritual tradition as well. A fascination with pain—almost to the point of the pathological—can be seen to mark Baroque spirituality in its Spanish and French expressions alike. In New Spain suffering is what would elicit the compassionate identification of the Virgin and saints with one's present poverty; in New France it is what would prepare one for the royal glories of heaven. French spirituality in the New World would offer many examples of self-abnegation as the crowning achievement of one's missionary labors. It would nourish rich metaphors of divine majesty and heavenly glory. But the French would never be successful at sinking their roots into the indigenous culture and geography of New France, creating a folk tradition similar to that of the Spanish in New Mexico. Despite heroic efforts by individual missionaries, the French were singularly unsuccessful at converting the Indians. Part of this may have been due to the cultural imperialism that tended to characterize the French mind. Bringing from France such elegant models of social and intellectual refinement, the more "primitive" culture of the Native Americans would to them indeed appear uncivilized by contrast. Marie of the Incarnation echoes a recurring theme when she writes to her son in 1668:

> It is a very difficult thing, not to say impossible, to make the little savages French or civilized. We have more experience of this than anyone else, and we have observed that of a hundred

that have passed through our hands we have scarcely civilized one.[55]

She especially laments the fact that her students so readily run off with their kinsmen into the woods, "finding more to please them there than in all the amenities of our French houses." With artless incomprehension, she could not imagine why the Indians should not want to become thoroughly French.[56] Herein lies much of the weakness of French Catholicism's lasting impact on American life and spirituality.

Yet the vision of people like Marie of the Incarnation is one highly representative of its time. Her juxtaposition of abasement and exaltation was a paradox lived out in her own experience. Elevating the divine splendor to ever new heights, she also entered into the most intimate relation with her God through the mystical marriage of the soul. Her spiritual director would rebuke her easy familiarity with God, praying as she did to her Divine Spouse and Chaste Love. "To think of treating with so sublime a Majesty in this way!" he scorned. But when she determined to abase herself still further in obedience to his counsel, she experienced a yet greater sense of divine acceptance—"like a queen who enjoys such an intimacy with her Divine Spouse."[57] Curiously the most humble servant has here become queen herself, reaching that estate most sought after by the French School. The goal of all servitude and abnegation was, after all, ultimately to be associated with the King Himself and His glory.

The pattern is revealed metaphorically in a vision disclosed to John Eudes by the French mystic Marie des Vallees (1590–1656), a contemporary of Marie of the Incarnation. Her mystical description of the Garden of the Blessed Sacrament sounds astonishingly like the court and gardens being designed at Versailles at the time. It was entered by a door of finely-wrought gold, on which these words were inscribed "Let none save Kings enter here, that is to say those clothed with the kingship and Divine qualities of Jesus." Inside the Garden were golden cups and crystal vases, hedges of red and white roses, seven circles of trees and vines—a regal setting for the meeting of one's sovereign Lord. Yet this was exactly the goal of all French devotion—to be "clothed with Kingship."[58] It was an image which transfixed the seventeenth-century mind.

But in the long run it was not one that would find lasting appreciation in the New World. Images of royalty would give place to more popular, democratic images in the American mind, especially as the eighteenth century wound its way toward revolution—in France and America. As settlers made their way across the Canadian landscape and into the American midwest, the rivers of America spoke not of convergence and royal authority, but of divergence, expansion, mobility. Any hope for a Catholic empire on this continent, bringing together New Spain and New France in a united whole, would be dashed not only by the course of Spanish and French politics in the New World, but by the sheer expanse of American geography itself. Two Jesuits, Eusebio Kino and Jacques Marquette, had each—in their explorations—lived for this dream. Kino had longed for the linking of New Spain and New France—from Mexico to the Hudson Bay—wishing that "the Catholic empire of the Catholic royal crown and of our Holy Mother, the Roman Catholic Church will be happily extended so that all the world may be one fold with one shepherd."[59] Similarly, when Marquette heard stories of a Great River from the Illinois Indians, his dream was that a Jesuit bridge might be effected between New France and New Spain, though he had no idea at first whether the mouth of the river would open onto the Atlantic, the Pacific, or the Gulf. As it happened, neither Jesuit saw his wish fulfilled. The future of the Catholic Church in North America lay instead with the English colonies. But New Spain and New France would nevertheless exert an influence on the character of the American Catholic Church, and much of this can be sought in the spiritual traditions to which they gave life.

These are Baroque traditions of spirituality, reflecting the rich and varied cultural milieus out of which they have grown. They are frequently marked by excess and severity, drawn at times even to the gruesome. But the traditions have roots deep in the respective landscapes from which they emerge, they each have been able eminently to provoke the mythic imagination and life of the spirit, and together they offer an important background for the fuller understanding of American Catholic Spirituality.

Mythic Landscapes:
The Desert Imagination of
Edward Abbey

"The further you go into the desert, the closer you come to God," says an ancient Arabic proverb. Maybe God, or maybe the devil—one never knows in the Sonoran desert of northern Mexico and southern Arizona. But it is clearly a locale of metaphysical extremes. Willa Cather repeated an old tale with roots deep in the mirage-soaked sand of that barren landscape in her novel *Death Comes for the Archbishop*.[1] It suggests the ambience of illusion on which the desert imagination thrives. Padre Junipero Serra, so the story goes, had arrived on foot one evening at an obscure monastery among the scattered western missions in that region. The brothers there could hardly believe that he and his companion had crossed—without guide or pack animals—the vast stretch of desert separating them from the mission they last had left. But Padre Junipero explained how they had been taken in by a poor Mexican family halfway through the desert the night before. A drunken muleteer, bringing in wood for the brothers and overhearing the tale, broke into laughter at the very idea, insisting that no one lived within twelve leagues of the sandy waste through which they had come.

Father Serra and his companion were then pressed to relate every detail of what had happened. They had set out with food and water across that implacably hostile desert of cactus and creosote bush. But by sunset of the second day, they had begun to lose heart, severely underestimating the way heat and distance increase geometrically in the desert sun. But then, in the distant waning light, they saw a stand of three tall cottonwood trees and hurried toward them. There an ass stood tied to a dead stump protruding from the sand, and nearby they saw a small house, its oven of brown clay near the door and strings of red peppers hanging on the wall. They called out and were met by an old Mexican, his face sunburnt and sheepskin coat stretched and worn. He greeted them with kindness, warmly inviting the weary friars to stay the night. Inside the adobe hut, the man's wife kneaded flatbread in a wooden bowl. Her child, scarcely more than an infant, pulled on the leg of a gangly lamb struggling for its freedom in the fenced yard outside. With these people the priests sat at table, shared in their simple evening prayers, and finally succumbed to a sweet weariness as the cool night breeze swept across the sand. The next morning the friars found everything as before, with food set for them on the table, though the family had gone to care for their flock in the nearby hills. Thus the two fathers had come, refreshed, to the monastery's gates.

The brothers had never heard of a settler and his family in the alkali flats. So the next day all went back into the wilderness. The three tall trees they eventually found, and even the dead stump. But the ass was nowhere to be seen, nor the house, nor the oven. Only shimmering waves of heat rose from the salt-cracked ground and receded into the empty horizon. The two friars suddenly fell to their knees and kissed the blistered earth, as they realized at last what Family had indeed met and fed them there.

Such a story is perhaps too quaintly pious to be instructive, yet too old to be dismissed entirely. It offers us at least a context for considering the mystique of the desert and its perennial appeal to the human imagination. From the desert fathers of late third-century Egypt to Edward Abbey in the American Southwest today, the desert has exerted its fascination on writers. It demands, yet also defies, understanding.

Edward Abbey is an unavowed naturalist—a desert rat with voracious curiosity—who has spent his life describing, defending, and ultimately abandoning all efforts to understand the desert.[2] He's an anarchist out of the 1920's and a would-be Luddite, wary of gasoline fumes and cement-and-steel jungles. He thrives on the large doses of loneliness known only to fire lookouts employed by the Forest Service. He is never more vivid than when he writes about the saltgrass harshness of Death Valley or the rough sandstone arches near Moab, Utah. His books provide an impassioned and wonderfully irreverent entrance to that elusive wildness which Father Serra found in the barren terrain west of the Superstition Mountains.

The desert's compelling indifference, its sparse simplicity and constant proximity to death, even its expressions of senseless joy amid the brief intensity of life—all these form the turbid complexity of any desert hermeneutic.[3] What *does* the damn thing mean? Abbey asks. All answers are fraught with paradox; but he can't resist continually returning to the question. "Something about the desert inclines all living things to harshness and acerbity," he writes.[4] It strips reality of any easy meanings. It absolutely refuses to explain itself. Yet this very indifference to the questions it raises—the unbearably callous uninterest itself—is the incongruous attraction that desert exerts on the imagination. The human mind is drawn by an irresistible grace to utterly senseless wonder.

In learning to love what remains to him an indifferent, perverse, even untamed and hostile reality, Edward Abbey has moved unknowingly along that narrow, torturous path of an apophatic mysticism. The way of negation, the ancients termed it—finding God on the backsides and in the shadows of things, like Moses gazing with terror from the cleft of the rock. On a float trip down Glen Canyon in 1963, before the "damning" of the Colorado, Abbey takes a hike one afternoon under a wine-dark sky up the deep, sculptured gorge of the Escalante, where its crystal waters join the Colorado. He is fascinated by the huge tapestried walls of the canyon, hundreds of feet high, the reefs of rich ruddy sand, the clear song of a canyon wren. "Is this at last the *locus Dei?*" he cries.

> There are enough cathedrals and temples and altars here for a Hindu pantheon of divinities. Each time I look up one of the secretive little side canyons I half expect to see not only the cottonwood tree rising over its tiny spring—the leafy god, the desert's liquid eye—but also a rainbow-colored corona of blazing light, pure spirit, pure being, pure disembodied intelligence, *about to speak my name.*[5]

The sheer and unyielding grandeur of this wasteland incessantly attracts his attention in the way a more docile, ordered beauty never could. Yet these flights of mystic fantasies are never long for Abbey. He shuns the screen of words and veil of ideas that too often form a "mental smog," obscuring one's vision of the world itself. Father Serra's easy entry to the desert's preternatural grace is for Abbey too accessible and cheap—too bent on didactic recitation. It lacks the earthy harshness that might lend it life. So back down the Escalante's canyon he comes to the river, to the boat and his friend Newcomb, to the smell of frying catfish. "There's God for you!" he exults. A return to kataphatic simplicity— the holy in the ordinary, if anywhere at all. Back to red, baked earth. But all the while a larger vision lies half-formed in the mind. The afternoon sun has touched and opened the quiet contradictions filling the desert terrain. Later, in his sleep, soul and body stand peering up steep canyon walls, still searching the vacant sky for *deus absconditus.*

Edward Abbey is always at his best when he's attempting this difficult movement from description to meaning, from the naturalist's fossilized rock to the philosopher's interpretative stone. For him the latter is never more than the scantest suggestion that the desert's mystery may unfold itself to human comprehension. Yet his detailed accounts of the exiguous, often grotesque, unyieldingly tenacious forms of life in the desert inevitably lend themselves to brooding contemplation. The creosote bush and saguaro cactus, the turkey vulture and spadefoot toad— each of these speaks, in medieval bestiary form, to a mystery greater than itself. But, he insists, each refers to nothing *but* itself. The actual, the tangible, the real is the only paradise he seeks.

Abbey is never very comfortable with his own eye for the sacramental. He reacts with fierce suspicion even while being drawn to every symbolic form. That's why he writes with such compelling charm. His ambivalence to the desert's pull is as old as St. Anthony, as current as last week's protest of strip mining at Black Mesa. It contains both worlds—the contemplative and activist, the search for semiotic meaning and the demand for militant action.

Take his characterization of the creosote shrubs, for example, scattered in bleached randomness across the desert's floor. The creosote bush is a small, tangled-branched shrub with strong-smelling olive-green leaves. It grows where little else will. In fact, it doubly secures its survival by secreting a poison from its roots, killing any other plant (including its own offspring) which might encroach on its territory. In this way the individual bush preserves "a perimeter of open space and a monopoly of local moisture sufficient for survival."[6] This clever, malignant adaptivity of the plant to its environment assures to the panorama of desert vegetation an essential scarcity and meagerness. Things there are boldly outlined by nothingness. And it is this abstract quality of thinned scantiness that most appeals to Edward Abbey.

> It seems to me that the strangeness and wonder of existence are emphasized here, in the desert, by the comparative sparsity of the flora and fauna: life not crowded upon life as in other places but scattered abroad in sparseness and simplicity, with a generous gift of space for each herb and bush and tree, each stem of grass, so that the living organism stands out bold and brave and vivid against the lifeless sand and barren rock.[7]

The saguaro cactus is yet another variation on the same theme. Like the chapter on Economy in Thoreau's *Walden*, it stands in a relation of stark, inventive simplicity to the rocky soil where it grows. Rising to a height of fifty feet or more after two hundred years, the photogenic saguaro with its lumbering arms is supported by an amazingly shallow root system—spread out in the shape of a huge fan around its trunk. In this way the root hairs can absorb the largest amount of water whenever rare cloudbursts flood the surrounding desert bed. The trunk of the cactus is also accordion-pleated longitudinally so that the pleats slowly unfold as moisture is absorbed. A healthy saguaro can swill a ton of water up its gorge in the hours following a single downpour.[8] Yet the mechanism succeeds (the capillary action of the roots, the distending of the ribbed trunk, the storage of enough water for the dry months ahead) only so long as the saguaro enjoys a lavish measure of space.

For millennia the desert has spoken to passing wanderers and hermit saints of spatial simplicity, but it also speaks of death. Its indifferent silence is a compelling teacher. A scholar once asked St. Anthony of Thebes, the first anchorite, "Father, how can you learn of God when you don't have any *books* out here?" Anthony stretched his arms toward the wind-carved rocks and gravel expanse, replying, "My book is the nature of created things, and anytime I want to read the Word of God, it's right there before me."[9] He read freely from this open book, but a frightening volume it could be. In the desert one always feels the close proximity of death. If the absence of life-giving water in itself weren't enough, there is also an abundance of predators in this grisly landscape: the stalking silence of a mountain lion downwind of its prey; the dragon-like menace of the gila monster and five-inch tarantula couched between rocks; the sidewinder rattler concealed in camouflage. These all serve God in their own macabre way. To enter the meaning of the desert is to become the predator's mark, to know oneself as object of the hunt. Yet even this status becomes a metaphor of God's uncommon way with us. Francis Thompson's hound of heaven, ever in patient pursuit, lovingly stalks its prey. In the desert one begins to understand what French spiritual writers of the seventeenth century meant when they spoke of being "victim" of God's devouring love.

Abbey recounts his stopping to rest at midday atop a lonely ravine, the heat too oppressive to move. Minutes later, as he lifts his hat from his shaded eyes, he sights a bald, redheaded vulture soaring high overhead. Masters of effortless flight, these primeval birds can sail for hours on imperceptible currents of air, hovering in contemplation. Abbey senses himself as the object of this bird's attention. It has singled out his form, hoping death will soon turn his flesh to food. Knowing that he is hunted, savored, Abbey studies the circling pattern of flight and quietly slips into dream:

> See those big black scrawny wings far above, waiting? Comfort yourself with the reflection that within a few hours, if all goes as planned, your human flesh will be working its way through the gizzard of a buzzard, your essence transfigured

into the fierce greedy eyes and unimaginable consciousness of a turkey vulture. Whereupon you, too, will soar on motionless wings high over the ruck and rack of human suffering. For most of us a promotion in grade, for some the realization of an ideal.[10]

It is the simultaneous threat and promise of death that hangs adrift in the desert sky. Its passing shadow on my face stirs life where I feared there was life no longer.

The inscrutability of the desert's emptiness raises questions that have no end. It speaks in Spartan scarcity of death's propinquity, and finally as well of a joy unreasoned—as if the scant life it did possess would burst with exultation. It is curious how some cactus blooms will open only one day in a single year, but in that one skyburst of beauty atone for a calendar's worth of gaunt plainness. As park ranger at the once-remote Arches National Monument, Abbey painstakingly assumed the editorship of cactus-flower research while bored and weary tourists drove on through the night to Denver. He studied, for example, the prickly pear with its splendid colors of violet, saffron, and bright cerise—golden stamens reaching for the sun. Insects could scarcely resist its unrestrained seduction.

> I have yet to look into one and not find a honeybee or bumblebee wallowing drunkenly inside, powdered with pollen, glutting itself on what must be a marvelous nectar. You can't get them out of there—they won't go home. I've done my best to annoy them, poking and prodding with a stem of grass, but a bee in a cactus bloom will not be provoked; it stays until the flower wilts. Until closing time.[11]

There's a drunken festivity in the desert's succinct, but reckless splendor. Another distinctive cactus, known to Mexicans as *la reina de la noche* (the queen of the night), also opens but once a year, its huge white, fragrant flowers revealing their magnificence only to the moonlit dark of night. This is a senseless glory, on display for no one, reveling in mute and undirected praise.

The spadefoot toad is just as rash in its short, but joyous life. Buried for months in the parched mud of a dry waterhole, the hibernating toads will spring to life with a sudden rain, the males singing in mad cacaphony for all they're worth. They mate, deposit eggs, and watch the pool fill with tadpoles before evaporation begins the cycle anew in a few days' time.[12] They sing, claims Abbey, "out of spontaneous love and joy, a contrapuntal choral celebration of the coolness and wetness after weeks of desert fire, for the love of their own existence, however brief it may be, and for joy in the common life."[13] A haunting, lethal melody it finally is. They sing despite the fact that their splendid uproar is surely luring all the "snakes and ringtail cats and kit foxes and coyotes and great horned owls" to the scene of their short-lived exaltation.

It makes no sense, this outrageous lust for life. But the desert draws a ravishing edge of beauty around its deathly pale. In its tenuous short-supply of life, it sings life all the more. From the ancient monks at Scete, west by desert sand from Alexandria, to Anasazi cliff-dwellers who carved their life from Arizona sandstone walls, to Paolo Soleri's desert fantasies at Arcosancti today, the same fascination with desert waste still stirs.[14] In sultry imagination, if not in palpable reality, the wilderness and solitary place are made glad, and the rejoicing desert blossoms as a rose. I hear it singing—this loud, brash, insistent cry; it thunders from a God I cannot fully comprehend, and echoes in Edward Abbey's coarse, cracked voice. In wistful fear, I almost think it calls my name.

5 | The Puritan Reading of the New England Landscape

"In seventeenth-century England and America the sacred meanings of time and space were so intimately joined, the Puritan myths of destiny so closely tied to Puritan symbols of place, that the full significance of neither element can be appreciated apart from an analysis of their relationship."[1]

Landscape is first of all an effort of the imagination—a construed way of seeing the world which is distinctive to a people, their culture, and even their anticipated means of encountering the holy. Landscape is never simply something "out there"—a picture postcard vista of towering pines on the upper Maine coast or a quaint New England village in autumn. The very choice and framing of the scene is itself a construction of the imagination. Landscape is always an expectation which is brought to the environment, an interpretative lens placed over an otherwise dull, placeless void. As poet Wallace Stevens put it, "We live in the description of the place and not in the place itself."[2] One's active reading of the landscape, therefore, is an on-going way of nurturing meaning in the world, something integral to the process of "dwelling" in a place so as to make it one's own. The Puritans offer an excellent example of this universal habit-of-being in their own distinctive reading of the New England landscape in the seventeenth and eighteenth centuries.

For Puritan consciousness, the terrain from Cape Ann to the Connecticut River Valley formed a continuous volume from which God's majesty and grace could be read. The Puritans were nearly as rich in their study of thunder clouds and plowed fields as they were in their analysis of scripture. Cotton Mather attended not only to the details of biblical exegesis, but also to scientific observations of the environment which he saw to fit perfectly into the biblical scheme of creation. In his study of natural phenomena presented to the Royal Society, he spoke of the unanimity of all God's revelation.

131

> Chrysostom, I remember, mentions a *Twofold Book* of GOD;
> the Book of the *Creatures*, and the Book of the *Scriptures*: GOD
> having taught first of all us, by his *Works*, did it afterwards,
> by his *Words*. We will now for a while read the *Former* of these
> *Books*, 'twill help us in reading the *Latter*: They will admirably
> assist one another.[3]

Whether examining the history of earthquakes or the typology of Nehemiah, he would approach the subject with a definite hermeneutic for its understanding. The notion of covenant—applied to scripture and nature alike—could serve multiple ends in explaining not only the Puritan conception of the divine-human encounter and the structuring of society, but their relationship to the land as well.

All of Puritan experience was structured by a configuration of meaning read off the slate of God's surrounding handiwork. The ideal layout of the New England village, the specter of the Massachusetts sky and its changing seasons, even the revolving turmoil of the surrounding wilderness—all these formed a mandala in which one could contemplate the fearsome and glorious visage of the divine. "A genuine reading of the book of nature is an ascension to the mind of God," declared Johann Alsted, the encyclopedist whose scientific reflections served the New England mind for over a century.[4] Gazing out on the morning sun over Cape Cod Bay or into the dark forests west of Concord the trained Puritan eye saw not only the dim and varied silhouette of a covenanting God, but also a mirror of his own moral condition. Look on the world, urged John Cotton, as "a mappe and shaddow of the spirituall estate of the soules of men."[5] The landscape served as catechist, carefully drilling the catechumen in lessons of the holy.

Jonathan Edwards celebrated this exercise of the analogical imagination with a gift of poetic expression not commonly enough recognized as Puritan. He wrote in his *Observations:*

> We have shown that the Son of God created the world for this
> very end, to communicate Himself in an image of His own excellency. . . .
> So that, when we are delighted with flowery meadows
> and gentle breezes of wind, we may consider that we see only
> the emanations of the sweet benevolence of Jesus Christ.
> When we behold the fragrant rose and lily, we see His love
> and purity. So the green trees and fields, and singing of birds,
> are the emanations of His infinite joy and benignity. The easiness and naturalness of trees and vines are shadows of His

beauty and loveliness. The crystal rivers and murmuring streams are the footsteps of His favor, grace, and beauty. When we behold the light and brightness of the sun, the golden edges of an evening cloud, or the beauteous [rain]bow, we behold the adumbrations of His glory and goodness; and in the blue sky, of his mildness and gentleness.[6]

For Edwards, the Massachusetts landscape was bursting with spiritual insight. Secondary causes tended quickly to dissolve as God's immediate hand became everywhere apparent.

But Edwards also found more than the mild gentleness of Christ as he looked out onto the distant Berkshires from the manse at Northampton. "There are also many things wherein we may behold His awful majesty," he added, "in the sun in his strength, in comets, in thunder, in the hovering thunder-clouds, in ragged rocks and the brows of mountains." One could easily make a study of the sundry interpretations of thunderstorms found in the New England Puritan marriage of theology and meteorology. Cotton Mather, for example, spoke at length on the awesome subject of *Brontologia Sacra*, the Sacred Lessons of Thunder.[7] The same Northeastern seacoast, therefore, could be read in two ways—as expression of glory or impulse to terror. This ambiguity of the landscape and the divine countenance alike is a theme that echoes like clap thunder across the entire Puritan experience. It expresses itself in a series of tensions that New England Congregationalists regularly encountered in their reading of the environment in which they lived. Their conceptual mapping of the terrain west from Boston offered lessons in the very framework of Puritan covenant theology.

Fear and Grace in Puritan Spirituality

A brief description of that theology, and the spirituality to which it gave rise, is necessary before going on to explore its implications for the cultural geography of New England. The Puritan grasp of Christian truth was one which above all laid hold of the majestic and untamed God of Calvinism. Of course, in doing so it risked being utterly overwhelmed by that which it sought to apprehend. John Calvin had opened the Puritan imagination to the vast landscapes of fear, double-edged as they are by splendor and awe.

He demanded that they contemplate, with steady, unblinking resolution, the absolute, incomprehensible, and transcendent sovereignty of God; he required men to stare fixedly and with-

out relief into the very center of the blazing sun of glory. God
[to the Puritan] is not to be understood but to be adored.[8]

The metaphors of blazing sun, raging sea, and crashing thunder were
among those most often used by the New England Puritans in speaking
of their God. Here it was that they sensed themselves to be met by the
God of Abraham on the plains of Mamre—struck dumb, lost in amazement, yet also strangely loved. This was a God inscrutable in his decrees, unpredictable as Nantucket weather, sometimes—it would
seem—holding the devil at too long a leash. Only harsh, masculine pro-
nouns could be used to address the immensity of such grandeur. Yet in
the midst of this *mysterium tremendum*, it was possible also to be surprised
by grace.

From this fixed image of the divine flowed all the corresponding
Puritan doctrines of predestination and providence, original sin and human depravity, even the glories of irresistible grace. Such a God of wondrous majesty filled the Puritan heart with intense anxiety as well as
hunger. The soul was driven to introspective meditation and the abandonment of self. It traveled well the valleys of dark despair, as it longed
all the while for the splendor of a God beyond its sinful reach. This was
a spirituality drawn from the *Institutes* of Calvin and Luther's commentary on Galatians. But it reached back still further to the *Confessions* of
Augustine, to another tortured soul who had stumbled onto grace by
the painful route of self-knowledge and a fierce Manichaen sense of divine power.[9]

What kept the Puritans from flying headlong into the flame of
God's consuming majesty, however, was their concept of covenant. The
covenant became the means by which a mysterious, unpredictable God
of glory could be seen to act with unerring dependability. Central to
Puritan thought was the conviction that this very God of inaccessible
light, who dwells beyond the Cloud of Unknowing, had voluntarily
chosen to limit his majesty so as to enter into covenant with human subjects. The God who could be tamed by no one had tamed himself,
pledging to honor the mutual obligations of covenant. The God who
was *everywhere* in unmitigated splendor promised to be *here* [in New En-
gland] in a particular way, with and for his people. So long as the faithful
remained true to the terms of this manner of binding God to themselves,
they could generally be assured of the divine blessing as they read it off
the landscape in which they lived. In the beauty of a Gloucester sunrise,
the expanse of fields planted in winter rye, they received tokens of God's
loving care, always undeserved and always an occasion for wonder. As

God's covenant people, they knew themselves to be sons and daughters of royalty—rapt in awe and bound by love.[10]

When John Newton, the erstwhile slave ship captain and hymn writer, wrote of "grace that taught my heart to fear, and grace my fears relieved," he summarized the double impulse of Puritan spirituality. Confronted by the enormity of sin, as viewed over against the demanding splendor of God's excellence, the soul is driven by grace to fear and from fear to grace reclaimed. It is a theme that can be traced through all Puritan accounts of conversion, through all the devotional manuals that frequented the homes of the pious in New England. God's being is disclosed to human perception under the aspects of both shadow and brightness, a specter of divine sovereignty which was at once awful and glorious.[11]

Two short stories by Nathaniel Hawthorne may serve best to describe this tension that forms the marrow of Puritan spirituality. They also demonstrate the tendency of the post-Puritan mind to drive apart the two poles of fear and grace which characterized the piety of this people. "Rappaccini's Daughter" offers the perspective most popularly attributed to the dour New England spirit. Its elusive, principal character is the tall and emaciated Dr. Giacomo Rappaccini who, clad in deathly black, cultivates behind his house in Padua a walled garden of dark and poisonous herbs. From these noxious plants he supposedly distills healing elixirs. But like some cold, Genevan deity of dark imagination, "he cares infinitely more for science than for mankind."[12] When a young man is drawn by reckless love to his pale and beautiful daughter, the lad learns to his horror that the girl has all her life been the object of her father's studied experimentation. Nourished from her birth by the poisons of a deadly plant created by him, the girl's life has been so imbued with the herb's inscrutable evil that her loving touch could mean nothing but death. It is this metaphor of "infinite monstrousness" that William Shurr has used to characterize the literary Calvinism he finds so influential on American writers from Hawthorne and Melville to Dreiser and O'Neill. They all, he says, are Rappaccini's children, fearfully drawn to the unfathomable malice of a God who toys with absolute power.[13] The image is only dimly Puritan, of course, emphasizing God's fearsome potency entirely apart from any concern with covenant. Unfortunately, it is an image advanced as definitive by every American literary anthology which uses Jonathan Edwards' sermon, "Sinners in the Hands of an Angry God," as its sole example of the malignant Puritan mind.

This commonly-accepted stereotype of Puritan piety is balanced, if not corrected, by yet another Hawthorne tale, entitled "The Artist of the Beautiful." It is the story of a fragile apprentice clockmaker, in love with his master's daughter, who devotes the whole of his impassioned, meticulous labor to the fashioning of a mechanical butterfly whose beauty would give her pleasure. Despite the menacing cynicism of his master and the swarthy bluster of a blacksmith who in the end wins his girl, he ultimately succeeds in creating this thing of beauty. A butterfly—seemingly alive—possessed of the most intricate workings, lightly flies from a jewel box of traced pearl when opened. "It is impossible to express by words the glory, the splendour, the delicate gorgeousness which were softened into the beauty of this object."[14] The wondrous mechanism was one in which its creator took perfect, near-infinite delight, even as it finally was crushed in the hand of an infant bearing the taint of Adam's sin. This sheer pleasure taken in the splendor of beauty itself is a grace also distinctively Puritan. Edwards wrote immeasurably more about the excellence of God's beauty than he ever dwelt on the horror of divine omnipotence. The capacity of humans to grasp, by an aesthetic (almost sixth) sense of the heart, the very glory of God would form the height of Puritan devotion at its best.[15] In the communion meditations of Edward Taylor, the ravishing love of a matchless God would be celebrated with poetic felicity, lifting the Puritan soul to the sublime.

These two stories, with their alternative themes of terror-ridden might and loving resplendence, constitute a pattern that recurs continually in the Puritan perception of spirituality and landscape. The brooding mystery of Dr. Rappaccini and the frail, but exquisite radiance of the apprentice, Owen Warland, are both inexorable elements of the Calvinist encounter of God. Neither can be separated from the other. The covenantal means by which the two are related can be seen theologically and geographically in the "Personal Narrative" of Jonathan Edwards, written in 1740. There he described "a season of awakening" that had occurred in his boyhood, some years before going to college. He and a few other schoolmates had "built a booth in a swamp, in a very retired spot [along the floodplain of the Connecticut River], for a place of prayer." There, in the solemn aloneness of the western Massachusetts landscape, he spent time in reflection on the "horrible doctrine" of God's sovereign decrees, a truth that had always plagued him with an awareness of his own sin. But as he further read the scriptures and imagined himself alone in the mountains (in the nearby Berkshires), this vision of divine sovereignty became an "exceedingly pleasant, bright, and sweet" doctrine. Not long after this, he had a similar experience while walking alone across the expanse of his father's pasture land.

As I was walking there, and looking upon the sky and clouds, there came into my mind so sweet a sense of the glorious *majesty* and *grace* of God, as I know not how to express. — I seemed to see them both in a sweet conjunction; majesty and meekness joined together: it was a sweet, and gentle, and holy majesty; and also a majestic meekness; an awful sweetness, a high, and great, and holy gentleness.[16]

This vivid experience of fear being wed to gentle grace meant a change in Edwards' future way of reading the inscape of the Massachusetts' sky. That which he once had feared became that by which he found himself most loved. Even hair-raising electrical storms took on new meaning in light of this new-found perception. He said that since that time

scarce any thing, among all the works of nature, was so sweet to me as thunder and lightning; formerly nothing had been so terrible to me. Before, I used to be uncommonly terrified with thunder, and to be struck with terror when I saw a thunderstorm rising; but now, on the contrary, it rejoiced me. I felt God, if I may so speak, at the first appearance of a thunderstorm; and used to take the opportunity, at such times, to fix myself in order to view the clouds, and see the lightnings play, and hear the majestic and awful voice of God's thunder, which oftentimes was exceedingly entertaining, leading me to sweet contemplations of my great and glorious God.[17]

Such profound spiritual insight is far removed from the customary caricature of the austere Puritan encounter of God. It contrasts significantly, for example, with Leon Kellner's distorted image of the Calvinist worldview. He urged that

Calvinism is the natural theology of the disinherited; it never flourished, therefore, anywhere as it did in the barren hills of Scotland and the wilds of North America. The Calvinist feels himself surrounded by naught but hostile powers; his life is a perpetual conflict from his very birth. The farmer who has to keep up a constant struggle against untoward phenomena, against the refractory soil, against drought and frost, against caterpillars and a host of other insect plagues . . . is naturally inclined to the belief from the outset that God . . . is a well-meaning but unquestionably a rigorous, cold being who rules

the world with some great purpose unknown to the inhabitants
of the earth.[18]

Indeed, the world, as well as the God, of the Puritans could be harsh.
But majesty was, for them, always framed by grace within the context
of covenant. God could also be met in rain and gently falling snow, not
only in drought and killing frost. The effort theologically to maintain
this balance and to spell out its implications for life in the New England
village would occupy three generations and more of Puritan believers.
It would be given expression spatially and geographically in the Puritan
structures of identity and place, as this spirituality continued to pervade
the landscape of the North Atlantic coastline. Three specific ways by
which the theology of covenant would be mirrored in the concrete experience of Puritan life can be considered here.

The Centripetal Focus of the New England Village

The first way in which Puritan covenant theology was given
expression geographically was in the tendency to symbolize the covenant relationship in the typical spatial pattern of the Puritan village. To
belong to the people of God was to live within the boundaries of the
proclamation of God's covenant love. Hence, the preferred layout of the
New England town radiated out concentrically from the meeting house
at its center to the boundaries of grace located on the edge of the surrounding wilderness. Patterned after instructions in the Pentateuch for
the placement of the tabernacle and its adjacent tents of the tribes of
Israel, this centripetal focus of space gave expression to the close bonds
of covenant. God's people were expected to dwell in proximity to the
place of meeting. But these boundaries of grace always lay in tension
with the foreboding and tempting landscape *beyond* the camp. Indeed,
such boundaries even seemed inimical to the divine call to inherit the
earth and to extend the Gospel beyond all horizons. Boundary could
serve simultaneously (and paradoxically) as both limit and challenge.
The New England village, therefore, assumed great symbolic importance to the Puritans, as a mythic as well as social and commercial center. Its physical configuration was, and still is, immediately recogniz-
able, pointing as it did to an ordered reality borrowed from the realm
of the holy.

This characteristic American landscape of the Puritan town plan is
one closely akin to Samuel Butler's Erewhon. Having never existed in
detailed perfection, it can nevertheless be described in mythic symbol-

ism by nearly everyone. At its center is the pointed spire of an old Congregational church, set in its framework of white clapboard houses, fronting onto a well-grazed village green or common. Huge elm trees reach from its quiet streets into the clear, blue sky. Cultivated fields nearby gradually give way to the dark and distant forest. To everyone the scene says "New England." This is a symbolic landscape which forms a central part of the American iconography—an image of the closely-knit, family-centered, and God-fearing people we would like at times to think we are. It can speak of many things, but the quaint Yankee village is quintessentially American—having been romanticized in the prints of Currier and Ives, reconstructed in museum gothic at Old Sturbridge in Massachusetts, and still approximated in remote locales like Lyndon Center, Vermont.[19] The archetypal village is one which, even in its non-existence (as a precisely-observed pattern), has exercised a profound, mythic influence on the American understanding of "placed" existence.

Environmental historian John R. Stilgoe traces the roots of this contrived New England landscape back to the original German meaning of the word *landschaft*. It suggested

> a collection of dwellings and other structures crowded together within a circle of pasture, meadow, and planting fields and surrounded by unimproved forest or marsh. . . . The word meant more than an organization of space; it connoted too the inhabitants of the place and their obligations to one another and to the land.[20]

The most common *landschaft* form was the concentric type, found usually in England and Western Europe. It was this spatial model which the Puritans brought with them from the Old World. Here, at the midpoint of the circle formed by the covenanting community, the Puritan saint could mythically share in the primitive cry of the Kwakiutl neophyte, "I am at the Center of the World!"[21] The circle formed the orb of God's special providential care. In ancient England, the midpoint of the village had been marked by a tree or vertical staff known as a roland. This served as "the objectified essence of *landschaft*"—a *universalis columna* like Jacob's ladder, connecting earth with heaven, a cosmic axis placing one at the symbolic navel of the earth. The pagan May-pole or unhewn tree would later be replaced by the Celtic cross, but the spatial conception of proximity to a sacred center remained the same.

In the New England village—like that of Ipswich, Massachusetts, founded in 1634—the old white meeting house on the village green would serve as the geographical and symbolic center of the town. There the community-forming Word of the Lord was preached and signified as sacred time converged with sacred space each Puritan sabbath. All roads radiated from this axis. The graveyard stood adjacent to the church. The town common functioned as a training field for the militia and occasional grazing ground for animals. In later years the nearby town hall and schoolhouse would be joined by a village inn, a general store, and eventually the grange building. In this way the fabric of colonial society was woven from threads all meeting at the center.[22]

The ideal pattern was first delineated in the mid-1630's by the anonymous author of an essay entitled "The Ordering of Towns."[23] This early-American model for town-planning exemplifies perfectly the hierarchical and centripetal notion of space that characterized the early New England mind. Its author proposed a paradigmatic townscape of six concentric circles set within a six-mile square. Optimally every Puritan village would be laid out in this manner. At the innermost circle would be the meetinghouse where the faithful gathered regularly to worship. As towers and spires were added to the simple New England churches after 1699, this symbolism of the church as ancient roland or *axis mundi* would be enhanced even further. In the second concentric circle, surrounding the meeting house on its village green, were the houses of the congregation members, "orderly placed to enjoy comfortable communion." This proximity to the house of meeting and to each other was considered crucially important on both social and theological grounds. Reverence for communal authority and respect for the Body of Christ could be nourished, it was thought, only by physical closeness to the symbolic center of God's rule. The "visible saints," therefore, could be identified geographically as well as in terms of their godly lives and personal narratives of conversion. In 1635 the Massachusetts General Court would even rule that "no dwelling house shall be built above half a mile from the meetinghouse in any new plantation."[24] Efforts to enforce the law, of course, proved hopeless, given the endlessly-beckoning quantities of space afforded by the New World. But the concern to maintain a traditional sense of confinement in space would continue to dominate the Puritan mind, even though ultimately it would prove their undoing.

The third circle composing the paradigmatic New England village was a ring of common fields whereon the typical Puritan husbandman managed his livestock. This was bounded, still further out from the center, by a fourth area where "men of great estate" could be granted 400-acre lots and a fifth ring where free-standing farms would raise crops on which the town could thrive. The sixth and final sphere in this spatial pattern is the most interesting of all. It was composed of "swamps and rubbish waste grounds" which, while owned by the town and included within its limits, were deliberately never occupied. This was a terrain serving primarily mythical purposes.

> The outer circle of wilderness, cursorily bounded and dimly perceived, would provide the surrounding disorder within which the town would find its identity.[25]

This was the threatening and chaotic *yin* which functioned as foil and contrast to the dominant *yang* of structured Puritan society. Wildness formed the containing border that gave meaning to the ordered life within. Hence, even though it was carefully shunned—an area about which one sought to know nothing—it was just as carefully mapped, lest one forget the value of propriety by disregarding the threat of chaos. Indeed, after the manner of the ancient Taoist symbol of the circle half dark and half light, the Puritan village even maintained a pinpoint of chaos near its center, in addition to its surrounding margin of incoherence. This was the early New England cemetery, invariably weed-grown and unkept, its stones half-toppled—a curious patch of disarray in the midst of well-laid order. Stilgoe observes that "seventeenth and eighteenth century graveyards were contrived disorders that clearly warned everyone of the fiery, chaotic wilderness of Hell."[26] The time-honored *I-Ching*, with its classic Chinese balance of attracting opposites, could have found no better expression than this symbolic arrangement of the New England village.

But in Puritan consciousness, it was order that clearly triumphed. A spirituality built on the firm ties of covenant theology could best be given spatial expression in the principle of containment. Hence, the first generation of Puritan settlers were ever concerned to remind each other of the virtue of propinquity. Living in proximity to the nucleus of the community was a sign of owning the covenant. Accordingly, those who lived "beyond the camp of Israel," remote from the means of grace, were scorned as "outlivers," dwelling in self-imposed exile from the house of meeting. Some towns, like Andover, even levied a fine of twenty shillings for each month that such defectors lived beyond the village pale. In this way they sought to nurture the ideal of "neighborly living."[27] Edward Johnson, in his *Wonder-Working Providence of Sion's Saviour in New England* (1654), offered a commentary on the layout of Massachusetts towns, as he surveyed the early history of Puritans in that region. Villages like those at Water-Towne and Newberry were particularly the object of his reproach because of their tendency toward geographical dispersion. The village of Water-Towne, strung haphazardly along the branches of the Charles River,

> hath caused her inhabitants to scatter in such manner, that their Sabbath-Assemblies prove very thin if the season favour not, and hath made this great Towne (consisting of 160. Families) to shew nothing delightful to the eye in any place.[28]

Similarly, the town of Dorchester was hopelessly stretched out like "a winged-serpent," slithering its way north toward Boston Harbor. How could such formlessness help but give rise to dissension and disharmony, Johnson asked. While the preferred model of the Puritan townscape may thus have been followed more in the breach than in the observance, the hope of containment still remained strong throughout the first generation. Eyes were turned away from the threatening wilderness to the sacred center where order and meaning dwelt. Beyond the town lay only bewilderment and disorientation in the dark forest— the home of malevolent forces and savage Indians, the landscape of fear.[29] All roads, therefore, led home—into the village, toward safety. The road to elsewhere was not yet imagined. No Whitmanesque wanderlust was able yet to lure young or old beyond the town. The carefree "song of the open road" would not be heard until the late eighteenth and nineteenth centuries, on the far side of the dissolved Puritan synthesis. But, as will be seen later, the seeds of discontent would be sown very early.

A Chosen Place and A Pilgrim People

A second way that covenant theology influenced the Puritan reading of the New England landscape relates to the measure of permanence by which Puritans attached themselves to the land. Were they to be conceived as a covenant people continually in transit, given to impermanence, finding their locus in God alone? Or were they a people assured by the covenant of a place to call their own, so that New England became an inheritance parallel to Israel's claim on Canaan? In other words, was the nature of the Puritan covenant to be understood primarily in Mosaic or Davidic terms? God's covenant with Moses in the Old Testament had been grounded in the experience of the exodus and wilderness wandering, always anticipating but never arriving in the land of promise. It was a conditional covenant, dependent upon the faithfulness of God's people, never to be taken for granted (cf. 1 Kgs 9:4–7). The Old Testament covenant with David, by contrast, had been grounded in the settled experience of Jerusalem and the divine assurance that the throne of David would never fail. This covenant was unconditional, permanent, resting on God's irrevocable word (cf. 2 Sam 7:14–16). The question, then, was how the American Puritans were to conceive of their own covenant with God.

They found themselves in a tension between their conviction of New England as God's chosen place and their identity of themselves as God's pilgrim people. From John Winthrop's sermon aboard the *Arbella*, even before the faithful had landed at Massachusetts Bay in 1630, the certainty was firm that God had meant them to be a "City upon a Hill" in this new place. *God* had chosen the land for them, not they themselves. But this confidence rested uneasily with yet another Puritan conviction that they were ever to remain "pilgrims and strangers" in the world—their faith nurtured by the exigencies of exile. John Calvin had compared the life of the children of God on this earth to that of a bird flitting from one branch to another, never resting for long in any single nest.[30] Pride in the chosenness of God's New Israel in America, therefore, would continually be accompanied by grave cautions against sinking one's roots too deeply and presuming too recklessly upon God's gracious placement of his people.

Exegetically this tension could be found in two very different texts often expounded from Puritan pulpits. The one, in Hebrews 11:10–16, insisted that the descendants of Abraham were ever to be a wandering people, whereas the other, in 2 Samuel 7:10, spoke of the covenant community as being planted in the land and having to move no more. In the first generation of Puritan settlers, the emphasis fell most on the former theme of "the world as a place of passage, and not as a place of habitation." Robert Cushman reminded his fellow pilgrims at Plymouth in 1622 that

> we are . . . in all places strangers and pilgrims, travelers and sojourners, most properly, having no dwelling but in this earthen tabernacle. Our dwelling is but a wandering, and our abiding but as a fleeting, and in a word our home is nowhere but in the heavens—in that house not made with hands, whose maker and builder is God.[31]

The notion that "home is nowhere" would become a cautionary slogan rehearsing for Puritans in America their separation from the ecclesiastical errors of the European past. John Cotton would instruct his people at Massachusetts Bay that "Christ is not bound to any place." Rome may long have doted on Peter's Chair, Jerusalem may have bragged of her privileges, the Reformers may have prided themselves on their stronghold in the Palatinate, but Christ, he insisted, had left them all, to go "abroad in the fields" as a pilgrim.[32] In such fashion, the praise of a certain holy placelessness would come to characterize much of Puritan piety.

With the uprooting from home and the Atlantic passage fresh in mind, it was not surprising that the first generation of American Puritans emphasized the motif of wandering pilgrimage. Yet soon the concern would turn to the permanence of Canaan's new plantation, asking how New England was finally to be conceived as home. Sidney Mead suggests that the question for Americans has always been how to be placed, but also free—how to balance these conflicting metaphors of plantation and pilgrimage. Americans, he says, have always tended to understand freedom as primarily a dimension of space. To explore the possibilities of being human has been to possess unbounded freedom of movement over new terrain.[33] But this impulse would be matched also by the concern to claim as an inheritance that land over which one's feet have trod (Jos 14:9). Pilgrims would become pioneers and pioneers, settlers. Increasingly the land would prove inviting in its own right.

Furthermore, if events were divinely foreordained, as Calvinist Puritans surely believed, then the site of the eventual settlement of God's people could be no accidental affair. One Puritan divine argued this point to the extreme, when he insisted that God "has decreed when and where every man that comes into the World shall be Born; and where he shall live, in what Country, and in what Town; yea, and in what House too. . . . "[34] From this perspective, the New England map offered a scaled topography of the divine decrees. This sense of God's predetermined placement of God's people could in time lend itself to a presumptuous pride in possession, leading ultimately to ideas of manifest destiny. The certainty of a chosen locale for a chosen people could result in a bold triumphalism on the part of some Puritan writers. Cotton Mather recalled, for example, the way God had gone before the *Mayflower* pilgrims so as to prepare a place for them in the vicinity of Plymouth.

> The Indians in these parts had newly, even about a year or two before, been visited with such a prodigious pestilence, as carried away not a *tenth*, but *nine parts* of *ten* (yea, 'tis said, *nineteen* of *twenty*) among them: so that the woods were almost cleared of these pernicious creatures, to make room for a better growth.[35]

God's predestination and providence could thus be brought into service in legitimating the Puritan confiscation of Indian land.

In this way, the principle of pilgrim placelessness urged by the earliest Puritan settlers to New England gradually gave way to an alternative principle of destined occupation of the land. While this may have been justified initially by a sense of divine call to yet further placement—carrying the Gospel to the uttermost parts of the world, it later gave way to all the wanderlust and land fever of colonial expansion.[36] The geography of the promised land was an ever-broadening phenomenon in the mythos of the seventeenth-century Puritan mind. The New Canaan may have been at first limited in the Puritan imagination to Massachusetts itself, but it soon outgrew such limits. In 1630, John Cotton had understood God's promise to be entirely fulfilled in the Puritan plantation along the coast between Salem and Plymouth. He preached a sermon on a text from 2 Samuel 7:10, where Yahweh had proclaimed, "I will appoint a place for my people Israell, and I will plant them, that they may dwell in a place of their owne, and *move no more.*"[37] Further migration into the interior of New England was at that time unthinkable. In fact, Puritan writers penned carefully-reasoned defenses of their having come this far, and no farther.[38] They felt keenly the accusations of those back home in England who viewed them as irresponsible drifters. But the lure of geographical expansion quickly dissolved this initial reluctance to pass over into the land beyond the Berkshires. Soon there were at least "three interior Canaans" which came to absorb the imagination of Puritan settlers. The Connecticut River Valley first drew Thomas Hooker and a small exodus from Massachusetts Bay in the year 1636. There Hartford would be established along "the delightful banks of the Connecticut." Others would look still further west to the Hudson River Valley, described as "the true garden of New England."[39] Some would point beyond even the Hudson to the unexplored area of the Great Lakes. As early as 1637, Thomas Morton was speaking of "the Great Lake of Erocoise" [Lake Superior] as "the principallst place for a plantation in all New Canaan . . . the prime seate for the Metropolis" of this new world.[40] Thirst for the freedom and opportunity afforded by unbounded space thus continued to drive the Puritans westward, even as it had originally prompted their passage over the sea.

It was a movement accepted only with reluctance by many. The Puritan sense of contained and structured "place" warred continually with the fascinating, if dangerous allure of unrestricted "space." As much as first-generation Puritans urged living close to the town center, with its fixed security, there remained (and increased) a fascination with the chaotic wilderness beyond. Nathaniel Hawthorne would later portray vividly this tension in his novel *The Scarlet Letter*. There the double-edged promise and temptation of wilderness served as literary structure to his story while it also revealed most deeply the Puritan dilemma. Hester Prynne, the woman whose adultery and willful silence had largely excluded her from the covenanting community, dwelt physically and emotionally on the margin of Salem's life. She lived in a small thatched cottage "on the outskirts of the town, within the verge of the peninsula, but not in close vicinity to any other habitation."[41] She had been driven to the edge of wilderness by her moral deviance, but that same wilderness also gave to her (and to her daughter) a strange vitality. It offered energy as well as exile. She was inexorably drawn to it, if always by a joy mixed with dread. Like Arthur Dimmesdale, the town minister and illicit father of her child, she knew the dark forest to be the haunt of that tall black man who urged unwary travelers to sign his heavy book.

But if the forest was a type of moral waste, it could also be a symbol of intoxicating freedom. In the novel's climactic forest scene, Hester cries out to Dimmesdale, himself damned by the confining bounds of Salem, "Wither leads yonder forest-track? Backward to the settlement, thou sayest! Yes, but *onward*, too. Deeper into the wilderness. . . . There thou are free!" She urges him toward a reorientation in spatial structure that would offer individual freedom, if also at the expense of covenant identity. "Leave this wreck and ruin," she exults. "Begin all anew!"[42] But the binds of covenant prove finally too strong for Hester and Dimmesdale alike. The loss of place is a possibility too frightening to envision, despite whatever new life may be afforded by open-ended space. It is this essential tension that may at last disclose the genius of Puritan spirituality—a subtle tension of fear and grace discerned even in the New England landscape.

The Jeremiad: Restoring the Ambiguity of Landscape

The Puritan synthesis showed clear signs of dissolving even before the turn of the eighteenth century. Puritan spirituality would not be able indefinitely to hold in tension the twin themes of majesty and grace. The sense of amazement at the grandeur of a covenanting God would cease to hold the Puritan imagination in quite the same way as it once had. The hazardous Atlantic crossing and the first hard years of tentative settlement could soon be forgotten. New Englanders no longer lived in a completely unsettled world resting tenuously on the sovereign finger of an Almighty God.[43] Geographically this meant that believers who had previously lived close to the house of meeting—faithful in owning the covenant—could more and more be found scattered far beyond the traditional boundaries of grace. Puritans who had rehearsed the pilgrimage motif in their light-handed touch on this passing age would come increasingly to feel at home in the world, reaching ever westward in the desire for more land. In the second and third generation of American Puritan life, therefore, the question arose of how the people of God were to recover the wellsprings of faith, seeing the landscape once again as filled with splendor, alive with God's electric presence—both terrifying and glorious.

The tradition of the jeremiad came to be used as a way of reviving the imagery on which the double impulse of Puritan spirituality had thrived.[44] Those who had begun to presume on the blessing of a gracious God were reminded that the benefits of covenant rested on the obligations of covenant. That which God had granted could also be taken away. As the prophet Jeremiah had warned the naively-confident people of Jerusalem in his own day, the double-edged spade of the divine gardener could pluck up as well as plant (Jer 1:10). One, therefore, could never presume upon safety of location. A breach of covenant could lead to a loss of place. John Cotton, preaching in England on the celebrated text of 2 Samuel 7:10, even before John Winthrop had sailed for America, had added a harsh Mosaic warning to its confident Davidic promise. Despite the assurances of being planted and moving no more, he said, "if you rebell against God the same God who planted you will also root you out again."[45] The theme would be echoed many times in the history of New England, particularly on those Days of Humiliation when times of affliction and disaster were used to recall the demands of covenant. On the morning of October 30, 1727, for example, Cotton Mather preached a sermon on "The Terror of the Lord," referring to an earthquake which had struck the New England coastline the night before. "The Glorious GOD has *Roared out of Zion*," he said.

> We have the last Night heard the terrible *Roaring;* with general and uncommon Terror, heard the awful Repetition of it. Who is here of you, among them who felt the *Earth trembling* under them, that said not . . . *Lord, my Flesh trembles for fear of Thee, and I am afraid of thy Judgments! The Lion hath roared; Who will not fear?*[46]

On one level, the jeremiad served simply as warning, as an exercise in discipline. It offered an occasion for driving home those moral concerns that could ordinarily go so easily unheard. In the sermon just mentioned, Cotton Mather would take the opportunity to rebuke those who often slept in church, observing happily that the recent earthquake assured the careful attention of them all. He went on to speak of intemperance and unchastity and the failure of sabbath observance as still further causes of the seismic anger of the Lord. But the tradition of the jeremiad ought not to be associated with moralizing tendencies alone, as if it functioned solely as a means of social control.

On a deeper level, the jeremiad expressed also a fervent longing for God. It was an expression of piety as well as an exercise in discipline. Its chief aim was the re-encounter of a living God, not simply the alteration of behavior. Cotton Mather himself could speak with "wonderment" of the great mercy of God which also was revealed in the recent tragic events. Like Puritan divines from Michael Wigglesworth and Edward Johnson to Jonathan Edwards and David Brainerd, he sought most to rediscover the God whom William Ames had described as passing all comprehension in his mercy and grace. All of these sought a reorientation to landscape, a renewal of fiery images once sparked by the crashing of waves on the flint rocks at Newport, by the driving sleet carried on winter winds over the Chatham lighthouse, by the tall, oppressive hardwoods of upper Maine, choking out the sun on the dark path west toward Mount Katahdin. They sought to meet there once again the God of John Calvin, untamed and fierce. No measured, housebroken deity was this, but the God of all ages bursting onto their staid horizon with glory uncontained. This was the God exalted in the Bay Psalm Book and later in the hymns of Isaac Watts, whose brightness fills the whole realm of nature, whose "love so amazing, so divine, demands my soul, my life, my all." It was the God of Edward Taylor, whom he implored to blow over the coal of his chilly, fireless heart, to enflame in him the love of God's consuming light.[47] It was a God finally found on the crusted, outer edges of the New England landscape, devouring all syrupy nature mysticisms in the white heat of his commanding Otherness. The jeremiad, in short, was an endeavor to restore the ambiguity of landscape, to see in earth, sky, and sea the terror-fraught and overawing beauty of a loving God.

Conrad Cherry remarks that "New England was most ambiguous when it was liveliest as a symbol."[48] Any symbolic landscape is always multivalent in its meanings. Indeed, it is when a symbol is most able to engage the imagination that it is most abounding in ambiguity. Surely this was the case in early seventeenth-century New England. The wilderness, for instance, could simultaneously evoke dissimilar, even opposite, images in the Puritan mind. William Bradford stepped off the *Mayflower* into what he described as a "hideous and desolate wilderness," starting what Roderick Nash speaks of as a "tradition of repugnance."[49] Yet John Winthrop could see only promise as he gazed onto the shore of Massachusetts Bay from the deck of the *Arbella*. "There came a smell off the shore like the smell of a garden," he said. It was the smell of luscious strawberries that he would soon find in abundance. Wilderness could thus mirror, at the same time, both the majesty and grace of a sovereign God. It could be understood as a threatening "hedge," limiting and containing the people of God, and it could function also as a training ground of faith, offering access to God's mercy.[50] Thomas Shepard would underscore the threatening, chaotic character of wilderness, insisting:

> A wilderness notes a desolate, solitary place, without Inhabitants, and where there is nothing but confusion and disorder . . . there's no man passing through, no man dwelling there, but it's deserted and forsaken of men. . . . [51]

It was a place one sought most to avoid. But Thomas Hooker found hope and joy in the same rugged terrain which Shepard viewed only as "wild and uncouth woods." Hooker spoke of passing through "a vast and roaring Wilderness" so as to "possess that good land which abounded with all prosperity, [and] flowed with Milk and Honey." Another could speak of the Lord Christ as

> having egged a small handful of his people forth in a forlorne Wildernesse, stripping them naked from all humane helps, plunging them in a gulph of miseries, that they may swim for their lives through the Ocean of his Mercies, and land themselves safe in the armes of his compassion.[52]

Such was the ambiguity that the wilds of New England offered to the early Puritan settlers. It was seen to contain constant reminders of both the lordship and the benevolence of Christ.

But as the second and third generation found themselves more firmly established in the land, the edge of ambiguity would soon be dulled. Wilderness would lose much of the threatening, provocative character it once had held. In part, the Puritans became victims of their own success. Launching deeper into the forest, they turned to the task of redeeming the wilderness, making it blossom like the rose (Is 35:1). They followed the impulse to put down roots, to plant and to build, to turn chaos into order. In draining swamps, reclaiming land, constructing neat houses, and laying out ordered streets, they found themselves able to manage what they first had feared. Years later, when Timothy

Dwight, the grandson of Jonathan Edwards, traveled across New England, he was attracted most to the "perfect neatness" of sprightly towns and "the numerous churches which gem the whole landscape."[53] It was the landscape fashioned by human industry that moved him most. Thomas Cole's famous landscape painting of "The Oxbow" turn in the Connecticut River could demonstrate the later Puritan attitude toward the land. On the right bank of the river were carefully manicured fields and distant houses, basking in the sun west of Mount Holyoke, while on the left bank thunderclouds hovered over the thick brush and tangled wilds of an untamed land. Increasingly the children and grandchildren of the Puritan fathers and mothers would come to draw their mythic images from the right side of the picture alone.[54] Yet, ironically, it was the unmastered wilderness that originally had been the source of their strongest images of a sovereign God. In managing the land, they had begun to lose the energies of their richest symbolic life.

The practitioners of the jeremiad, therefore, would be the ones to attempt the restoration of a lost ambiguity. Realizing how symbolically important the fierce wilderness had been, Edward Johnson, for example, reminded his people of the harsh exigencies involved in the planting of Concord, the first inland town. Clambering over fallen trees, wading through watery swamps, their arms and legs torn by brambles, they sought a haven from the bitter storms to which Massachusetts Bay was subject. They sweltered in the hot summer sun, the driving snow later dissolving on their backs in winter, as they struggled to survive under the leadership of their pastor John Jones.

> In Desart's depth where Wolves and Beares abide,
> There Jones sits down a wary watch to keepe. . . . [55]

It was a tale of unrelieved affliction, but Johnson had no doubt that their souls had thrived in inverse proportion to the harshness of the land. Their imagination could root itself deeply in the soil of that wild and savage place.

In a similar way, Michael Wigglesworth responded to the drought of 1662 by recalling the trials of earlier pilgrims in the "places wilde and waste" of Eastern Massachusetts. The vehement poetry of his "God's Controversy with New England" was aimed at regaining a glorious sense of God's mercy mixed with his justice. He has God declare:

> But hear O Heavens! Let Earth amazed stand;
> Ye Mountaines melt, and Hills come flowing down:
> Let horror seize upon both Sea and Land;

Let Natures self be cast into a stown.
I children nourisht, nurtur'd and upheld:
But they against a tender father have rebell'd.[56]

Wigglesworth loved the equivocal landscape of the North Atlantic coast. He was stirred by its harshness and its beauty both. "Ah dear New England!," he cried, "dearest land to me." He longed to share the double-vision of its power with the sluggish souls belonging to his care. This was the same impulse that would later drive Cotton Mather to remind the settled people of Boston that "the rabid and howling *Wolves* of the *Wilderness*" still prowled the city's edge at evening. Seeking to regain the imaginative power of an earlier naivete, he warned of the dragons, droves of devils, and fiery flying serpents that also dwelt beyond the fragile bounds of ordered life.[57] The preachers of the jeremiad, from Wigglesworth to Mather, knew that if ambiguity could be restored to landscape—its provocative contradictions crashing into the structured world of a domesticated people—then the multivalent richness of God's own nature could also be regained.

■ ■ ■ ■ ■ ■ ■ ■ ■ ■ ■ ■ ■ ■ ■ ■ ■

In the most creative Puritan reading of the New England landscape there was always a bi-polarity of emphasis. On the one hand, there were terrifying images of the divine majesty—mirrored in hundreds of stories about earthquakes, losses at sea, dread Indian captivities, and blight on the grain. But, on the other hand, the faithful narrative of God's grace in delivering the elect from drought, pestilence, and the threat of the Atlantic passage could be heard in every other pulpit from Narragansett to New Haven. Both anger and blessing would be read from the ambiguous sky and fields of New England. The same landscape invited settlement and bade the pilgrim to pass on quickly before the gathering shadows of night. Hawthorne's Hester Prynne would seek salvation on a middle landscape between town and forest, within the grace-filled environs of a covenant community. But Hermann Melville, gazing out on the roiling sea three days from New Bedford, would insist that "in landlessness alone lies the highest truth."[58] Both insights were drawn from a common Puritan source of mythic energy. In either case, the holy could always be found along the uncertain edges where ordered and chaotic life converged. There it was that a watchful eye was kept so as to search for God's passing, like Moses hidden in the cleft of the rock. In all these ways, therefore, tensions in the New England landscape gave expression to the possibilities and problems of life under the covenant. Puritans found themselves caught between being centered and being scattered, placed and uprooted, frightened and enchanted by the same beauteous and rugged space in which they dwelt. Such is the subtle and convoluted hermeneutic that Puritans brought to the landscape of New England.

Mythic Landscapes:
Galesville, Wisconsin:
Locus Mirabilis

The unwatched gates of Eden lay in anonymity along the great river north of La Crosse, Wisconsin. U.S. Highway 53 boldly led the way to a paradise Augustine had once declared inaccessible to fallen humanity. A Mobil station and a Shur-Save grocery stood on either side of the road in the place where flaming seraphim had once been set. To the profane eye, of course, the landscape looked no different from the gently-rolling Wisconsin prairie we'd been driving through all morning. But according to the visionary insight of a nineteenth-century prophet and local eccentric, we had just entered God's first garden. John Locke had known that in the beginning all the world was America, and here in Trempealeau County in the American heartland the Rev. D. O. Van Slyke had seen traces of humankind's first home.

This itinerant preacher for the Methodist Episcopal Church had made his own way to the bluffs overlooking the Mississippi River on a snowy night in November of 1854. Shortly before his death thirty years later he published a pamphlet entitled *The Garden of Eden*, claiming on the basis of scripture and topography that the locale surrounding Galesville, Wisconsin—the place of his long and erratic ministry—was indeed the scene of primeval paradise.[1] Van Slyke's story bears retelling. It is a good tale in its own right, but more than that it is a case study in American mythopoesis, an example of how humans invariably see the sacred not just in the cosmic but in the particular. We long to see our ordinary dwelling places transformed into the *axis mundi*.[2]

Several years before this trip to Wisconsin, I'd come across a copy of Van Slyke's pamphlet. I was intrigued by the number of people like him who had discovered in southwestern Wisconsin the intimate abode of the holy. Frederick Jackson Turner and Frank Lloyd Wright, for example, had each been nurtured in their youth by the smoky-orange sunsets and prodigious farmlands of "God's native country." A fascination with the American frontier and the impulse behind organic architecture both took shape in the promised land. Indeed, the town and promise of Arcadia can still be found along Route 95 not far north of Galesville.

I set out with my family on a sunny morning late in June on a carefree search for Eden. The road lay roughly parallel to the Mississippi; the distant bluffs on the Minnesota side loomed high on the borders of paradise. It was not until we turned off onto a spur leading to the river itself that I began to enter the mystery of Van Slyke's insistent vision. The bluffs both beyond the river and behind the highway formed a long crescent. They offered a sense of enclosure—a notion of the limits or boundaries of Elysium. One could begin to think of the terrain as hedged-in, set apart, as if for a purpose. (The first requisite to a sense of the sacred in a given locale may be the hint of an opening framed by closure.) It was from this threshold that I could think my way into the grandly provincial mind of the venerable Methodist divine—entering his mystery, submitting to his own skewed vision of the world.

The Mississippi here seemed to double back on itself in places, as if hesitant to continue its flow to the sea. Bright green algae floated gently in the side pools along the banks. I became aware of a greater variety of trees, more frequent calls of birds, an unusual lushness to the ferns and mosses. I found myself listing trees (noting hardwoods, willows, white pines, and sugar maples) and watching for portents. Before the dew had fully dried, my children and I climbed Brady's Bluff in the state park near the Mississippi. We were perfectly alone, climbing in silence, when I noticed on the trail ahead a doe and fawn dash into the trees to the left. The children didn't see them. Only I did. Was it because only I had submitted to the strangeness of the place, I wondered. I had tried earlier to engage my ten-year-old daughter in the mystery— describing the Genesis account of a garden east of a great, long river (the Euphrates mentioned in Genesis 2:14 meaning "long river"), with three lesser rivers flowing into it. By Van Slyke's reckoning, the Black, Trempealeau, and La Crosse rivers perfectly fit the biblical account. But she thought the idea silly, seeing very little in that Wisconsin landscape on a hot summer day to inspire notions of paradise. But I myself was unable to relinquish the aberrant vision of D. O. Van Slyke. I set out for Galesville to ask some questions.

The fellow wearing a John Deere cap and pumping gas at the Mobil station didn't laugh when I asked about the Garden of Eden. That was the first hopeful sign. He even suggested I look up Elsie Docken, the town postmistress. "She can tell you all the old stories," he said. However, the postmistress had had a death in the family the night before and was not at work that day. So, referred by others, I went on to the Pres-

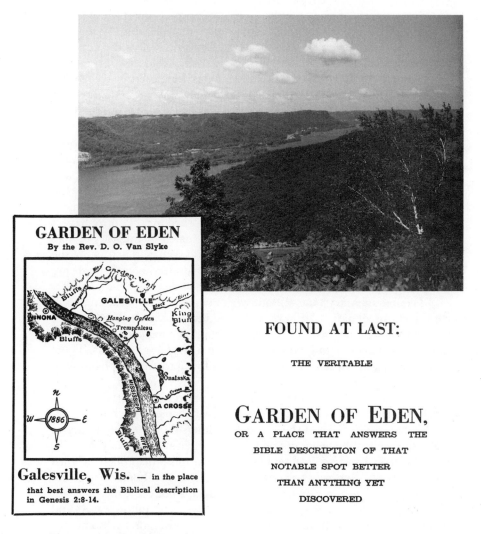

GARDEN OF EDEN
By the Rev. D. O. Van Slyke

Galesville, Wis. — in the place that best answers the Biblical description in Genesis 2:8-14.

FOUND AT LAST:

THE VERITABLE

GARDEN OF EDEN,

OR A PLACE THAT ANSWERS THE
BIBLE DESCRIPTION OF THAT
NOTABLE SPOT BETTER
THAN ANYTHING YET
DISCOVERED

The banks of the Mississippi River in Trempealeau County, Wisconsin, the site of the Garden of Eden according to the Rev. D. O. Van Slyke, nineteenth-century Methodist preacher.

byterian Church around the corner, the Mill Road Cafe (a local watering hole), and even the Galesville Bank. Everyone knew a little, but no one very much about the curious Mr. Van Slyke. I learned that the bank distributes copies of his pamphlet, as a way of promoting the town. The drug store sells fifteen-cent post cards stamped "Galesville, Wisconsin: Garden of Eden." And the Gale Packing Company prints the same epithet on every box of vegetables it ships across the Midwest. Strangely, here was a myth that no one really understood, but nearly everyone still remembered. The public identity of the town somehow remained tied to the dream of an erratic visionary who was never seen as more than a fool in his own lifetime.

By late afternoon, however, the patience of my wife and children was wearing thin and they were anxious to get on with our vacation. I left them at the town laundromat, with a promise to return quickly, and hurried to track down one last source. What had begun as a brief stop in a small Wisconsin town had become a detective adventure with more at stake than I knew. I was hooked—as if absorbed in a Dorothy Sayers mystery rich in geographical detail. I was fascinated by the story of Van Slyke and intrigued also by my own fascination. What archetypes of the American experience were being revealed that afternoon through my participation in a nineteenth-century vision of Eden?

I contacted Mary Jane Hilton, whose name had been coming up in conversations all day. Within twenty minutes I was at her farm and we were poring together over old newspaper clippings and county histories. She was delighted to find someone as drawn to the tale as she was. There on the paper-strewn table in Mrs. Hilton's living room, the phantom of D. O. Van Slyke began to assume flesh.

He was born in 1819 and called to the ministry at the age of twenty-seven. He left New York state shortly thereafter to explore more promising spheres of service in the West. But things didn't go any better in Galesville, where he never got on with the other members of the Methodist Episcopal society. He said he had tried more than once "to turn the rascals out," but had been outnumbered by the stubborn devils who never gave him a minute's rest. One summer a notice in the *Galesville Transcript* offered a reward for the return of sheets, pillow cases, and underclothing stolen from Mrs. Van Slyke's clothesline by "some evil disposed person or persons." The local ruffians apparently had no mercy on the eccentric clergyman. After several frustrating years, he heeded Lincoln's call for volunteers in the spring of 1862. He served as chaplain of Company C, 30th Wisconsin Infantry, but the hate, stupidity, and carnage he witnessed in the war made him further disillusioned. Moreover, in June 1863, while a bloody siege occupied Vicksburg and troops from both sides were converging on the small town of Gettysburg, Pennsylvania, his six-year-old son was found floating face down in a pond back home. By all appearances, chaos reigned in the world of D. O. Van Slyke. When he returned from the Civil War it was with a bellyful of anguish. He seemed irretrievably thrown off center. Viewed locally as a crackpot, even senile, he was asked finally to return his license as deacon and elder of the church.

He took to reading his Bible alone and walking along the bluffs overlooking the river. The solace he failed to find in people he hoped to find in the land. Then one day in 1886 a pattern presented itself to him, suggesting a sense of "placed" meaning he had never before known. Galesville took on new meaning. This stubborn, unresponsive place now appeared, in God's strange choosing, to have been all along "the first habitation of man." On the American continent, here "in the heart of the New World," was the geography sketched in Genesis. Wasn't this region known for its dry, balmy weather and well-watered fields? Hadn't Wisconsin cheese and Arcadia creamery butter taken first place at the recent World's Exposition in Philadelphia? Hadn't the Indians spoken of the land as once notorious for rattlesnakes and plentiful with fruit trees? Who could study its configuration of rivers, its central placement on the 90th meridian, without recognizing the features of paradise? Van Slyke unexpectedly found himself at the center of the world. One who had been denied so long a meaningful place to dwell was granted the vision of a place where all meaning had once cohered.[3]

Trapped in the cramped, attentuated experience of paradise lost, searching for the path back to Eden along the worn walkways of his own narrow world, what was sought suddenly became apparent. The story is characteristically American. The American urge to discover origins deeper than Europe's history—the impulse to plot the center of the world in the backwaters of the American landscape—is replicated in innumerable towns of unrenown, from Galesville to Watervliet to Ipswich. Each of them exert their own bold claim to universality. If one takes Highway 83 north from Laredo toward Abilene, through the desert of southwest Texas, one passes near three county seats with very little to commend themselves to the world's attention. Yet Crystal City prides itself as "The Spinach Capital of the World," Uvalde is known locally as "The Honey Capital of the World," and Rocksprings claims the typonym of "The Angora Goat Capital of the World."[4] It is a pattern not at all infrequent. In college I remember hitchhiking through Castroville, California, then a tiny spot on the map north of Monterey. Waiting by a huge field of olive-green plants, I leaned a soggy sleeping bag against the post of a scrolled-iron sign stretched over the road outside of town. The sign read "Castroville, California: Artichoke Capital of the World." I could have been standing beside the omphalos at Delphi, the wry claim to centripetence was no less pronounced.

The place of apparent inconsequence becomes invariably, in mythic insight (and, later, in marketing design), the navel of the earth. The appeal to cosmic significance is always tenuous, given to ambiguity, subject to dispute. But it persists nonetheless. The neon boomtown of Grants, New Mexico bills itself optimistically as "The Uranium Capital of the World," even as radioactive dust from nearby mine tailings slowly threatens the environment. The people of Ridgeway, Illinois continue to think of their town as "The Popcorn Capital of the World," despite the title having been transferred to a larger producer of popcorn elsewhere. What is this passion for world-centeredness that reappears across the American land? Storefront Chambers of Commerce thrive on plastic claims of universal notoriety. Yet there is more here than mere business hype alone. It also reveals a deeper quest for dwelling at the center. It is the human longing for a *locus mirabilis*, a place of extraordinary import found amid all that is common and profane. D. O. Van Slyke is thus culturally typical in his slant particularity. Eden beckons beyond the corner gas station on all the blue highways of America.

What drew me to Van Slyke and his vision? His stubborn independence, his role as dreamer and village fool, his Kierkegaardian sense of always being misunderstood, his ability to see what others never saw. Yet throughout the day in Galesville, even I wavered between fascination with his vision (*wanting* to believe along with him) and the need simply to accept what was there without trying to see beyond it. I was torn between Van Slyke's obsession and the needs of my family; between the appeal of Eden and the need to find a place to stay that night; between the vision of paradise and the reality of the parking ticket I found on my car at the end of the day. It seemed, indeed, that I had stood forever at that particular point of decision.

Our last stop on the way out of Galesville was the town cemetery, a cluster of white stones leading up a hill to the cliff overlooking the town. The children climbed with me, and near the crest we found his stone—a rough-hewn granite obelisk, flattened on top. Van Slyke had cut it himself with hammer and chisel and hauled it to the cemetery in a wagon shortly before he died in 1890. Jutting six feet out of the hill, it stands awry at a seventy-degree angle, a fitting memorial to a man whose vision had also been oblique. Taking in the view from his stone, I searched the frame houses and brick buildings below, and I tried one last time to discern the lineaments of Eden. But to my great poverty, I saw nothing particularly profound—only the charmed Wisconsin land-scape.

I did, before leaving, think to stand the children in front of the stone and bless them in the name of the place and in the memory of this grand eccentric. They smiled, of course, indulging their whimsical fa-ther. But before we walked down to the car, they took a second look from the brow of the hill themselves. Who, at last, can resist the pros-pect of paradise? We wistfully seek an arcane cosmos through every leaf and branch, longing for the ordinary to be revealed as holy.

6

The Correspondence of
Spiritual and Material Worlds
in Shaker Spirituality

"Thingness is a scandal to the conceptualist," said Marshall McLuhan. Yet religion dies when the former is made to yield to the latter.[1]

One Sunday afternoon in June 1856, Hannah Cohoon received a vision at the Shaker Community where she lived in Hancock, Massachusetts. Drifting over the Berkshire hills, it was a simple, but vivid scene of a recently-deceased sister bringing to her a gift of beautiful apples in a small basket. She would later make an inspirational drawing of the gift in watercolor and ink, remembering this vision of heavenly apples in the most palpable detail.

> I noticed in particular as she brought them to me the ends of
> the stems looked fresh as though they were just picked by the
> stems and set into the basket one by one.[2]

Curiously, what was central to her vision was not the psychic phenomenon of spectral apparition, but the careful observation of freshly-picked apple stems. It was this sensitivity to particulars that would generally characterize the Shaker perception of the holy. Theirs was a spirituality in which the supernatural would be given very earthy specificity. "Don't carelessly pass over small things," they warned each other.[3] To know God is to be attentive to the presence of heaven in every leafstalk and sprig.

These were a people who regularly communed with spirits while at the same time they bent wet strips of maple to make oval boxes with expert care. They lived in two worlds with equal vigor. They practiced a macro and micro spirituality brought into mesh by their conviction that the millennium had already arrived. These were believers who walked in a foreign land while trying to realize the New Jerusalem in their midst, reconstructing it in every detail. Shaker theology, therefore, would always be concerned to join visionary place to material place, the heavenly sphere to the most tangible, earthy realm, the world of angels to the world of well-turned table legs. In Shaker thought, visionary and craftsman were always one—the two worlds joined in correspondence.

The Shaker experience has been the longest lived and perhaps most imaginative of all the American experiments in communitarian living. Tracing their roots to Georgian England in the years before the American Revolution, they began as a group of "Shaking Quakers," living in the shadow of poverty cast by Manchester's textile mills. Their keen expectation of the second coming of Christ was spurred on by Ann Lee's profound experience of that reality in 1770. She became their spiritual leader and accompanied eight others to the American colonies some four years later. Eventually settling near Albany, New York, they thrived in the first half of the nineteenth century—teaching a gospel of Christlike simplicity, celibate community life, and a notion of worship that embraced ecstatic dancing as well as the work of one's hands.[4] By the eve of the Civil War their numbers had risen to a height of nearly 6,000 members, spread across nineteen communities from Maine to western Kentucky. The decline of frontier revivalism and rise of an urban, industrial economy would eventually reduce the viability of Shaker communities. After two centuries of communal life in America, only a handful of sisters in two New England communities would remain, with the Book of the Covenant closed to any further membership. The Shakers are now remembered most for their simple and finely-wrought furniture, their closeness to the land, and their call for a spiritual life which, like their dancing, was as carefully patterned as it was joyous.[5]

The Shaker Principle of Correspondence and the Overlapping of Worlds

The most compelling question about Shaker spirituality is how they were able to hold together so well the disparate concerns of two separate worlds. Curtis Cramer, a brother at the North Union Shaker community near Cleveland, Ohio, could write in his diary about thinking of heavenly things as he sharpened knives and began scalding kettles to use in the butchering of hogs. "How many bright angels attended our meeting last night!" he mused, while giving himself wholly to the ordinary tasks of trimming and drysalting meat.[6] Somehow he found no contradiction between living in a supersensual world, peopled with spirits, and attending with loving care to the smallest of earthy details. Mother Ann, after all, had enjoined her followers to "Do your work as if it would last a thousand years and as if you would die tomorrow."[7] In such a way, both worlds could be taken at the same time with utmost seriousness. This was because an overlapping of the two spheres had already occurred in the Shaker spiritual imagination. They tried to duplicate in their studied attention to detail a quality of life already glimpsed through a higher, spiritual perception. In every common task they sought to reify their vision. It was as if they carried within them a map of the New Jerusalem, a model of how things ought to be, and then proceeded to realize on earth the specificity of that heavenly realm. In some cases, they even perceived the layout of Shaker villages as conforming to a heavenly design situated directly above the terrestrial landscape.[8] The most mundane experience, therefore, could be seen to correspond to a celestial archetype.

This conception of the world of visible, tangible things as being in some way a counterpart of a larger spiritual pattern has deep roots in the history of western and eastern spirituality. In ancient Egypt and Babylon the topography of earth was seen to echo a superterrestrial reality. The Nile, or Tigris and Euphrates Rivers, were understood to be modeled after heavenly rivers. Huge cities had their starry prototypes. In Chinese mythology, the entire landscape was an emblem of the heavenly sphere.[9] As a result, in such a society one would experience a complete absence of tension between sacred and profane. Living in a symbolic universe, all meaning would cohere in the immediacy of corresponding worlds. As the Shakers understood it, "Heaven and earth are threads of one loom."[10]

What this meant in the praxis of Shaker life was that all spatial relationships and ordinary experiences would become sacramental, pointing beyond themselves to a larger and more powerful reality. The geographical configuration of Shaker villages, with their various families, outbuildings, and central meetinghouse, would symbolize an order introduced from beyond. Angles, shapes, and colors all served to indicate the pattern of an apocalyptic vision. One cultural geographer has observed:

> In imitation of the Holy City of Jerusalem, which according to the Scriptures was 'laid foursquare,' the layout of [Shaker] village, garden, and field followed a rectangular pattern. The idea of orthogonalism was carried to extreme: the Believers were to extend the right hand first, to lead with the right foot, kneel on the right knee. One was not to reach diagonally across the table.[11]

Every action and structure served as an allusion to the archetypal reality now present in their midst. The meetinghouse, where the faithful met for worship and dance, was always painted white, with interior trim of a "heavenly blue." When possible, the building was also covered with a gambrel roof, its sloping edges suggesting the dome of heaven itself.[12] No detail would be neglected in this concern to recognize the figurative world as a sign and shadow of a yet grander sphere.[13]

Many strains of thought converged in the early nineteenth century to support this Shaker theory of spiritual correspondence. Mother Ann Lee had been a member of a small society of Quakers in England who were influenced by the Camisards, or French Prophets. These had fled Catholic persecution in France, having survived for years as an ecstatic sect in the Cevennes mountains. There they related the symbolic imagery of the Apocalypse to current events and received their own clarifying visions of an age to come.[14] But the application of this otherworldly similitude to concrete social structures would not occur until the Shaker heirs of this tradition had made their way into the Hudson River Valley of New York. There they were influenced still further by Puritan, Transcendentalist, and even Swedenborgian ideas of spiritual correspondence. In all of these currents of thought, the reciprocal overlapping of spiritual and natural worlds would be emphasized.

Puritan theology, for example, with its emphasis on the New England commonwealth as a fulfillment of Old Testament typology, had always looked upon ordinary phenomena as emblematic or representative of divine, archetypal events. The pictorial emblems of John Bunyan and Francis Quarles had given the Puritan imagination the expectation of discerning images and shadows of the holy in their everyday experience.[15] The Transcendentalists would develop this notion even further, as Emerson and his colleagues understood "each piece of the world capable of being fitted to a multiplicity of spheres."[16] The Transcendentalist contemplation of nature led inevitably to an awareness of universal being, even as Plotinus had found within himself images that corresponded to distant constellations. The Harvard Shaker community was a scant fourteen miles from Emerson at Concord and Bronson Alcott's Fruitlands experiment was situated only two miles to the west. The Shakers in Massachusetts could not help but be influenced by the Transcendentalist presence.

Even the notions of correspondence held by Emmanuel Swedenborg (1688–1772) would enter into Shaker theology by way of Frederick Evans, a leading Shaker spokesman in the mid-nineteenth century. Swedenborg, like Ann Lee, had emphasized the divine inspiration of human instruments through the reality of the second coming and had seen himself to be continually moving between the two worlds of natural and spiritual experience. Evans even made the claim that Ann Lee had viewed Swedenborg as her own "John the Baptist." The Shaker similarity to the Swedish thinker's ideas can be seen in one of the believer's descriptions of how heaven and earth intersect. She wrote:

> The light which is established in the heavens or invisible world, is closely connected with the light which is established on earth; and they who walk in the light which is manifest on earth, are compassed about by those who walk in the same light, although in the invisible world.[17]

Resulting from all these converging currents of thought, therefore, would be the clear Shaker conviction that life in this world was a vast and comprehensive antetype—a copy or mask—of yet another world, to which one sought to conform his or her experience in every detail.

The Concreteness of
Shaker Visionary Experience

Having examined briefly this Shaker conception of correspondence and some of its sources in the history of ideas, a better understanding can now be gained of Shaker visionary experience and craftsmanship alike. What intrigues the observer of this unique group is the extent to which its mystical encounter of the holy is pervaded by earthy detail and its meticulous artistry, in shop and field, given to the service of the sacred. The Shaker phenomenon plainly contradicts those who would contrast ethereal fantasy and sober-minded workmanship as opposite poles of the spiritual experience. Indeed, it may often be the visionary who reaches for the most specific image with which to concretize his or her vision. C. S. Lewis and J. R. R. Tolkien have each spoken of that deep human need to explore a "secondary universe" in search of the beauty or concord which is not supplied in the actual world. Yet the visitor to such sidereal spheres invariably comes back to a universe of ordinary wardrobes, London attics, and common village life, where what has been experienced is now made operable in new and specific forms.[18] Hence Joseph Smith in the 1820's moved directly from his celestial encounter with the angel Moroni to town planning and the mapping of Zion.[19] This attention to hard-minded and sensible detail in the description of mystical experience is particularly manifest in Shaker visionary narratives.

While the Shakers, especially in the early period, were persecuted

The Shakers were not the only religious community to emphasize the principle of geographic correspondence in the nineteenth century. This drawing of the Salt Lake Valley in Utah shows how the Mormons understood their own place of settlement to be a "spiritual double" of the Holy Land in Palestine. Published in William E. Smythe, *The Conquest of Arid America*, 1900. Reprinted by the University of Washington Press, 1969. Used by permission of the Denver and Rio Grande Western Railroad Company.

as wild-eyed fanatics, given to hallucination and frenzied worship, their accounts of actual visions were extraordinarily this-worldly in focus. Mother Ann Lee, for example, spent one morning at Watervliet (near Albany) softly speaking in tongues as she sat in a chair, seemingly withdrawn entirely from her surroundings. On waking, however, she gave an account of a spectral world highly material and concrete. "I felt myself," she said, "walking with Christ in groves and valleys as really as if he had been here on earth."[20] Mother Ann's visions had almost always been specific in this way. She spoke even of having seen America and its people in mystical insights received while still in England. The Square House at Harvard, Massachusetts, into which the Shakers would later move, had appeared to her in dreams on several occasions.[21] Shaker visions were invariably of the most palpable sort—simple, emblematic gifts received from Christ, the angels, or deceased members of the community.

During the period of revival known as "Mother Ann's Work," filling the decade between 1837 and 1847, such visionary experiences became more prominent than ever.[22] Usually the gifts received were pictorial images of fruit trees, flowers, or doves, shared verbally with others, or sometimes mimed and less often reproduced in drawings. Predictably they were unremarkable icons, drawn from rustic, ordinary life. One sister received from Mother Ann, "a pail [sic] blue silk handkerchief with white fringe, & a little song book." Still another wrote by inspiration a naively-simple poem, plainly decorated with unpretentious trees and flowers.

> In various forms, and colours too,
> I now have sent my love to you,
> Knowing it will your spirits cheer,
> For it is from your Mother dear. . . .
>
> This pretty gift I send to you,
> That you at times may sit & view,
> This emblem of a higher sphere,
> And bring your feeling to it near.[23]

This unaffected simplicity is the chief mark of Shaker spirituality. It borders on the trivial, yet profoundly suggests that the kingdom of God is a reality "hidden from the wise and understanding and revealed unto babes" (Mt 11:25).

Two Shaker narratives can serve to indicate further the simple earthiness that characterized Shaker mystical perception. Nathan Williams was a brother at the New Lebanon community in New York who found himself far from his Shaker family one spring in the 1840's. Work had taken him to Washington Mountain, where he was felling trees and drawing mill logs, but also longing for home. One day he dreamed that he had returned to "the Pleasant City," though it was not quite the same as he had remembered it. A spirit guide explained that he had actually come in his vision to the New Jerusalem, a "city set upon a hill," not unlike his own village north of the Catskills near the banks of the Hudson. There were buildings on either side of the street, all white as snow, flanked by rows of large maple trees, similar to those in New Lebanon itself. He met Father Eleazar, a departed saint, sitting on the front porch of his house. "I told him I was glad to see him," said Williams, and added—as if lazily twisting a piece of saw grass between his fingers, "You've got the pleasantest place that I ever saw."[24] Father Eleazer took him around back to show him his vegetable garden, ripe with herbs in early spring, and even picked a few "little cucumbers" for him to take back to Sister Eliza. This is a fascinating narrative, revealing typical references to allegorical gardens and the Holy City, while at the same time pervading the air of heaven with a homely presence drawn straight out of Columbia County back home.[25] Nathan Williams' spiritual encounter was as soil-centered as it was sublime.

A second Shaker narrative shows a similar playfulness and homely ease in describing the presence of the holy. Abijah Worster had been one of the original members of the Harvard, Massachusetts community when he died at the age of ninety-six in 1841. He was one of the last to have known Mother Ann personally. His funeral, therefore, was one of great ceremony, attended—it was said—by many of his old friends gathered from the spirit world. Those who witnessed this vision spoke of the Eternal Father, the Eternal Mother, Christ, and Mother Ann all serving as pall bearers for the occasion.[26] People stepped back to make room for the heavenly guests; and when the grave had been covered with earth, they all were led by Christ and Mother Ann in a lively dance, rejoicing at the homecoming of their brother.

> At the close of the dance the Godhead crossed hands forming a seat for Father Abijah, and giving a glad shout spread their wings and ascended, followed by the heavenly host to Mother's mansion, where a banquet was in waiting to welcome the last of the first Fathers in Harvard to his final home.[27]

This image of the members of deity joining in a child's "fireman's carry" so as to bear home one of their own evokes warmly-remembered scenes of summer picnics and barn raisings—a vision of heaven rooted in careful attention to the playful and mundane. It summarizes yet again the richly concrete character of Shaker visionary experience.

The Reification of the Holy in Shaker Craftsmanship

"It is an essential characteristic of being human that we feel the urge to reify experience," writes geographer Yi-Fu Tuan.[28] Human beings seek tangible expression for the most valued gifts of their imagination. This is particularly the case in a communitarian society like the Shakers', who lived with the conviction that the long-awaited millennium had come, that distinctions between this world and the next had already begun to collapse. They sought to make real, in their workshops and fields, the substance of that new epoch which now had dawned. Much has been written on Shaker craftsmanship and the philosophy of work which underlay it, but these themes acquire new significance in light of their intimate relationship to a corresponding spiritual world, glimpsed through visionary experience and modeled after the work of one's hands. Thomas Merton grasped this when he remarked that "the peculiar grace of a Shaker chair is due to the fact that it was made by someone capable of believing that an angel might come and sit on it."[29] Merton insisted that William Blake, the English poet, artist, and visionary, offered the best angle of perception for understanding Shaker creativity. He, too, had received visions of the New Jerusalem and longed, through his drawings and poetry, to portray "the real and eternal world of which this vegetable universe is but a faint shadow."[30] Blake urged that being a Christian demanded one's also being a poet, painter, musician, or architect. It meant reifying one's experience of the holy in concrete form.

Shakers thus looked upon the material thing, fashioned by assiduous manual labor, as serving a dual purpose. By fulfilling most simply and perfectly its function in this world—whether it be a straight-backed chair, a patterned quilt, or a well-pruned fruit tree, it also became emblematic of the simplicity and perfection of that world to which this one dimly corresponds. Things could, in themselves, carry one more deeply into the multi-dimensional reality made present by the second coming of Christ. This emphasis on "bethinged existence" and the power of artifacts to enhance life's meaning would be still further developed in the twentieth-century thought of existentialist philosopher Martin Heidegger. The material thing, he said, is what can draw all of experience together in a sense of gathered presence. "Thing is an opener of world."[31]

Its "thingness" does not consist merely in its objectivity, its distance from the individual as subject. The power of a thing lies in its ability to assemble reality in an interplay of earth and sky, ordinary and noumenal experience. Heidegger describes, for example, the association of meanings found in an old pair of peasant work shoes.

> Out of the dark opening of the worn-out interior of the shoes stares the toil of work-paces. In the firm [massive] heaviness of the shoes, the tenacity of [plodding step] is stored—the [plodding step] over the far-spread and uniformly matched furrows of the field, over which the harsh wind halts. On the leather lies the dampness and the saturation of soil. From under the soles slips the loneliness of the country-road in the fading evenings. In the shoes reigns the suppressed call of earth, its silent giving away of ripening grain and its unexplained refusal in the barren fallows of wintry fields. All through this implement the uncomplaining anxiety for the security of bread, the wordless joy of an overcome distress, the shiver at the arrival of a birth and the shudder at the threat of death are drawn. To earth belongs this implement and in the world of a peasant is it preserved.[32]

To this poignant description of the shoe's gathered presence, the Shaker would only have added the truth also embraced by the one originally making the shoe. The loving attention to the tanning of leather and double-sewing of soles, the simple cut of the shoes, lending them a perfection grounded in function—these things would have enhanced still further the thing's power as opener of world. The Shaker would argue that manufactured things ought ever to evince the pattern of eternity, a pattern marked by simplicity, by meticulous care, by a sense of what is inherently fitting.

The Shaker believers stood within that time-honored tradition of St. Benedict of Nursia, who had understood work as but another form of prayer. Both worship and labor involved a sharing in the celebrative and creative act of God's own freedom. *Laborare* and *orare* were mimetic devices used to bring to this world an order drawn from yet another. A Shaker writer in the late nineteenth century said:

> There is as much worship in good workmanship done in the right spirit, as in any other act; the spirit of the thing done and not the act itself is the key to tell whether anything done be worship or not, but God, the master workman, who has made

the minutest insect with as much care as the mammoth ele-
phant, sets us the example of good works. Imitation is the sin-
cerest praise.[33]

Shaker handiwork was clearly a matter of imitating God's own highest
plan for each particular implement. "The thing made had to be precisely
what it was supposed to be," observed Thomas Merton. "It had, so to
speak, to fulfill its own vocation. The Shaker cabinet maker enabled
wood to respond to the 'call' to become a chest, a table, a chair, a desk."[34]
The pattern of the millennium was thus put into Shaker furniture at its
making and could later be read back out by those sensitive to the fullness
of its meaning.

The famous Shaker chairs, like those produced by the Mt. Lebanon
community throughout the nineteenth century, could be seen in themselves to summarize Shaker values and expectations. Material culture
scholar Jules David Prown has discerned how readily a cluster of meanings could be read from a single given chair.

> Chairs are particularly revealing of cultural values because
> they so easily become human surrogates. We use such human
> analogues as feet, legs, back and seat in our descriptive ter-
> minology for chairs. It is not unreasonable to speculate that
> aspects of an object that seem to echo the human anatomy may
> reflect in abstract terms the way in which individuals in a so-
> ciety perceive themselves.[35]

Moreover, in light of the Shaker theory of spiritual correspondence, a
chair can even more profoundly reflect a particular perspective of
heaven. Built to last a thousand years, made light so as to be hung from
wall pegs when not in use, carved from sturdy hardwoods whose only
ornament was the beauty of their own natural grain—Shaker chairs offered a catechism in wood for those who would study the dreams that
prompted their making.

If the crafted piece thus became a primary means by which Shaker
values were mimetically expressed, then one also understands more
readily the emphasis of the Believers on anonymity in workmanship.
The Millennial Laws, drawn up by the Shakers between 1820 and 1845,
did not allow any craftsman "to write or print his name on any article
of manufacture, that others may hereafter know the work of his
hands."[36] One did his or her finest work, not to be flattered by compli-
ments that appeal to personal vanity, but solely to express the spiritual
life as that could be read from the simplicity and deftness of the thing

made. The Shakers knew that unselfconsciousness in art was generally a precondition of its quality. As Alan Gowans points out, "The more consciously and deliberately you set out to 'create a work of art,' the more unlikely you are to produce much of lasting significance."[37] Shaker artisans focused, therefore, on the essential thing itself—its possibilities and needs—instead of on the creative exercise of their own egoistic designs. The concern of a Shaker gardener, for example, would be to ask how he could more effectively attend to the needs of a plant he was encouraging to grow.

> A tree has its wants and wishes, and a man should study them as a teacher watches a child, to see what he can do. If you love the plant, and take heed of what it likes, you will be well repaid by it. I don't know if a tree ever comes to know you; and I think it may; but I am sure it feels when you care for it and tend it; as a child does, as a woman does.[38]

What becomes apparent here is that, in Shaker thought, "means" can often assume far more importance than "ends." Emphasizing the immediate thing and its needs is recognized finally as the only route to achieving larger and more ethereal ends. Hence, the identity of the Shaker horticulturist or stonecutter, blacksmith or weaver, was inevitably secondary to the product he or she produced. It is true that individual Shaker artisans would be remembered by name. Brother Theodore Bates of Watervliet was the inventor of the flat broom. Sister Tabitha Babbitt of Harvard created the first circular saw. Yet the reason for attaching their names to their gifts was not to celebrate their individual artistic genius, but rather to recall that it is through specific instruments of God's own choosing that millennial gifts are shared.

In short, the Shakers invariably sought access to the holy through the particular and sensorial. As they understood it, this is what the advent of the millennium had already achieved. They also knew, with Nietzsche, that "the more abstract the truth is that you would teach, the more you have to seduce the senses to it."[39] It is this which gives to Shaker spirituality its winsome earthiness. They could even discover the whole of the Christian life to be summarized in the mundane act of baking a cake. In a recipe for Mother Ann's Birthday Cake, usually prepared around February 29, the anniversary of the foundress' birth, the preparer of the cake was advised to

> cut a handful of peach twigs, which are filled with sap at this season of the year. Clip the ends and bruise them and beat [the]

cake batter with them. This will impart a delicate peach flavor to the cake.[40]

Suggested here is not only a keen sensitivity to subtle shadings of taste and an awareness of sap already flowing at this time through late-winter twigs, but also the firm confidence that even the smallest task of baking a cake should be done with the most loving care and attention to detail.

"A Man can Show his religion as much in measureing onions as he can in singing Glory Halalua," wrote one believer in his diary.[41] The fulfillment of one's vocation in attending even to the most menial tasks and inconsequential things was ultimately, to the Shakers, an exercise in worship. This was because every concrete thing could be seen to disclose the pattern of the heavenly sphere. The smallest action, the least green onion, took part in a vast mimesis of paradise. June Sprigg indicates the extent to which this could be carried in Shaker life.

> The Shakers saw their homes as the nearest thing to heaven here on earth, which meant primarily that their conduct was to imitate heavenly perfection as nearly as possible. But it also often meant that the actual physical environment of the Shaker village was shaped to some heavenly ideal: lines were perfectly straight, not crooked; angles were exactly right; deceitful workmanship was forbidden; and all was kept pure, clean, and orderly.[42]

One Shaker carpenter spoke metaphorically when he described the loss of his tape measure as an insurmountable hindrance to his task of perfectly fitting lids to wooden boxes. "I can go no further in my work without it, for positive exactness is required not only in inches, but in the sixteenths and thirty-seconds of an inch."[43] He knew this was true in woodcraft because it had first been recognized as true in theology.

Shaker Rituals of Travel and the Sanctification of Place

The Shaker spiritual world was one filled with green-sloped mountains and verdant valleys spread with fields of corn—roasting ears ready for the picking. Its nearby woods could be combed for lobelia, pennyroyal, and other wild herbs. It was as variegated and diversified as the familiar hills of upstate New York. Visionary insight opened onto such a world. Conversely, the earthly peaks and hollows of New England and New York served often as a metaphorical landscape, hinting of spiritual

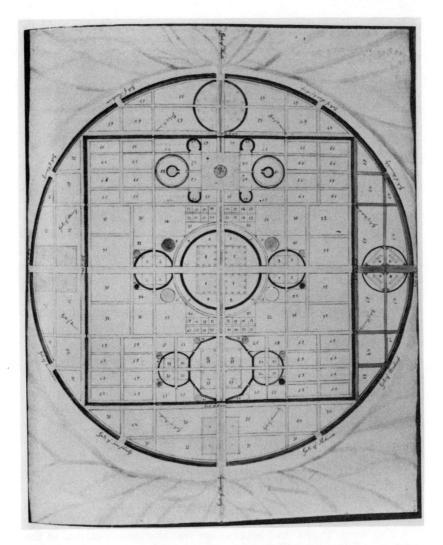

A Shaker inspirational drawing by a brother in the Mt. Lebanon, New York community, dated March 16–21, 1843, entitled "Explanation of the Holy City with Its Various Parts and Appendixes Pointed Out." This is a map of the twelve-square-mile section of the spiritual terrain encompassing Mt. Lebanon and Hancock Shaker villages. The square and circular patterns seen in this heavenly sphere were duplicated architecturally in the barns, gardens, and dwelling houses of its earthly antetype. Reproduced in the Philadelphia Museum Bulletin LVII:273 (Spring 1962), p. 95. Used by permission.

realities just beyond them. One of the most common Shaker symbols for true humility, for example, was the image of coming down into the valley from the heights.

> The mountain top of prideful self-exaltation is barren and windswept; the valley to which we descend when we see ourselves rightly is blessed with well-worked soil to bring forth fruit in abundance. It is the farmer's image of bottom land, rich and fertile.[44]

In Shaker imagination, these two worlds of meaning would never be far apart. It is where they finally touch that the observer understands most clearly the nature of the Shaker religious experience. The point at which the intersection of corresponding worlds was regularly rehearsed in Shaker ritual activity, particularly during the period known as "Mother Ann's work," may offer the last and most fruitful area for examining these two poles of Shaker spirituality.

Ritual is the life force of any vital and continuing community. If *myth* is what "stories" world with sacred events and meanings, it is *ritual* which draws individuals into a contemporary and dynamic relationship with what has been declared most holy.[45] Those ritual behaviors which powerfully absorb a group, therefore, provide the greatest insight to the dominant metaphors that structure myth and generate dogmas within the religious community. In Shaker thought, it was the metaphor of "travel" which would serve as the organizing principle by which deepest meanings were structured. The most engaging rituals in Shaker life were those that gave expression to the spiritual notion of "traveling in the Gospel." This accords very well with the place-oriented character of Shaker spirituality already described. The Shakers "traveled"—symbolically moving from place to place—so as to realize the continuity that exists between the present world and the world of the Spirit now breaking through it.

The word "travel" in Shaker usage was also closely related to the idea of "travail." As Robley Whitson observes, "To travel in the Gospel, thus, embraced three levels of meaning: movement from one locus to another, arduous and sometimes painful labor, and the labor of childbirth."[46] To travel ritually, through the movements rehearsed in Shaker worship, meant to journey between two worlds—one that was dying and another that was struggling to be born. The Shakers identified readily with the Apostle Paul's insistence that "the whole creation has been groaning in travail together until now" (Rom 8:22). The spiritual life, as they saw it, was a matter of entering into the travel/travail of two intersecting worlds, moving deliberately from the one into the other. Three particular ritual activities would express most profoundly this experience encompassed by travel imagery. The fact that each of these rituals was at times closed to outside observers would indicate still further the sacral character ascribed to them by the Shaker community. Such travel rituals included the Shaker dances, the ceremonies attending the selection of a Holy Mount in the 1840's, and the sacral processions conducted within the Shaker villages during that same period. They each provide an engrossing perspective on how Shaker believers used categories of place and movement to orient themselves with respect to the holy.[47]

The Shaker meetinghouse was the topographical and symbolic center of the village, the most sacred place within the microcosm formed by the community's buildings and fields. The various dwelling houses situated around it were those of the North, South, or West Families, named according to their respective placement to the meetinghouse and its Center Family. At this axial point of Shaker worship the "travel-rites" of dancing gave symbolic expression to the idea that all the surrounding world was to be claimed for the glory of God. The dawn of the millennium had meant that all geographical realities had to be reconceived. It was remembered that Yahweh had promised ancient Israel, "Every place that the sole of your foot will tread upon I have given to you" (Jos 1:3). The Shakers, in their millennial fervor, saw themselves ritually to be fulfilling that promise as they tred with lively step over the whole of the meetinghouse floor, reaching toward all the cardinal directions and symbolically circling the whole of creation as they "labored" in dance. The space enclosed by the meetinghouse walls became the site on which a cosmic drama in miniature was reenacted—the travail of the Spirit finally concluded in a new creation, the declaration that the earth was now to be made new.

Roger Grainger has described well the mythic importance of the place where ritual such as this transpires.

> The "ritual ground," whether it be a clearing in the forest, a field on the other side of the river or any sort of sanctuary or church building, is distinguished from all other locations because of what happens there. This is the place set aside for dying in order to live, chosen to be a heaven and hell, the scene of a cosmic or supra-cosmic journey.[48]

On the Shaker meetinghouse floor, the cosmic journey traced in dance was one that symbolized the coming together of corresponding worlds. The "square order shuffle," for example, was a pattern received through visionary insight and carried out in coordination with the four points of the compass. It gave visual expression to the foursquare order of the New Jerusalem so recently revealed. Ring dances were later added as an echo of Ezekiel's vision of "a wheel within a wheel." This superimposed geometric form was a choreographic representation of a cosmic truth not yet fully realized. Still other "step song" marches were performed in double file, as the believers passed over neighboring fields and orchards, across highways, claiming for the Lord and Mother Ann the symbolic boundaries of the new land of Zion.[49] Patterned dance was thus a way of ritually circumscribing the perimeters of paradise.

In the early 1840's, during the outpouring of the Spirit associated with "Mother Ann's Work," revelations were received in many communities instructing the faithful to clear ground atop a nearby hill in preparations for still further blessings and gifts to be sent by God. A rectangular "feast ground" was to be laid out on the Holy Mount, with a central area fenced off and marked by a large Fountain Stone. This particular site—an omphalus-like point of connection between spiritual and material worlds—would be the fountain source from which the reality of the millennium could be received. It was to be surrounded by carefully-planted trees, with a tall pine sometimes rooted at its center. To this hallowed ground, the entire community would come each spring and fall, dancing around "the center of the earth" as it had been ritually set apart. The approach to the Holy Mount was frequently lined with rows of huge maple trees, the route eventually giving way to a narrow, labyrinthine path twisting to the summit. This semi-annual ascent to the holy hill would be remembered in Shaker diaries as a richly sacramental experience.

> It was a holy, a joyful day,—lifted above earth and earthly tasks and burdens; the long climb, its rocks and cliffs, its stumbling places and its dark, forest depths, all typical of the hard, burdened, shadowed path through earth life, up the spiritual steeps of redemption. . . . But at the top,—the long, glad day of spiritual feasting and joy![50]

On reaching the top of the sacred hill, the faithful would join in singing and dancing around the Fountain Stone, as spiritual or imaginary gifts were shared with all who had come. Spiritual clothing was put on and spectacles worn that enabled one more clearly to see spiritual things. Sometimes the spirits of Native Americans would attend the festivities, the sisters would pantomime the dipping of cleansing water from the holy fountain, and a box of spiritual guns from George Washington might even be passed out to the brethren. It was an occasion for ecstasy. Usually the day would end with a spiritual feast—the long, imaginary tables on the holy hill laden with bowls of celestial wine, sweet cakes of love, large clusters of grapes, and golden plums "picked from the Saviour's vine." The day was characterized by excess, yet—as always—the Shaker experience of the holy would be cast in the most vivid and earthy images.[51]

A third ritual expression of the Shaker effort to enter into the travel/travail of earth's millennial redemption is found in a series of walking or marching exercises begun in 1842. These involved a ritual journey around the circumference of the Shaker village, passing through its shops and dwelling houses, up and down the fields and meadows that formed the backdrop of ordinary Shaker life. It was a ritual activity as ancient as human experience. Parading the periphery of a space, so as to claim it in the name of cosmic powers for the use of a given community, reaches back beyond the circling of Jericho by the children of Israel. Paleolithic peoples had ritually set apart sacred locales with a ring of stones. Even timber wolves mark their terrain by stalking its borders and leaving their scent. Throughout much of Christian history, the tradition of annual Rogation Days has carried on the practice of processionally encompassing a plot of ground, claiming it for the blessing of God.[52] The Shakers in the 1840's would enter into this legacy by urging the exercise of rituals known as "The Midnight Cry" and "The Cleansing Gift."

In "The Midnight Cry," a group of twelve believers, carrying lamps in their right hands, would march through all the rooms of every building in the village, singing as they went and rousing others to join them. Like the faithful virgins ready to meet the bridegroom in the Gospel parable, they called on the world to recognize the sudden arrival of its Lord. Sometimes they pantomimed the sweeping of brooms as they walked and sang:

> Awake from your slumbers, for the Lord of Hosts is going
>   through the land,
> He will sweep he will clean his holy sanctuary.
> Search ye your Camps, yea read and understand
> For the Lord of Hosts holds the Lamps in his hand.[53]

In a similar way, "The Cleansing Gift" would be observed each fall, as a band of singing brothers marched in procession through every room of the workshops, barns, stables, and hogpens, while another band of sisters traversed every corner of the schoolrooms, dairies, and wash-houses. In the afternoon, the men would take out across the fields and pastures, as the women passed over the yards and gardens, symbolically cleansing and claiming the entire space for the Lord of Zion. Sometimes in spring they traveled the whole length and breadth of their fields, sowing invisible seeds of love and humility in the black and rock-ribbed earth. Every place that was tread by the soles of their feet seemed to blossom in the promise of God's new reign.[54]

■ ■ ■ ■ ■ ■ ■ ■ ■ ■ ■ ■ ■ ■ ■ ■

In summary, the reclamation of space would prove to be a central theme in Shaker spirituality. The already-realized second coming of Christ meant for them that the present world had been overlaid by another reality. Believers in this truth could discern the presence of that vivid, millennial kingdom in every earthy detail. The "thingness" of world and "felicity of space" thus assumed great importance in their apprehension of the holy. While the Shakers had consciously separated themselves from the mainstream of American culture, they sought nevertheless to possess once again the charmed places and things of this earth, cleansed and made new by the Spirit.[55] For the Shaker believer, working the grist mill at Canterbury, New Hampshire or stacking hay in the Round Barn at Hancock, Massachusetts, the world was both more and less than it seemed to be. Experiencing a correspondence of worlds, he or she would perceive reality with a double vision.

> Earthly, natural forms are to him as the shadows of the actual, spiritual facts. Fruit and flower, landscapes, works of art and literature, whatever brightens, gladdens or uplifts humanity are to him ten-fold more real when seen and felt through the sense of the interior, spiritual being. To him is the right to the life and glory of the spirit land, for, in a sense true of no other, is he the child of the Divine Father and Mother. This opening of the spiritual world into the earthly life of Believers was so actual and practical that it lifted the communistic toiler into the life of spirit spheres, and no longer was there a question of the possibility of angel communication. It was a natural, every day fact.[56]

Such a spirituality of stark and stunning simplicity, lived as "natural, every day fact" was what the followers of Mother Ann Lee had hoped most to realize in their lives. It was a gift as simple as a basket of freshly-picked apples—suggesting, from one point of view, the glorious advent of the millennium and, from another, simply nothing other than itself. In the vision of God, after all, the two points of view were unmistakably one. "For now we see through a glass, darkly; but then face to face" (1 Cor 13:12). The Shakers tried simply to reach through the glass, so as to behold the world from both sides in tandem vision. In doing so, they found it more than twice as grand than all they once had thought.

Mythic Landscapes: Liminal Places in the Evangelical Revival

Fundamentalism was imaginatively provocative for me, as a youth, so long as it remained aniconic, liminal, marginal to the world. But in recent years, much of Fundamentalism has taken on the marks of an iconic, comfortably-settled majority. Therein, for me, lies the loss of its magic.

I was ten years old the afternoon men came to the vacant lot across the street and began driving huge steel stakes into the ground. There on the dead grass where I'd chased kites and fielded grounders all my life, they had erected by evening a three-poled tent of milk-gray canvas. In the warm August weather, its side awnings were left rolled up, revealing neat rows of folding chairs and large wood shavings strewn over the ground.[1] The sudden emergence of this massive, if makeshift place—precisely where there had been no place the day before—enthralled us neighborhood children. Later that night we crossed the road to see the revival, my parents and I. And to a ten-year-old child without money, its excitement was as grand as a circus—perhaps even grander, with its laced edge of obscure mystery. I watched bare light bulbs hanging precariously from wires in the top of the tent as a woman played a small, portable organ and the evangelist traced with violin bow the high, wavering notes of "The Old Rugged Cross" on the flat edge of a hand-saw held between his knees. Brother and Sister Thomas, they were called, if I remember well. They sang duets, preached with an energy which seemed evoked by the tent itself, and gave an invitation that brought people sobbing out of their chairs and down to the front. I sat there mystified, caught up in a power I didn't understand but knew to be intensely real to these people. The melody of the hymns, the high and haunting sound of the saw, swept out of the tent and through the Florida night air, across our house, into the neighborhood beyond, and over the landscape of America. On that night, in that liminal place, I knew myself to have stood for a moment on the edge of some universal reality. It was my first, but not last, encounter with the spirituality of the evangelical revival.[2]

For years now I've been asking myself how to retrieve that experience of growing up on the margins of Southern evangelicalism. How do I discover the second naivete of which Paul Ricoeur speaks—the hard-won ability to reclaim the vitalities of myth on the far shore of critical suspicion? How can I be there again, without also denying all that I have since become? In asking these questions, I'm intrigued that the process of memory seems so often linked to a sense of place. Recalling the physical environment, the concrete details of a given placed experience, can be the most vivid way of reviving forgotten and intensely powerful images. St. Ignatius Loyola, in his *Spiritual Exercises*, for this reason emphasized the reconstruction of place and application of the five senses in one's reading of the Gospel stories. In such a way, as he well knew, the reading would become a remembering—the rich remembering of *anamnesis*, a remembering that creates, that invites simultaneity and the deepest participation.

As I remember, then, the places that form the context of my earliest encounters with God—places distinctive to the experience of the evangelical revival—I remember them as places charged with liminality. They were places that were, at the same time, *not* places—places caught in transition, existing only on the margins of a structured world. A tent used as a revival hall, a furnace room housing a Sunday School class, a storefront serving as church, a barracks as evangelistic center, a dance hall as place of worship—these were the sites that filled my childhood imagination with the power of a God upsetting all structure and questioning all places once thought secure. These were places bristling with ambiguity, each used for a purpose utterly different from their original design. As a result, their multivalent sense of place left the air that much more charged with possibilities for imagining alternative selves, for rethinking the structures of one's own being.

The concept of liminality, as used by anthropologists Arnold van Gennep and Victor Turner to describe the transitions involved in rites of passage, is rooted in the Latin word *limen*, meaning "threshold."[3] It describes the experience of movement involved in having left one place, one conventional state of being, and not yet having arrived at another. One is caught "betwixt and between"—no longer a child, for example, but not yet either an adult. Such threshold experiences force us to question old identities and entertain new ones, even as Janus, the Roman god of doorways, looked continually in two directions at once. The everyday awareness of liminality comes to us often in the context of travel. The hour or two spent on an airplane between stops can occasion considerable imaginative freedom, characterized as it is by a sense of passage and unstructured time. How many of us have adopted new personae on such occasions?—remarking to the person in the next seat that we worked as a teacher of Greek folk dancing and happened to live in a Benedictine monastery, when indeed we were nothing of the sort. We all have been irresistibly drawn to such creative playfulness. To view it as merely deceitful is to miss entirely the power involved in the imagination of vicarious selves. This juxtaposing of conflicting identities is very much also an exercise in faith. And nowhere is that exercise made more possible than in places of liminality. Hence, the dynamics of conversion—the abundant possibilities for significant personal change—may be intricately tied in the tradition of the evangelical revival to the magic of marginal places. We can explore more fully the implications of this by reference to three characteristics of liminal (placed, yet also unplaced) experience as found in Scripture and the history of American revivalism.

1. The first conviction of a biblically-informed spirituality of the revival is that God, as a God of aniconic freedom, can never comfortably be contained in any one place. Yahweh dwells in thick darkness (I Kgs 8:12), beyond the control and predictability of those who would anchor the holy in secure and accustomed structures. God is always essentially beyond knowing, beyond being placed. The sacred groves and high places of Baal are thus attacked because of their mechanical claims of guaranteeing the divine presence—of promising what can never be produced at will. Containing God in any given object or place is always subject to biblical ridicule (Is 44:9–20). Yet a tension is thrown into this theology by the very mystery of revelation itself. The God who can be located by no one is nonetheless made known by a free act of God's own self-placement. God chooses to be disclosed in proximity to Eden, the burning bush, Sinai, the tabernacle and temple. The God who surpasses all fixed contexts is at the same time revealed in the particularity of place. Hence, a biblical dialectic persists between placement and freedom, iconic and aniconic imagery, temple theology and the theology of a boundless God.[4] In the tradition of American revivalism, the latter term has always been the one most emphasized.

From the eighteenth century, when John Wesley began preaching in the fields at Bristol and George Whitefield, the Grand Itinerant, carried on his own ministry in cottages, barns, and marketplaces up and down the Atlantic coast, the revivalist tradition has celebrated the power of a God not limited by the confines of meeting house and parish. The impulse of the revival has invariably involved a spatial as well as social and theological departure from existing church structures. In the Great Awakening, the deviation from fixed ecclesiastical locations became the most celebrated and controversial mark of the New Light experience. Gilbert Tennent, in his sermon on *The Dangers of an Unconverted Ministry* (1740), urged hungry souls to cross over parish boundaries in order to receive the spiritual nourishment they might not find at home. Other enthusiastic preachers followed Whitefield's example by exhorting in the streets or in open fields, contradicting the established patterns that questioned such "Gospel rambles." Indeed, in 1741, the Old Light faction in Philadelphia denounced this "Wonderful Wandering Spirit," given as it was to ranging "here and there, and every where . . . hating bounds and limits." Throughout the decade, anti-itinerancy laws would be passed in local communities from Connecticut to the Carolinas.[5] The reorientation of space has ever been an offending characteristic of revivalist spirituality. The revival declares God too often to have been domesticated and house-broken in the process of being restricted to a limited geography of grace.

In my youth I felt keenly the appeal of this bold and itinerant spirit. The small Bible church of which I was a part met for a time in an abandoned storefront and even, for several months, in an old Army barracks, unoccupied since the Second World War. A great, liminal energy was generated by both places. Here I discovered a God who was too un-tamed, too unpredictable and demanding to be contained in the cultivated interior of a traditional sanctuary. The temporary, ersatz character of the sites themselves offered a sense of immediacy in worship that was appropriate to a God who "tabernacled" with his people. It was a former shoe store, in the shopping center next to the Public Market down the street, that served for a while as our place of worship. I remember the scrape of Samsonite chairs on the bare concrete floor and especially the large glass windows that occasioned both embarrassment and fascination. Just sitting there was a defiant proclamation to the world that God had supplanted all merchandise and usurped every claim to stubborn secularity. We sang songs with lusty voices and exulted in the incongruity of God's strange presence.[6]

But the barracks adjacent to the old airfield across the lake from our house offered even more vivid associations. Several frame buildings had been thrown up by the Army Air Corps in the 1940's and were scheduled to be demolished, but we were allowed to hold services there in the summer of 1954. Government-issue olive-green paint was peeling off the walls and ceilings in huge sheets. We children found spent rifle cartridges in the hall and dug .45 caliber bullets out of sand bags stacked nearby at an old pistol range. The place still harbored a forgotten urgency, a sense of danger and robust masculinity—things not lost on any of us, especially eleven-year-old boys feverishly pushing their way to manhood. More exciting even than this was a series of missionary meetings held in the barracks that summer. Tommy Titcomb, a veteran missionary from West Africa, spoke of living in the Congolese jungle, eating monkey meat, and obeying Christ to the ultimate extent. He told grisly tales of primitive tribes whose pagan rites made them file down the front teeth of their children. I was transfixed by the violence and daring alike, reading still more adventures in his weathered face and intense eyes. On Saturday night, at the close of the meetings, he invited forward those who felt called to foreign missionary service and I stepped out to embrace all the fierce hazards of abandonment. I was suddenly claimed by a God who reveled in exotic and unfixed places.

2. A second conviction of a revivalist spirituality is that the liminal experience of being in transit—of being caught between one place and another—forms a primary metaphor of the encounter with God. Significant character change—the "turning around" process of *metanoia*—often occurs in situations of displacement or transition. Here it is, on the marginal ground between places once held certain, that the Spirit of God often sets up camp. This is the place where "threshold beings" take form. It is a phenomenon apparent in many of the conversion accounts listed in Scripture, as well as in the history of American revivalism. Early Christians were not inappropriately characterized as people of the "Way," a people involved in passage and movement (Acts 9:2; 18:25). Paul's conversion experience occurred in transit—on the road between Jerusalem and Damascus, in a transitional state that allowed a rethinking of his antipathy to the people of the "Way." The experience brought with it a radical spatial disorientation, alleviated only three days later, after Paul had met Ananias and entered a new community of meaning (Acts 9:1–22). Similarly, the Ethiopian minister of finance mentioned in Acts 8 is overtaken by Philip while traveling south from Jerusalem by chariot. As they ride together, discussing the prophet Isaiah, a wadi is sighted from the road—its waters flowing down from the Judean hills—and the Ethiopian eunuch is drawn, by the serendipity of the passing moment, to request his own baptism (Acts 8:26–40). Frequently the suggestive context of being *en route* is the occasion by which spiritual transformation occurs. It's a pattern repeated again and again in the history of the American revival.

One can almost put it down as a principle that conversion in the American experience is predominantly a peripatetic affair.[7] People influenced by the revival are people caught in motion. Jonathan Edwards was profoundly moved by the grace of Christ while walking the countryside near Northampton, having dismounted from his horse in a wild and remote area. David Brainard encountered an "unspeakable glory" as he also walked in a "dark thick grove," along the Connecticut River

Valley. Peter Cartwright was walking in a horse-lot near a cave behind the family cabin in Logan County, Kentucky, when he, too, was struck by the divine presence. Charles Finney plotted his own conversion by means of a similar movement from the woods near his home to the road into town and on to the law office where he worked, all occurring on the day of October 10, 1821. The experience of transition appears to be rich in possibilities for personal, spiritual change. John Newton aboard ship in a violent sea, Sojourner Truth on her way back to her master's house, Billy Sunday waiting on a curb near a vacant lot—all these are occasions for dramatic conversion.[8] William James offers a classic example of this threshold experience in his reference to the religious conversion of Henry Alline in 1775. In remembering his experience, Alline paid most careful attention to where it occurred.

> As I was about sunset wandering in the fields lamenting my miserable lost and undone condition. . . . I returned to the house, and *when I got to the door, just as I was stepping off the threshold*, the following impressions [of God's presence] came into my mind like a powerful but small still voice.[9]

The spiritual experience of passage from one state of consciousness to another is often mirrored in the simultaneous passage from one particular place to another.

My own sense of appropriating a conscious and responsible faith in my childhood is indelibly associated with a furnace room behind the choir of the church where we finally settled. It was the location of Mr. Flinn's sixth grade Sunday School class, a place chosen with shrewd insight. None of us twelve-year-olds, of course, wanted to be considered part of the Sunday School, with its wing of pastel-painted rooms where the "children" pasted and cut. We were too old to be associated with children, though not yet old enough to be classed with teenagers. So our liminal status was given recognition by a liminal place. We had graduated from flannelgraph boards to furnace filters.[10] Furthermore, a new content came with the new terrain. On the first day, Mr. Flinn carried us straight into the regions of hell, describing with graphic detail the Lake of Fire as depicted in the Book of Revelation. Curiously, as I remember it now, my response was not primarily one of fear, but, instead, one of being let in on something really big. This wasn't your usual Sunday School pap about lambs and cardboard mangers. This was thoroughly adult, life-and-death stuff. Mr. Flinn was treating us like persons old enough to make decisions about God for themselves. For the first time, Sunday School was about something that genuinely mattered. I was impressed. In this transitional place, halfway between the sanctuary and the regular classrooms, I began to work out the lineaments of my own encounter with God.

3. A last conviction, anchored also in biblical faith, is that the revival experience—at its best—will always demand one's identifying with the marginal, unplaced peoples of this world. The liminal experience of the revival necessarily makes one sensitive to dispossessed and uprooted peoples everywhere. Victor Turner uses the term "communitas" to speak of that peculiar quality of social bonding that is formed among liminal subjects, a relationship not dependent upon similarities in class, rank, wealth, or social status. Young people involved in Ndembu initiation rites, fellow pilgrims making their way to Canterbury, commuters on a New York subway that breaks down in a power failure—all these discover a sense of comradeship that is spontaneous and concrete, one not shaped by the customs, laws, and norms of social structure.[11] People in such contexts are naturally made sensitive to others whose identity may be defined outside the institutionalized structures of society. Their experience of liminality allows them to entertain connections they might not have imagined before.

Biblically, this notion is grounded in the experience of Israel as a displaced people—never far removed from the memory of their own journey through the wilderness, their own encounter with exile. This means that their pleas for justice will invariably include a particular concern for those who, like them, have been victims of dislocation. The homeless, especially widows and orphans, will be singled out for deliberate care (Ex 22:22–24). Cities of refuge will be designated as centers of sanctuary for those in flight (Num 35). The precepts of the year of Jubilee will pointedly connect social righteousness with the disenfranchisement of place (Lev 25).

The same dynamic is also found in the history of American revivals. The social impact of the Evangelical Awakenings has by now been well documented, indicating its own propensity toward ministering to alien and displaced persons.[12] The spirit of revival has, at various times, driven David Brainerd to work among Native Americans in Massachusetts or Charles Sheldon to question labor conditions in Topeka, Kansas. It has prompted Theodore Dwight Weld to anti-slavery activities in Ohio and Phoebe Palmer to slum reform in New York City. Revivalism, despite its ethereal, other-worldly ethos, has been rich in possibilities for radical social change. I think back, for example, to a dance hall at a migrant labor camp which became another site in the formation of my early grasp of faith. There I witnessed first-hand the risks of discipleship, the social consequences of the revival. Marv Renstead was the lay preacher who took me with him every Sunday morning one winter to hold services at a large labor camp near Orlando. Men from Haiti and the Bahamas were brought in and housed there, so as to pick oranges in the groves nearby. They lived in shanties covered with sheets of corrugated tin. I never understood why they were paid so little or abused so much. Each week the acrid smells of lard, stale cigarette smoke, and urine clung to my clothes all the way home. I went along to play the accordion, while Marv preached—and organized, always asking questions, as he did, about living and working conditions. He would have done Joe Hill proud, Marv would. I remember him as a crazy mix of Billy Sunday and Saul Alinsky. He preached with an unmeasured passion and had a way of making enemies with great ease. One night the Ku Klux Klan chased him for hours through the groves—driving his 1944 Hudson at full throttle, without lights, to avoid being caught. They would have killed him if they could. This was one "nigger lover" who had gone too far in demanding civil rights for alien blacks. But Marv survived, and so did my faith.

In fact, the most meaningful communion service I have ever known occurred in the camp dance hall one Sunday morning at the end of the season that year. After the crap games had been driven out and the chairs set up in the large, empty hall, I began, as usual, playing "Amazing Grace" and "What a Friend We Have in Jesus," practically the only songs I knew. The seats were filled; Marv preached. Then we formed a circle of huge black men with wide Caribbean smiles, a bald white agitator, and an ingenuous thirteen-year-old accordion player. Tears flowed freely as we all passed a jelly-jar glass of Welch's grape juice and several slices of white sandwich bread. I was hugged so much that day that it hurt. But I never remember being encountered so much by the real presence of Christ as on that day in that liminal place. There the revival became inescapably for me a matter of love molded in the shape of justice.

As I look back now, the threshold experience of the revival has formed me more than I knew. Its liminal places led me to openings that have been nurtured all of my life. These include a deep appreciation for anti-structure, for the incapacity of any fixed place or institution fully to contain the holy. They involve the expectation of being found by God in the disconcerting moments of transition and movement in my life, as well as the discovery of the Holy Spirit on the margins of society, at those points where the people of God embrace the pain of others. I have willingly yielded to this impact of the revival on my manner-of-being. But I've learned also its limits. There was always, in my past, a sense of tentative transience even to the most exciting events of the tent and storefront—an awareness that even here the faithful had not fully caught the glory for which they grasped. They all harbored a fear that the power wouldn't last. And, indeed, it didn't. Brother and Sister Thomas took down the tent and moved on. Tommy Titcomb returned to Africa. Our enthusiastic congregation suffered two major church splits, one caused by the minister's leaving his wife and three children to run away with the church secretary. He began selling used cars in a town nearby, while the church divided over what to do next. Mr. Flinn, my Sunday school teacher, was arrested for pretending to be a doctor in "Colored Town" on the far side of the city, and even Marv Renstead left home and was indicted on charges in Tennessee that I never understood. All my grandest heroes would never quite fulfill their promise. But I loved them deeply nonetheless. They were people who had been touched by angels, but who finally were too frail to hold for long the power of God. They stood wavering on the threshold, torn by a bold hesitance. They were like us all. I see their faces still as I strain to remember the haunting melody drawn from the edge of a hand-saw by the violin bow of a traveling evangelist. They live somewhere, in a liminal stretch of memory, beyond the limbus of my own well-ordered world. I recall the strange half-places of yesterday and I'm with them once more.

7 | Precarity and Permanence: Dorothy Day and the Catholic Worker Sense of Place

"Poverty has many faces. People can, for example, be poor in space alone. Last month I talked to a man who lives in a four-room apartment with a wife, four children, and relatives besides. He has a regular job and can feed his family, but he is poor in light and air and space."[1]

On May 1, 1933, the sixteenth anniversary of the Russian Revolution, a new penny newspaper went on sale in Union Square in the East Village of Manhattan. It was hawked by students and shirt-sleeved workers, looking much like the socialist radicals nearby who sold copies of the Communist paper, *The Daily Worker*. But these unlikely prophets were harbingers of the New Catholic Left in America. They could be found as often at Mass as at the meetings of striking workers. They read papal encyclicals as well as Kropotkin's revolutionary pamphlets. They practiced spiritual works of mercy even as they staffed bread lines for the unemployed. They were a people of paradox—given to the most utter precarity and transience as they identified with those displaced people most affected by the Great Depression. Yet, at the same time, they emphasized the concrete and material importance of place in achieving the dignity of unhoused people as well as in realizing the sacramental presence of the Mystical Body of Christ. Finding their way between un-Christian socialists, on the one hand, and the majority of unsocial Christians, on the other, they sought to give placement to those who were uprooted and to uproot those who were ensconced in overly-secure places.

Hence, a paradoxical tension between place and placelessness can be seen to distinguish the urban-centered spirituality of the Catholic Worker Movement. A celebration of the impermanence and detachment which characterized primitive Christianity is found right alongside the personalist conviction that full human dignity requires a place of one's own, a profound sense of rootedness in space. In the first issue of *The Catholic Worker*, its editor Dorothy Day emphasized the precarious na-

189

ture of the enterprise just launched by herself and Peter Maurin, the French peasant who would be the movement's intellectual gadfly.

> This first number of *The Catholic Worker* was planned, written, and edited in the kitchen of a tenement on Fifteenth Street, on subway platforms, on the El, the ferry. There is no editorial office, no overhead in the way of telephone or electricity, no salaries paid. . . .
>
> Next month someone may donate us an office. Who knows?
>
> It is cheering to remember that Jesus Christ wandered this earth with no place to lay his head. *The foxes have holes and the birds of the air their nests, but the Son of Man has no place to lay His head.* And when we consider our fly-by-night existence, our uncertainty, we remember (with pride at sharing the honor) that the disciples supped by the seashore and wandered through cornfields picking the ears from the stalks wherewith to make their frugal meals.[2]

Within the context of this spirituality, being without a place would become a badge by which true identification with Christ could be discerned. "The main thing is not to hold on to anything," Dorothy Day would explain simply.[3]

Yet, at the same time, the importance of one's being rooted in a place that could nourish personal freedom was also seen to be primary in the Catholic Worker theology of place. Emmanuel Mounier, the French personalist who would influence much of the New Catholic Left in this century, insisted that "space is liberty." Our existence as full human beings is grounded in the richness of our experience of space. "Tell me where you are to be found," he said, "and I will tell you who you are."[4] Accordingly, the pages of *The Catholic Worker* are filled with cases of homeless people who are aided in their quest for dignity through the acquisition of place. Dorothy Day describes, for example, a black and Puerto Rican woman of twenty-two named Felicia, whose husband had lost two fingers in a machine shop. For a while she lived in the hall outside the apartment of her husband's parents, then they found a two-room tenement on Eldridge Street.

> It was a hideous scabrous place, with the plaster falling off the walls, and the toilet out of order in the halls, and cold water, and the halls smelled of rats and cats.

She feared for the lives of her three children there. Finally, they were able to move to a flat that was adequate to their needs, they even acquired furniture, and the woman assumed a degree of pride and wholeness once again in her life. The story concludes, "You can see Felicia has some sense of dignity, now that she is a householder, with a place of her own."[5] In such a way, the Catholic Worker Movement would persistently concern itself with the particularities of place—responding to the "tragedy of a landless people, homeless, meagerly fed, housed like animals rather than like creatures made in the image and likeness of God."[6]

It is a peculiar paradox, this tension between the idealist's celebration of placelessness and the materialist's attention to the concrete demands of placement. Yet both are indelibly a part of the Catholic Worker conception of Christian faith. Dorothy Day spoke of "this life of attachment and detachment" in which property (and place) becomes that which is to be revered as the substance of God's providence and grace, yet must also be readily offered back to God lest it become an end in itself.[7] The tension is one between precarity and permanence. It can be seen to rest upon a Christology that embraces the wandering, homeless Jesus of early Jewish Christianity and, at the same time, the Jesus who is discovered in the tangible particularity of one's cross-town neighbor. It is a tension found in two of Dorothy Day's favorite saints—Benedict Joseph Labré and Thérèse of Lisieux—the one continually wandering in abject poverty and the other consecrating the most common things in life at her convent near the French coast of Normandy. It is a tension which ultimately is found to hinge upon a liturgical as well as Christological center. In the mystery of the Eucharist, with its encounter of the Mystical Body of Christ, that which is natural, ordinary, and physical is joined with that which is supernatural and divine. A rich earthiness, a sharpened sensitivity to the spatial and temporal needs of others, necessarily derives from the real presence of the incarnate Lord, uniting the faithful with all who are members (actually or potentially) of his Mystical Body. Hence, a liturgical reality transcending time and space becomes the very means by which those categories of human freedom can be taken seriously and concretely.

Dorothy Day and Peter Maurin: The Lived Experience of a Theology of Place

This dialectical tension between precarity and permanence can be observed most readily in the lived experience of Dorothy Day and Peter

Maurin themselves. Their lives were constantly pulled between the desire of the unsettled to be settled and the discomforting need of the settled to be unsettled. In short, they were sojourners with an anchor in tow. Dorothy Day's autobiography, *The Long Loneliness*, can be outlined geographically as a movement from the streets of Manhattan to the protective seclusion of Staten Island and back again. Her life was a passage from confused impermanence to the temporary security afforded by marriage and householding and on, at last, to a bold and voluntary placelessness.[8]

Dorothy Day had been born in 1897, the daughter of an erratic and itinerant sports writer. He gave her, if nothing else, a lust for printer's ink and travel. Her own career as a journalist began with the *Call* and *The Masses*, two socialist newspapers based in Greenwich Village. There she reported on strikes and meetings of the I.W.W., went to jail with women demanding suffrage, and even interviewed Leon Trotsky shortly before the Bolshevik Revolution. Late at night in a nearby bar she would listen to Eugene O'Neill quoting "The Hound of Heaven" through shots of Irish whiskey. Like Francis Thompson, she was in pursuit of a meaning she could discover only in being found by that which she was herself pursued. The next few years brought a tragic love affair ending with an abortion, a misguided marriage lasting only a few months, and a degrading experience of being arrested with local prostitutes in Chicago. She seemed aimlessly floating at sea, without a place of mooring. In an autobiographical novel written at this time, entitled *The Eleventh Virgin*, her principal character was a mirror of Dorothy Day's own experience.

> There were afternoons when she walked the streets, or took bus rides, watching the women shopping on Fifth Avenue, looking at the homes of all those people who accepted permanency as the undercurrent of their lives. Those women were buying things to take home to their husbands—to their babies probably. Why couldn't she too have a home, a husband, and babies?[9]

Her life seemed to lack any personal and geographical center that could be the occasion for a deeper sense of meaning.

But such a center finally was gained in 1925 when she bought a cottage on Staten Island with money obtained from the sale of movie rights to her novel. That was the year she also began living with Forster Batterham, an anarchist and naturalist who shared her love of the earth and the sea. They fished together, walked for miles on the lonely beach, and studied sunsets on the bay near Sandy Hook as Dorothy was more and more awakened to joy. There she conceived a child. And the mystery of that experience of co-creation led her to the Creator of all things. Her conversion was a response to the wondrous ordinariness of giving birth. For the first time in her life she was given roots, confined to a place, and she found it oddly glorious.

> I was enchained, tied to one spot, unable to pick up and travel from one part of the country to another, from one job to another. I was tied down because I was going to have a baby. No matter how much I might sometimes wish to flee from my quiet existence, I could not, nor would I be able to for several years. I had to accept my quiet and stillness, and accepting it, I rejoiced in it.[10]

Her discovery of a fixed location in which meaning could cohere became both the occasion and the product of her religious conversion. To encounter God was to have known the experience of being placed.

Yet, ironically, that very placement would lead once more to an agonizing uprooting. Forster Batterham, her common-law husband, had been reluctant to bring a child into the world at all, convinced as he was that every form of government—from family to state—tended to rob people of their freedom. He particularly rejected the church with its sanctioning of all other forms of social control. Thus, when Dorothy determined to have their daughter baptized in the Roman Catholic Church and when she herself began attending Mass, it meant giving up the man she had loved so much and the place they had shared together. She was forced to embrace an even higher conception of placement and meaning. Having found in Christ a new center to her life, all other centers would now derive their significance from that focus alone. Hence, once again she could launch out into a certain precarity, knowing that the world now possessed an *axis mundi*. She came to know, with Emmanuel Mounier, that "man's permanence is ultimately in adventure." The movement of faith turns always from the pain of dislocation to the tranquility of placement. But it drives on still further to voluntary impermanence—to the abandoning of security for the sake of love.

Moving back to Manhattan with her child, Tamar, she began searching for a way to relate her new-found faith to the displaced masses for which her socialist years had given her love. Four years later Dorothy Day would cross paths with an extraordinary man, a wandering French peasant by the name of Peter Maurin. Preaching a gospel of agriculture, his shirt pockets stuffed with the labor writings of Charles Pé-

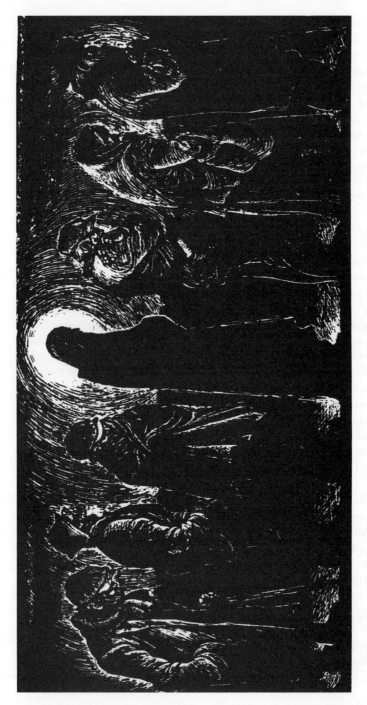

"The Christ of the Breadlines" (1950), one of Quaker artist Fritz Eichenberg's many woodcut engravings done for *The Catholic Worker*. Used by permission. ©Fritz Eichenberg Trust/Licensed by VAGA, New York, N.Y.

guy, wearing clothes he had not changed in three days, he seemed to many a holy fool in the tradition of Francis of Assisi or Benedict Joseph Labré. Yet his threefold program keenly appealed to Dorothy's own conception of social change and Catholic action. He called for round-table discussions as a means toward "clarification of thought," houses of hospitality to make possible the works of mercy, and "agronomic universities" where labor and study could be joined on communal farms.[11] "Cult, Culture, and Cultivation," he called it—a conviction that truth is discovered through the personal exchange of people who refuse to distance themselves from the land and the dignity of their common work (their *liturgia* in the deepest sense).

Peter Maurin exemplified the spirit of voluntary placelessness that Catholic Worker spirituality sought to espouse. He traveled continually, identifying with displaced persons wherever he went—sleeping in flophouses more often than not. Once invited to the home of a Columbia University professor, the wife mistook him for the meter-reader and sent him down to the basement. He was thrown out of more than one meeting to which he had come to speak, being mistaken for a Bowery bum. To his delight, the Catholic Worker houses of hospitality were regularly filled with a piebald assembly of street people, students, labor activists, and utopian socialists. The whole kingdom of God embraced in a ship of fools. He reveled in the very incongruity of it all, knowing the Church itself to be preeminently "a sign of contradiction" in the world. He was a man without need of place, and hence without status, offering to the world an alternative measure of things. Dorothy Day once recalled:

> When we all lived together under one roof in the houses of hospitality, he seldom had a room of his own. Returning from trips around the country, he never knew whether there would be a bed for him. The younger editors had their own desks and were jealous of their privacy. But Peter not only had no place to lay his head but had no place for his books and papers—aside from his capacious pockets. He had no chair, no place at table, no corner that was particularly his. He was a pilgrim and a stranger on earth, using the things of this world as though he used them not, availing himself of only what he needed and discarding all excess baggage.[12]

While Peter Maurin denied the necessity of a place for himself, he nonetheless spoke untiringly of the importance of a place for others. He urged a return to the land and manual labor as a primary source of human dignity. His "Green Revolution" involved a vision of the revival of subsistence farming in a village setting. In a decentralized economy of this sort, property-owning farmers and craftsmen would be able to recover once more the spiritual nature of work, something prohibited by the mechanized labor system of modern society. If naively romantic, even medieval, his cry of "Back to Christ—Back to the Land!" demonstrated all the same his unshaken confidence in the importance of place for the renewal of human hope. Voluntarily abandoning any location for himself, he insisted on the crucial value of "being placed" for those who were involuntarily cast into exile.[13]

Theological Roots:
A Christology of Intentional Simplicity

The Catholic Worker theology of place has deep roots in a Christology that reaches back to the beginnings of the Christian experience and is renewed in the late medieval movement of the Spiritual Franciscans. It is this Christological foundation that lends definition and support to the notions of precarity and permanence discussed here. The Jesus who is pictured in the pages of *The Catholic Worker*—from Dorothy's regular column "On Pilgrimage" to the woodcut engravings of Fritz Eichenberg—is a Jesus marked by poverty, wandering itineracy, and hiddenness. He is the Jesus celebrated in the early Syriac asceticism of Jewish Christianity, a Jesus who had no place to lay his head, who could be found only in the hiddenness of poverty.[14] Francis of Assisi emphasized the same motif in the thirteenth century, pointing to a Christ without possessions or place—one who had joined himself to "Lady Poverty." Dorothy Day and Peter Maurin would accentuate these themes of ancient Syriac and Franciscan spirituality as they shared their own vision of Christ in the world. This can be observed most effectively in the way Dorothy depicted the Christ-like lives of two of her favorite saints.

Benedict Joseph Labre (1748–1783), often remembered as "the beggar of Rome," was an idiosyncratic saint whose vocation had been that of wandering all over Europe. He slept in the corners of abandoned buildings and had no possessions other than a ragged cloak and a few books. One writer described him as "a rock of prayer crawling with lice," "a sort of patron saint for failures."[15] It was this eccentric figure that Dorothy Day chose to introduce to the readers of *The Catholic Worker* through a series of letters pseudonymously written in 1939 and 1940. They were signed by a contemporary vagrant workingman named Ben Joe Labray, who spent his time, like many others in the depression, "trying to get enough to eat from day to day and a flop at night." He had worked once on the Sixth Avenue subway as a mucker and had rolled cement at Boulder Dam. He wrote on one occasion from a migrant labor camp near Salinas, California, where he picked lettuce and celery with Filipinos. At another time his letter came from a jail in Pittsburgh where detectives from the Pennsylvania Railroad had locked him up for riding the freights. He said,

> I feel I'm representing the great number of unemployed throughout the country. I work off and on and keep going, looking for work. Some call me hobo; some would label me a migratory worker; some would call me plain bum. . . . [But] I keep thinking of my unemployment as a vocation . . . a vocation to homelessness.[16]

Out of his experience he would offer advice to transients in New York City, suggesting they try the Local Homeless Relief Bureau on Lafayette Street for a bed; they would surely be picked up, he warned, if they tried to sleep in the parks. He carried a rosary and spoke of faith where he could. But more often he met with abuse, ending up in Bellevue Hospital once with broken ribs and a broken jaw for speaking on behalf of striking workers in a shipyard.

Ben Joe Labray, "your lay apostle on the bum," was a vivid expression of that "harsh and dreadful love" described by Fr. Zossima in *The Brothers Karamazov*, a love that expended itself in caring for both the deserving and the undeserving poor. "Ben Joe Labray" wrote always with the greatest sensitivity to place, recognizing that the tramps and migrant workers he met derived what self-respect they had from proximity to the land. A letter received in the spring of 1940 expressed this insight with great artistry, showing the author's keen eye for physical details.

> I'm writing this in a little country schoolhouse where I will sleep tonight, and writing by the light of a tin wood-stove. You see, I've walked the highway all day and my feet are blistering. The nearest town of any size is thirteen miles off, and when dusk fell I spotted this little school. . . .

Hoping no one will see the smoke and send for a sheriff, he asks if they had gotten his last letter from a road camp where he had been assigned to a chain gang on a charge of vagrancy. He speaks of his release and subsequent efforts to find food at rescue missions in the next city. Then he concludes.

The stove light is glaring now and I must cease writing for fear someone will detect me. Police cars may pass and I'd rather be spared another thirty days. Now I'm looking at the ears of corn that decorate the schoolroom and am becoming more hungry. What a life! Excuse this composition book paper, but it's all I can get around here. I'll remember to pray for the work and ask you to pray for the large number of people that I meet on the road. I'll write from the berry country—if I make it. God bless you.

Ben Joe Labray[17]

Other saints frequently quoted in the pages of *The Catholic Worker* included Francis of Assisi and Teresa of Avila, in addition to eulogies paid to St. Joseph the Carpenter and St. Isidore the Farmer. But Dorothy's own favorite saint above all others was the Little Flower, Thérèse of Lisieux, the young French nun who became exceptional for the unexceptional simplicity of her devotion. Here again the Catholic Worker Movement found its Christological center summarized in a figure of remarkable inconsequence. St. Thérèse of the Child Jesus (1873–1897) was a Carmelite nun who had entered the convent in Lisieux at the age of fifteen. She died nine years later, having written an autobiography that took the world by storm—due to the charmed simplicity with which she described her spirituality of "the Little Way." This woman often pictured with a bouquet of roses, so affectionate with others and given to boundless enthusiasm, was most sensitive to those everyday situations which she saw to open one to "the sacrament of the present moment."[18] She understood prayer as essentially a matter of paying loving attention to the smallest of details. At her canonization, a scant twenty-eight years after her death, Pius XI remarked that she had achieved sanctity "without going beyond the common order of things."

Dorothy Day first learned of St. Thérèse in the maternity ward of Bellevue Hospital. The woman in the bed next to hers noticed that she had chosen to name her daughter Tamar Teresa and asked which saint she had been named after. Dorothy took pleasure in pinning to the baby's nightshirt a medal of the Little Flower, given by this woman whose explanation of her daughter's name suddenly brought new preeminence to her. Dorothy would later write a book on Thérèse and invite people to reflect on the social implications of her teachings. "The significance of our smallest acts"—that, she said, is what the Church has most to learn from this saint. The little things we do are filled with the greatest consequence.

Martyrdom is not gallantly standing before a firing squad. Usually it is the losing of a job (and so the means of a life) because of not taking a loyalty oath, or buying a war bond, or paying a tax. Martyrdom is small, hidden, misunderstood.[19]

The hiddenness of Christ, made apparent even in the least of one's actions, would become central to Catholic Worker spirituality. Indeed, seeing Christ in one's neighbor—in that very family on Bleecker Street, evicted from their tenement flat and sitting amid their scraps of furniture on the sidewalk—was the heart of the gospel itself.

If we hadn't got Christ's own words for it, it would seem raving lunacy to believe that if I offer a bed and food and hospitality for Christmas—or any time, for that matter—to some man or woman or child, I am replaying the part of Lazarus or Martha or Mary, and that my guest is Christ. There is nothing to show it, perhaps. There are no halos already glowing round their heads—at least none that human eyes can see. It is not likely that I shall be vouchsafed the vision of Elizabeth of Hungary, who put the leper in her bed and later, going to tend him, saw no longer the leper's stricken face, but the face of Christ. . . .

If everyone were holy and handsome, with "alter Christus" shining in neon lighting from them, it would be easy to see Christ in everyone. . . . [But] He is disguised under every type of humanity that treads the earth.[20]

The task demanded of each Christian is the recognition of the hiddenness of Christ—particularly in those who may be homeless or displaced. The intentional simplicity of Benedict Joseph Labré and Thérèse of Lisieux thus exemplifies the Christological premise on which the Catholic Worker theology of place is founded.

Praxis: Situating the Unplaced and Unplacing the Situated

The working out in practice of this theology of place involves an inescapable dialectic for the spirituality of the Catholic Worker Movement. Even as a distinction is maintained in radical Catholic thought between voluntary and involuntary poverty (the one affirmed and the other denounced), the implications of the principle extend also to voluntary and involuntary placelessness. Dorothy Day proclaimed:

> Poverty is a strange and elusive thing. . . . I condemn poverty
> and I advocate it; poverty is simple and complex at once, it is
> a social phenomenon and a personal matter. Poverty is an elu-
> sive thing, and a paradoxical one.[21]

Christian praxis demands, on the one hand, *the securing of place* for
some (so as to relieve the impoverishment of poverty) and, on the other
hand, *the taking away of place* from others (to the extent that it offers a
false security and an obstacle to faith). This puts the Catholic Worker
in the position of advancing a rich sacramentality and an exacting asceticism at one and the same time. The essential goodness of all created
things—of place and property—is clearly extolled, while simultaneously a caveat is raised about the tendency to use those things for a purpose that distorts their goodness. Place is that which can enhance and
enrich one's very being, opening one to a greater spaciousness. But it
also can become that which isolates one from others, serving to limit risk
and growth. Every metropolis, with its sprawling suburbs neatly separated from its inner-city neighborhoods, witnesses to the problems of
place that Catholic Worker spirituality seeks to address.

The concern to speak out against the placelessness of the poor was
a chief priority of Catholic Workers in the depression years of the 1930's.
"On the fringes, by the rivers, on almost every vacant lot," wrote Dorothy Day, "there was a Hooverville, where the homeless huddled in
front of their fires."[22] She freely borrowed pages from *The Grapes of
Wrath* as she described, in the poignant style of muckraking journalists,
the plight of migrant peoples. In 1940, for example, she traveled
through California's San Joaquin Valley, portraying the experience of
unemployed farm workers there. At a roadside camp outside Marys-
ville, she found the characters of Ma Joad and her brooding son Tom to
have been lifted out of fiction into reality.

> Down in the hollow, back of the road, there are forty families
> encamped. Down on either side of the highway, nestled under
> the levee of the Feather River, there are more families. Many
> of the camps are surrounded by water and mud. The stars are
> reflected in the pools of water in the fields and the orchards.
> Last week there was a bad flood up here so that most of the
> roads were under water. . . .
>   It is so sad to see this constant coming and going,
> hundreds of thousands of people on the move from place to
> place.[23]

These were people without a place of their own, and without the consolation and worth that place brings. These were the people—both urban and rural—for whom *The Catholic Worker* wrote in its first issue in 1933.

> For those who are sitting on park benches in the warm spring sunlight.
> For those who are huddling in shelters trying to escape the rain.
> For those who think that there is no hope for the future, no recognition of their plight,—this little paper is addressed.[24]

The precise means by which these displaced people were to be situated in a space of their own, however, was not always clear. Catholic Workers often disagreed on how dignity could best be restored through change of place. Some favored an anti-urban, anti-industrial flight to the land as the best option. This was Peter Maurin's program for a Green Revolution, influenced as it was by certain anarchist and distributist ideas. But others aimed at reclaiming and humanizing the structures of habitat found within the city itself. Hence, Catholic Worker communities usually tried to do both—setting up farming communes out on the land and establishing houses of hospitality within metropolitan centers. Maryfarms were begun by the New York community at Easton, Pennsylvania and later at Newburgh, New York, but the pulse of the movement could invariably best be felt at the Worker houses on Mott and Chrystie Streets in Manhattan.

For her own part, Dorothy Day could never give up her first love of the city. The sound of tugboats and barges on the East River, gulls wheeling warm gray and white over the Staten Island Ferry, children on their way to school, with a radio performance of *Tosca* drifting through the open window—these were the joys of New York. "I do love cities!" she cried.[25] She saw light where others spied only squalor and ugliness. On her way to Mass she could speak of "that splendid globe of sun, one street wide, framed at the foot of East Fourteenth Street in early-morning mists."[26] But she admitted that the actual reclamation of the city, making it habitable for the poor, always proved more difficult than she hoped. The cycle of sweat-shop wages, exorbitant rents, and relentlessly-crowded conditions seemed inevitably to make life in the city intolerable. The lure of the land, therefore, was continually felt. It provided opportunity for periodic retreats, if not also for the building of alternative communities. Communal farms seemed to offer new beginnings simply through their acquisition of new space.

Peter Maurin had been the one most supportive of experiments on the land. He had considered himself a peasant all of his life, remembering the old stone house in Languedoc where he had grown up as a child. Sheep had been kept in the basement. His family had worked that farmland in the south of France for fifteen hundred years. He was a medievalist, calling for a romantic Catholic agrarianism which could counter the capitalist spirit of mechanized labor. But at the most profound level, his insight lay in that awareness of the intricate web of meanings which binds human existence to place and land. Contemporary marginal farmers like Wendell Berry have since echoed that same sensitivity.

> How you act *should* be determined, and the consequences of your acts *are* determined, by where you are. To know where you are (and whether or not that is where you should be) is at least as important as to know what you are doing, because in the moral (the ecological) sense you cannot know *what* until you have learned *where*.[27]

This personalist perspective on the return to the land—this sensitivity to the "where" of one's being—is important because what Maurin and Day both sought most was not so much an elaborate program for social reconstruction as a fuller sense of personal wholeness obtained through a responsible proximity to the soil. None of the communal farms proved to be unqualified successes, no more than did the urban houses of hospitality. The farms often had poor soil, some of the people never worked as hard as others, and disputes invariably broke out. At the Worker houses in New York, organization was seldom as effective as some wanted, nor as unstructured as others preferred. Confusion seemed to reign much of the time. By strict canons of sociological evaluation, therefore, the Catholic Worker experiments were far from exemplary. But the movement never sought to be judged primarily by its effectiveness at community organization and social control. Its goal was always the person. It preferred to be judged in "little ways," by those small increases in personal dignity that accrue from the responsible use of land and the pride taken in the work of one's hands. Success could be measured only to the extent that Christ was recognized in each individual whose life had been touched.

Biblical Displacement and Prophetic Action

If half of the Catholic Worker strategy was to situate the unplaced, whether in a renewed urban or rural setting, the other half was to unplace the situated, disturbing those who had secluded themselves in protective enclaves, cut off from vulnerability and growth. Here some of the prophetic, revolutionary impulse of the New Catholic Left is disclosed. Peter Maurin had warned that the Catholic Church possessed a powerful social force not unlike dynamite, but that Catholic scholars had always failed to blow it. Now was the time, he urged, to drive the money changers out of the temple—to spiritually dislocate those people who had become bound to the financial and bureaucratic corridors of power.[28] This was a language, of course, that never ceased to unnerve the cardinal archbishop of New York, but Maurin and Day would insist that it gave expression to the evangelical counsels of the Church. One thrust of the gospel, as they saw it, is to dislodge those who had barricaded themselves in sacred confines, impervious to the needs of others.

An important strain of biblical theology, traced through the Hebrew prophets, had primarily underscored the freedom of God in spatial terms. God is not confined to place—particularly not to those places where people of influence and power might want to keep God "on call." Even the temple of Solomon could not guarantee God's accessibility (1 Kgs 8:27). God had chosen instead to be primarily accessible to those without power and voice, to those without a place of their own.[29] To presume, therefore, that one's place of social or religious consequence might in itself assure the protection and blessing of heaven was folly of the highest sort. Much of New Testament thought continued this tendency to separate the guarantees of God's covenant from the occupation of particularly-favored sites. It would question the prominence traditionally given to Jerusalem, the temple, and even the land of Israel.[30] W. D. Davies has observed that the New Testament theology of place turned away from all fixed geographical points, seeing the presence of Christ alone to constitute the sacredness of a place.

> The New Testament finds holy space where Christ is or has been: it personalizes "holy space" in Christ, who, as a figure of History, is rooted in the land; he cleansed the Temple and died in Jerusalem, and lends his glory to these and to the places where he was, but, as Living Lord, he is also free to move wherever he wills.[31]

What this suggests is that in the primitive Christian conception of things, the God of Jesus Christ was ever engaged in displacing those who had become falsely secure in their attachment to territorial zones of power. In biblical understanding, place could never become a guard against risk and change. Self-protection and security were not accepted as the proper or primary functions of place, because the presence of Christ would finally make every locale open to radically new possibilities.

For Dorothy Day, one practical expression of this theology would mean taking part in certain symbolic activities which raised questions about one's occupation and use of space. She would on occasion deliberately put herself in the place of danger, so as to challenge those whose attachment to places of security had distorted their understanding of truth. In the 1950's, for example, she participated in protests against the annual Civil Defense air raid drills in the city of New York. During these mock drills, all citizens were required by law to seek the illusive safety of underground shelters during a hypothetical nuclear strike. Sirens rang eerily through the empty city streets. The people of Manhattan sat underground in strained silence, knowing that Strategic Air Command Bombers flew overhead, terrified by the threat of Communist attack, imagining apocalyptic scenarios in which the world might end. But not Dorothy Day. On June 15, 1955, in the third consecutive year of such drills, Dorothy and several other Catholic Workers walked to City Hall Park on Lower Broadway. There they intended to protest to the mayor the absurdity of pretending that the city could be preserved from nuclear explosion by hiding twenty feet under the sidewalk. When the sirens began to sound, they were joined by members of the War Resisters League and the Fellowship of Reconciliation. But all were promptly arrested. They were taken to jail, one would presume, for the crime of not adequately having sought their own self-preservation. The judge, in fact, declared them "guilty of the murder of three million people," alleging this to be the number of those who would have been lost had they not sought shelter in an actual attack.[32] Each summer for the next several years Dorothy Day would continue sitting on park benches during the annual drills, accepting the arrest and jail sentence that followed her action. She simply insisted that there is no place of safety in nuclear warfare. To urge others to act as if there were was merely to engage in psychological manipulation, furthering the increase of Cold War hysteria, without protecting life at all. Her conviction, of course, was that sometimes occupying the "wrong place" can clearly be one's Christian duty, even as Thoreau had insisted that jail is, on occasion, the most honorable place where one can be found. The place where Christ is discovered is not the place of safety and self-defense, but rather the place of risk. An editorial in *Commonweal*, that summer of 1955, spoke of the way in which this woman challenged the accepted opinions of her day.

Dorothy Day's vocation has been a radical vocation. She has witnessed to the uncomfortable, the not "respectable," truths of Christianity. The example of her life rebukes most of us for our complacency.[33]

A similar illustration of opposition to an un-Christian perspective of sacred and profane space can be found in Dorothy Day's trip to Clarence Jordan's Koinonia Farm the following spring. There on the red earth of southern Georgia, eight miles southwest of Americus, a communitarian experiment had been established. Jordan was a Southern Baptist minister and Greek scholar who had brought together blacks and whites to work the land and live in community—something the white citizens of Sumter County were not ready to accept in 1956. While half of the county's population was black, many of these were still sharecroppers, working on land owned by whites. All of them were segregated. Therefore, when Jordan went so far as to help two Negro students in their attempt to enter a previously-segregated college in Atlanta, the Knights of the Ku Klux Klan responded with violence. Fences were cut, sugar poured into gas tanks, bullets fired into the roadside stand where the Koinonia community sold its eggs and produce. It was made clear that the space of Sumter County was conceived by its people of influence as segregated space.

Within this context, Dorothy Day went to Koinonia Farm herself over the Easter weekend of that year. She was concerned to show her solidarity with Jordan and his people, even asking to serve as a sentry guard at the entrance to the farm on the night of Holy Saturday. Members of the community had regularly been keeping watch to prevent further vandalism. But a strange Easter Vigil it would be. Sitting in a station wagon under the floodlight at the roadside vegetable stand, she waited in the silence of a warm Georgia night, praying. Only crickets and tree-toads stirred. And then she heard the distant, whining tires of a pick-up truck on Highway 49. Its headlights came faster as she instinctively hid herself beneath the open windows of the car. A shotgun blast rang out and the station wagon was riddled with pellets as the truck sped away. But Dorothy escaped unharmed. She had experienced her first encounter with Southern vigilante justice. It was perhaps a reckless, almost theatrical action, this effort to identify heroically with black and white farmers in the South. At least such an action could be so conceived, if it were not commensurate with the rest of her whole life. But she had always insisted on the need for the poor and the exiled to be guaranteed a place of their own. She had ever spoken out against those who would isolate themselves in protective locales excluding all others. [34]

Many of these attitudes toward place and placelessness found in Dorothy Day and Peter Maurin are informed by the personalist philosophy of Emmanuel Mounier. His Christian understanding of property, for example, is directly transferable to the Catholic Worker perception of space. [35] Mounier had argued that property is the human being's extension of himself or herself. Property (or place) can be that by which one's being is expanded or limited. In capitalist societies, however, the tendency is for property (or place) to be used simply as the physical extension of one's sphere of control. It becomes a protective shell, making oneself less vulnerable to the intrusion of the world. Hence, the bomb shelters of New York City, stocked with supplies of food and water, symbolized spatially the protective control sought by American society as a whole. By using property (or space) in a protective, defensive manner, one becomes unavailable to the outside world. His property insulates and isolates him. In a similar way, the white citizens of Sumter County, Georgia sought to isolate themselves spatially and socially from their black neighbors. In contrast, Mounier argued that the Christian possession of property involves the use of goods (the employment of space), not for self-protection and preservation, but for self-exposure. It becomes an occasion for vulnerability and risk. In this way, it truly makes possible an extension of the person, an expansion of one's being. It was this openness to personal growth that Dorothy Day most sought, in the fear-ridden streets of New York and the threatening roadsides of Georgia alike. The civil disobedience and prophetic action inspired by Catholic Worker spirituality was rooted in an implicit theology of place and property—one that finally would find expression in the liturgical life of the Church.

The Eucharist, the Senses, and the Mystical Body of Christ

The point at which permanence and precarity, attachment and detachment, come most closely together in the life of the Church is in the celebration of the Eucharist. There the body of Christ is made concrete and physical through the mystery of the real presence and the gathered community of the faithful. Yet, in that same sacramental act, the believers receiving the body of Christ are also united with his Mystical Body, of which all men and women are members—actually or potentially. The impulse of Holy Communion, therefore, is to force the Church inward to the place where Christ is met spatially around the

altar (in his own body and blood received by his people) and then outward to all places where the crucified Christ continues to suffer in the
physical experience of the displaced and disinherited. An attachment to
the place where one is joined to the sufferings of Christ must drive
Christians to a renunciation of their own easy security so as to embrace
the pain of others—in all the specific places where they, too, suffer. Eu-
charistic theology is necessarily a theology sensitive to place.

Mel Piehl has observed: "For [Dorothy] Day, the Eucharist in particular was the foundation of spiritual life, connecting the spiritual and
material. She rejoiced in the use of bread and other common elements
in Catholic ritual." She once wrote:

> I loved all the physical aspects of the Church. They showed
> that man was body and soul, and could learn through his
> senses. The sacramentals which attuned one to accept the sac-
> raments with intensified faith also delighted me. It was easy
> to accept the teaching that all water had become holy since
> Christ was baptized in the Jordan.[36]

She knew that places, too, could become sacred through their association with Christ and his Mystical Body. She was above all aware that it
is often the suffering connected with a place that gives it meaning. People outside the Church, for that matter, without any awareness of sacramental theology, could readily grasp this.

> Often there is a mystical element in the love of a radical for his
> brother, for his fellow worker. It extends to the scene of his
> sufferings, and those spots where he has suffered and died are
> hallowed. The names of places like Everett, Ludlow, Bisbee,
> South Chicago, Imperial Valley, Elaine, Arkansas, and all
> those other places where workers have suffered and died for
> their cause have become sacred to the worker.[37]

If this is the case in the world at large, then surely the sharing in Christ's
suffering through unity with his Mystical Body will doubly compel one
to identify with those striking lumbermen in Everett or struggling farmworkers in Imperial Valley. For this reason, therefore, the centrality of
the Eucharist would remain crucial in Catholic Worker spirituality.

The mystery of the Mass was so important for Dorothy's own spirituality because it became the means by which her senses could grasp
the holy. She had always possessed a great appreciation for what T. S.
Eliot had described as "the grace of sense."[38] Her writing is consistently

engaging because it reflects so often the concrete and earthy world of
her senses. Hers was a deeply incarnational spirituality. To a person
who once had inquired, with obsequious reverence, if she had received
ecstasies and visions in her life of prayer, she responded, "Hell no, the
only visions I have is of unpaid bills!"[39] Her encounters with God were
always rooted in very ordinary experience. From the farm of her daughter and son-in-law in Vermont, she could write with profound simplicity of her most recent experience with Christ: "As I washed and teased
wool for the comforter I had finished last month . . . I thought of God's
goodness and the sacramentality of things."[40] She most commonly was
brought to God through her sensing of the things of God's world—especially those things she could smell.

In her writings she both extolled creation and decried the condition
of the poor by reference to her nose. She loved driving to the farm at
Easton because of the good smells it brought.

> Coming down at night from the city, the warm, sweet smell
> of the good earth enwraps one like a garment. There is the
> smell of rotting apples; of alfalfa in the barn; burning leaves;
> of wood fires in the house; of pickled green tomatoes and baked
> beans, than which there is no better smell, not even apple
> pies.[41]

The smells of earth drew her to God. But the smells of poverty led her
also to compassion for others. As she passed through the cheap lodging
houses and dingy restaurants of New York, she was appalled most of all
by their offense to the senses.

> Above all, the smell from the tenements, coming up from
> basements and areaways, from dank halls, horrified me. It is
> a smell like no other in the world and one never can become
> accustomed to it. I have lived with these smells now for many
> years, but they will always and ever affront me. I shall never
> cease to be indignant over the conditions which give rise to
> them. There is a smell in the walls of such tenements, a damp
> ooze coming from them in the halls. One's very clothes smell
> of it. It is not the smell of life, but the smell of the grave.[42]

Yet it was the Mass which continually drove her back to such places.
The sensate encounter with Christ through the species of bread and
wine made her alert in all her senses to every place where Christ suffers.

Dom Virgil Michel, the Benedictine liturgist of St. John's Abbey

Rear view of St. Joseph's house at 223 Chrystie Street, by Rita Corbin. Published in the September 1954 issue of *The Catholic Worker*. Used by permission.

who often wrote for *The Catholic Worker*, had said in speaking of the Eucharist that "incorporation in Christ means also con-corporation with all the members of the Mystical Body."[43] No one could enter into the heart of the liturgical spirit, he argued, without having been seized by a passion for the realization of social justice in every specific locale. In his view, Catholic action was simply a matter of prolonged worship. If "liturgy" meant literally the work (*ergon*) of the people (*leitos*), then it was not finished until it paid specific attention to where and how that work was completed in the world.[44] Hence, he regularly concerned himself with cooperatives, distributism, rural communal life, personalism, and all things human—speaking out strongly in support of Dorothy Day and her work. As he insisted in the pages of *The Catholic Worker:*

> One cannot steep oneself in the true meaning of the Mass as corporate worship to be participated in by all and enact the dedication of oneself to God with Christ in the sacrificial prayer of the Mass, and yet remain a cold-blooded individualist in one's life outside the precincts of the altar.[45]

Dorothy Day had herself recognized very early the crucial centrality of the Eucharist. Only there was love made thoroughly concrete and sensual. All compassion grew from that source. From this center she could summarize her entire vocation.

> When one loves, there is at that time a correlation between the spiritual and the material. Even the flesh is energized, the human spirit is made strong. All sacrifice, all suffering is easy for the sake of love. . . . This is the foundation of the Catholic Worker Movement.[46]

■ ■ ■ ■ ■ ■ ■ ■ ■ ■ ■ ■ ■ ■ ■ ■ ■

The spirituality of Dorothy Day was intimately connected with space. It carried her to all places, to anywhere that people suffered. It was fitting, therefore, that at her funeral all the people from all the places would return to her. Native Americans, Mexican farmworkers, blacks and Puerto Ricans sat alongside the cardinal archbishop of New York in the small Nativity Catholic Church near the Bowery. They had come from migrant camps in California, from communal farms in Georgia; others came from one-room apartments in Greenwich Village; some even wandered in from whiskey-soaked cots on Third Street. It was supposed to have been a private service, but over five hundred people came. When the priest asked that only the "family" follow the plain wooden coffin out of the church, three hundred people lined up behind it. Through the years they had all been made to feel "family." That happens when one pays such close attention to the "where" as well as the "how" of loving.[47]

All of her life Dorothy Day would plead for poverty and precarity, seeing herself drawn at the same time to an unhesitant affirmation of God's creation and a light-handedness with respect to the use of its goods. As one of her editors once wrote, "It seems that these two diverse states, permanence and precarity, have both assumed a strange but integral part of the Catholic Worker's existence."[48] On the twenty-fifth anniversary of the newspaper's founding, they received notice from the New York Transit Authority that St. Joseph's House on Chrystie Street, their main headquarters, was to be torn down to make way for a new subway connection. Not uncharacteristically they responded by saying, "We consider this something of a 'sign' from God, a most appropriate gift on our twenty-fifth anniversary. The gift of precarity to insure our permanence."[49] Like Francis of Assisi, they had learned to find in transience and homelessness a paradoxical sign of God's determined faithfulness. In letting go of place, they found themselves able to embrace it more profoundly than ever—in Jesus Christ, to them the Lord of all places.

PART 3 | Method and Perspective in Studying American Spirituality and Place

If we speak of a healthy community, we cannot be speaking of a community that is merely human. We are talking about a neighborhood of humans in a place, plus the place itself: its soil, its water, its air, and all the families and tribes of the nonhuman creatures that belong to it. If the place is well preserved, if its entire membership, natural and human, is present in it, and if the human economy is in practical harmony with the nature of the place, then the community is healthy.

—Wendell Berry, *Sex, Economy, Freedom, and Community*

Each place its own mind, its own psyche. Oak, madrone, Douglas fir, red-tailed hawk, serpentine in the sandstone, a certain scale to the topography, drenching rains in the winter, fog off-shore in the summer, salmon surging in the streams—all these together make up a particular state of mind, a place-specific intelligence shared by all the humans that dwell therein, but also by the coyotes yapping in those valleys, by the bobcats and the ferns and the spiders, by all beings who live and make their way in that zone. Each place its own psyche. Each sky its own blue.

—David Abram, *The Spell of the Sensuous*

There are men charged with the duty of examining the construction of the plants, animals, and soils which are the instruments of the great orchestra. These men are called professors. Each selects one instrument and spends his life taking it apart and describing its strings and sounding boards. This process of dismemberment is called research. The place for dismemberment is called a university.

A professor may pluck the strings of his own instrument, but never that of another, and if he listens for music he must never admit it to his fellows or to his students. For all are restrained by an ironbound taboo which decrees that the construction of instruments is the domain of science, while the detection of harmony is the domain of poets.

—Aldo Leopold, *A Sand County Almanac*

8 | The Ephemeral Character of Place: Problems in Articulating an American Sense of Sacred Space

Alongside the Church of St. Lucy at Bronxwood and Mace Avenues in the North Bronx stands a stone grotto. It has an artificial spring patterned after the sanctuary at Lourdes in France. The result is a poor copy at best. Yet people in the neighborhood have claimed the site as their own. Migrants in the area from Jamaica, Trinidad, and Puerto Rico, along with African Americans from the South Bronx, regularly come to the place, honoring it as sacred. Many of them are not even Catholic. They gather in plastic milk jugs the "holy water" that flows from a pipe between the rocks, speaking of its healing properties, even filling their car radiators with it for protection on the road home. What appears to be ordinary New York water from a Hudson River aqueduct is received with the sign of the cross and used as a way of securing blessing in a profane urban habitat.

Robert Orsi tells this story to college students in a course he teaches on American urban religion, using it to raise questions about the nature of religious experience and the way we define places thought to be sacred. His students regularly balk at the idea that a shallow imitation, an ersatz place of this sort, could ever be considered an authentic religious site. Their inclination is to insist that "*religion* is private and interior, not shamelessly public; mystical, not ritualistic; intellectually consistent and reasonable, not ambivalent and contradictory."[1] They want to identify religious experience as unlike anything else, divorcing it from the ordinary realities of everyday life.

This narrative and the characteristic responses of Orsi's students point us toward the third part of this book and the methodological concerns it addresses. These include three important questions raised

215

by many of the geographical narratives considered thus far. How, for example, do we grasp the elusive character of any American sacred place, torn as it is between religious thirst and cultural conditioning, spirit and matter, the transcendent and the immanent? Secondly, how should we study spirituality as an academic discipline, taking seriously the cultural milieu within which religious experience inevitably emerges? And thirdly, how do we acknowledge (particularly within the study of Christian spirituality) the peculiar tension between place and placelessness that characterizes a religion committed simultaneously to the incarnation and to a God who is radically Other? These form the focus of the next three chapters. My concern in this first one is to explore the ineffable character of any place perceived to be holy.

D. H. Lawrence was deeply moved by his experience of the desert and mountain terrain near Taos, New Mexico, when he first arrived there in 1922. He spoke of this New World landscape as offering him his first "permanent feeling of religion." "It is curious," he admitted, "that it should be in America, of all places, that a European should really experience religion." Yet, as he insisted, "the moment I saw the brilliant, proud morning shine high up over the deserts of Santa Fe, something stood still in my soul, and I started to attend."[2]

What is it about the expansiveness of American space that has so often captured the European mind and the imagination of others as well? A religious sensitivity to place is an enduringly significant dimension in the mythos of American life, yet it remains extremely difficult to define. How do we understand the sacred as somehow "lingering" at a particular site? How do we differentiate (if at all) between the terms "space" and "place," as if these categories of spatial experience were different in the religious impact they exerted? How can we even talk about attachment to sacred places in a culture that has always celebrated freedom of movement, shunning the restraints and ties of a limited domain? And how, for that matter, can we regard spirituality as in any way "place-specific," given the Platonic sympathies with which the Western mind has usually approached all things spiritual?

"Space is the central fact to man born in America," urges poet Charles Olson.[3] Americans have been a people obsessed with space, molded by their continuing quest for a passage to India, their longing to see America as the garden of the world, their expansion across a vast frontier. All these have been extensions through space that functioned even more importantly as extensions of the imagination. In the twentieth century, Americans experienced an increasing scarcity of space, felt especially in large cities and sprawling suburban areas. Simultaneously, they sought an expansion of interior space in the open, clean, functional lines of architects like Louis Sullivan and Frank Lloyd Wright. As inhabitants of the Space Age, their attention was turned to the occupation of outer space, while their fascination with consciousness led to the deeper exploration of inner space. Americans still seek the "wide-open spaces" of a remembered past, replayed in the western motifs of the *Star Wars* trilogies and multiple generations of *Star Trek* expeditions. In every possible way, they commit themselves to the "conquest of space." To orient oneself in relation to spatial categories seems to be characteristically American.

This same preoccupation with the spatial environment equally applies to American religious life.[4] This book has been an effort to suggest the importance of such a dimension in the study of American spirituality. Students of religious experience in American culture have not often enough taken into account the stubbornly recurring theme of ordinary, "placed" existence, as it forms the milieu of the divine-human encounter. Attention to the earthbound context of American spiritual traditions has lagged behind investigations into American spiritual biography and other devotional literature. In this area, researchers in the study of spirituality can profit especially from listening to what cultural geographers and analysts of material culture are saying about the interaction of environment and human perception.[5] The study of religious experience in American culture demands a careful consideration of the places that shape and contain that experience. Yet difficulties inevitably arise in trying to articulate the ways in which perception is molded by the places to which we are drawn.

The sacredness of a place may be highly ephemeral, subjective, and hard to define. A special experience that one has at a place perceived to be sacred usually proves to be unrepeatable. Going back to the site never guarantees one's being able to return to the experience. The place itself doesn't readily retrieve the memories that people have of it. Jack Turner tells a hair-raising story of crashing his small plane in the Maze district of Canyonlands National Park in the wild expanse of southeast Utah. Wandering down into the Maze, he was startled at dusk by a line of dark torsos seen on a wall near the canyon floor. Rigid with fear, his mind at first did not compute the meaning of these strange figures. It took a moment for him to recognize them as "just pictures," paintings left by an ancient people in the middle of nowhere. Yet he says he will never forget the initial terror and awe of his experience there. I know something of what he must have felt, having myself approached those same figures by moonlight in the middle of an April night.

Two months later Turner went back with friends to the same site, expecting to recover the mystery he had first found there. Yet it wasn't the same.

> The pictographs were still wonderful, but now they were just things we were visiting. I had become a tourist to my own experience. I tried unsuccessfully to recapture the magic of those first moments. I took notes, but they exceeded my power of description. I kept photographing. . . . But what I sought could not be captured with photography or language. Indeed, the more we talked, described, and photographed, the more common they seemed. Everyone was appreciative, impressed, but the unmediated, the raw, and the unique was history.[6]

Our attachment to any place arises from what we experienced there and, subsequently, from what we retain of it in our memories. The power of memory may be even more important than the continuing physical reality of the site itself. "Is it possible," asks landscape architect Robert Riley, "that the greater power of place lies not in inhabiting it but in remembering it?" He thinks, for example, of Marcel Proust's attentiveness to the evocative power of small, almost stray stimuli—like the smell of madeleines and tea—"to unlock the whole, great, internal complex of landscape remembered and landscape experienced."[7] Given the ephemeral character of our experience of place, what we make of a site in the body's memory of its particulars and the mind's construction of its meaning is often a tangled skein. Access to what we encountered there is difficult. It shares the ultimate impenetrability of all spiritual experience.

The American Penchant for Mobility and Placelessness

One obvious problem in articulating a sense of sacred space in the United States has been the penchant of American culture for mobility and placelessness. Can it actually be argued that the same passion for place, discerned in so many traditional cultures, is also to be found in American consciousness, known as the people of the United States are for their relentless transience, their perennial "Song of the Open Road"? "I am glad I shall never be young without wild country to be young in," exclaimed Aldo Leopold in his *Sand County Almanac*. "Of what avail are forty freedoms without a blank spot on the map?"[8]

Americans are fascinated by *space*, but their attachment to particular *places* may often be negligible. For people in the United States, "to stay in one place for life is usually interpreted as being unambitious, unadventurous—a negation of American values."[9] Geographer Wilbur Zelinsky identifies an almost deliberate placelessness as intrinsic to the American mind. "The love of change and of all forms of mobility, an innate restlessness, is one of the prime determinants of the structure of American national character."[10] Or as Gertrude Stein put it, "In the United States there is more space where nobody is than where anybody is. This is what makes America what it is."[11]

American people, throughout the modern period, have been ambivalent in their attachment to place. Richard Rubenstein observes that the national experience of people in the United States has generally been nomadic in orientation. Americans have felt little awareness of being rooted to place or region, little sense of love for the land. America has no holy places, he argues.[12] People have been too much in transit to attend to the enduring mystery of where they dwelt. The Wendell Berrys in American culture, he would say, have been few and far between.

Similarly, Wayne Fields suggests that Americans have been "more a people of highways than of places," the destination never being quite so important for them as the journey itself. "From the restless Boones and Leatherstockings of the first decades of nationhood through the Jack Kerouacs and Easy Riders of the 1950's and 1960's," an image of the proudly untethered traveler runs throughout our literature and popular culture.[13] North Americans may finally be not unlike the South American Apapokuva, a people known for centuries to have wandered over the terrain of northwestern Brazil and Peru, constantly in search of a Perfect Land.[14] The recurring theme of incessant American movement has been undeniable, whether documented by Frederick Jackson Turner or yesterday's statistics from the Federal Housing Authority.

But it can be argued that, while Americans are continually physically in passage, their quest is always psychically for an Odyssean sense of home. Theirs is an insatiable thirst for place—one never fulfilled but always sought. David Sopher has observed that, a century ago, when (as today) one American in five changed residences within a year, "one of the most widely treasured household icons was a plaque or sampler carrying the words 'Home Sweet Home.'"[15] Americans have never seemed to long so much for home as when they have committed themselves most firmly to leaving.

Edward Everett Hale created a most poignant example of that in Philip Nolan, the fictional army officer that most of us may recall as "The Man Without a Country." The classic short story was written during the Civil War, in 1863, as a call to patriotism. In Hale's historical fiction, the misguided Lieutenant Nolan, court-martialed for backing Aaron Burr, cries out in a fit of frenzy, "Damn the United States! I wish I may never hear of the United States again!" His wish is granted; he is put aboard a ship and never again allowed to see his native land or even to hear a word of it. As he is dying, an old friend comes to visit him in his stateroom. There he finds that Nolan, remorseful after fifty-six years of exile, has made a shrine out of his berth. A picture of Washington is swathed in the Stars and Stripes. A great map of the United States, carefully drawn by hand, shows a geography half a century old. The broken man, driven by his thirst for a sense of place now lost, had sought to create, within the narrow space left to him, an ersatz homeland—a partial and dimly remembered experience of having "dwelt" in a place rich in meaning.[16]

There *is* an American attachment to place, paradoxically nurtured by the very fact of incessant American movement. It isn't accidental, then, that a renewed interest in the study of place has arisen at the very time when American life makes "displaced" living an increasingly common experience. Art historian Vincent Scully observes that "it is only when the gods finally begin to die completely out of the land and when many human beings begin to live lives totally divorced from nature—at the beginning, that is, of the modern age—that landscape painting, picturesque architecture, and landscape description . . . become the obsessive themes of art."[17] People are drawn to nature in direct proportion to their sense of separation from it.

Even more today, as we find ourselves moving beyond the modern age—with its Enlightenment quest for the universal and homogeneous, with its attraction to the utilitarian functionalism of "space"—do we begin to discover a postmodernist fascination with the idiosyncratic eccentricities of "place." Our focus is more on local, unpredictable places characterized by their difference, rather than by their uniformity. If the modern American city became "a blueprint for placelessness, for anonymous, impersonal spaces, massive structures, and automobile throughways," the postmodernist impulse has stirred a renewed interest in specific regional and historical styles.[18] Vernacular sites and ethnic neighborhoods—"people places" known for their folk allusions and distinctive sense of place—have in recent years assumed far more interest in city planning.[19] Many people have bemoaned the loss of places set aside as public commons, the absence of porches, stoops, and vest-pocket parks where folks can readily congregate and chat, where the human community can be realized. On the other hand, this renewed quest for place has also expressed itself in an individualistic and elitist tendency, as others seek escape from the *danger* of public commons, withdrawing to the sanctuary of protected homes and gated communities in "Fortress America."[20] In either case, the allurement of the generalities of space has yielded to the appeal of the particularities of place.

The American Tension between Space and Place

All this raises yet another question as to what extent human beings experience the sacred as a matter of expansiveness (celebrated in the freedom of *space*) or as a matter of safe enclosure (identified in the security of *place*). Both of these spatial categories appear in the stories Americans like to tell of themselves. Yi-Fu Tuan speaks of a tension between spaciousness and containment as a universal dialectic in human experience. "The ideas of 'space' and 'place' require each other for definition. From the security and stability of place we are aware of the openness, freedom, and threat of space."[21] I would propose diagramming the respective poles of this tension in American cultural life in the following way. In each case—for space and place alike—a continuum stretches between a tendency to attract and a tendency to repel, suggesting positive and negative dimensions of each experience.

The vertical axis in the diagram indicates the range of mythic energies exerted by the concept of space in the American experience. It expresses the more neutral, impersonal, and analytical notion of space as *topos*, described in chapter two. At the top of the continuum, one discovers freedom, the celebration of the limitless possibilities of an expanding frontier. Frederick Jackson Turner described this notion in the 1890's when he wrote of the western frontier as an escape valve for the narrow confines of eastern Ameri-

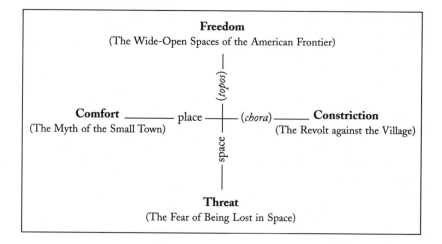

can cities. In his 1960 presidential nomination address, John F. Kennedy similarly spoke of space as a new frontier that would carry the American imagination to the moon and beyond. Spaciousness, freedom of movement, joie de vivre—all these are characteristics of "space" at its best.

Yet at the bottom of the same continuum, one discerns a frightening sense of infinite space without limits, lacking any comforting point of reference, something deeply threatening to the human psyche. The fear of being "lost in space," for example, appeared in the agoraphobic reports of nineteenth-century settlers as they moved across the endless western plains. A few early diary entries even described this god-awful, treeless expanse as a "Great American Desert." After the same pattern, Stanley Kubrick's film, *2001: A Space Odyssey*, stands in a long line of science-fiction movies confronting us with the horrors of being helplessly cast into outer space, subject to a technology beyond our control. Even biblical images of hell as outer darkness or a bottomless pit describe the abode of the damned as a terrifying space without parameters or spatial confines.

The horizontal axis in the diagram represents, by contrast, both the appeal and the anxiety provoked by "place" in the American experience. It embraces the more dynamic and personally engaging conception of place as *chora*. At the left end of this polarity, one finds the distinct comforts and assurances of place proclaimed in the American myth of the small town as a font of virtuous life. From Thornton Wilder's *Our Town* to the Alabama village described in the film *Fried Green Tomatoes*, folklore traditions have celebrated the sense of togetherness and stability, the memory of an enveloping community of support so often associated with village life.

On his travels in search of Middle America, Charles Kuralt was drawn to Arrol's drugstore in the town of Arcola, Illinois. There he noticed 162 coffee cups on the wall behind the counter, inscribed with the names of customers who regularly stopped for a morning chat. He learned that the only way to receive a signed cup of one's own was to have bought a hundred cups of coffee and sipped it there with the other regulars. By the hundredth cup, the newcomer was finally recognized as a part of the community. Such is the staying power of life in a small American town. You know you're in a small town, Kuralt says, if you dial a wrong number and talk for fifteen minutes anyway. You know you're in a small town if you can't walk for exercise because every car that passes you offers you a ride. You know you're in a small town if you missed church on Sunday and the preacher sends you a get-well card.[22]

If "place" is a source of profound comfort, however, it also offers a disconcerting sense of constrictiveness, as the right end of the horizontal axis suggests. For every folktale that celebrates the virtues of small-town American life, there is another story reminding us of its small-mindedness and pressures to conform. Sinclair Lewis, in his novel *Main Street*, wrote of being suffocated by the closeness and predictability of life in Gopher Prairie. "It is dullness made God," he lamented. Hence the myth of the ideal small town struggles continually with a corresponding revolt against the village. The place that bestows the closeness of nurturing life can also smother and confine.

These tensions stretch across the whole fabric of American religious life. Thomas Merton could celebrate the seclusion and closeness of monastic life in his autobiography, *The Seven Storey Mountain*, even as he spoke in his journals of chafing under the confining restrictions placed on him by Abbot James. Thoreau, in his essay, "Walking," described the inevitable pull of the wild and open spaces to the West, even when his own actual encounter with unbounded terrain on Mt. Katahdin left him speechless and terrified. One readily discovers spatially oriented experiences of God at both ends of the two axes formed by space and place. In each case, an encounter with the holy expresses itself in a *via negativa* and *via positiva*. To grasp this wide range of the spatial dimensions of spiritual experience is to understand something of the complexities involved in the study of American spirituality.

The Platonic Rejection of Space
in Western Spirituality

But a sensitivity to place of this sort has often been ignored in the past because of the antimaterialist tendency in much of Western religious thought. A substantive reason for the neglect of attention to the "placed" character of spiritual experience has been the propensity for studies in spirituality to overlook the ordinary, embodied, material context of the faith event. While recent researchers from Carolyn Walker Bynum to Margaret Miles have made significant progress in documenting the importance of the body in the study of spirituality, Harold Turner's call for a systematic attentiveness to questions of place remains largely unanswered.[23] "We need a theology of space itself, as a basic category or dimension of human existence. . . . We have here an extensive lacuna in theological thought that becomes apparent when we consider the considerable attention given to the category of time, and therefore of history, as also to the philosophy of history. We have forgotten that history always has a geography, and that each is essential to the other."[24]

The history of Christian spirituality expresses a persistent tension between the impulse of the incarnation—with its affirmation of flesh and world, its concrete placing of redemption in first-century Judea—and the impulse of an otherworldliness fostered by Gnostic-Manichaean sources. Too often the latter has been emphasized at the expense of the former. Not a few Christians since Marcion have sought escape from the entanglements of matter. In his monumental study of Christian mysticism, Bernard McGinn acknowledges the significant contribution of Platonic thought to the Christian ideal of ascent to a heavenly realm, but he insists that Christians, at their best, have always anchored their ascent in Christ and the community that formed his body.[25] He also urges that alongside the image of ascent in the history of Christian mysticism are equally powerful, earthbound images of desert and sea. Nonetheless, in ascetical theology the traditional pattern of purgative, illuminative, and unitive stages of the spiritual life has inadvertently implied a vertical movement away from the world in the journey toward God. "As a result," argues Friedrich Wulf, "the word *spirituality* still carries with it today the flavour of the enfeebled, the ascetically dematerialized, and the aesthetically esoteric."[26]

An example of the triumph of Platonism in the Western spiritual tradition can be found in a story told of Petrarch, the fourteenth-century Renaissance humanist. Taking a day away from his conscientious work on letters, he decided to climb Mount Ventoux in southern France. The view was beautiful. From its summit of some 6,000 feet he could see the chateau country of Avignon thirty miles distant. At first he took delight in being "free and alone, among the mountains and forests." But as he stood in the thin wonder of the Provence air atop the peak, he felt pressed to open the pages of Augustine's *Confessions*, which he had brought along in his pocket. There he read with chagrin the Bishop of Hippo's accusing words: "Men go to gape at mountain peaks, at the boundless tides of the sea, the broad sweep of rivers, the encircling ocean, and the motions of the stars: And yet they leave themselves unnoticed; they do not marvel at themselves."[27]

"I was abashed," Petrarch later wrote in remorse, "and I closed the book, angry with myself that I should still be admiring earthly things who might long ago have learned . . . that nothing is wonderful but the soul."[28] He hurriedly left the mountain's crest, reflecting on how the world's beauty can divert men and women so easily from their proper concerns.

This is the influential heritage of Platonic inwardness. Possessing a deep reaction to the thingness of things, the placeness of place, it seeks to move immediately to the ultimate, the spiritual, the One. Under such influences, Western spirituality has frequently and wholeheartedly abandoned the "common places" of everyday human experience.

Yet the concrete ordinariness and insistence of place will ever reassert itself in the human psyche. The impulse to discover the holy in the corporeal experience of one's physical environment is a universal phenomenon, rooted in the human manner of being-in-the-world. "The body is the first proselyte the soul makes," wrote Thoreau in his journal.[29] Our spiritual experiences are never wholly unrelated to the "placed" character of our physical existence. We are creatures ultimately discontented with the full-scale Cartesian separation of subject and object. It is the tangible ordinariness of everyday life that we want most to be informed by the holy. We recognize, therefore, the simplest and most common place often to be that most laden with power. "The founders of mysteries know well," writes Werner Jaeger, "that the deepest secrets are found only in things that are seemingly obvious."[30] The plain givenness of our occupation of space is the inescapable context of our experiencing the sacred.

In the journey beyond the age of modernity, human beings increasingly express a vague longing for God's presence in the world. Their quest is for an authentic sense of place and the experience of dwelling meaningfully in a fragmented universe. Contemporary men and women, no less than their forebears, still hunger for the power of myth and place. In the shadow of Devil's Tower in eastern Wyoming, on the Staten Island Ferry looking back toward Lower Manhattan, along the main streets of small towns throughout the Midwest, even in the ceremonial center of suburban shopping malls—the quest goes on for a centered place, a place of empowerment and community where, even today, one might discern in ordinary landscapes the "camouflage of the sacred."[31] "From the dawn of man's imagination," writes Eudora Welty, "place has enshrined the Spirit."[32] In human longing, the phenomenon continues.

The problem, however, is that the path that goes back to the burning bush has been lost. Only frustration arises from our trying to return to a magical, imagined past where the landscape once pulsed with energy. Going back to a premodern age is impossible. If there is hope for a genuine rediscovery of the spirit, it will not be found in looking back to an innocence once lost, a simplistic return to the paradise of Eden. It will demand a reaching back into the spiritual practices and critical insights gathered by the whole of the Western (and Eastern) spiritual tradition. It will require a metanoia, a turning away from efforts to manage the mystery of God by means of abstract Enlightenment reasoning or by an accumulation of individual spiritual techniques. It will even necessitate an attentiveness to the questions of power, gender, and ethnicity that cultural studies have posed, requiring us to test our motives and listen carefully to voices long silenced in the past. Only then may it be possible to encounter, by grace, a second naivete—a renewed sense of wonder glimpsed within the myriad landscapes of the holy.

Nikos Kazantzakis told the story of a monk who had desired all of his life to make a pilgrimage to the Holy Sepulcher—to walk three times around it, to kneel, and to return home a new person.[33] Through the years he had saved what money he could, begging in the villages nearby, and finally, near the end of his life, had set aside enough to begin his trip. He opened the gates of the monastery, took his staff in hand, and with great anticipation set out on his way to Jerusalem.

But no sooner had he left the cloister than he encountered a man in rags, sad and bent to the ground, picking herbs. "Where are you going, Father?" the man asked.

"To the Holy Sepulcher, Brother. By God's grace, I shall walk three times around it, kneel, and return home a different man."

"How much money do you have, Father?" inquired the man.

"Thirty pounds," the monk answered.

"Give me the thirty pounds," said the beggar. "I have a wife and hungry children. Give me the money, walk three times around me, then kneel and go back into your monastery." The monk thought for a moment, scratching the ground with his staff, then took the thirty pounds from his sack and gave the whole of it to the poor man. Then he walked three times around him, knelt, and went back through the gates of his monastery. He returned home a new person, of course, having recognized that the beggar was Christ himself—not far away at the Holy Sepulcher but right outside his monastery door, in a place he might never have thought sacred.

Pilgrimage, more often than not, is a very elusive enterprise. As Emerson wrote in his essay on self-reliance, "Traveling is a fool's paradise. We owe to our first journeys the discovery that place is nothing."[34] In a sense, Emerson is right. The sacred place never guarantees a thing. Going to Jerusalem does not automatically grant the pilgrim wisdom or zeal. "The real voyage of discovery consists not in seeking new landscapes," wrote Marcel Proust, "but in having new eyes."

And yet the mystery of being given new eyes (in this case, being able to glimpse the holy in the beggar outside one's door) is inescapably connected to the reality of the place to which one is drawn. The monk's encounter would have been impossible apart from Jerusalem as a demonstrable physical site *and* his resolute intention of going there. Through the years the man's longing had been stirred by the detailed accounts he had heard from other pilgrims reporting on their trips to the Holy Land. The place, as a result, had burned its way into his heart. Only because of his envisioning the holy place *there* in all of its particulars, at that distant point, therefore, could he discover it *here*, in the equally vivid ordinariness of home.

St. Columba of Iona, in the Celtic tradition, spoke of three kinds of authentic pilgrims: those who were able to plan and sustain an actual pilgrimage, those who had intended to do so but were prevented by injury or death, and those whose situation never allowed them to leave home but whose longing for the place brought them to it as surely as those who had made the trip.[35] We are told that in fifteenth-century Europe, spiritual handbooks were written to instruct armchair pilgrims on how to pass through all the stages of pilgrimage without ever having to leave home.[36] Oddly enough, it seems, the experience of place is simultaneously distant from and proximal to the place itself. We invariably come to "know" a place as sacred on the basis of multiple levels of perception, intricately intertwined.

All this underscores the intimate, even sacramental, relationship of imagination and place in human experience. Place operates powerfully in the imagination because of the concrete specificity, the "otherness" that it also bears. Jerusalem, for example, is a sacred place, not only because of the particular mythic meanings attached to it (as "a city whose builder and maker is God"), but also because of the geophysical appeal it exerts as a spring-fed mountain fortress in a desert terrain, as well as its long history of conflict, from ancient Babylonians and Jews to Latin Crusaders and Ottoman Turks. Place operates, as we have seen, in multiple ways—as a construct of the imagination reaching for the sublime, as a phenomenological reality exerting its own array of intersubjective influences and affordances, and as a dense cultural fact participating in a variety of competing claims and interpretations. We have not understood the place until we have taken into account each of these concerns.

John Kirtland Wright, a celebrated American geographer of an earlier generation, spoke of the importance of stretching the mind as widely as possible in pursuing an understanding of the mysteries of place: "What distinguishes the true geographer from the true chemist or the true dentist would seem to be the possession of an imagination peculiarly responsive to the stimulus of *terrae incognitae*, both in the literal sense and more especially in the figurative sense of all that lies hidden beyond the frontiers of geographical knowledge."[37]

If this is true of geographers, it applies just as well to theologians. To grasp something of the ephemeral character of place is to risk a never-ending range of questions about the nature of human experience and its relation to the divine. Bridging the chasm between a people's encounter with God and the concrete topography in which that occurs demands the most imaginative and disciplined insight. The theologian, ultimately, must be a geographer as well as archivist and celebrant of the spirit.

9

Edwards and the Spider as Symbol: Reflections on Spirituality as an Academic Discipline

People who live within walking distance today of the post office in the village of East Windsor, Connecticut, call it Taylor Brook. Overgrown with weeds and thorn bushes, it's a large gully with a little water flowing through it, located about two hundred yards south of the old homestead where Jonathan Edwards grew up. Half a mile to the west, the Connecticut River runs slowly toward Old Saybrook and the sea. In the first decade or two of the eighteenth century, young Jonathan liked to build huts along this brook, setting aside places for studying spiders and praying, two of the things he seemed to enjoy most. In various ways the spider became, for Edwards, an "image of divine things," a symbol drawn from everyday life that could summarize important themes in his spirituality.

A place is often declared sacred or a spirituality gradually takes shape because of the symbol-making process by which humans make sense of the world around them. This essay is an effort to explore that process, reflecting on how the study of spirituality as an academic discipline is necessarily interdisciplinary in its attentiveness to the lived experience of theological insight within a selected cultural context.[1] I confess, like Edwards, my own fascination with the joint-legged creatures of the class Arachnida, equipped as they are with silk glands and multiple spinnerets, poison ducts and a sucking stomach for storing the liquefied tissue they draw from their prey.

Several years ago I had a student leave class one day in an ecstatic state. (Would that this happened more often!) In an undergraduate class on nature and theology, we had just participated in a micro-hike. Everyone had spent the last forty-five minutes on the grass outside the classroom building, paying attention to the two-

229

foot-diameter circle formed by a string attached to a tent stake. Thinking the exercise ridiculous, this student had put his tent stake in the middle of a patch of dead grass and had decided to go to sleep. But just as he was dozing off, he noticed a spider climbing onto the top of the iron stake. The spider looked around from that vantage point, then shot out from its rear end a length of web and pulled it back in.

The student had never seen this before and was intrigued. He watched then as the spider shot a length of web over to his hand and began to walk across it toward him, while he lay there perfectly still. Reaching his hand, the spider looked around once again and spun out another line, this time to the boy's forehead, walking up it toward him. By now the class was nearly over, and the student couldn't wait to tell somebody about what he had just experienced. After carefully disconnecting the spider and its web from himself, he ran up to me, exuberant over the fact that, for the first time in his life, he had watched a spider spin its web—*and* he had been still enough for it to spin its web on *him!*

Caught up in the spider's performance of a quiet, methodical, deliberate consciousness, the student was able to see mirrored his own inchoate desire for quiet and deliberate action in his life. The spider as symbol invited a corresponding performance on his part, a mimetic practice allowing him entry into what almost approximated an experience of "theater." He could briefly imagine living in the subjunctive mode, as if the world of his imagination were now one in which he could actively participate. This performative function of a symbol is what makes it particularly important in the task, not only of living out, but also of understanding and analyzing a given spirituality.[2]

The symbol of the spider, especially as found in the work of Jonathan Edwards, offers a way of reflecting on the symbol-making and symbol-interpreting process that is central to the study of spirituality (or "lived religion") as an academic discipline. The metaphor of the spider offers a fine image of the web-spinning, interdisciplinary character of spirituality, as it connects various historical, anthropological, psychological, and myth-and-symbol concerns in exploring the human search for self-transcendence.[3] It also exemplifies how a particular metaphor, especially one drawn from nature, is able to carry over (*meta-phora*) abstract theological ideas into concrete, lived experience.[4]

Researchers concerned with the function of symbol in theological discourse, from Tillich to Ricoeur and Tracy, argue that symbols are the quintessential language of theology: They readily invite participation.[5] Ricoeur says it is the "double intentionality" of a symbol, conveying a literal, obvious meaning on one level and a deeper, analogical meaning on another, that makes it most effective. The symbol embodies what it also conceals, opening the imagination to multiple layers of meaning. As Maura Campbell says, "a symbol is not merely a concept-bearer, but an experience-bearer."[6]

Nature symbols in particular seem to be the stock in trade of writers throughout the history of Christian spirituality—from Gregory of Nyssa's emphasis on Moses and the mountain of unknowing to Teresa of Avila's insistence that nothing surpasses water imagery in describing the spiritual life. Bernard McGinn reflects on the "ocean" and "desert" as recurring symbols of mystical absorption, while Andrew Louth uses the image of "wilderness" to discuss a variety of spiritual writers in the Christian tradition. From the hexameral literature in the early church to St. Bonaventure's *Tree of Life*, from medieval bestiaries to Puritan typologists such as Milton and Bunyan, Christian spirituality lives and breathes through symbols drawn from nature.[7]

The spider is a particular symbol that recurs repeatedly in this history, from Augustine's *Enarrationes* on the Psalms to Horace Bushnell's essay on spiders and pests in his *Moral Uses of Dark Things* (1868).[8] The number of theologians and clergy who have played a part in the history of arachnological research is remarkable. They include the Rev. Dr. Thomas Muffet (father of "Little Miss Muffet") in sixteenth-century England, Jonathan Edwards in colonial Massachusetts, Anglican priest Octavius Pickard-Cambridge (one of the fathers of British arachnology), and Princeton-trained theologian Henry McCook, who wrote the definitive nineteenth-century text, *American Spiders*.[9]

Throughout the history of this curious preoccupation with eight-legged arachnids is an awareness that the spider serves as a highly multivalent symbol, admired *and* loathed at the same time. Augustine praised the spider as an exemplar of quiet contemplation, yet also observed that its moral weakness (lying in wait for insects) justifies its expulsion from Paradise.[10] We praise the industry of spiders, the beauty and pattern of their weaving. But we also are repulsed by their venom, their seemingly nefarious ways of trapping their victims.

In mythology, the spider is often very wise, sensitive, and skillful, like Charlotte in E. B. White's children's book *Charlotte's Web*. There is the honored Spider Woman of the Navajo, teaching her people the art of weaving and connecting each of them to her by an invisible thread. But in the classical tales of Ovid, the spider is also Arachne, punished by the goddess Minerva for her stubborn pride. The spider is Anansi the Trickster and the cunning web-spinner of Mary Howitt's poem who invites the fly into her parlor; she is the enemy-mother in Freudian symbolism who would take us back into the womb, binding us tightly to the impotence of infancy.[11] All these images of delight and horror, creativity and seductiveness, Rudolf Otto's *mysterium tremendum* and *fascinans*, are contained in this one symbol of the spider.

Jonathan Edwards's writings about spiders are a spiritual case study in the transformation of thought into action through the symbol-making process and in the ways in which doctrine and life are joined in a web of mutual interconnectedness. In Edwards's case, his eighteenth-century Reformed theology of a Sovereign God found metaphorical expression in the delight (and risk) that a spider takes in ballooning out on a filament of web borne by warm air currents on a fall day.[12]

The symbol of the spider appears most prominently in two different sections of the Edwards corpus.[13] One is a collection of Spider Papers, probably penned in 1720 (when he was sixteen years old) and written with unfulfilled hopes of being published in England. They reported on his meticulous observations of "flying spiders," including hand-drawn illustrations of how the spider floats on the air, seemingly buoyed up by the lightness of its web. He goes on to draw from these observable facts a powerful symbol of his Calvinist theology, showing how it exemplifies "the exuberant goodness of the Creator, who hath not only provided for all the necessities, but also for the pleasure and recreation of all sorts of creatures, even the insects."[14] Here Edwards invites his reader (Judge Paul Dudley of the Royal Society) to imagine himself in the place of the spider, possessed of that capacity for delight, that interior sense or "taste" for Being that every good Calvinist draws from his contemplation of the world as a *theatrum gloriae Dei.*[15]

Edwards's second use of the spider as symbol is found, of course, in his infamous sermon of 1741, "Sinners in the Hands of an Angry God."[16] Through this one sermon, the image of the spider has become virtually a defining metaphor in the history of American spirituality, a shorthand form for characterizing the intensity and grimness of the whole revivalist tradition. Once again, Edwards employs the spider as symbol to encapsulate certain strands of Calvinist theology and motivate his listeners to decisive action. Here the spider is at great risk, held in the fingertips of a Sovereign God over raging flames. The readers or listeners are encouraged to imagine themselves in the place of the spider, fully aware of that towering uncertainty, the horrible threat of nonbeing that forms the human dilemma of all who have failed to exercise that delight which God had meant for their highest existence.

In both the earlier and later uses of this spider image, the observer is encouraged to enter as participant into the spider's performance, imagining himself or herself in its place, as it symbolically mirrors the observer's *own* performance of delight and horror, respectively. In the first case, the multifaceted symbol suggests, for the subsequent reader of the Spider Letter, an interior shift from the mere intellectual "concept" of conversion to an intimate sharing in that aesthetic sense of delight that Edwards would later define as the clearest mark of a conversion experience. In the second case of the "Sinners" sermon of 1741, the listener is drawn into a vicarious identification with the spider dangling over the flames, evoking the interior transmutation of an abstract doctrine of hell into a deep Kierkegaardian sense of the human condition at risk before God, without refuge, forced at last to decide.[17]

The examination of Edwards's spirituality, in these two instances, becomes a study of human participation in symbols, asking how theological constructs are creatively turned into motivating energies. Spirituality as an academic discipline may have much to learn from the history of myth and symbol analysis in American Studies, as it explores the dominant narratives and images by which a given community repeatedly structures meaning for its common life.[18] Indeed, there may be important parallels between American Studies and spirituality as two still relatively young disciplines searching for adequate methodologies in doing research. Both are "field-encompassing fields," viewed with some suspicion by scholars in traditional disciplines because of their interdisciplinarity.

American Studies began in the 1950's and 1960's as a body of scholarship concerned with interpreting the principal symbols that capture the energy of American cultural experience. Henry Nash Smith, Leo Marx, and Alan Trachtenberg analyzed symbols of the garden, the frontier, even Brooklyn Bridge, for example, showing their role in the construction of American identity.[19] This myth-and-symbol school in American Studies was initially very influential, but it had serious limits, too. It tended toward sweeping generalizations based on a few elite literary texts. It tended to celebrate free-floating ideas without rooting them enough in specific social and

historical contexts. It was prone to emphasizing American excep-
tionalism and lacked the discipline of a critical theory of culture.[20]
As a result, American Studies gradually turned its attention to social
anthropology and cultural studies as a corrective to earlier patterns
of research.

Similar criticisms might be made of Christian spirituality as a
nascent academic discipline. It has attended primarily to mainstream
voices in the history of the tradition (largely ignoring what R. Laur-
ence Moore describes as the "outsiders"). Its tendency has been to
focus on disembodied ideas, apart from the complexity and ambiguity of their cultural settings. It has granted privileged status to
Christianity in a way that both minimizes the importance of comparative studies and fails to deal critically enough with Christian
practice itself. If the field expects to be taken seriously as an academic
discipline, these are concerns that it should continue to address.

One might argue, to this end, that myth and symbol studies can
be useful in examining the way a particular spirituality moves from
symbolic meaning to communal practice. But the critical perspective of cultural studies will also be necessary in observing how this
simultaneously emerges as a social construction of reality. It is important to ask about the *interiority* of the symbol, as it engages the
participation of those shaped by the myth, and *also* how this symbolic process of identification is played out in particular cultural
settings with their own privileged centers, circulations of power, and
ways of constructing human subjectivity. Highly prominent symbols
and "master narratives" not only give shape to a community's spirituality. They also channel and solidify its power, imposing silences
and constraints on those excluded from the symbolic order.[21]

In looking at Edwards's use of the spider in his 1741 sermon, for
example, one must ask not only how the symbol is employed to
invite participation in a Calvinist theology of the human dilemma
but also how various social and political tensions are subtly being
addressed at the same time. Edwards may have been doing some
weaving himself, in other words, trying to catch a variety of flies in
his mid-eighteenth-century, western Massachusetts web. Silent but
nonetheless present in this text are dissident church members with
whom Edwards had been in conflict since the completion of a new
church building three years earlier. A major contention over seating
in the new sanctuary had arisen in Northampton in 1738. Contrary
to Edwards's wishes, the new seating pattern ranked members of
the congregation according to wealth, no doubt giving preference to
those who had contributed most to the new building. As a result,

Edwards began preaching against "contention and a party spirit," attacking those "seated high in a place that is looked upon hungrily by those that sit round about."[22]

Also present but silent in this text are the parents of young people who were unhappy over the minister's practice of publicly addressing their children's courtship behavior. Edwards had recently been critical of the practice of bundling. (His eventual dismissal from the Northampton Church would occur a decade later in connection with another case of sexual impropriety concerning young people secretly reading a midwife's manual.) Moreover, even beyond the walls of the church, unseen but pervasive, are Quabaug and Narragansett Indians threatening from the northwest, as hinted at by Edwards's reference in his text to "the bow of God's wrath [being] bent, the arrow made ready on the string." A major fortification of the town in response to Indian attack had been made a generation earlier, and the nearby village of Southampton would have to be abandoned over the winter of 1748 because of Indian raids.[23] Given the highly precarious position of the spider in this sermon, therefore, one has to ask whom the spider represents. Which voices are being empowered to speak and which ones are being silenced by the use of the same symbol?

Similar questions could also be asked of Edwards's earlier Spider Papers. The October 31, 1723, date that he gave to the finished text of his letter, only recently discovered in the manuscript collection of the New York Historical Society, indicates that the work was not written (as earlier thought) when Edwards was twelve years old but after he had completed both bachelor's and master's degrees at Harvard. This would mean that the young theologian (and amateur naturalist) was writing about the "delight" he observed in flying spiders at about the same time that he had met the attractive Sarah Pierpont and was beginning to notice the "exceeding sweet delight" that she took in the glories of God while "walking in the fields and groves" around New Haven.[24]

All these are questions that careful historical and cultural analysis demands of us. We can never assume, in some naively pious way, that the operation of symbols within a spirituality is simply a reflection of theological categories. They are inextricably bound up with specific social and historical contexts, even with questions of contest and exchanges of power, sexuality and the body. Spirituality as an academic discipline, therefore, has to combine an imaginative sensitivity to the symbol-making process along with the hard-nosed task of cultural criticism. It has to remember the caution of Roland

Barthes that myth and symbol often serve to legitimize as universal what may be only local, to sanction as transcendent or natural what is actually socially determined, to proclaim as "value neutral" what is heavily laden with political interest.[25] Spiritualities are unquestionably involved in masking various forms of hegemony and ideology, their disguised agendas often hidden under the surface of theological description.

An excellent example of the balanced work for which I argue here can be found in Rowan Williams's study of the spirituality of Teresa of Avila.[26] In analyzing her experience of the spiritual life, he attends naturally to questions of power that arise from her Jewish background and the investigations of the Inquisition. He considers questions of sexuality and the body, the construction of subjectivity within the cultural milieu of sixteenth-century Spain, the manner in which voices are heard and suppressed, and the polysemous way by which meanings are exchanged from various points of view—all without any explicit reference to the methodological paraphernalia of cultural studies as such. He asks these questions intuitively, as they arise from the subject he studies.

Scholars attentive to these questions in the study of American spirituality, for example, include Robert Orsi, Ann Taves, Ann Braude, Leigh Eric Schmidt, Jenny Franchot, and others. They anchor their investigation of Catholic devotionalism or nineteenth-century Spiritualism or Easter piety in a disciplined cultural analysis. That *has* to be done, and it *can* be done without falling into a cultural reductionism that excludes theological questions as irrelevant. Bob Orsi could not write about the construction of women's identity in connection with the Shrine of St. Jude in Chicago, for instance, without also exploring the Catholic American theology of suffering. The two are inseparable. Cultural studies need not push God out of the analysis. It can provide instead an important way of weaving (or, if one prefers, "incarnating") spiritual experience into the warp and woof of culture.

In focusing, then, on the symbol-making character of a given spirituality—asking how that operates in facilitating the transition from theology to cultural expression—this essay argues that we have to do both. We must attend to the interior operations of the symbolic life *and* to the larger cultural web by which that is always and inevitably formed and reformed.

Spirituality as an academic discipline is the study of an intentional community's mode of engagement with life, the way it makes the transition from "knowing" to "living" in its appropriation of the truth it practices. This necessarily includes the symbols that the community uses to embody its deepest convictions, as well as the ritual performances that express that symbolic reality in mimetic action. Understanding the symbol-making process requires the most disciplined skills of observation and analysis, the careful work of poet and critic alike.

A. R. Ammons, the American poet, touches the heart of the matter when he writes of the mysterious way of a spider with its web. "It is / wonderful / how things work," he says.

> I will tell you
> about it
> because
> it is interesting
> and because whatever *is*
> moves in weeds
> and stars and spider webs
> and [if] known . . . is loved.[27]

That, finally, is the goal of Christian spirituality (if not other spiritualities as well)—to make the transition from knowing to loving, from conceptualization to engagement. The goal of spirituality as an academic discipline is to analyze the process by which all this occurs, bringing to the task as much imaginative reflection *and* critical insight as possible.

10 | The Imagined Landscape: A Tension between Place and Placelessness in Christian Spirituality

In the history of Christian thought, landscape operates as a function of the imagination. The call to a life of abandonment to God is often experienced as the call of a particular place evoking that spirit of abandonment. Athanasius, in his *Life of Antony*, tells how the first of the desert fathers sought out a high and remote hill in the upper Thebaid of Egypt. It was a site marked by clear, sweet water, with a few untended date palms and wide plains beyond. We are told that "Antony, as if stirred by God, fell in love with the place."[1] St. Basil the Great described the chosen location of his own meditation as "a lofty mountain overshadowed with a deep wood, irrigated on the north by cold and transparent streams." "My highest eulogy of the spot," he exclaimed, "is that . . . it bears for me the sweetest of all fruits, tranquillity."[2]

Bernard of Clairvaux spoke enthusiastically of the site chosen for his Cistercian monastery in the Aube Valley of northeastern France, "That spot has much charm, it greatly soothes weary minds, relieves anxieties and cares, helps souls who seek the Lord greatly to devotion, and recalls to them the thought of the heavenly sweetness to which they aspire."[3] William of Malmesbury could even exult in the desolate land cultivated by the monks of Thorney, located "in the middle of wild swampland." It impressed him as a veritable "image of paradise."[4] In each case, the experience of God was connected to an imagined experience of place. The spiritually conceived landscape is one that metaphorically represents and concretizes the experience of faith generated there.

Consciously or unconsciously, these sites of vivid encounter with God were also, of course, a particular reflection of cultural taste. None of them, despite their seemingly untouched beauty,

238

their remoteness and inaccessibility, offered the pure touch of un-
sullied nature that we sometimes imagine to be the surest channel
of contact with the divine. Antony, Basil, Bernard, and William had
each brought with them into the wilderness, along with their tools,
a sackload of cultural interpretations. Simon Schama urges in *Landscape and Memory* that "landscapes are culture before they are nature; constructs of the imagination projected onto wood and water
and rock."[5] We live in a natural world framed by the stories we tell,
though we prefer to think of it as a *tabula rasa*. We walk continually
through a terrain manufactured by the human imagination, dwelling
as much in our interpretation of the place as in the place itself.

I write these words, for example, on a high outcropping of rock
overlooking the village of Ojo Caliente in northern New Mexico. It
is an ancient healing site, described by Spanish explorer Cabeza de
Vaca as a place sacred to the local inhabitants when he passed
through in the 1530's. He named it "Hot Eye" because of the
bubbling waters of the mineral springs that fascinated him. I have
come here myself for two days of rest and prayer, looking out onto a
scene that I frame according to my own particular needs. Weary of a
long and demanding semester, I picture before me a landscape as
free and empty—as soothing and tranquil—as any that Bernard or
Basil might have sought. I have positioned myself on a rock, with a
juniper tree to the right and a pair of piñon pines to the left, gazing
toward the beautiful snow-capped mountains of the Sangre de Cristo
range in the distance.

Consciously *excluded* from my view are the water tank and supply sheds behind the old hotel down below. I ignore the trucks full
of oil and lumber, slipping into lower gear as they head up Highway
285 toward Taos. I forget that I am hiking on Bureau of Land
Management land and that the mountains toward which I am gazing
are lined with ski trails at the Sipapu Ski Area near Tres Ritos. On
my way back to Santa Fe tomorrow, I'll pass by Los Alamos, where
the Manhattan Project was begun in 1942, and will sleep tomorrow
night at the state capital, where the legislature yesterday voted
overwhelmingly to approve the carrying of concealed weapons. This
place, therefore, necessarily speaks to me with an unavoidable ca-
cophony of voices. Despite all this (I marvel at the mystery), it still
is able to heal. Yet try as I might, I have no contact here with an
idealized experience of nature that is not already culturally constructed.

On the other hand, neither can I imagine myself as "standing over" the place, constructing it (and framing its meaning) wholly apart from the simultaneous process of its "constructing" me. Michael Taussig speaks of the "contact sensuosity" by which a place transfers its qualities of embodied wildness onto human beings by means of mimetic ties.[6] My contact with the place involves a process of imitation, an awareness of the intersubjective connections that I share with the whole sensuous lifeworld of which I am a part in this instance. I speak as an echo of its voices.

The composition of a place, therefore, is far more complicated than we tend to think. It doesn't come as a preexistent given. It "happens" as a dynamic exchange: my culturally formed imagination interacting with the embodied contact that I experience in (and with) the place. While in this chapter I primarily emphasize the importance of cultural construction, I do not want to suggest that the human social world is the *only* source of meaning and value in defining the significance of place. That's why, in chapter two, I stressed the importance of David Abram's application of phenomenology to ecological thinking. Yet my principal contention here still stands: We have no entrée to a world that exists apart from what we make of it or how we participate within it.

Michael Pollan, an editor at *Harper's Magazine,* says that the only world to which we have access anymore is one that he calls "second nature."[7] Any notion of a "first nature," untouched by human influence, persists only in the imagination. He argues from his experience as a Connecticut gardener, having observed the persistent struggle of cultural forces playing across the fields of the old farm that he purchased a few years ago near the town of Cornwall. In perpetual conflict with insects and rodents, the unpredictability of the weather, and the natural history of the land itself, he realizes his naivete in ever thinking that he might have lived there communing with nature on a purist level apart from the inescapable intrusions of culture. Even smog in Yosemite Valley, for that matter, is not a recent phenomenon. Its earliest Ahwahneechee inhabitants regularly practiced periodical burnings in order to maintain its meadows. Our relationship to nature has always been a product of cultural intervention. We have no retreat to an idealized communion with the natural world. The doors to Eden have closed.

What this means is that identifying our fabricated images (and illusions) of the places we occupy is as important as identifying the places themselves. The symbolic meanings (the stories) we attach to them are the secrets that tell us most about who we are. There we encounter the deepest identities, the unacknowledged values, the blind ideologies, even the destructive idolatries of our daily experience. But consciously recognizing the images we project onto the places around us, much less *letting go* of them, is no easy task. That's why the Christian tradition has always maintained a tension between place and placelessness, between the importance of attaching meaning (and remembrance) to particular locales and the danger of misusing the places to which we lay claim. To imagine our possession of place as an end in itself, as a guarantee of our possession of truth, is ever a temptation. The need to abandon false images and to question our cultural constructions of place emerges, therefore, as a recurring motif in the history of Christian thought—today no less than in the past. The relinquishment of twisted cultural perceptions about how places can and cannot be used, for instance, is essential to the resolution of the current ecological crisis. Reconsidering our images of place—how we perceive ancient forests and the habitats of endangered species, how we respond to sites of urban and rural poverty around the world—may determine who we will be and what will survive.

Christian spirituality has traditionally offered two ways of dealing with the religious imagination: celebrating its power, on the one hand, and criticizing its limits, on the other. These two approaches are known respectively as the kataphatic and apophatic traditions. The one multiplies images with abandon, delighting in their endless heterogeneity. The other is radically critical of all images, warning of their inability ever to contain the mystery of the holy. If the kataphatic tradition rejoices in discerning the presence of God in the singularity and "thisness" of various places, the apophatic tradition exercises prophetic judgment in demanding the placeless and imageless character of a transcendent God. Apophatic criticism also emphasizes the inevitable human propensity toward self-delusion. Being able, therefore, to *affirm* images of place and to know how to *judge* them are both essential skills in living a spiritual life and in practicing the academic discipline of spirituality.

The concern of this chapter, therefore, is twofold. It underscores the importance of the imagination in constructing every place that we enter and the equal importance of critical insight in deconstructing every imagined place. Both of these, ultimately, are spiritual exercises, practiced in the kataphatic and apophatic traditions, respectively. Building on the distinction between place and placelessness in Christian spirituality, the chapter argues first for the imaginative significance of space and landscape in the spiritual life, setting up the tension that these mutually correcting spiritualities try to resolve. In the process, it makes suggestions for a constructive theology of place. Secondly, the chapter emphasizes the apophatic discrimination of the image-making process, critically evaluating the limits of the imagination itself, while stressing the perennial need to reflect on our manifold constructions of the meaning of place.

The Christian Imagination and a Theology of Place

As this book has maintained, one readily discerns the prominence of place in the history of the Christian spiritual life. Origen's Alexandria, Thomas Becket's Canterbury, Luther's Wittenberg, Emerson's Concord, Thomas Merton's Gethsemani—each place becomes inescapably a part of the truth discovered there. Religious experience is invariably centripetal in its tendency. The experience of the holy is perceived to occur at a sacred center, an *axis mundi* where heaven and earth, the sacred and the profane, intersect. God is there, "at the still point of the turning world," as T. S. Eliot observed.

Yet religious experience is also subsequently centrifugal in its impulse, as argued earlier in this work. The believer necessarily reaches beyond the sacred place of initial encounter to expect God in every other place as well. Jeremiah cautions the people of Israel against associating God exclusively with the Temple, pointing to the divine presence even in exile in Babylon (Jer. 29:7). Jesus exhorts his followers to move beyond the city of Jerusalem, beyond even Judea and Samaria, to the ends of the earth in their witness to his presence (Acts 1:8). In scripture and the history of spirituality alike, one finds a continuing tension between place and placelessness, between the local and the universal. God is *here*—in this place at Bethlehem, Lourdes, Iona, even Boston and Salt Lake City. But, at the same time, God is *not* here—not limited exclusively to this place, not *only* here.

In his *Magnalia Christi Americana*, Cotton Mather spoke of his native Boston as a site chosen by God some three score and ten years earlier. This "outcast Zion," previously scorned by callous visitors as "Lost-town" because of its sad and mean circumstances, had become by 1702, "*The* Metropolis of the whole English America." Mather knew that Christianity had necessarily reached beyond its Middle Eastern and European margins, extending the power of the Gospel to a bold and new terrain. "The Church of God must no longer be wrapped up in Strabo's cloak; geography must now find work for a Christianography in regions far enough beyond the bounds wherein the Church of God had, through all former ages been circumscribed."[8] His quest for a "Christian geography," reaching to the New England coast and beyond, is emblematic of the perennial (and insatiable) religious thirst for place.

Daniel L. Smith writes of the forced migration of Jewish exiles in 586 B.C.E. Pressed into political detention and disenfranchisement, theirs was the anguish of the landless as they trod the long road toward Babylon.[9] This is a recurring theme in Old Testament theology, this yearning for home, for the land of promise. Yahweh is disclosed, not just anywhere, but at shrines located in Shechem, Hebron, and Beersheba, at the Temple in Jerusalem. Israelite hill farmers discover Yahweh in the tilling of the soil they had been given, in proximity to great oak trees where the stories of holy history are repeated. As the J Source in the Old Testament makes clear, "The religion of the Yahwist's epic is a religion of the earth."[10] The God of Old and New Testaments is one who tabernacles with God's people, always made known in particular locales. When Paul celebrates the "scandal of the Gospel," this is a reality geographically rooted in Jesus, a crucified Jew from Nazareth, of all places. The offense, the particularity of place, becomes intrinsic to the incarnational character of Christian faith.

To sharpen the dialectic, however, biblical theology also insists upon the supralocative character of the divine-human encounter. Yahweh differs from the mountain and fertility gods of the ancient Canaanites, refusing to be bound to any single geographical locale. The "high places" pretending to capture the divine presence must be torn down as idolatrous in the extreme. The prophet Nathan warns David, as he plans to build the Temple, that no one can presume to build a house for God. Yahweh, the one who dwells in thick darkness, will not remain "on call" in Jerusalem, at the behest of the king (II Sam. 7). A theology of transcendence will never be fully comfortable with place. Hence, the tension between place and placelessness remains a fiercely vigorous one, struggling to understand the truth of a great and transcendent God revealed in the particularity of place.

These undeniable spatial dimensions of religious experience call us to the need for a fuller theology of place, especially if we are to understand the role the imagination plays in constructing the places we inhabit and the meanings we attribute to them. Conversion narratives, for example, provide an opportunity for analyzing our perception of the immediate environment in the psychodynamics of change.[11] In the effort to recall and describe a vivid encounter of the holy, one instinctively reaches out to the senses, anchoring the experience in the memory of place. Hence, Paul's conversion is associated with a particular point on the Damascus Road. Constantine tells of a vision seen in the sky over Milvian Bridge. Augustine's life is changed in a garden of the Villa Cassiciacum outside of Milan. John Wesley's heart is "strangely warmed" at a prayer meeting on Aldersgate Street in eighteenth-century London. Bonhoeffer's apprehension of "religionless Christianity" takes shape in Tegel prison. Repeatedly, it is place that lends structure, contextuality, and vividness of memory to the narrative of spiritual experience. Yet, until recently, in biblical and historical studies, questions of time have always taken precedence over questions of place.[12]

A textual analysis of words for "place" in biblical and rabbinical usage can be helpful in recognizing the role that spatial categories play in the theological reflection of early Christians and Jews. It also suggests a starting point for developing a more comprehensive theology of place. In biblical usage, the words for "place" (*maqom* in Hebrew and *topos*, especially *chora*, in Greek) seldom refer to an empty, indifferent location, abstractly conceived. They speak, instead, of a place where events of human and divine significance have occurred—a dwelling place, a place of meeting, a site for the gathering together of being. In Hebrew thinking, therefore, "not to have one's place is to cease to be."[13] Far from being a neutral, inert container of experience, place is an integral aspect of existence.[14]

It is not altogether surprising, therefore, to find in rabbinical Judaism the notion of place as an extension of the divine presence, a way of describing God's immanence in the world without compromising the divine transcendence. This is similar in ways to the personification of *Sophia* in Second Temple Judaism. The word *maqom* becomes a name frequently used for God among the Tannaim.[15] Yahweh is preeminently "Place," that which incorporates and defines, even making room for all other spaces. The Psalmist had spoken of "the Lord as our dwelling place" (Ps. 90:1), but the rabbis come to describe God's "place" as filling (even constituting) the world, in the same way as the divine light (*shekhina*) and the divine word (*memra*). Arguing as to whether God is the dwelling-place of the world, or the world is the dwelling-place of God, they affirm the former, insisting that all places acquire meaning through their participation in *God* as place.[16]

What this line of argument does is to integrate the experience of God into the natural world of placed existence. One can still speak of divine transcendence but without having to dissociate God entirely from the spatial and material dimensions of creation. In this way, the rabbis inherently understood a wisdom much later expressed by Friedrich Nietzsche, when he said, "The more abstract the truth is that you would teach, the more you have to seduce the senses to it."[17] To speak at all of a God who is "Wholly Other" is ultimately to communicate in concrete categories of space and time.

In the search for subsequent efforts in the history of Christian thought to explore the parameters of a theology of place, we can suggest briefly a number of motifs by which the religious imagination is able to "create" places or landscapes that become embodied means of experiencing the divine presence. These categories of immanence function within a larger theology of transcendence to give sacramental value to the world of the ordinary.

1. John Calvin, among others, spoke of the natural world as a *theatrum gloriae Dei*, a theatre full of wonders in which God's glory becomes apparent. God puts on the garments of alpine meadows and thunderclouds reflected in mountain lakes as a way of luring all of creation back to God's love. Every creature, and ecosystem as well, not only participates in the "stage settings" for the great drama of divine revelation but also shares in its praise.[18] The earth, as Hildegard of Bingen affirmed, provides a great green access to the heart of God. This idea finds vivid expression in the medieval depiction of the charted world as the Body of Christ. In the thirteenth-century Ebstorf map, for example, the earth is drawn as a large, circular body, with the head of Jesus at its top (in the east, near paradise) and the feet in the west at the bottom, pointing towards an America still unknown.[19] Christ stands with the Antipodes at his left hand, the joining of Europe and Asia at his right, inviting the reader of the map "to see with his eyes and touch with his hands concerning the Word of Life" (I John 1:1). In such a way, geography becomes a natural corollary of any deep interest in the incarnation.

2. Another theme echoing through the whole of the Christian tradition, from Antony of Egypt to Jonathan Edwards, is the notion of nature as a "second book," offered alongside the first book of scripture as a way of reading the presence of the Holy. The compelling landscapes of creation constitute a volume accessible to all. Even Thomas Browne, a seventeenth-century Puritan, declared that "surely the Heathens knew better how to joyne and read these mysticall letters, than wee Christians, who cast a more careless eye on these common Hieroglyphicks, and disdain to suck Divinity from the flowers of nature."[20] Drawn from references to a double-sided scroll in Ezekiel 2:9 and Revelation 5:1, this metaphor of the

second book has had an enduring influence in the Christian theology of nature. Raymond of Sabunde in the fifteenth century could even go so far as to suggest that the second book is less subject to misinterpretation than the first.

3. A still more central motif, developed in the theology and iconography of the Eastern churches, is the dignity granted to matter in general as a result of the doctrine of the incarnation. In response to those criticizing the veneration of icons in the Eastern tradition, John of Damascus argued, "I do not worship matter. I worship the Creator of matter who became matter for my sake, who willed to take his abode in matter, and who through matter wrought my salvation."[21] Because of the sacramental mystery of Christmas, the material world of places and things assumes new significance. As Teilhard de Chardin proclaimed in his "Hymn to Matter," "I acclaim you as the divine milieu, charged with creative power, . . . as the clay moulded and infused with life by the incarnate Word."[22] All aspects of the material world are seen to shine in the glow of the Cosmic Christ. The created world of place and time shares fully in the redemptive hope of those awaiting the final consecration of matter (Rom. 8:22-23).

4. Developing a Christian theology of place requires reckoning with the impact of Gnostic and Manichaean ideas on the history of Christian thought, as mentioned previously. Their repudiation of the natural world has had more influence than it should, despite their views having been consistently rejected by the church. Irenaeus, the second-century bishop of Lyons, produced a rich theology of creation in his reaction to the Gnostic belief that an evil Demiurge gave form to the material world as we know it. He stressed instead that God's own hands were intimately involved in molding the earth and bringing it to redemption.[23] Augustine took a similar position in his opposition to Manichaean dualism in the fifth century, extolling "the loveliness of the earth and sea and wide airy spaces," in his reaction to those who would deny the beauty of the natural world.[24] Francis of Assisi's exuberant celebration of all creatures appears in bold contrast to the dark rejection of nature found among the Cathari in the thirteenth century. Francis knew, like Aquinas after him, that *a*sensuality is a vice in the Christian order of things.

One begins to suspect that the distinctive contribution of Christianity may lie in its refusal to dematerialize the world of matter. Maurice Leenhardt, a Christian missionary who worked for forty-five years with the Canakas of New Caledonia, asked a convert among the Canakas how he thought the coming of Christianity had changed the thinking of his people over the years. Leenhardt himself suggested that the new element Christianity might have brought was the notion of spirit. But the convert said no. "What Christianity brought was the conception of body. Before Christianity came, the Canakas had no notion of themselves as distinct persons. The new notion enabled them to grasp the notion of space, and thence distance, separation, and personhood."[25]

A deep respect for place, in all of its various aspects, undergirds the wholeness of the Christian revelation. "The greatest sin of the age," wrote Nicholas Berdyaev, "is to make the concrete abstract."[26] The imaginative work of tying spiritual experience to the constructions of place we inhabit is one of our primary ways of securing meaning in our lives.

5. There is even, in the history of Christian thought, a tendency to celebrate the most diminutive and utterly ordinary dimensions of nature as sacramental signs of the divine glory. Meister Eckhart insisted, "If I spent enough time with the tiniest creature—even a caterpillar, I would never have to prepare a sermon. So full of God is every creature."[27] Similarly, Augustine directed the human imagination toward ants and worms in the contemplation of God's glory.[28] The prophet Micah gave blessing to Bethlehem as the source of the Davidic hope, not in spite of but *because* of its being least among all the places of Judah (Micah 5:2). Valuing the dignity-in-specificity of the created world becomes an important witness here to the reality of a God intimately engaged in all God has made.

If one carries this principle to its natural conclusions, it becomes rich in implications for environmental awareness and action. The value of species diversity and the integrity of endangered ecosystems, for example, assume theological significance, as well as economic and political concern, in the light of this truth. If a theology of place necessarily begins with creation and the incarnation, it properly ends with an attention to questions of poverty and eco-justice.[29] Moreover, if we live, inescapably, in our "constructions" of place (as opposed to some idealized and neutral place wholly separate from the imagination), we become—more than ever—morally responsible for how we construct and maintain them.

Placement and Displacement in Kataphatic and Apophatic Traditions

Having argued for the kataphatic importance of "place" in the study of Christian spirituality, we go on, then, to ask how "place-

lessness" counterbalances the tendency to "locate" God too specifically. God as *deus incarnatus* may be accessible to human experience,
yet God as *deus absconditus* is also "free," unbounded by human
efforts to assure the divine presence in any locale. There is an
inescapable tension here between our human need for assurances
(even guarantees) of God's presence and the absolute freedom of
the divine being, in whom place itself coheres. This is where the
tension between kataphatic and apophatic traditions in Christian
spirituality comes into play.[30] They serve both to sanction and to
keep watch over the work of the human imagination in the cultural
construction of place.

Spirituality in the kataphatic tradition makes deliberate use of
metaphor and image in contemplating the divine. It is highly oriented to place and thing. Here the imagination is directed "according to the image" (*kata-phasis*) of the created world and is led to God
by way of spatially conceived analogies. This tradition expresses a
keenly sacramental sensitivity to all the details of the natural world.
Franciscan and Ignatian spiritualities are good examples. By contrast, the spiritual life as practiced in the apophatic tradition turns
the imagination "away from the image" (*apo-phasis*), emptying the
mind of all efforts to comprehend the holy. Seen in the Byzantine
and Dionysian traditions, from the Cappadocian fathers to the author of the *Cloud of Unknowing*, it never denies the value of the
natural world but cautions that the use of human language (grounded
as it is in time and space) is never sufficient to grasp the mystery of
God.[31]

The apophatic tradition, therefore, is very different from Gnostic or Manichaean thought in its emphasis upon placelessness. The
latter rejects the world of matter on principle, whereas the former
offers a prophetic reminder that God, as *deus absconditus*, is never
wholly available to us. There is no place where the presence of the
divine can be guaranteed.

The differences between these two approaches to the operation
of the human imagination are readily apparent in their respective
attitudes toward place, as hinted already. The impulse of kataphatic
spirituality grows out of biblical efforts to anchor the divine presence in particular places and in connection with material things.
Bethel, Shiloh, the shore of the Sea of Galilee, the ark, the tabernacle, the breaking of bread—all of these engage the senses in their
suggestiveness of God's immanence. Prayer takes shape in the movement from the reconstruction of place in the imagination to the

meeting of God in the human heart, through a process of interior pilgrimage.[32]

With a palpable place or thing as a starting point for contemplation, the imagination is led beyond and through the sacramental object to God alone. With no promise that the place or thing will in itself ensure access to the divine being, at this point the mind and body begin their approach to the divine. There is always the danger, of course, of focusing on the exterior place as an end in itself, as if proximity to the place of the holy could substitute for the inner experience of the holy. Simply traveling to Medjugorje in Yugoslavia is, in itself, no assurance of encountering the presence of God.

Royal theologians under Solomon and his successors sought to guarantee the presence of Yahweh at the temple in Jerusalem, associating the throne of the king with the cultic center of divine power. Their effort was to connect the political stability of the kingdom with the life of prayer. But prophets like Jeremiah resisted this presumption that God's ritual presence could be controlled in any way whatever. They demythologized sacred space, attacking the myth of Zion and defending the elusive presence of a God who refuses to be bound to any location (Jer. 7:4).[33] Stephen would do the same thing in his speech before the Sanhedrin, desacralizing the Temple and reminding his listeners that "the Most High does not dwell in houses made with hands (Acts 7:48)."[34]

This is the impulse of apophatic spirituality, with its concern to affirm the limits of God's accessibility to human understanding. Its object is to lead the believer into a process of abandonment, stripping away all images by which God is known. There God is met, not as an object to be understood, but ultimately as a mystery to be loved. This is characterized traditionally as "negative theology." Its encounter with God is dependent upon the negation of the self and all its efforts to manipulate access to the divine being.[35]

An apophatic sensitivity, to the extent that it is drawn to place at all, gravitates toward places of emptiness, threat, loss, and disconnection. The apophatic tradition, in fact, makes frequent use of mountain and desert landscapes in teaching the relinquishment of control that is necessary for approaching God. The experience of Moses going into the desert, ascending Mt. Sinai, and entering a dark cloud of unknowing is a theme repeated by mystical writers from Gregory of Nyssa to John of the Cross.[36] The mountain, like the desert, is a place of abandonment. There one is stripped of egocentric concerns, carried by the fierce landscape itself into an emptiness only God can fill. The retreat to the desert in the history of spirituality is not an accidental choice of landscape. Its desiccated barrenness, its sparsity of images, and its utter indifference to human life has the effect of driving the believer out of self and into the elusive presence of a wilderness God.[37]

Hence, we reach the ironic conclusion that apophatic spirituality (with its radical disdain of images) may employ landscape metaphors just as much as kataphatic spirituality. The places chosen are those that suggest surrender, renunciation, and the *via negativa*, but they are places nonetheless—vindicating our contention that place is an indispensable means for describing the experience of God.

If the apophatic tradition is important in the task of criticizing all images, it also becomes helpful in the work of deconstructing the places of the imagination that we regularly inhabit. It forces us to attend to what our images mask as well as disclose. Apophatic criticism, for example, would make it impossible for us to imagine cities without slums, even though major highways skillfully manage to avoid pockets of poverty. Idealized conceptions of Jerusalem as the Holy City, from an apophatic perspective, would have to be tested by the political realities of dying Palestinian youths and a culture of fear. The forty-four Native American sacred sites listed as threatened in recent proposals to Congress would have to be recognized not simply as romantic tourist spots but as terrain where religious liberties must be guaranteed. Places constructed in the imagination regularly require the deconstructive work of apophatic criticism.

In other words, the places to which an apophatic sensitivity would point us are those that people often dismiss as "non-places." These include run-down neighborhoods where children are at greater risk of violence and disease, nursing homes where the old are easily forgotten, even rural enclaves where aching poverty can be romanticized as "closeness to the land." To a large extent, these are places that don't exist in the everyday imagination of the American middle class.

French anthropologist Marc Augé says that "non-places" are, by definition, places of inherent disconnectedness, primarily to be passed through. For middle- and upper-class Europeans and Americans, he says, "the real non-places of supermodernity [are] the ones we inhabit when we are driving down the motorway, wandering through the supermarket or sitting in an airport lounge waiting for the next flight to London or Marseille." These are sites that strip us of our identity, where we become anonymous, where we have a sense of being present and yet not present at the same time. They include turnstiles, tollbooths, checkout counters, hotel lobbies, and information desks.[38] Personal individuality, relationships, and history make no sense in locations of this sort. They are places empty of personal meaning.

But they suggest still other "non-places," where the sense of dissociation is higher and where we may experience a greater loss of control and surrender of selfhood. Hospitals and drug rehabilitation centers, where people visit or stay only briefly, for example, can foster this sense of deep confusion and marginality. A dread of death or fear of rejection becomes part of their non-placedness, promoting a general disorientation. For the person in such a context, the internal work of imagining the place—constructing it in a way that somehow makes it habitable—is profoundly important. Perceiving oneself as proactive, assuming responsibility for one's own health and contributing to the health of others in the same setting, is often a way of attributing new identity to the place. One ceases to be a patient "acted upon" by a hostile location and becomes, instead, a participant in a mutual sphere of healing. It is the *imagined* place, not the idealized or naked place itself, where we commit ourselves to living.

Terrence Tilley, in a lecture on "Dying Children and Sacred Space," speaks of the experience of hospitalized children in a cancer ward as a case in point. He reflects, for example, on the institutionalized tension they encounter between private place and public space, feeling as if they were always on display, an object continually open to view. "Sick children come to recognize their bodies as public spaces," he says. They remain exposed to the gaze, the prodding, and the inquiries of people they do not know. Often their first reaction, on meeting strangers, is automatically to bare their wounds.[39] In the unreality of the hospital ward, their bodies are no longer their own. As a result, they are forced to imagine new ways of coping with their situation, new interpretations of their place that allow them somehow to live within it.

The apophatic character of such places reminds us of the universal, recurring experience of placelessness and loss that we all confront at times in our lives. But it also teaches us about the process of constructing and deconstructing places of the imagination—the theme with which this chapter began. Whether we are attending to the formation of a spirituality or the effort to negotiate unfamiliar terrain, the role of the imagination in the composition of place is equally important.

The medical staff, the parents, and the children in this situation, for example, go about the task of culturally constructing the hospital space in extremely different ways. The professional staff perceives the oncology ward as a space where diseases are scientifically diagnosed, treated, and cured. Their medical training has made them confident of their power to heal. They fully anticipate the success of their work. The parents, on the other hand, look on the same hospital site as an esoteric and intimidating space where their children may nonetheless be healed. They want to cooperate in every way with the curative process, while they remain deeply committed to protecting their children from as much fear and pain as possible. Despite the fact that these two parties come from very dissimilar viewpoints, they share the temptation to deny what is happening. Neither of them can imagine the ultimate death of the children. Hence, they unconsciously join together in constructing a space of the imagination where they mutually refuse to admit that the patients are dying. They cope with the children's disease (both professionally and personally) by practicing a "mutual pretense," assuring each other that the sick will eventually be cured.

Meanwhile, the children themselves are torn by this process. They want to protect their parents (and even their doctors) from the despair they see in their eyes, so they, too, go along with the pretense. They shelter the people they love from the truth that the adults are unable to receive. But for their own survival—as *they* come to terms with the hospital space and with their own dying—the children need honesty and reliable information. They need a space where this can happen. And they find it by setting up a secret place of their own: usually outside the entry to the bathroom, where they stand in small groups together waiting for lab procedures to begin.

Tilley comments on what he observed: "The bathroom was the only secret space left to them. It was the only space where they could slip a space for truth into a world of pretense. There the older children could play the role of guides to the younger. There the youngsters could learn the truth of their situation and learn how to become guides to those younger than they. There, in a space where pretense was suspended, the children could play the roles of truth-tellers."[40] The children, in other words, could become the adults their parents and doctors were not yet able to be, constructing a space of their own with a far greater degree of honesty and trust.

This is a story that speaks poignantly to the experience of grace, as well as to the spiritual power of the human imagination. In the empty spaces of our lives—in those apophatic moments of tragic loss—we too are invited to new possibilities never before imagined.

There in the deserts of placelessness ("without form and void"), where we survive by denial and pretense, the Spirit of God moves like a wind over the dry arroyos of chaos, and the imagination constructs new places in which to dwell.

The imagined landscape is the only one that we inhabit. "We live in the description of a place and not in the place itself," Wallace Stevens declared. Despair persists and hope is born in the places framed by the limits and conceivabilities of our culture. The imagination is what makes possible our fullest entry into the material world through which our bodies move. Through the imagination we create and we destroy, we fear and we dream, we sin and we repent. Questions of place and its conceptual construction, therefore, are unavoidably questions of spirituality.

From a Christian theological perspective, the cultural construction of place requires a hermeneutics of suspicion—a warning that God ultimately stands beyond all places and times and cultural forms, beyond all the brokenness of human language. The tradition admonishes us that human beings possess profound resources for fooling themselves, for living in denial, for betraying the dignity (and the places) of others. The preeminence of placelessness in prophetic thought calls men and women to a God who stands alongside displaced peoples everywhere, a God who is known more clearly in exile than in the security of any given locale, a God who refuses ever to be pinned down.

The difficult task is to remain creatively alive and responsible in the everyday places that our imagination allows us to perceive in ever new ways. We always find it easier to move to a new place of imagined splendor than to root ourselves in the unconceived possibilities of the familiar. For this reason, Christianity has historically been ambivalent about the benefits of pilgrimage in the spiritual life. The idea of journeying to an intrinsically sacred site (even to the Holy Sepulcher) to draw from its spiritual energies has been highly suspect. Gregory of Nyssa, one of the great theologians in the apophatic tradition, roundly denounced pilgrimage. "You who fear the Lord," he said, "should praise him in the places where you now are. Change of place does not guarantee one's drawing nearer to God. Wherever you find yourself, that is where God will come to you."[41] Augustine said the same thing when he insisted that "we go to God not by walking, but by loving." These are theologians anxious to emphasize the truth of Psalm 84:5—"Blessed are they who have highways in their hearts." An *attitude* of pilgrimage, they thought, is far more important than pilgrimage itself.

The ability to recreate our images of the world around us—to reconstruct the ordinary by the power of the imagination—may be the highest grace we are given. It allows us to treat everything around us with a new respect and justice and love. The best pilgrimage is one from which we return to find that we have never left home.

Such was Thomas Merton's experience one March afternoon in 1958. He was walking in downtown Louisville, not far from the monastery at Gethsemani, where he had lived for fifteen years. He had looked on his cloistered life up until that point as a pilgrimage of sorts, a way of escaping the profanity of life in the secluded safety of a holy place, but as he approached the corner of Fourth and Walnut he suddenly saw everything differently. "As if waking from a dream," he later wrote in his journal, he recognized the unhallowed and ordinary people around him as his own, as the people he had been given to love.[42] He was forced to rethink the nature of his vocation, to give up his "separateness" from the world, the distance on which he had long prided himself. He went back to the monastery, of course, but he returned home with new eyes. Having reconceived the meaning of the places of his life, he could walk for the first time into what he had newly imagined. That perhaps is the deepest mystery of place, the truth that we are free to enter all that we've received as a gift, all that we're able to imagine. That is what allows us finally to create—sometimes even to recreate—the most common and most ordinary places of our lives.

My effort in this book has been to invite myself (and others) to those landscapes of the sacred that we dismiss so easily because we have not learned to recognize them. They are the ones closest to home. I think of Richard Nelson's exquisite book, *The Island Within*, in which he shares his love for an island not far from where he lives in the Pacific Northwest. His concern is to illuminate the obvious, to lift up what is not seen because it is always seen. "I undertook this work," he says, "not as a travel guide but as a guide to non-travel. My hope is to acclaim the rewards of exploring the place in which a person lives rather than searching afar, of becoming fully involved with the near-at-hand, of nurturing a deeper and more committed relationship to home, and of protecting the natural community that sustains all who live there."

I could not wish for anything better in thinking of my own desires for this book. As Nelson discovered in his work among Koyukon elders in the far north, "There may be more to learn by climbing the same mountain a hundred times than by climbing a hundred different mountains."[43] That is the approach to "sacred place" that I have sought to emphasize in these pages. To see the same place in a hundred different ways is much harder (and infinitely more rewarding) than visiting a hundred different places and never seeing any of them.

Notes

Preface to the Johns Hopkins Edition

[1] Pat Conroy, *The Prince of Tides* (New York: Bantam Books, 1987), p. 1.

[2] I have reflected on this in more detail in *The Solace of Fierce Landscapes: Exploring Desert and Mountain Spirituality* (New York: Oxford University Press, 1998).

[3] See Robert A. Orsi, *The Madonna of 115th Street: Faith and Community in Italian Harlem, 1880–1950* (New Haven: Yale University Press, 1988) and *Thank You St. Jude: Women's Devotion to the Patron Saint of Hopeless Causes* (New Haven: Yale University Press, 1998); and Colleen McDannell, *The Christian Home in Victorian America, 1840–1900* (Bloomington: Indiana University Press, 1994).

[4] See Edward Linenthal, *Preserving Memory: The Struggle to Create America's Holocaust Museum* (New York: Penguin Books, 1997).

[5] Theodore Hiebert, *The Yahwist's Landscape: Nature and Religion in Early Israel* (New York: Oxford University Press, 1996).

[6] See "Environment and Art in Catholic Worship" (1978) and "Built of Living Stones: Art, Architecture and Worship" (2000), both issued by the National Conference of Catholic Bishops in Washington, D.C.

[7] These include Eric Hirsh and Michael O'Hanlon, eds., *The Anthropology of Landscape: Perspectives on Place and Space* (Oxford: Clarendon Press, 1995); Dolores Hayden, *The Power of Place: Urban Landscapes as Public History* (Cambridge: MIT Press, 1995); Doreen Massay, *Space, Place and Gender* (Minneapolis: University of Minnesota Press, 1994); Stephen R. Higley, *Privilege, Power and Place: The Geography of the American Upper Class* (London: Rowman & Littlefield, 1995); Barbara Ching and Gerald W. Creed, eds., *Knowing Your Place: Rural Identity and Cultural Hierarchy* (New York: Routledge, 1997); and David Seamon, *Dwelling, Seeing and Building: Toward a Phenomenological Ecology* (Albany: State University of New York Press, 1992).

[8] Rowland A. Sherrill, "American Sacred Space and the Contest of History," in David Chidester and Edward T. Linenthal, eds., *American Sacred Spaces* (Bloomington: Indiana University Press), p. 324.

[9] Philip Sheldrake's *Spaces for the Sacred: Place, Memory and Identity* (London: SCM Press, 2001) is published in the United States by the Johns Hopkins University Press.

[10] From Wendell Berry, "The Thought of Something Else," in *Collected Poems* (San Francisco: North Point Press, 1985), p. 55.

Introduction

[1] For an account of the social and natural history of the Ghost Ranch area, see Dan Flores, *Horizontal Yellow: Nature and History in the Near Southwest* (Albuquerque: University of New Mexico Press, 1999), pp. 201–251, and Lesley Poling-Kempes, *Valley of Shining Stone: The Story of Abiquiu* (Tucson: University of Arizona Press, 1997).

[2] See Michael Taussig, *Mimesis and Alterity: A Particular History of the Senses* (New York: Routledge, 1993).

[3] Quoted in Edward Relph, *Place and Placelessness* (London: Pion Limited, 1976), p. 43.

[4] Yi-Fu Tuan, *Topophilia: A Study of Environmental Perception, Attitudes, and Values* (Englewood Cliffs, New Jersey: Prentice-Hall, 1974).

[5] See Joachim Wach, *Sociology of Religion* (Chicago: University of Chicago Press, 1944), p. 84 f.

[6] Yi-Fu Tuan, "Geopiety: A Theme in Man's Attachment to Nature and to Place," in David Lowenthal and Martyn J. Bowden, eds., *Geographies of the Mind: Essays in Historical Geography in Honor of John Kirtland Wright* (New York: Oxford University Press, 1976), pp. 13–14.

[7] Christian Norberg-Schulz, in his *Genius Loci: Towards a Phenomenology of Architecture* (New York: Rizzoli International Publications, 1979), p. 5, quotes Heidegger extensively in his effort to understand the "spirit of place."

[8] Martin Heidegger, "An Ontological Consideration of Place," in *The Question of Being* (New York: Twayne Publishers, 1958), pp. 19, 26. Cf. Christian Norberg-Schulz's discussion of "Existential Space" in his *Existence, Space and Architecture* (New York: Praeger Publishers, 1971), pp. 17–36.

[9] Sam Keen, "The Restoration of a Sense of Place: A Theological Reflection on the Visual Environment," *Ekistics: Reviews on the Problems and Science of Human Settlements* 25:151 (June 1968), p. 422. See also Peter Berger, *The Homeless Mind* (New York: Random House, 1973).

[10] Paul Tournier, *A Place for You: Psychology and Religion* (New York: Harper & Row, 1968), p. 37.

[11] Simone Weil, *The Need for Roots* (1952), quoted in Edward Relph, *Place and Placelessness* (London: Pion Limited, 1976).

[12] Walter Lowrie, *A Short Life of Kierkegaard* (Garden City, New York: Doubleday, 1961), pp. 35–36.

[13] Eudora Welty spoke of the importance of "Place in Fiction" in her collection of essays and reviews entitled *The Eye of the Story* (New York: Random House, 1978), pp. 116–133. For a discussion of places in the literary imagination, see Phillip C. Muehrcke and Juliana O. Muehrcke, "Maps in Literature," *Geographical Review* 64:3 (July 1974), pp. 317–338.

[14] See James H. Kunstler, *The Geography of Nowhere: The Rise and Decline of America's Man-Made Landscape* (New York: Simon & Schuster, 1993), pp. 219–222.

[15] "In sum, the themed milieu with its pervasive use of media culture motifs that define an entire built space increasingly characterizes not only cities but also suburban areas, shopping places, airports, recreation spaces such as baseball stadia, museums, restaurants, and amusement parks." See Mark Gottdiener, *The Theming of America: Dreams, Visions, and Commercial Spaces* (Boulder, Colorado: Westview Press, 1997), p. 4.

[16] See Karl Ann Marling, ed., *Designing Disney's Theme Parks: The Architecture of Reassurance* (Montreal: Canadian Centre for Architecture, 1997).

[17] Norman O. Brown, *Life Against Death: The Psychoanalytical Meaning of History* (Middletown, Connecticut: Wesleyan University Press, 1959), pp. 202–233.

[18] Adolphe Tanquerey, *The Spiritual Life: A Treatise on Ascetical and Mystical Theology* (Tournai, Belgium: Society of St. John the Evangelist, Declee & Co., 1932).

[19] Karl Rahner, ed., *Encyclopedia of Theology: The Concise Sacramentum Mundi* (New York: Seabury Press, 1975), p. 1624.

[20] Edward Kinerk, S. J., speaks of "a former professor of historical theology [who] once described spirituality as a 'glob' area. He explained this rather inelegant label by pointing out that spirituality enjoys an unlimited wealth of resources but possesses no tools for getting those resources organized." See his article, "Toward a Method for the Study of Spirituality," *Review for Religious* 40 (1981), p. 3.

[21] Carolyn Osiek, "Reflections on an American Spirituality," *Spiritual Life*, 22 (1976), p. 230. The first three issues of the *Christian Spirituality Bulletin*, 1 (Spring and Fall 1993) and 2 (Spring 1994), included several articles by Philip Sheldrake, Rowan Williams, Bernard McGinn, Walter Principe, Bradley Hanson, and Sandra Schneiders, exploring

very carefully the nature of spirituality as a discipline. See also Sandra Schneiders, "The Study of Christian Spirituality: Contours and Dynamics of a Discipline," *Christian Spirituality Bulletin* 6:1 (Spring 1998), pp. 1–12.

[22] William James, *The Varieties of Religious Experience* (New York: New American Library, 1958), p. 45.

[23] Sir Edwyn Hoskyns, Cambridge Sermons, quoted in Gordon S. Wakefield, ed., *The Westminster Dictionary of Christian Spirituality* (Philadelphia: Westminster Press, 1983), p. 362.

[24] Adrian J. Ivakhiv, *Claiming Sacred Ground: Pilgrims and Politics at Glastonbury and Sedona* (Bloomington: University of Indiana Press, 2001).

1 Axioms for the Study of Sacred Place

[1] N. Scott Momaday, quoted in Barry Lopez, *Arctic Dreams: Imagination and Desire in a Northern Landscape* (New York: Charles Scribner's Sons, 1986), p. ix.

[2] Cf. Jan Morris, *The Matter of Wales: Epic Views of a Small Country* (New York: Oxford University Press, 1984), p. 91.

[3] The story is taken from the author's article, "The Breviary in the Woods," in *The Christian Century*, 100:18 (June 1, 1983), pp. 564–566.

[4] William Faulkner, "The Bear," Part 1.

[5] The idea of proposing axioms for the study of landscape is taken from Peirce F. Lewis in his essay on "Axioms for Reading the Landscape," in D. W. Meinig, ed., *The Interpretation of Ordinary Landscapes: Geographical Essays* (New York: Oxford University Press, 1979), pp. 11–32.

[6] Quoted in Martin Marty, *The Public Church: Mainline-Evangelical-Catholic* (New York: Crossroad, 1981), p. 95.

[7] Joseph Campbell, *The Mythic Image* (Princeton, New Jersey: Princeton University Press, 1974), p. 184.

[8] Mircea Eliade, *The Sacred and the Profane* (New York: Harper & Row, 1961), p. 20.

[9] *Ibid.*, pp. 37, 63. Cf. Eliade's discussion of sacred places in his *Patterns in Comparative Religion* (New York: New American Library, 1958), pp. 269–271, 369–387.

[10] Eliade, *Patterns in Comparative Religion*, p. 369. Gerardus Van der Leeuw adds: "We *cannot* make shrines and *cannot* select their 'positions,' but can never do more than merely 'find' them." *Religion in Essence and Manifestation* (Gloucester, Massachusetts: Peter Smith, 1967), II, p. 398.

[11] Richard L. Rubenstein, "On the Meaning of Place," in Rolfe L. Hunt, ed., *Revolution, Place, Symbol* (Journal of the First International Congress on Religion, Architecture and the Visual Arts, New York City

and Montreal, August 26 through September 4, 1967), 1969, pp. 148–150.

[12] Cf. Job 20:9 and Ps 103:16. In Job 8:18, the place of the wicked denies him, saying, "I have never seen you."

[13] Cf. Van der Leeuw's chapter on "Sacred Space" in *Religion in Essence and Manifestation*, II, pp. 393–402. One can compare stories told of the "calling" power of the spring of Kastalia at Delphi or even the irrepressible Tivoli fountain in Rome. Jean Piaget wrote that "the child behaves as if nature were charged with purpose." David Lowenthal relates this to the dynamics of geographical perception in his "Geography, Experience, and Imagination: Towards a Geographical Epistemology," in *Man, Space, and Environment*, eds. Paul W. English and Robert C. Mayfield (New York: Oxford University Press, 1972), p. 224.

[14] Peter Matthiessen, *Indian Country* (New York: Viking Press, 1984), p. 7. Navajo writer Pauline Whitesinger, speaking in relation to the Big Mountain controversy in 1986, said: "In our tongue, there is no word for relocation. To move away is to disappear and never be seen again."

[15] Hans Mol, *Meaning and Place: An Introduction to the Social Scientific Study of Religion* (New York: Pilgrim Press, 1983), p. 4.

[16] Cf. William A. Lessa and Evon Z. Vogt, *Reader in Comparative Religion: An Anthropological Approach* (New York: Harper & Row, 1972), pp. 381–412 and Emile Durkheim, *The Elementary Forms of the Religious Life* (New York: Collier Books, 1961).

[17] Carlos Castaneda, *A Separate Reality* (New York: Simon & Schuster, 1971) and *Journey to Ixtlan* (New York: Simon & Schuster, 1972).

[18] Eliade, *Patterns in Comparative Religion*, p. 370. The ancient Greeks spoke of sacred spaces as *abaton*, inaccessible ground, says W. Brede Kristensen in *The Meaning of Religion: Lectures in the Phenomenology of Religion* (The Hague: Martinus Nijhoff, 1960), p. 357.

[19] Cf. John R. Stilgoe, *Common Landscape of America, 1580–1845* (New Haven: Yale University Press, 1982), p. 221.

[20] Wendell C. Beane and William G. Doty, eds., *Myths, Rites, Symbols: A Mircea Eliade Reader* (New York: Harper & Row, 1975), I, p. 128.

[21] Lynn White, Jr., in his article on "The Historical Roots of Our Ecologic Crisis," *Science*, 155:3767 (March 10, 1967), p. 1205, argues that "by destroying pagan animism, Christianity made it possible to exploit nature in a mood of indifference to the feelings of natural objects."

[22] Cf. Walter Harrelson, *From Fertility Cult to Worship* (Garden City, New York: Doubleday & Co., 1969), chapter one; Harvey Cox, *The Secular City* (New York: Macmillan, 1965), chapter one; and Walter Brueggemann, *The Land* (Philadelphia: Fortress Press, 1977), pp. 184–185.

²³ Cf. Mircea Eliade, *The Quest: History and Meaning in Religion* (Chicago: University of Chicago Press, 1969), p. 126. The argument here and following is also informed by Paul Ricoeur's *The Symbolism of Evil* (New York: Harper & Row, 1967).

²⁴ Paul Ricoeur, *The Symbolism of Evil*, pp. 347–357.

²⁵ Joseph Campbell, *The Hero with a Thousand Faces* (Princeton, New Jersey: Princeton University Press, 1968), p. 249.

²⁶ Annie Dillard, *Teaching a Stone to Talk: Expeditions and Encounters* (New York: Harper & Row, 1982), p. 70. An example of the contemporary effort to rediscover an ancient magic is found in Starhawk's *The Spiral Dance* (New York: Harper & Row, 1979). It offers a series of exercises for "creating sacred space," drawn from the traditions of witchcraft and Goddess Religion.

²⁷ Jonathan Z. Smith, *Map Is Not Territory: Studies in the History of Religions* (Leiden: E. J. Brill, 1978), p. 308.

²⁸ David Sopher, "The Landscape of Home," in D. W. Meinig, ed., *The Interpretation of Ordinary Landscapes*, p. 138.

²⁹ Cotton Mather, *Magnalia Christi Americana, or the Ecclesiastical History of New-England,* reproduced from the edition of 1852 (New York: Russell and Russell, 1967), I, pp. 91–99.

³⁰ Representing indestructibility, the power of purification, and periodic regeneration, respectively, the stones, water, and trees become an *imago mundi,* as if one were standing at the very heart of the universe. Eliade, *Patterns in Comparative Religion*, p. 269.

³¹ Cf. W. Y. Evans-Wentz, *Cuchama and Sacred Mountains* (Chicago: Swallow Press, 1981).

³² Louis Agassiz, another American naturalist, would later say he had once spent the summer traveling—only to have gotten halfway across his back yard. Regarding the Transcendentalist doctrine of correspondence see Catherine Albanese, *Corresponding Motion: Transcendental Religion and the New America* (Philadelphia: Temple University Press, 1977).

³³ Edward Relph discusses the rise of modern landscape painting and its significance in his book, *Rational Landscapes and Humanistic Geography* (Totowa, New Jersey: Barnes & Noble Books, 1981).

³⁴ Cf. David Lowenthal, "The American Scene," *Geographical Review*, 58:1 (1968), pp. 65–66.

³⁵ Mircea Eliade, *The Sacred and the Profane*, p. 40.

³⁶ Quoted in Jonathan Z. Smith, "Earth and Gods," *The Journal of Religion*, 49:2 (April 1969), p. 111. Joseph Smith similarly spoke through revelation of Independence, Missouri, as "the center place," the site in the land of promise for the city of Zion. Cf. Joseph Smith, *History of the*

Church of Jesus Christ of Latter-Day Saints, ed. B. H. Roberts (Salt Lake City: Deseret Book Co., 1978), I, p. 89.

[37] Van der Leeuw, *Religion in Essence and Manifestation,* II, p. 400, and Jonathan Z. Smith, *op. cit.,* pp. 112–113. Cf. Ernst Cassirer, *op. cit.,* II, pp. 54–55, 90–91 and Brevard Childs, *Myth and Reality in the Old Testament,* Studies in Biblical Theology Series, no. 27 (Naperville, Illinois: Alec R. Allenson, Inc., 1960), pp. 84–90, for discussions of Jerusalem as the navel of the earth.

[38] Cf. Mason Lowance, *The Language of Canaan: Metaphor and Symbol in New England from Puritans to Transcendentalists* (Cambridge, Massachusetts: Harvard University Press, 1980) and R. W. B. Lewis, *The American Adam* (Chicago: University of Chicago Press, 1955).

[39] Cf. Charles L. Sanford, *The Quest for Paradise: Europe and the American Moral Imagination* (University of Illinois Press, 1961), p. 111.

[40] Quoted in William Cronon, *Changes in the Land: Indians, Colonists, and the Ecology of New England* (New York: Farrar, Straus, and Giroux, 1983), pp. 34–35. Cf. Peter Carroll, *Puritanism and the Wilderness* (New York: Columbia University Press, 1969), pp. 55f, and Larzer Ziff, *Puritanism in America* (New York: Viking Press, 1973), p. 46. Ziff quotes the seventeenth-century English playwright John Marston, who in 1605 satirized on the London stage the current extravagance of claims that all things in America were marvelous. One of his characters said, "I tell thee, golde is more plentiful there than copper is with us. . . . Why man, all their dripping pans and their chamber pottes are pure gold . . . and for rebies and diamonds, they goe forth on holydayes and gather 'hem by the sea-shore."

[41] Joseph Campbell, *The Hero with a Thousand Faces,* p. 4.

[42] David Stein, "The Cottonwood Tree," *At the Door:* Quarterly Newsletter of the Chicago Catholic Worker Community (Fall 1985).

[43] Henry Adams, *The Education of Henry Adams* (New York: Heritage Press, 1918), p. 354. There had been a similar reaction to the huge Corliss steam engine on display at the Philadelphia Centennial Exposition in 1876. Newspapers reported strong men to have been moved to tears. Walt Whitman stood by the hour watching the sublime movement of the great pistons. Cf. John F. Kasson, *Civilizing the Machine: Technology and Republican Values, 1776–1900* (New York: Grossman Publishers, 1976), p. 164.

[44] Cf. Vincent Vycinas, *Earth and Gods: An Introduction to the Philosophy of Martin Heidegger* (The Hague: Martinus Nijhoff, 1969).

[45] Yi-Fu Tuan distinguishes the non-specificity and freedom of *space* from the commitment and encompassing security evoked by *place.*

"'Space' is more abstract than 'place.' What begins as undifferentiated space becomes place as we get to know it better and endow it with value." *Space and Place: The Perspective of Experience* (University of Minnesota Press, 1977), p. 6. Cf. Walter Brueggemann, *The Land*, pp. 5–6.

[46] Cf. Martin Buber, *I and Thou* (Edinburgh: T. & T. Clark, 1966), pp. 7f, and Paul Tournier, *A Place for You*, pp. 13, 42.

[47] Norberg-Schulz observes that in Roman thought, every independent being (or place) had its genius or guardian spirit, determining its character or essence. *Genius Loci: Towards a Phenomenology of Architecture*, p. 18.

[48] Lawrence Durrell, *The Spirit of Place: Letters and Essays on Travel* (New York: E. P. Dutton & Co., 1969), p. 156.

[49] Russian literary critic Victor Shklovsky uses the word *ostranenie* (the idea of "making strange" a given concept) in arguing that the goal of the poet is always that of occasioning an utterly novel view of the world. Cf. Victor Erlich, *Russian Formalism: History—Doctrine* (The Hague: Mouton & Co., 1955), p. 151.

[50] T. S. Eliot, *The Complete Poems and Plays, 1909–1950* (New York: Harcourt, Brace & World, Inc., 1971), p. 145.

[51] Wendell Berry, *Recollected Essays, 1965–1980* (San Francisco: North Point Press, 1981), pp. 230–244.

[52] Charles G. Finney, *Memoirs* (New York: A. S. Barnes & Co., 1876), pp. 12–21.

[53] Brevard Childs, *Myth and Reality*, p. 93. Walter Harrelson adds that Hebrew holy places were holy only "in virtue of the deeds of salvation associated with them." *From Fertility Cult to Worship*, p. 36.

[54] Van der Leeuw, *Religion in Essence and Manifestation*, II, p. 402.

[55] Walter Brueggemann, *The Land*, pp. 3, 185. Gerhard Von Rad, in *The Problem of the Hexateuch and Other Essays* (New York: McGraw-Hill Book Co., 1966) similarly emphasizes the crucial importance in the Hexateuch of Yahweh's land.

[56] Oscar Handlin, *The Uprooted* (1951), quoted in Edward Relph, *Place and Placelessness*, p. 40. Eric Dardell, in his book *L'Homme et La Terre* (1952), further describes this need to be "placed." "Before any choice, there is this place which we have not chosen, where the very foundation of our earthly existence and human condition establishes itself. We can change places, move, but this is still to look for a place, for this we need as a base to set down Being and to realise our possibilities—a *here* from which the world discloses itself, a *there* to which we can go." Quoted in Relph, *op. cit.*, p. 41.

[57] Harvey Cox, "The Restoration of a Sense of Place," pp. 422–423.

[58] Brueggemann, *op. cit.*, pp. 15–16.

[59] Campbell, *Hero with a Thousand Faces,* p. 169. Dietrich Bonhoeffer wrestled with this tension in the last years of his life. He refused to deny the visible nature of the church, like those understanding it purely as a spiritual force. The church must occupy a definite space in the world. But this, he said, could no longer be a privileged space, segregated from the world, relegated to some secret enclave. The church must exist in the midst of the common ways of life, wholly belonging to the world. Cf. F. W. Dillistone, *Traditional Symbols and the Contemporary World* (London: Epworth Press, 1973), pp. 94–95, and Dietrich Bonhoeffer, *Letters and Papers from Prison* (New York: Macmillan, 1953), pp. 208–220.

[60] J. B. Jackson, "The Order of a Landscape: Reason and Religion in Newtonian America," in D. W. Meinig, ed., *The Interpretation of Ordinary Landscapes*, pp. 156–157.

[61] Cf. Ray Allen Billington, ed., *The Frontier Thesis* (New York: Holt, Rinehart, & Winston, 1966), and William Warren Sweet, *The Story of Religion in America* (New York: Harper & Row, 1950) for discussions of the frontier, revivalism, and the Turner thesis.

2   Giving Voice to Place: Three Models for Understanding American Sacred Space

[1] E. V. Walter, *Placeways:* A Theory of Human Environment (Chapel Hill: University of North Carolina Press, 1988), pp. 120–123.

[2] Aristotle, *Physics*, 209a. See Max Jammer, *Concepts of Space* (Cambridge: Harvard University Press, 1969), pp. 17–21.

[3] Plato, *Timaeus*, 49a, 51a.

[4] The western Apache frequently speak of the land as "stalking people" or "going to work on them," playing tricks so as to reconnect them to their roots. The land and the teaching stories connected with it have a way of "shooting them with arrows," calling the people back to an identity (and responsibility) that they share with the entire landscape. See Keith H. Basso, *Wisdom Sits in Places: Landscape and Language among the Western Apache* (Albuquerque: University of New Mexico Press, 1996), pp. 38–41, 58–64.

[5] Mikhail Bakhtin recognizes the joining of time and place when he speaks of the "chronotopes" that serve as monuments to a community's shared life and identity. These are "points in the geography of a community where time and space intersect and fuse." They are recognized in the defining narratives that rehearse a people's experience of "space becoming charged and responsive to the movements of time and his-

tory." See Mikhail Bakhtin, *The Dialogic Imagination: Four Essays*, ed. M. Holquist (Austin: University of Texas Press, 1981), p. 7.

[6] See Rowland A. Sherrill, "American Sacred Space and the Contest of History," in David Chidester and Edward T. Linenthal, eds., *American Sacred Space* (Bloomington: Indiana University Press, 1995), pp. 323–325. From another point of view, however, to attend to intimate perceptions of place is to share in the characteristic American propensity (from Jonathan Edwards to Mary Oliver) for regarding nature as personally instructive, as a source of spiritual insight. See Catherine Albanese, *Nature Religion in America* (Chicago: University of Chicago Press, 1991).

[7] Charlene Spretnak observes that poststructuralist thinking "spawns books and articles that perceive only a one-way creative power; the projection by humans of their 'social constructions' onto nature. All this seems exceedingly odd—and more than a little pathological—to traditional native peoples." They insist, by contrast, that there is a two-way process of communication between the human and more-than-human worlds. See Charlene Spretnak, *The Resurgence of the Real: Body, Nature, and Place in a Hypermodern World* (New York: Routledge, 1999), pp. 27–28.

[8] See John Muir, "My First Summer in the Sierra," in *Nature Writings* (New York: Library of America, 1997), p. 292.

[9] Gary Snyder, *The Practice of the Wild* (New York: North Point Press/Farrar, Straus & Giroux, 1990), pp. 103, 114–115.

[10] David Abram observes that "many indigenous peoples construe awareness, or 'mind,' not as a power that resides inside their heads, but rather as a quality that they themselves are inside of, along with the other animals and the plants, the mountains and the clouds." David Abram, *The Spell of the Sensuous: Perception and Language in the More-Than-Human World* (New York: Vintage Books, 1996), p. 227.

[11] Paul Ricoeur, *The Symbolism of Evil* (New York: Harper & Row, 1967), 347–357.

[12] A brief survey of methodological approaches to the study of American sacred places is given in the introduction and notes to Chidester and Linenthal, *American Sacred Space*, pp. 1–42. Douglas Burton-Christie canvasses a wide body of literature relating spirituality and place in his article, "A Sense of Place," *The Way* 39:1 (January, 1999), pp. 59–72. Ethnographic approaches are outlined in the introduction to Steven Feld and Keith H. Basso's *Senses of Place* (Santa Fe: School of American Research Press, 1996).

[13] Mircea Eliade, *The Sacred and the Profane: The Nature of Religion* (New York: Harper & Row, 1961), pp. 20–29.

[14] Eliade's own intellectual roots and political outlook had been shaped by the same antimodern pessimism and romanticism that gave rise to European fascism. Cultural studies approaches, by contrast, have been deeply committed to exposing the ways by which dominant cultures often silence the voices of difference. See Robert Ellwood, *The Politics of Myth: A Study of C. G. Jung, Mircea Eliade, and Joseph Campbell* (Albany: State University of New York Press, 1999).

[15] Bernyce Barlow, *Sacred Sites of the West* (St. Paul: Llewellyn Publications, 1996), p. 35.

[16] Astronomer John Eddy of the High Altitude Observatory at the National Center for Atmospheric Research in Boulder, Colorado, affirmed these alignments in his own observation of the summer solstice at Medicine Wheel, Wyoming, in June of 1972, building on the earlier work of British astronomer G. S. Hawkins. See John Eddy, "Medicine Wheels and Plains Indian Astronomy," in *Native American Astronomy*, ed. Anthony E. Aveni (Austin: University of Texas Press, 1977), pp. 147–169.

[17] Different attitudes toward the site can be found among First Nations people themselves. The Cheyenne, for example, perceive the circle as too sacred to enter, tying offerings of their own in a stand of small, wind-whipped spruce trees nearby.

[18] James J. Gibson, quoted in Dolores LaChapelle, *Sacred Land, Sacred Sex: Rapture of the Deep: Concerning Deep Ecology and Celebrating Life* (Sky Land, North Carolina: Kivaki Press, 1992), p. 108.

[19] Mircea Eliade, *The Sacred and the Profane*, p. 26.

[20] D. H. Lawrence, "The Spirit of Place," in *The Symbolic Meaning*, ed., Armin Arnold (New York: Viking Press, 1964), pp. 20, 18.

[21] In speaking of "synchronistic events" and "miracle healings" in 1959, Jung mentioned "numinous spots" like the cave and underground spring at Lourdes. See *The Letters of Carl G. Jung*, 2 vols., ed. Gerhard Adler (Princeton: Princeton University Press, 1979), 2:500. Cf. Daniel C. Noel, "Soul and Earth," *Quadrant* 23:2 (1979), pp. 62–63.

[22] James A. Swan, *Sacred Places* (Santa Fe: Bear & Co., 1990); James A. Swan, ed., *The Power of Place: Sacred Ground in Natural & Human Environments* (Wheaton, Ill.: Quest Books, 1991); and Winifred Gallagher, *The Power of Place: How Our Surroundings Shape our Thoughts, Emotions and Actions* (New York: Poseidon Press, 1993).

[23] Stephen F. De Borhegyi describes the history and devotion of the site in *El Santuario de Chimayo* (Santa Fe: Spanish Colonial Arts Society, Inc., 1956).

²⁴ Jonathan Z. Smith, *Map Is Not Territory* (Leiden: E. J. Brill, 1978), p. 308.

²⁵ See the first chapter of Jonathan Z. Smith, *To Take Place: Toward a Theory in Ritual* (Chicago: University of Chicago Press, 1987). Elsewhere he argued, "There is nothing that is inherently sacred or profane. These are not substantive categories, but rather situational or relational categories." Jonathan Z. Smith, *Imagining Religion* (Chicago: University of Chicago Press, 1982), p. 55.

²⁶ Victor and Edith Turner observe that "the holiest pilgrimage shrines in several major religions tend to be located on the periphery of cities, towns, or other well-demarcated territorial units. Peripherality here represents liminality and communitas, as against sociocultural structure." Victor and Edith Turner, *Image and Pilgrimage in Christian Culture* (New York: Columbia University Press, 1978), p. 241. See also Victor Turner, *Dramas, Fields, and Metaphors* (Ithaca: Cornell University Press, 1974).

²⁷ See Robert A. Orsi's books on *The Madonna of 115th Street: Faith and Community in Italian Harlem, 1880–1950* (New Haven: Yale University Press, 1988) and *Thank You, St. Jude: Women's Devotion to the Patron Saint of Hopeless Causes* (New Haven: Yale University Press, 1996).

²⁸ John Eade and Michael J. Sallnow, eds., *Contesting the Sacred: The Anthropology of Christian Pilgrimage* (London: Routledge, 1991), pp. 5–6, 7, 10 (emphasis added). At the Shrine of Our Lady of Lourdes in France, for example, they have identified at least three different discourses expressed there: a miracle discourse, spoken by desperate pilgrims seeking cures; a sacrifice discourse, encouraged by the shrine staff and practiced by seasoned pilgrims who perceive their suffering as a sharing in Christ's sacrifice on the cross; and an economic discourse, exercised by the townsfolk who attend carefully to the presence of visitors as part of the tourist trade. See Eade and Sallnow, pp. 10, 17.

²⁹ Edward T. Linenthal, *Sacred Ground: Americans and Their Battlefields* (Urbana: University of Illinois Press, 1991), pp. 55–62, 187–199. Linenthal's subsequent book on the Holocaust Museum in Washington, D.C., documents the tensions between Holocaust survivors who feared a second victimization in the murder of their memory and others in Washington who did not want a building focused on grief and repentance to compete with the larger national monuments nearby on the Mall. See Edward T. Linenthal, *Preserving Memory: The Struggle to Create America's Holocaust Museum* (New York: Penguin, 1997).

³⁰ Timothy Matovina of Loyola-Marymount University, in a paper, "The Alamo and San Fernando Cathedral in San Antonio," given at the November 1997 meeting of the American Academy of Religion in San

Francisco, spoke of the Alamo as originally a mission, not a battle site—pointing out that the cathedral dates back a hundred years before the "sacral events" of 1836. Proud Tejanos still describe the cathedral as "the only unconquered place in town." Others tell of how they have "been left out of the story," as African Americans for the Alamo and the Irish Shamrock Society recall those of their number who died in the fighting at the old Spanish mission.

[31] See Mary Pat Dowling Beal, *Grotto Stories: From the Heart of Notre Dame* (Notre Dame, Ind.: Mary Sunshine Books, 1996). Robert S. Brown discusses the role of college and professional football in occasioning national mourning, community bonding, and healing in his doctoral dissertation, "Football as a Rhetorical Site of National Reassurance: Managing the Crisis of the Kennedy Assassination," Indiana University, 1996.

[32] Since Castro's revolution in 1959, the number of Cubans in Miami has grown to over half a million, with this shrine becoming the sixth largest Catholic pilgrimage site in the United States. See Thomas Tweed, "Diasporic Nationalism and Urban Landscape: Cuban Immigrants at a Catholic Shrine in Miami," in Robert A. Orsi, ed., *Gods of the City: Religion and the American Urban Landscape* (Bloomington: Indiana University Press, 1999), pp. 131–154.

[33] See James S. Griffith, *Beliefs and Holy Places: A Spiritual Geography of the Pimería Alta* (Tucson: University of Arizona Press, 1992), pp. 105–110. Griffith has identified more than twenty variants of the narrative in the Arizona Folklore Archives. In one of the accounts of this "wishing shrine," an old man is said to have been killed there. "If you want anything real bad," the local people explain, "like if you want a new car or if you're in the third grade and want to pass into the fourth, you go there and tell the old man that if you get it you'll go and light a candle for him."

[34] While the American Indian Religious Freedom Act, passed in 1978, provided for the first time a guarantee of Native American religious rights, it lacked any ability to enforce what it had set up in principle. A Free Exercise of Religion Act, therefore, was introduced to the U.S. Congress in 1993, providing (among other things) the protection of forty-four sacred sites on federal land that were being threatened by tourism, development, mining projects, etc. What finally was passed in Congress in 1993 was a Religious Freedom Restoration Act, aimed at restoring religious liberties threatened by the Supreme Court's ruling in the 1990 *Employment Division v. Smith* case. This was ruled unconstitutional by the Supreme Court in 1997. A new Religious Liberty Protection Act was introduced in Congress in 1999 to try once again to assure

that only a compelling state interest can limit the free exercise of religion.

No one has written more thoughtfully on matters of litigation related to First Nations claims to sacred places than Robert S. Michaelsen of the University of California, Santa Barbara. See his "American Indian Religious Freedom Litigation: Promise and Perils," *Journal of Law and Religion* 3:1 (1985), 47–76; "Sacred Land in America: What Is It? How Can It Be Protected?" *Religion* 16 (July 1986), pp. 249–268; and "Dirt in the Court Room: Indian Land Claims and American Property Rights," in Chidester and Linenthal, eds., *American Sacred Spaces*, pp. 43–96.

[35] See Klara Kelley and Francis Harris, *Navajo Sacred Places* (Bloomington: Indiana University Press, 1994), pp. 143, 169–172.

[36] If sacred places are popularly understood to be clearly differentiated from surrounding terrain, if they are expected to function in a manifest way as a "center"—if one even anticipates a permanent physical structure of some sort to be the focus of attention there (like a church or temple)—then Navajo and Hopi plaintiffs obviously have no credibility when they speak of the San Francisco Peaks as intrinsically holy. To court justices operating under an essentially Eliadean conception of sacred place, these mountains appear to be a very diffuse and "ordinary" terrain, not at all marked off in any particular way as sacred, and therefore not necessarily requiring protection under First Amendment rights.

[37] John Eade and Michael Sallnow, *Contesting the Sacred*, p. 15. Chidester and Linenthal speak of any given "sacred" space as an "empty signifier," something "open to unlimited claims and counter-claims on its significance." Chidester and Linenthal, eds., *American Sacred Spaces*, p. 18.

[38] No more, that is, than a written text can be interpreted convincingly in any random manner. William L. Portier, in "A Church Polarized: Fault Lines in the History of American Catholicism," *U.S. Catholic Historian* 15 (1996), pp. 141–145, criticizes cultural analyses that reduce devotional practices in American life to mere cultural patterns alone.

[39] Tim Ingold, "Culture and the Perception of the Environment," in Elisabeth Croll and David Parkin, eds., *Bush Base: Forest Farm: Culture, Environment, and Development* (London: Routledge, 1992), p. 41. Ingold argues elsewhere that "the landscape, in short, is not a totality that you or anyone else can look at, it is rather the world in which we stand in taking up a point of view on our surroundings." See Tim Ingold, "The Temporality of the Landscape," *World Archaeology* 25:2 (1993), p. 171.

[40] See Edmund Husserl, *Cartesian Meditations: An Introduction to*

Phenomenology, trans. Dorion Cairns (The Hague: Martinus Nijhoff Publishers, 1960), and Edmund Husserl, "Epilogue," in *Ideas Pertaining to a Pure Phenomenology*, vol. 2, trans. Richard Rozcewicz and Andre Schuwer (The Hague: Martinus Nijhoff, 1989), p. 421.

[41] Tim Ingold, "Culture and the Perception of the Environment," p. 39.

[42] David Abram makes this distinction in *The Spell of the Sensuous*, p. 67.

[43] These affordances "exist as inherent potentials of the objects themselves, quite independently of their being put to use or realized by a subject." Tim Ingold, "Culture and the Perception of the Environment," p. 42. Gibson details his "theory of affordances" in his important study, *The Ecological Approach to Visual Perception* (Boston: Houghton Mifflin, 1979), pp. 127–143.

[44] Tim Ingold, "Culture and the Perception of the Environment," p. 42.

[45] See Adrian Ivakhiv, "Places of Power: Sacred Sites, Gaia's Pilgrims, and the Politics of Landscape: An Interpretative Study of the Geographics of New Age and Contemporary Earth Spirituality, with Reference to Glastonbury, England, and Sedona, Arizona," doctoral dissertation, York University, Toronto, 1997.

[46] David Abram says that "the perceiving body does not calculate logical probabilities; it gregariously participates in the activity of the world, lending its imagination to things in order to see them more fully." Abram, *The Spell of the Sensuous*, p. 58.

[47] Maurice Merleau-Ponty, *Phenomenology of Perception* (London: Routledge & Kegan Paul, 1962), p. 214.

[48] See Kristin Ann Hass, *Carried to the Wall: American Memory and the Vietnam Veterans Memorial* (Berkeley: University of California Press, 1998) and Jan D. Scruggs, *To Heal a Nation: The Vietnam Veterans Memorial* (New York: Harper & Row, 1985).

[49] Abram says, "My hand is able to touch things only because my hand is itself a touchable thing, and thus is entirely a part of the tactile world that it explores." To touch the name of my friend cut into the black granite wall was, in this respect, "to experience [my] own tactility, to feel [myself] touched by the [wall]." It is to recognize fully that my "surroundings are experienced as sensate, attentive, and watchful." Abram, *The Spell of the Sensuous*, pp. 68–69. The wall was the powerful medium of contact with my friend as our mutual interaction of person and place was joined in a single moment.

[50] Edward S. Casey, *Getting Back into Place: Toward a Renewed Under-*

standing of the Place-World (Bloomington: Indiana University Press, 1993), pp. 204–222.

[51] Jack Turner shares an engaging story of his own journey into the Maze in *The Abstract Wild* (Tucson: University of Arizona Press, 1997), pp. 3–18. See also N. Scott Momaday, "The Native Voice in American Literature," in *The Man Made of Words: Essays, Stories, Passages* (New York: St. Martin's, 1997), p. 14.

[52] See Douglas Burton-Christie, "Interlude: The Literature of Nature and the Quest for the Sacred," in *The Sacred Place*, ed. W. Scott Olsen and Scott Cairns (Salt Lake City: University of Utah Press, 1996), pp. 165–177; "Mapping the Sacred Landscape: Spirituality and the Contemporary Literature of Nature," *Horizons* 21:1 (Spring 1994), pp. 22–47; and "A Feeling for the Natural World: Spirituality and the Appeal to the Heart in Contemporary Nature Writing, *Continuum* 2:2–3 (Spring 1993), pp. 154–180. Much of my appreciation for the phenomenological approach argued in this paper is tied to a backpacking trip into the Maze with Doug Burton-Christie in the spring of 1998. This journey to one of the oldest and hardest to reach of all American sacred places was profoundly formative of my thinking.

[53] The Apache claim that places have their own way of "stalking" them with the power of their stories. "The land makes people live right," they claim. See Keith Basso, *Wisdom Sits in Places: Landscape and Language Among the Western Apache* (Albuquerque: University of New Mexico Press, 1996), pp. 37–70.

[54] Clifford Geertz, *Local Knowledge* (New York: Basic Books, 1983), pp. 19–35.

[55] W. G. Hoskins, *The Making of the English Landscape* (Harmondsworth, England: Penguin Books, 1970), p. 1. Walter Brueggemann's book, *Finally Comes the Poet: Daring Speech for Proclamation* (Philadelphia: Fortress Press, 1990), similarly reflects on the importance of the poet's artistry in the exercise of biblical hermeneutics. I would argue that the hermeneutics of place requires the same poetic sensitivity.

[56] David Abram, *The Spell of the Sensuous*, pp. 80–82. Abram argues that our language is "continually nourished by these other voices—by the roar of waterfalls and the thrumming of crickets. It is not by chance that, when hiking in the mountains, the English terms we spontaneously use to describe the surging waters of the nearby river are words like 'rush,' 'splash,' 'gush,' 'wash.'"

[57] Bruce V. Foltz, *Inhabiting the Earth: Heidegger, Environmental Ethics, and the Metaphysics of Nature* (Atlantic Highlands, N.J.: Humanities Press, 1995), pp. 49–50.

[58] See Lynda Sexson, *Ordinarily Sacred* (New York: Crossroad, 1982), and Kathleen Norris, *The Quotidian Mysteries: Laundry, Liturgy, and "Women's Work"* (New York: Paulist Press, 1998).

MYTHIC LANDSCAPES
The Ordinary as Mask of the Holy
[1] Dorothy Day, *On Pilgrimage: The Sixties* (New York: Curtis Books, 1972), p. 207.

[2] Dietrich Bonhoeffer, *Letters and Papers from Prison* (New York: Macmillan, 1962), p. 225.

[3] Wendell Berry, "A Country of Edges," in *Recollected Essays, 1965–1980* (San Francisco: North Point Press, 1981), p. 229.

[4] Herman Melville, *Moby Dick, or The Whale* (New York: Bobbs-Merrill Co., Inc., 1964), p. 220.

[5] Cf. Philip S. Watson, *Let God Be God: An Interpretation of the Theology of Martin Luther* (Philadelphia: Fortress Press, 1947), pp. 76–81.

[6] André Malraux, quoted in *Time*, March 19, 1984, p. 77.

[7] Lewis Thomas, *The Lives of a Cell: Notes of a Biology Watcher* (New York: Viking Press, 1974).

[8] G. K. Chesterton, *Orthodoxy* (London: Fontana Books, 1961), p. 63.

[9] Alice Walker, *The Color Purple* (New York: Washington Square Press, 1983), pp. 178–179.

[10] Paul Ricoeur speaks of the "is" and "is not" character of metaphor in his *The Rule of Metaphor: Multi-Disciplinary Studies of the Creation of Meaning in Language* (Toronto: University of Toronto Press, 1977), pp. 255–256.

[11] Lillian Hellman, *Pentimento: A Book of Portraits* (Boston: Little, Brown, and Co., 1973), frontispiece.

[12] Sam Gill, *Native American Religions: An Introduction* (Belmont, California: Wadsworth Publishing Company, 1982), p. 92. Cf. Frank Waters, *Masked Gods: Navaho and Pueblo Ceremonialism* (New York, 1950).

[13] Martin Luther, "The Freedom of the Christian," in John Dillenberger, ed., *Martin Luther: Selections from His Writings* (Garden City, New York: Doubleday & Co., 1961), p. 76.

[14] Annie Dillard, *Teaching a Stone to Talk* (New York: Harper & Row, 1983), pp. 11–16.

[15] Annie Dillard, *Holy the Firm* (New York: Harper & Row, 1977), p. 45.

[16] William Shakespeare, *King Lear* (V.iii. 11–17).

[17] *The Gospel of Thomas*, 95:26–28.

3 Seeking a Sacred Center: Places and Themes in Native American Spirituality

[1] Frank Waters, *Masked Gods: Navaho and Pueblo Ceremonialism* (Albuquerque: University of New Mexico Press, 1950), p. 17.

[2] Maria José Hobday, "Strung Memories," *Parabola: Myth and the Quest for Meaning*, IV:4 (1979), p. 4.

[3] Cf. Susanne Langer, as quoted in Robert P. Larkin and Gary L. Peters' article on "Sense of Place" in their *Dictionary of Concepts in Human Geography* (Westport, Connecticut: Greenwood Press, 1983), p. 217.

[4] Herman Melville, *Moby-Dick*, quoted in Frederick W. Turner, *Beyond Geography: The Western Spirit Against the Wilderness* (New York: Viking Press, 1980), p. vii.

[5] Sam D. Gill, *Native American Religions: An Introduction* (Belmont, California: Wadsworth Publishing Co., 1982), p. 29. The relation of religious thought and the environment among American Indians is discussed in Christopher Vecsey and Robert W. Venable's *American Indian Environments: Ecological Issues in Native American History* (Syracuse University Press, 1980), pp. 1–37.

[6] The difficulty of classifying and surveying Indian groups and their beliefs is discussed in Elisabeth Tooker, ed., *Native North American Spirituality of the Eastern Woodlands* (New York: Paulist Press, 1979), pp. 7–11. The further difficulty of deciding on a generic name for the native peoples of this continent is dealt with by Haig A. Bosmajian, in his article, "Defining the 'American Indian': A Case Study in the Language of Suppression," in James MacKillop and Donna W. Cross, eds., *Speaking of Words: A Language Reader* (New York: Holt, Rinehart, and Winston, 1978), pp. 95–100.

[7] Quoted in William Least Heat Moon, *Blue Highways: A Journey into America* (Boston: Little, Brown & Co., 1982), p. 206. Cf. Sam D. Gill, *op. cit.*, pp. 33–35. David R. Lee offers a broader phenomenology of the spatial notion of the circle and its center in his article, "In Search of Center," *Landscape*, 21:2 (Winter 1977), pp. 33–37.

[8] Cf. Leland C. Wyman, ed., *Beautyway: A Navaho Ceremonial* (New York: Pantheon Books, 1957), pp 36–37, and Peter Matthiessen, *Indian Country* (New York: Viking Press, 1984), p. 308.

[9] Cf. Sam D. Gill, *Sacred Words: A Study of Navajo Religion and Prayer* (Westport, Connecticut: Greenwood Press, 1981), pp 50–55.

[10] Nancy J. Parezo, *Navajo Sandpainting: From Religious Act to Commercial Art* (Tucson: University of Arizona Press, 1983), p. 1. The spiritual impact of the sand-painting ritual on the Navajo believer is vividly described in a story told by Gerry Armstrong in the Fall 1979 issue of

Explor, vol. 5, no. 2, published by Garrett-Evangelical Theological Seminary, p. 58.

[11] Quoted in Ray B. Browne and Marshall Fishwick, *Icons of America* (Bowling Green, Ohio: Popular Press, 1978), p. 6.

[12] Gladys A. Reichard, *Navaho Religion: A Study of Symbolism* (Tucson: University of Arizona Press, 1983), p. 152.

[13] Cf. Leland Wyman, *op. cit.,* pp. 36–37, for a discussion of these sacred peaks. Alfonso Ortiz describes the world of the Tewa Pueblos of New Mexico, similarly bounded by four sacred mountains, in his book, *The Tewa World: Space, Time, Being, and Becoming in a Pueblo Society* (University of Chicago Press, 1969), pp. 18–20.

[14] Cf. Sam D. Gill, *Sacred Words,* pp. 63–64.

[15] Catherine Albanese explores this concept, especially as it is developed by nineteenth-century Transcendentalists, in her book *Corresponding Motion: Transcendental Religion and the New America* (Philadelphia: Temple University Press, 1977), pp. 8–20.

[16] Cf. Mircea Eliade, *The Sacred and the Profane,* p 37.

[17] Cf. C. Gregory Crampton, *The Zunis of Cibola* (University of Utah Press, 1977), pp. 1–30.

[18] Dennis Tedlock, *Finding the Center: Narrative Poetry of the Zuni Indians* (New York: The Dial Press, 1972), p. 282. Cf. Sam Gill, *Native American Religions,* pp. 16–20, and Dorothea Leighton and John Adair, *People of the Middle Place: A Study of the Zuni Indians* (New Haven, Connecticut: Human Relations Area Files, Inc., 1966), pp. 11f.

[19] Cf. Matthew Fox, O.P., "Catholic Spirituality and the American Spirit: Notes for a Tricentennial Celebration," *Spiritual Life,* 22 (1976), p. 46.

[20] T. C. McLuhan, *Touch the Earth: A Self-Portrait of Indian Existence* (Outerbridge and Dienstfrey, 1971), p. 6.

[21] Jonathan Z. Smith, *Map Is Not Territory: Studies in the History of Religions* (Leiden: E. J. Brill, 1978), p. 291. Horace Miner's "Body Ritual Among the Nacirema," *American Anthropologist,* 58 (1956), pp. 503–507, offers a clever study of cleanliness among Americans, the "Nacirema" spelled backward.

[22] Lucien Levy-Bruhl, *Primitive Mentality* (New York: Macmillan, 1923), pp. 35ff. Cf. Dennis Tedlock and Barbara Tedlock, *Teachings from the American Earth* (New York: Liveright, 1975), pp. xiif.

[23] T. C. McLuhan, *op. cit.,* p. 23.

[24] The symbolism of colors and geographical directions vary considerably among Native American traditions. Cf. Gladys A. Reichard, *Navaho Religion: A Study of Symbolism,* pp. 147ff, and Yi-Fu Tuan, *Man and*

Nature Commission on College Geography Resource Paper No. 10 (Washington, D.C.: Association of American Geographers, 1971), p. 21.

[25] Frederick W. Turner recounts this story in arguing for the necessity of myth in his book *Beyond Geography,* pp. 11–13.

[26] John Neihardt, ed., *Black Elk Speaks* (Lincoln: University of Nebraska Press, 1961), p. 10.

[27] From a Native American perspective, the modern European attitude toward nature found among whites can be characterized as follows: "Nature is analogous to a machine; or in the more popular version nature is a machine. Nature is composed of hard, irreducible particles which have neither color nor smell nor taste. . . . Beauty and value in nature are in the eye of the beholder. Nature is dead *res extens,* perceived by the mind, which observes nature from a position of objective detachment. Nature in itself is basically a self-sufficient, self-enclosed complex of merely physical forces acting on colorless, tasteless, and odorless particles of hard, dead matter." J. Baird Callicott, "Traditional American Indian and Traditional Western European Attitudes toward Nature: An Overview," in *Environmental Philosophy: A Collection of Readings* (Pennsylvania State University Press, 1983), p. 235. Cf. Ake Hultkrantz on "Feelings for Nature among North American Indians," in his *Belief and Worship in Native North America* (Syracuse, New York: Syracuse University Press, 1981), pp. 117–134.

[28] Cf. Norman Bancroft-Hunt, *The Indians of the Great Plains* (New York: William Morrow & Co., 1981), pp. 112–117.

[29] Cf. Joseph Epes Brown, ed., *The Sacred Pipe: Black Elk's Account of the Seven Rites of the Oglala Sioux* (Norman: University of Oklahoma Press, 1953), pp. 31–43, and John Fire/Lame Deer and Richard Erdoes, *Lame Deer: Seeker of Visions* (New York: Simon & Schuster, 1972), pp. 174–182.

[30] Lame Deer, *op. cit.,* p. 212.

[31] Cf. Bryan R. Wilson, *Magic and the Millennium: A Sociological Study of Religious Movements of Protest Among Tribal and Third-World Peoples* (New York: Harper & Row, 1973), pp. 292ff, 416ff.

[32] Arthur C. Parker, *The History of the Seneca Indians* (Port Washington, New York: Ira J. Friedman, Inc., 1967), p. 34. (Originally published in 1926.)

[33] Cf. Campbell Grant, *Rock Art of the American Indian* (New York: Thomas Y. Crowell Co., 1967).

[34] George H. J. Abrams, *The Seneca People* (Phoenix: Indian Tribal Series, 1976), pp. 6–8.

[35] Mary José Hobday, "Seeking a Moist Heart: Native American

Ways for Helping the Spirit," in Matthew Fox, O.P., ed., *Western Spirituality, op. cit.,* p. 326.

[36] O. D. Von Engeln and Jane McElway Urquhart, *Story Key to Geographical Names* (New York, 1924), and John Rydjord, *Indian Place-Names* (Norman: University of Oklahoma Press, 1968).

[37] This story, frequently retold, appeared in Jeremiah Curtin's collection of *Seneca Indian Myths* (New York: E. P. Dutton & Co., 1923). Other selections of Seneca tales can be found in Jesse J. Cornplanter, *Legends of the Longhouse* (Port Washington, New York: Ira J. Friedman, Inc., 1963), and Morton T. Kelsey, ed., *Tales to Tell: Legends of the Senecas* (Pecos, New Mexico: Dove Publications, 1978).

[38] Walter Ong, S.J. has explored the dimensions of *Orality and Literacy* in his book by that title (London: Methuen & Col, Ltd., 1982) and his earlier work, *The Presence of the Word* (New Haven: Yale University Press, 1967).

[39] N. Scott Momaday, "The Man Made of Words," in Sam D. Gill, ed., *Native American Traditions: Sources and Interpretations* (Belmont, California: Wadsworth Publishing Co., 1983), p. 45.

[40] Belden C. Lane, "The Oral Tradition and Its Implications for Contemporary Preaching," *Journal for Preachers* (Easter 1984), pp. 20–21.

[41] Edmund Carpenter, Frederick Varley, and Robert Flaherty, *Eskimo* (University of Toronto Press, 1959), p. 4.

[42] Cf. Jules B. Billard, ed., *The World of the American Indian* (Washington, D.C.: National Geographic Society, 1974), pp. 80–88.

[43] Joseph Epes Brown, *The Spiritual Legacy of the American Indian* (New York: Crossroad, 1982), pp. 6–7.

[44] Asen Balikci, *The Netsilik Eskimo* (Garden City, New York: Natural History Press, 1970), pp. 205–207. Cf. Tedlock, *Teachings from the American Earth*, pp. 13f, where the sea goddess, according to other Eskimo accounts, is named Takanakapsaluk.

[45] Quoted in Annie Dillard, *Pilgrim at Tinker Creek* (Toronto: Bantam Books, 1974), p. 23.

[46] Arthur Conan Doyle, *The Memoirs of Sherlock Holmes,* quoted in Jonathan Z. Smith, *Map Is Not Territory,* p. 300.

[47] Mary José Hobday, "Seeking a Moist Heart," *op. cit.,* pp. 327–328.

[48] William Least Heat Moon, *op. cit.,* p. 174.

[49] William Carlos Williams, *In the American Grain,* quoted in Frederick W. Turner, *op. cit.,* p. x.

[50] Walt Whitman, "A Song of the Rolling Earth," from *Leaves of Grass* (New York: New American Library, 1954), p. 191.

MYTHIC LANDSCAPES
The Mountain That Was God

[1] N. Scott Momaday, *The Names: A Memoir* (New York: Harper & Row, 1976), p. 3.

[2] Lama Anagarika Govinda, *The Way of the White Clouds: A Buddhist Pilgrim in Tibet* (London: Hutchinson & Co., 1966), p. 212.

[3] Yi-Fu Tuan, *Space and Place: The Perspective of Experience* (Minneapolis: University of Minnesota Press, 1977), p. 89.

[4] John Jerome, *On Mountains: Thinking About Terrain* (New York: Harcourt Brace Jovanovich, 1978), pp. 14–16.

[5] Govinda, *op. cit.*, p. 214.

[6] The symbolism of the mountain in Hebrew thought is discussed in Robert L. Cohn's "Mountains in the Biblical Cosmos," in *The Shape of Sacred Space: Four Biblical Studies* (Chico, California: Scholars Press, 1981), pp. 25–33. A study of mountain imagery in Western thought is found in Marjorie Hope Nicholson's *Mountain Gloom and Mountain Glory: The Development of the Aesthetics of the Infinite* (New York: W. W. Norton & Co., 1963).

[7] Cf. Jerome, *op. cit.*, pp. 247–249, and Yi-Fu Tuan, *Topophilia: A Study of Environmental Perception, Attitudes, and Values* (Englewood Cliffs, New Jersey: Prentice-Hall, 1974), pp. 70–74.

[8] William Howarth, ed., *Thoreau in the Mountains* (New York: Farrar, Straus, Giroux, 1982), pp. 10–11. Thoreau urged that all colleges be placed at the base of a mountain. Thereby "some will remember, no doubt, not only that they went to the college, but that they went to the mountain. Every visit to its summit would, as it were, generalize the particular information gained below, and subject it to more catholic tests." Quoted in William J. Wolf, *Thoreau: Mystic, Prophet, Ecologist* (Philadelphia: United Church Press, 1974), p. 69.

[9] Cf. Mircea Eliade, *Patterns in Comparative Religion* (New York: Sheed & Ward, 1958), pp. 99–102, and Joseph Campbell, *The Mythic Image* (Princeton University Press, 1974), pp. 76–140. The mountain has always been the primal place of divine encounter—from the Sumerian ziggurat and Mount Olympus to the Temple of Heaven in Peking and Cambodia's Ankor Wat, from Sinai to the Mount of Olives.

[10] In the Kikuyu religion of Kenya, East Africa, the name for the snow-covered Mount Kenya is also the name most often used for God, "the possessor of brightness." Similarly, Christians among the Chagga peoples on the slopes of Kilimanjaro in Northern Tanzania sing a hymn to Jesus, "the Mountain full of eternal brightness." Cf. Carl Hallencreutz, "'Christ is the Mountain': Some Observations on the Religious Function of Symbols," in *Religious Symbols and Their Functions*, ed. Haralds

Biezais, Scripta Instituti Donneriani Absensis, X (Stockholm: Almqvist and Wiksell, Int., 1979).

4   Baroque Spirituality in New Spain and New France

[1] *McGraw-Hill Dictionary of Art* (New York: McGraw-Hill Book Co., 1969), I, p. 247.

[2] *The Autobiography of Venerable Marie of the Incarnation, O.S.U.: Mystic and Missionary,* translated by John J. Sullivan, S.J. (Chicago: Loyola University Press, 1964). pp. 90–92, 99–100, 128.

[3] Cf. John Tracy Ellis, *Catholics in Colonial America* (Baltimore: Helicon Press, 1965).

[4] Erich Isaac, "Religion, Landscape, and Space," *Landscape* IX (Winter 1960), p. 14, as quoted in David Sopher, *Geography of Religions* (Englewood Cliffs, New Jersey: Prentice-Hall, Inc., 1967), pp. 14–15.

[5] Marcelin Defourneaux, *Daily Life in Spain in the Golden Age* (New York: Praeger Publishers, 1971), p. 30.

[6] John Crow, *Spain: The Root and the Flower* (New York: Harper & Row, 1963), p. 4.

[7] E. Allison Peers, *Spain: A Companion to Spanish Studies* (London: Methuen, 1956), p. 7. Indicating still further the pride of the Spanish in their language as well as independence, Emperor Charles V was said to have spoken Italian to his mistresses, French to his friends, and German to his dogs; but in Spanish he communed with his God!

[8] Cf. William Fleming, *Arts and Ideas* (New York: Holt, Rinehart and Winston, Inc., 1963), pp. 461–467.

[9] Cf. Pierre Janelle, *The Catholic Reformation* (Milwaukee: Bruce Publishing Co., 1963), p. 104.

[10] *The Collected Works of St. Teresa of Avila* (Washington, D.C.: ICS Publications/Institute of Carmelite Studies, 1976), p. 190.

[11] Cf. Louis Cognet, *Post-Reformation Spirituality* (New York: Hawthorne Books, 1959).

[12] A careful study of spiritual writers in New Spain has yet to be made. Yet a catalogue of such figures would have to include the Colombian mystic, Sor Francisca Jesefa de la Concepcion, known popularly as Mother Castillo (1671–1742). Enrique Imbert speaks of her as *"the mystic of Spanish American letters."* Enrique A. Imbert, *Spanish-American Literature: A History* (Detroit: Wayne State University Press, 1963), pp. 92–93. E. Allison Peers also refers to Antonio de la Cruz and Gaspar de la Figuera as spiritual writers who worked, in part, out of their Mexican experience. Cf. *Studies of the Spanish Mystics*, III, pp. 38f and 222f.

[13] Ross Calvin, *Sky Determines: An Interpretation of the Southwest* (Albuquerque: University of New Mexico Press, 1965), p. 5.

¹⁴ Thomas J. Steele, S.J., *Santos and Saints: The Religious Folk Art of Hispanic New Mexico* (Santa Fe, New Mexico: Ancient City Press, 1982), pp. 109f, 121f. Cf. William Wroth, *Christian Images in Hispanic New Mexico* (Colorado Springs: Colorado Springs Fine Arts Center, 1982).

¹⁵ *Ibid.*, p. 60. Cf. Steele's article on "The Spanish Passion Play in New Mexico and Colorado," *New Mexico Historical Review* 53 (1978), pp. 239–259.

¹⁶ Cf. Marta Weigle, *Brothers of Light, Brothers of Blood: The Penitentes of the Southwest* (Albuquerque: University of New Mexico Press, 1976) and Earle R. Forrest, *Missions and Pueblos of the Old Southwest* (Cleveland: Arthur H. Clark Co., 1929), pp. 195–206.

¹⁷ For an account of the early sixteenth-century plays performed by Franciscan missionaries in Mexico see Robert Ricard, *The Spiritual Conquest of Mexico* (Berkeley: University of California Press, 1966), pp. 194–206. Cf. Leonard Ellinwood, *The History of American Church Music* (New York: Da Capo Press, 1970), pp. 3–9.

¹⁸ Henry Nash Smith, *Virgin Land* (Cambridge: Harvard University Press, 1978), pp. 174–183.

¹⁹ John Updike, *A Month of Sundays* (New York: A. A. Knopf, 1975), pp. 161f.

²⁰ Alice Corbin Henderson, *Brothers of Light* (1937), p. 49, quoted by Marta Weigel, *op. cit.*, p. 1.

²¹ His conversion is narrated in book III, chapters 4–5, 79–80 of his *History of the Indies* (1560). See *Bartolomé de Las Casas: A Selection of His Writings*, translated by George Sanderlin (New York: A. A. Knopf, 1971), pp. 80–94. For a documentary history of the colony of New Spain, see Charles Gibson, ed., *The Spanish Tradition in America* (New York: Harper & Row, 1968).

²² Cf. Henry R. Wagner, *The Life and Writings of Bartolomé de las Casas* (Albuquerque: University of New Mexico Press, 1967).

²³ Cf. Lewis Hanke, *All Mankind Is One: A Study of the Disputation Between Bartolomé de Las Casas and Juan Gines de Sepulveda in 1550 on the Intellectual and Religious Capacity of the American Indians* (Northern Illinois University Press, 1974).

²⁴ Cf. Gloria Giffords, *Mexican Folk Retablos* (Tucson: University of Arizona Press, 1974), pp. 27, 31, 71.

²⁵ Cf. Ernest Burrus, S.J., *Kino and Manje: Explorers of Sonora and Arizona* (Rome: Jesuit Historical Institute, 1971), p. 35. Padre Kino's achievements in mapping the landscape of lower California are further described in Fr. Burrus's *Kino and the Cartography of Northwestern New Spain* (Tucson: Arizona Pioneer's Historical Society, 1965).

²⁶ Thomas Steele sees the four-part structure of the apparition se-

quence to further suggest that the account was authentically Indian—
not composed by a European, for whom the narrative law of three
would have been much more mythically profound. See his *Santos and
Saints*, p. 99. Cf. Joseph L. Cassidy, *Mexico: Land of Mary's Wonders*
(Paterson, New Jersey: St. Anthony Guild Press, 1958).

[27] Donald Demarest and Coley Taylor, *The Dark Virgin* (Freeport,
Maine: Coley Taylor, Inc., 1956), pp. 208–212.

[28] Bamber Gascoigne, *The Christians* (New York: Morrow, 1977), p.
180.

[29] Winifred E. Wise, *Fray Junipero Serra and the California Conquest*
(New York: Scribners, 1967).

[30] John Lough, *An Introduction to Seventeenth-Century France* (New
York: David McKay Co., Inc., 1954), pp. 162–166. Cf. W. H. Louis *The
Splendid Century: Life in the France of Louis XIV* (Garden City, New York:
Doubleday & Co., Inc., 1953), chapter 2, "The Court."

[31] Quoted in Lough, *op. cit.*, p. 135.

[32] Lawrence Durrell, *The Spirit of Place: Letters and Essays on Travel*
(New York: E. P. Dutton & Co., Inc., 1969), p. 323.

[33] Cf. Yi-Fu Tuan, *Topophilia*, pp. 85–91.

[34] Quoted in Robert Brittain, *Rivers, Man and Myths* (Garden City,
New York: Doubleday & Co., Inc., 1958), p. 90.

[35] Cf. E. Estyn Evans, *France: An Introductory Geography* (New York:
Frederick A. Praeger, Publishers, 1967), and Ragnhild Hatton, *Louis
XIV and His World* (London: Thames & Hudson, 1972).

[36] Henri Bremond, *A Literary History of Religious Thought in France*
(London: S.P.C.K., 1936), III, p. 32.

[37] *Ibid.*, III, pp. 17, 77. Cf. Jean Gautier's study of "Oratorian Spirituality" in his book *Some Schools of Catholic Spirituality* (Paris: Desclée
Co., 1959), pp. 29–346, and Louis Cognet, *op. cit.*, pp. 56–115.

[38] Henri Bremond, *op. cit.*, III, p. 35.

[39] Cf. Jean Simard, *Une Iconographie du Clergé Francais au XVIIe
Siecle: Les Dévotions de L'École Francaise et les Sources de 'L'Imagerie Religieuse
en France et au Quebec* (Quebec: Les Presses de L'Université Laval,
1976), pp. 159–167.

[40] Quoted in Hilda Graef, *Mary: A History of Doctrine and Devotion*
(New York: Sheed and Ward, 1965), II, p. 41. At this same time in
seventeenth-century France, worship is increasingly subservient to cleri-
cal authority. Worship becomes more hieratic and the mass becomes
less familial, more distant from the average parishioner—who gradually
loses his right (which had been customary) to challenge his *curé*, to talk
to him in public, and to discuss his statements. With the obvious exception of the hymns, the faithful are reduced to silence. Worship has

become more solemn: a profound change, with far-reaching psychological implications." Georges Duby and Robert Mandrou, *A History of French Civilization* (New York: Random House, 1964), p. 305.

⁴¹ Jean Simard, *op cit.*, pp. 31–39 and Henri Bremond, *op. cit.*, III, pp. 464–469.

⁴² *The Autobiography of the Venerable Marie of the Incarnation*, p. 168.

⁴³ Cf. Cynthia P. Maus, *The World's Great Madonnas* (New York: Harper & Row, 1947), p. 531.

⁴⁴ Francis B. Thornton, *Catholic Shrines in the United States and Canada* (New York: Wilgred Funk, Inc., 1954), pp. 253–256.

⁴⁵ Jacques Marquette, *Voyages of Marquette in the Jesuit Relations*, 59, March of America Facsimile Series, number 28 (Ann Arbor: University Microfilms, Inc., 1966), p. 93.

⁴⁶ *Autobiography*, pp. 27, 131.

⁴⁷ Cf. Dale Van Kley, *The Jansenists and the Expulsion of the Jesuits from France, 1757–1765* (New Haven: Yale University Press, 1975), pp. 9–11, and Alexander Sedgwick, *Jansenism in Seventeenth-Century France* (Charlottesville: University Press of Virginia, 1977), pp. 193–207.

⁴⁸ Cf. R. F. Sheehan's article in *The Saturday Evening Post* (November 28, 1964) and Michael Novak's reference to the "Celtic heresy" of authoritarianism in *Commentary* (September 1965).

⁴⁹ So argues Desmond Fennell in his book *The Changing Face of Catholic Ireland* (Washington, D.C.: Corpus Books, 1968), pp. 124–129, 180.

⁵⁰ Joyce Marshall, ed., *Word From New France: The Selected Letters of Marie de L'Incarnation* (Toronto: Oxford University Press, 1967), pp. 83–84.

⁵¹ *Ibid.*, p. 170.

⁵² John Tracy Ellis, ed., *Documents of American Church History* (Chicago: Henry Regnery Co., 1967), I, p. 71.

⁵³ Cf. Richard Van Der Beets, *Held Captive by Indians: Selected Narratives, 1642–1836* (Knoxville: University of Tennessee Press, 1973), pp. 3–40. Marie of the Incarnation also relates Fr. Jogues's story with great detail in her letters, *Word from New France*, pp. 102–175.

⁵⁴ John Tracy Ellis, *Documents of the American Catholic Church*, I, p. 54.

⁵⁵ *Word From New France*, p. 341. As a young woman, prior to her entering the Ursulines, Marie had been married and had given birth to a son. Her husband died and her child was raised by others, yet the two remained close correspondents all of their lives.

⁵⁶ Fairness demands, however, that it be noted how the French, unlike the Spanish, never made a practice of slavery or forced labor in the New World. In fact, the charter of the Company of New France

declared that Indian converts had full rights to settle in France and own property there like any other French subject. Cf. W. J. Eccles, *France in America* (New York: Harper & Row 1972), p. 39.

[57] *Autobiography*, pp. 149–150, 175.

[58] Cf. Bremond, *op. cit.*, III. pp. 530–531.

[59] Martin E. Marty, *Pilgrims in Their Own Land: 500 Years of Religion in America* (Boston: Little, Brown, & Co., 1984), p. 92.

MYTHIC LANDSCAPES
The Desert Imagination of Edward Abbey

[1] Willa Cather, *Death Comes for the Archbishop* (New York: Alfred A. Knopf, 1927), pp. 281–283.

[2] Cf. Garth McCann, *Edward Abbey*, Western Writers Series, no. 29 (Boise, Idaho: Boise State University, 1977), p. 14.

[3] For studies of the biblical image of the desert see Shemaryahu Talmon, "The 'Desert Motif' in the Bible and in Qumran Literature," in Alexander Altmann, ed., *Biblical Motifs: Origins and Transformations* (Harvard University Press, 1966); John L. McKenzie, "Into the Desert," *The Way*, I:1 (January 1961), pp. 27–39; Robert L. Cohn, "Liminality in the Wilderness," in *The Shape of Sacred Space* (Chico, California: Scholars Press, 1981); and George H. Williams, *Wilderness and Paradise in Christian Thought* (New York: Harper & Brothers, 1962).

[4] Edward Abbey, *The Journey Home: Some Words in Defense of the American West* (New York: E. P. Dutton, 1977), p. 14.

[5] Edward Abbey, *Desert Solitaire: A Season in the Wilderness* (New York: McGraw-Hill, 1968), p. 176.

[6] *The Journey Home*, p. 72.

[7] *Desert Solitaire*, p. 26.

[8] Edward Abbey, *Cactus Country* (New York: Time-Life Books, 1973), pp. 52–61. Cf. Joseph Wood Krutch, *The Voice of the Desert: A Naturalist's Interpretation* (New York: William Sloane Associates, 1954), pp. 40–52.

[9] Yushi Nomura, *Desert Wisdom: Sayings from the Desert Fathers* (New York: Doubleday, 1982), p. 68. Cf. Susan A. Muto, "Living the Desert Experience," in *A Practical Guide to Spiritual Reading* (Denville, New Jersey: Dimension Books, 1976), pp. 58–95, and Donald Goergen, "The Desert as Reality and Symbol," *Spirituality Today* 34:1 (March 1982), pp. 70–79.

[10] *Desert Solitaire*, pp. 117–118.

[11] *Ibid.*, pp. 24–25.

[12] Cf. David Attenborough, *The Living Planet* (Boston: Little, Brown & Co., 1984), pp. 156–160.

[13] *Desert Solitaire*, p. 125.

[14] Cf. Martha Robbins, "The Desert-Mountain Experience: The Two Faces of Encounter with God," *Journal of Pastoral Care* 35 (March 1981), pp. 18–35.

5 The Puritan Reading of the New England Landscape

[1] Conrad Cherry, "New England as Symbol: Ambiguity in the Puritan Vision," *Soundings*, 58 (Fall 1975), p. 348.

[2] Quoted in Charles Mabee, *Reimagining America: A Theological Critique of the American Mythos and Biblical Hermeneutics* (Mercer University Press, 1985), p. 6.

[3] Cotton Mather, *The Christian Philosopher: A Collection of the Best Discoveries in Nature, with Religious Improvements* (1721) (Gainesville, Florida: Scholars' Facsimiles & Reprints, 1968), p. 8. George Williams, in his study of *Wilderness and Paradise in Christian Thought* (New York: Harper & Brothers, 1962), p. 103, remarks of Roger Williams that he "read the book of the wilderness with its emblems much as he read Scripture typologically, as though it were a vast palimpsest unrolled before him."

[4] Johann Alsted, *Encyclopaedia Scientiarum Omnium* (1630), quoted in Perry Miller, *The New England Mind: The Seventeenth Century* (Boston: Beacon Press, 1961), p. 209.

[5] *Ibid.*, p. 212. Miller argues that "the disposition to read sermons in brooks and morals in stones seems . . . to have become ingrained in the New England nature," transmitted later to Hawthorne and Emerson. *Ibid.*, p. 214.

[6] Jonathan Edwards, *Observations, etc.* Appendix, pp. 94–97. Quoted in Alexander V. G. Allen, *Jonathan Edwards* (New York: Burt Franklin Reprints, 1975), pp. 355–356.

[7] Cotton Mather, *Magnalia Christi Americana* (New York: Russell & Russell, 1967) (Reproduction of 1852 edition), II, pp. 363–372.

[8] Perry Miller, *Errand into the Wilderness* (New York: Harper & Row, 1964), p. 51. "The essence of Puritanism," adds Miller, "is the hidden God, the unknowable, the unpredictable." *Ibid.*, p. 93.

[9] Perry Miller began his study of *The New England Mind: The Seventeenth Century* with a chapter on "The Augustinian Strain of Piety" which he saw to be central to Puritan spirituality.

[10] The terms of covenant piety, including the narrative of personal conversion which came to be expected of those "owning" the covenant, are described in Edmund S. Morgan's *Visible Saints* (Cornell University Press, 1963) and Patricia Caldwell's *Puritan Conversion Narratives* (Cambridge University Press, 1983). On the significance of the sacraments of baptism and the Lord's Supper in covenant theology, see E. Brooks

Holifield, *The Covenant Sealed: The Development of Puritan Sacramental Theology in Old and New England, 1570–1720* (New Haven: Yale University Press, 1974).

[11] Strange it is that the terror of dislocation from God—the awesomeness of sin—becomes itself the antechamber of grace. Hence, the extraordinary paradox of an essential Calvinist truth: "that sin itself is the sublime, and that only its enormity puts men on speaking terms with God." Ann Douglas, *The Feminization of American Culture* (New York: A. A. Knopf, 1977), p. 245.

[12] Newton Arvin, ed., *Hawthorne's Short Stories* (New York: Vintage Books, 1946), p. 185. This stereotype is echoed in H. L. Mencken's wry comment that "Puritanism is the haunting fear that someone, somewhere might be happy."

[13] William H. Shurr, *Rappaccini's Children: American Writers in a Calvinist World* (Lexington: University of Kentucky Press, 1981).

[14] *Hawthorne's Short Stories*, p. 285. The influence of Puritan spirituality on Nathaniel Hawthorne has been studied in Michael Solacurico's *Province of Piety: Moral History in Hawthorne's Tales* (Harvard University Press, 1984) and Agnes Donohue's *Hawthorne: Calvin's Ironic Stepchild* (Kent State University Press, 1985).

[15] Cf. Jonathan Edwards's 1734 sermon, "A Divine and Supernatural Light," described by Perry Miller as offering "the whole of his system contained in miniature." *Jonathan Edwards* (New York: W. Sloane Associates, 1949), p. 44.

[16] Jonathan Edwards, "Personal Narrative," *The Works of President Edwards* (New York: S. Converse, 1829), I, p. 61.

[17] *Ibid.*, pp. 99–100.

[18] Quoted in William Shurr, *op. cit.*, pp. 10–11.

[19] D. W. Meinig describes the archetypal New England Village, along with the Main Street of Middle America and the California Suburb, as symbolic landscapes or idealizations of American communities. Cf. *The Interpretation of Ordinary Landscapes* (New York: Oxford University Press, 1979), pp. 164–192.

[20] John R. Stilgoe, *Common Landscape of America, 1580 to 1845* (New Haven: Yale University Press, 1982), p. 12.

[21] Mircea Eliade, *The Sacred and the Profane* (New York: Harper & Row, 1961), p. 36.

[22] John W. Reps describes the pattern of New England village planning in his book, *The Making of Urban America* (Princeton University Press, 1965), pp. 124–146. Cf. John Stilgoe, *op. cit.*, pp. 43–58, and Samuel Chamberlain's *The New England Image* (New York: Hastings House, 1962) for a photographic essay on the Yankee townscape.

[23] Found among the papers of John Winthrop Stilgoe analyzes this essay in his article, "The Puritan Townscape: Ideal and Reality," *Landscape*, 20:3 (Spring 1976), pp. 3–7. Sumner C. Powell, in his book *Puritan Village: The Formation of a New England Town* (Middletown, Connecticut: Wesleyan University Press, 1963), discusses the open field manorial village as a background to New England town-planning.

[24] Stilgoe, "The Puritan Townscape," p. 3. John Cotton proposed a statute by which "noe man shall set his dwelling house" more than "half a myle, or a myle at the farthest, from the meeting house of the congregation." Cf. Peter N. Carroll, *Puritanism and the Wilderness* (New York: Columbia University Press, 1969), p. 121.

[25] Stilgoe, "The Puritan Townscape," p. 4.

[26] Stilgoe, *Common Landscape of America*, p. 54. Cf. David Stannard, *The Puritan Way of Death* (New York: Oxford University Press, 1977).

[27] *Ibid.*, p. 44. John Cotton set it down as a maxim that "society in all sorts of human affairs is better than solitariness."

[28] Edward Johnson, *The Wonder-Working Providence of Sion's Saviour in New England: A History of New England, 1628–1651* (New York: Charles Scribner's Sons, 1910), p. 74.

[29] Yi-Fu Tuan, in his study of *Landscapes of Fear* (New York: Pantheon Books, 1979), suggests the importance of considering the relation of anxiety to place, though not referring in particular to the New England Puritan experience. Stilgoe observes in this respect that four-fifths of the women accused of being witches in the 1690's lived *beyond* the bounds of Salem village, on the edge of the seductive wilderness. Their placement in the landscape thus provoked as much fear as their behavior.

[30] Quoted in Ronald S. Wallace, *Calvin's Doctrine of the Christian Life* (Edinburgh: Oliver & Boyd, 1959), p. 128.

[31] Robert Cushman, "Reasons and Considerations Touching the Lawfulness of Removing out of England into the Parts of America," (London, 1622), quoted in Charles E. Hambrick-Stowe, *The Practice of Piety: Puritan Devotional Disciplines in Seventeenth-Century New England* (Chapel Hill: University of North Carolina Press, 1982), pp. 13–16. Larzer Ziff, in his *Puritanism in America* (New York: Viking Press, 1973), p. 41, suggests that, for the Puritan, "the [Old Testament] attachment of place to promise was abrogated by Jesus. America was a lawful place for settlement not because it was a promised land, but, on the contrary, because there was no longer such a particular locale—neither England nor America nor Canaan—and therefore all places were suitable for the elect. . . ."

[32] John Cotton, *A Briefe Exposition of the Whole Book of Canticles* (London, 1642), quoted in Hambrick-Stowe, *op. cit.*, p. 59.

[33] Mead says "the pioneer felt 'free' so long as he felt that he could move on when he could see the smoke from a neighbor's cabin or hear the sound of his neighbor's rifle." Sidney E. Mead, *The Lively Experiment: The Shaping of Christianity in America* (New York: Harper & Row, 1963), p. 12. The first chapter of Mead's book offers a brilliant discussion of the tensions of space and time confronting early American settlers.

[34] Quoted in Perry Miller, *The New England Mind: The Seventeenth Century*, p. 15.

[35] Cotton Mather, *Magnalia Christi Americana*, I, p. 51.

[36] John White, in *The Planter's Plea* (London, 1630), p. 3, said, "If it were then [as he has argued], the mind of God, that man should possess all parts of the earth, it must be enforced that we neglect our duty, and crosse his will, if we doe it not, when wee have occasion and opportunitie. . . ." But two generations later the Reforming Synod of 1679 complained that "there hath been in many professors an insatiable desire after Land, and worldly Accommodations, yea as to forsake Churches and Ordinances and to live like Heathen, only that so they might have Elbow-room enough in the world." Quoted in Hambrick-Stowe, *op. cit.*, p. 244.

[37] John Cotton, "God's Promise to His Plantations" (London, 1630), *Old South Leaflets* III:53 (Boston: Old South Meeting House, n.d.).

[38] Cf. John White, *The Planter's Plea; or The Grounds of Plantations Examined and Usual Objections Answered* (London: William Jones, 1630).

[39] John Underhill, quoted in Alan Heimert, "Puritanism, the Wilderness, and the Frontier," *The New England Quarterly*, XXVI (March–December 1953), p. 365.

[40] Thomas Morton, *New English Canaan* (Amsterdam: Jacob Frederick Stam, 1637), p. 97.

[41] Nathaniel Hawthorne, *The Scarlet Letter* (New York: Washington Square Press, Inc., 1955), p. 81.

[42] *Ibid.*, pp. 207–208.

[43] Hambrick-Stowe, *op. cit.*, pp. 54–90, observes that the Atlantic crossing stories came later to be replaced by Indian captivity narratives in the continuing pilgrimage motif of Puritan devotional literature.

[44] On the Puritan tradition of the jeremiad, see Perry Miller, "From the Covenant to the Revival," in *The Shaping of American Religion*, ed. James Smith and Leland Jamison (Princeton University Press, 1961) as well as his chapter on the jeremiad in *The New England Mind: From Colony to Province* (Boston: Beacon Press, 1961), pp. 27–39. Cf. Sacvan

Bercovitch, *The American Jeremiad* (Madison: University of Wisconsin Press, 1978), and Robert Bellah, *The Broken Covenant: American Civil Religion in a Time of Trial* (New York: Seabury Press, 1975).

[45] John Cotton, *God's Promise to His Plantations*, pp. 15–18.

[46] Cotton Mather, *Days of Humiliation: Time of Affliction and Disaster, Nine Sermons for Restoring Favor with an Angry God, 1696–1727* (Gainesville, Florida: Scholars' Facsimiles & Reprints, 1970), p. 288.

[47] Cf. Edward Taylor, "Sacramental Meditation One," *The Poetical Works of Edward Taylor,* ed. Thomas H. Johnson (Princeton University Press, 1943), p. 123.

[48] Conrad Cherry, *op. cit.,* p. 348.

[49] Roderick Nash, *Wilderness and the American Mind* (New Haven: Yale University Press, 1967), pp. 23–24.

[50] On Puritan conceptions of wilderness see the respective works by Alan Heimert and Peter Carroll already quoted.

[51] Thomas Shepard, *Eye-Salve, Or A Watch-Word from Our Lord Jesus Christ unto His Churches* (Cambridge, Massachusetts: Samuel Green, 1673), p. 3.

[52] Edward Johnson, *op. cit.,* p. 151. Thomas Hooker quoted from Peter Carroll, *op. cit,* p. 68.

[53] Quoted in J. B. Jackson's "A Puritan Looks at Scenery," in his book *Discovering the Vernacular Landscape* (New Haven: Yale University Press, 1984), pp. 59–60.

[54] Cf. John Conron, *The American Landscape: A Critical Anthology of Prose and Poetry* (New York: Oxford University Press, 1974), pp. 568–578 and illustrations 32 and 33, for the perspective of landscape painter Thomas Cole.

[55] Edward Johnson, *op. cit.,* p. 112.

[56] Michael Wigglesworth, "God's Controversy with New England," quoted in Conrad Cherry, *God's New Israel: Religious Interpretations of American Destiny* (Englewood Cliffs, New Jersey: Prentice-Hall, 1971), p. 50. Cf. John Cotton, *Gods Mercie Mixed with His Justice*, 1651 (Gainesville, Florida: Scholars' Facsimiles & Reprints, 1958).

[57] Cotton Mather, quoted in Nash, *op. cit.,* p. 29.

[58] Quoted in Conrad Cherry, "New England as Symbol," p. 360.

MYTHIC LANDSCAPES
Galesville, Wisconsin: Locus Mirabilis

[1] D. O. Van Slyke, *Found at Last: The Veritable Garden of Eden, or a Place that Answers the Bible Description of That Notable Spot Better Than Anything Yet Discovered* (Galesville, Wisconsin: The Galesville Republican, 1886).

² American myth has repeatedly been drawn to the theme of the lush garden found in the New World. Henry Nash Smith, in his book *Virgin Land* (Cambridge: Harvard University Press, 1978) pp. 123–260, speaks at length of the image of America as the "Garden of the World." The tradition began as early as Columbus himself, writing to the Spanish treasurer of the "verdant and luxuriant" growth found on the island of San Salvador—the fruit trees, the beautiful mountains, and gentle inhabitants that so impressed him. Cf. Giles Gunn, ed., *New World Metaphysics* (New York: Oxford University Press, 1981), pp. 6–9. Mircea Eliade speaks of the theme of primordial paradise as found in a variety of cultures in his *Myth of the Eternal Return* (New York: Pantheon Books, 1954), pp. 16, 91, 121.

³ The American quest for paradise is studied in David W. Noble, *The Eternal Adam and the New World Garden: The Central Myth in the American Novel Since 1830* (New York: George Braziller, 1968); Charles L. Sanford, *The Quest for Paradise: Europe and the American Moral Imagination* (University of Illinois Press, 1961); and R. W. B. Lewis, *The American Adam* (University of Chicago Press, 1955).

⁴ Cf. Berton Roueche, *Special Places: In Search of Small Town America* (Boston: Little, Brown & Co., 1982), p. 89, and Charles Kuralt, *Dateline America* (New York: Harcourt Brace Jovanovich, 1979), pp. 101–102.

6　The Correspondence of Spiritual and Material Worlds in Shaker Spirituality

¹ J. S. Whale, *Christian Reunion: Historic Divisions Reconsidered* (Grand Rapids, Michigan: William B. Eerdmans Publishing Co., 1971), p. 59.

² Quoted in Ruth Wolfe, "Hannah Cohoon: Shaker Spirit Painter," *Art and Antiques* (May/June 1980), p. 94. Her drawing can be seen in Edward Deming Andrews and Faith Andrews, *Visions of the Heavenly Sphere: A Study in Shaker Religious Art* (Charlottesville: University Press of Virginia, 1969), pp. 90–91.

³ Millennial Laws, IV:20, found in Edward Deming Andrews, *The People Called Shakers* (New York: Dover Publications, Inc., 1963), p. 287.

⁴ Ann Lee (1736–1784) was viewed by many of her followers as a feminine expression of the Word of God first revealed in Jesus Christ. Their emphasis on the equality of the sexes, along with their pacifism and early tendency toward enthusiasm in worship led to their being persecuted in New York and Massachusetts. Mother Ann was herself dragged for several miles behind a wagon over icy roads by a hostile mob shortly before her death.

⁵ Known more precisely as "the United Society of Believers in Christ's Second Appearing," the Shakers' history and theology are de-

scribed in the works of Edward and Faith Andrews already mentioned. See also their *Work and Worship: The Economic Order of the Shakers* (Greenwich, Connecticut: New York Graphic Society, 1974) and *The Gift to be Simple: Songs, Dances and Rituals of the American Shakers* (New York: Dover Publications, Inc., 1940). Henri Desroche offers a sociological perspective in his book on *The American Shakers: From Neo-Christianity to Presocialism* (Amherst: University of Massachusetts Press, 1971). June Spriggs has a fine survey of Shaker attitudes toward space, time, and simplicity in her book, *By Shaker Hands* (New York: Alfred A. Knopf, 1975). The best study of Shaker spirituality is found in Robley E. Whitson, ed., *The Shakers: Two Centuries of Spiritual Reflection* (New York: Paulist Press, 1983).

⁶ Caroline B. Piercy, *The Valley of God's Pleasure: A Saga of the North Union Shaker Community* (New York: Stratford House, 1951), p. 150.

⁷ Quoted in Edward D. Andrews and Faith Andrews, *Religion in Wood: A Book of Shaker Furniture* (Bloomington: Indiana University Press, 1966), p. 5.

⁸ An inspirational drawing made at the Mt. Lebanon, New York, community in 1843 shows "the Plan of the City of the New Jerusalem" as "a perfect [pattern] of the High City of the Holy Selan in the Heavens [which is] right over this the Holy City on Earth." Cf. David Sellin, "Shaker Inspirational Drawings," *Philadelphia Museum Bulletin*, LVII:273 (Spring 1962), pp. 95–96.

⁹ Catherine Albanese surveys this history of the doctrine of correspondence in her book *Corresponding Motion: Transcendental Religion and the New America* (Philadelphia: Temple University Press, 1977), pp. 615.

¹⁰ Quoted in June Sprigg, *By Shaker Hands*, p. 5. The duplication of other-worldly perfection was particularly seen in the copying of geometric forms thought to be characteristic of the heavenly sphere. Edward Andrews indicates, for example, the frequency of the hexagonal shape in the construction by the Shakers of their "holy mounts" in the 1840's. Constantinos Doxiades, in his study of *Ekistics: An Introduction to the Science of Human Settlements* (New York: Oxford University Press, 1968), pp. 133–146, shows how the hexagonal form is one of the most optimal designs for ekistic regions anywhere in nature, from insect to human settlements.

¹¹ R. Louise Fletcher, "Shakerland: A Topographic History," *Landscape*, 21:3 (Spring-Summer 1977), p. 38. June Sprigg observes how "the actual physical environment of the Shaker village was shaped to some heavenly ideal: lines were perfectly straight, not crooked; angles were exactly right; deceitful workmanship was forbidden; and all was kept pure, clean, and orderly." *Op. cit.*, p. 74. Mircea Eliade speaks of the

cross-cultural phenomenon of celestial archetypes of territories, temples and cities in *The Myth of the Eternal Return* (New York: Pantheon Books, 1954), pp. 6–12.

[12] The Shaker meetinghouse was also designed as spaciously as possible, without supporting pillars to interrupt this space for dancing. In such a way, a certain "felicity of space" was achieved within the hall of worship. Sprigg, *op. cit.*, p. 76. Cf. Herbert Schiffer, *Shaker Architecture* (Extort, Pennsylvania: Schiffer Publishing, Ltd., 1979).

[13] Calvin Green and Seth Wells, two of the earliest Shaker theologians, would insist that "the natural world, and the things therein contained, were, from the beginning, wisely designed as figurative representations of spiritual things to come." *A Summary View of the Millennial Church, or United Society of Believers, Commonly Called Shakers* (Albany: C. Van Benthuysen, 1848), pp. 125–126.

[14] Cf. Rene Francois Rohrbacher, *Histoire Universelle de L'Eglise Catholique* (Paris: Gaume Freres et J. Duprey, 1859), vol. 26, pp. 407–410.

[15] For a study of emblematic imagery in the Puritan consciousness, see George Monteiro and Barton Levi St. Armand, "The Experienced Emblem: A Study of the Poetry of Emily Dickinson," *Prospects: The Annual of American Cultural Studies*, ed. Jack Salzman (New York: Burt Franklin and Co., 1981), pp. 184–280.

[16] Albanese, *op. cit.*, p. 96.

[17] Quoted from Shaker medium Paulina Bates, in John McKelvie Whitworth, *God's Blueprints: A Sociological Study of Three Utopian Sects* (London: Routledge and Kegan Paul, 1975), pp. 55–57. Frederick Evans spoke of both Emerson and Swedenborg in his *Autobiography of a Shaker and Revelation of the Apocalypse* (Glasgow: United Publishing Co., 1888), referring to the latter as the angel from heaven predicted in Rev. 18:1 (p. 41). Cf. George F. Dole, ed., *Emmanuel Swedenborg: The Universal Human and Soul-Body Interaction* (New York: Paulist Press, 1984), pp. 27f.

[18] Cf. C. S. Lewis, *Of Other Worlds: Essays and Stories* (New York: Harcourt, Brace & World, Inc., 1966) and J. R. R. Tolkien, "On Fairy-Stories," in *Tree and Leaf* (London: Allen & Unwin, 1964). W. H. Auden pursues the same theme in his *Secondary Worlds* (London: Faber and Faber, 1968).

[19] The manner in which Mormon religious thought was given spatial expression is analyzed in Richard H. Jackson's "Religion and Landscape in the Mormon Cultural Region," in *Dimensions in Human Geography*, ed. Karl W. Butzer (University of Chicago Department of Geography Research Paper 186, 1978), pp. 100–127.

[20] Quoted in Anna White and Leila S. Taylor, *Shakerism: Its Meaning and Message* (Columbus, Ohio: Press of F. J. Heer, 1904), p. 361.

[21] Mother Ann told her followers that "while I was in England, I knew, by the revelation of God, that God had a chosen people in America and I saw some of them in vision, while I was in England; and when I saw them in America, I knew them." Quoted in Diane Sasson, *op. cit.*, p. 27.

[22] The revival began in August 1837 when several children at the Watervliet society reported receiving visions and being guided by angels from place to place in a joyous Spirit Land. Cf. Andrews, *Visions of the Heavenly Sphere*, pp. 15–16. The decade of the 1840's was one of great turmoil and religious creativity generally. Initiated by the financial panic of 1837, it brought to prominence the millennial expectations of William Miller, the utopian socialist fervor of the Fourierist phalanxes, and the spiritualist enthusiasm associated with the "Rochester Knockings."

[23] Edward D. Andrews and Faith Andrews, *Visions of the Heavenly Sphere*, pp. 37, 48. The Andrews point out that during the Kentucky revival there had been many such visions "in which the sun, moon, stars, mountains, rivers, plains, vegetables, fruits, animals and a thousand particular things and circumstances in nature were used as emblems of things in the spiritual world" (p. 9).

[24] Diane Sasson, in her study of *The Shaker Spiritual Narrative*, examines a number of such visionary accounts. Cf. pp. 41–43. Distinguishing various kinds of mystical encounters, she observes of the Shakers that "auditory experiences most often occur outdoors: on the road, on a mountain top, in a field, [whereas] pictorial visions tend to occur indoors" (p. 63).

[25] The recurrence of allegorical gardens in visionary experience can be seen in most religious traditions. A. Bartlett Giamatti indicates that "the place of perfect repose and inner harmony is always remembered as a garden . . . an earthly paradise." Quoted in Jule Scott Meisami, "Allegorical Gardens in the Persian Poetic Tradition: Nezami, Rumi, Hafez," *International Journal of Middle East Studies*, 17:2 (1985), p. 229. On the mythic significance of the Holy City in visionary insight, see James Dougherty, *The Fivesquare City: The City in the Religious Imagination* (Notre Dame, Indiana: University of Notre Dame Press, 1980).

[26] By mid-nineteenth century, many Shakers had come to speak of Mother Ann as sharing a complete equality with Christ, seeing him to have become incarnate again in a woman. Greater emphasis was also placed at this time on the role of Holy Mother Wisdom in the divine economy. Cf. Robley Whitson, *op. cit.*, pp. 48f, 211.

[27] Quoted in Edward R. Horgan, *The Shaker Holy Land: A Community Portrait* (Harvard, Massachusetts: The Harvard Common Press, 1982), p. 75.

[28] Yi-Fu Tuan, "The Significance of the Artifact," *Geographical Review*, 70:4 (October 1980), p. 462.

[29] Thomas Merton, "Introduction" to Edward D. Andrews and Faith Andrews, *Religion in Wood: A Book of Shaker Furniture* (Bloomington: Indiana University Press, 1966), p. xiii.

[30] William Blake, quoted in *ibid.*, p. xiv.

[31] Heidegger's essay on "The Thing" is included in his book *Poetry, Language, Thought* (New York: Harper & Row, 1971), pp. 165–186. Cf. Gaston Bachelard's *The Poetics of Space* (Boston: Beacon Press, 1969) in which he examines the philosophical significance of drawers, wardrobes, closets, and other places in which "things" are kept.

[32] Quoted in Vincent Vycinas, *Earth and Gods: An Introduction to the Philosophy of Martin Heidegger* (The Hague: Martinus Nijhoff, 1969), p. 243.

[33] *The Shaker Manifesto*, XI:2 (1881), pp. 29–30.

[34] Merton, *op. cit.*, p. ix.

[35] Quoted in Cara S. Sutherland, "Shaker Chair Demonstrates Idealism, Progress," *The Shaker Messenger* 8:2 (Winter 1986), p. 8. Cf. Charles R. Muller and Timothy D. Rieman, *The Shaker Chair* (Winchester, Ohio: Canal Press, 1984).

[36] Millennial Laws, II:XII:4. Quoted in Andrews, *The People Called Shakers*, p. 274.

[37] Alan Gowans, "Spiritual Functionalism in Shaker Furniture," in Andrews, *Religion in Wood*, p. 19.

[38] Elder Frederick Evans, quoted in Andrews, *Work and Worship*, pp. 48–49.

[39] Friedrich W. Nietzsche, *Beyond Good and Evil*, epigram #128 (Chicago: Henry Regnery Co., 1955), p. 82.

[40] Quoted in Amy Miller and Persis Fuller, *The Best of Shaker Cooking* (New York: Macmillan, 1970), p. 228.

[41] Quoted in Sprigg, *op. cit.*, p. 95.

[42] *Ibid.*, pp. 72–74. Father James Meacham, the early organizer of the Shakers in America, wrote: "All work done, or things made in the Church . . . ought to be faithfully and well done, but plain and without superfluity." Quoted in Andrews, *Religion in Wood*, p. 7.

[43] Quoted in Sprigg, *op. cit.*, p. 87.

[44] Robley Whitson, *op. cit.*, p. 258.

[45] Ronald L. Grimes, in *Beginnings in Ritual Studies* (Washington, D.C.: University Press of America, 1982), p. 55, defines ritual in the

following way: "Ritualizing transpires as animated persons enact formative gestures in the face of receptivity during crucial times in founded places."

[46] Robley Whitson, *op. cit.*, p. 86.

[47] Diane Sasson notes the frequency of the journey motif in Shaker narratives. "Narrators typically recount experiences of travel and travail. They often must traverse a wilderness or swamp; some climb mountains or cross rivers. They must surmount obstacles, overcome dangers, and avoid temptations. . . . At the end of the journey [they] arrive at a holy setting. . . . When the visionaries see a house, they most often describe it as plain and white and square in shape. In other visions the holy place appears as a paradisiacal garden or the New Jerusalem." *Op. cit.*, p. 64.

[48] Roger Grainger, *The Language of the Rite* (London: Darton, Longman, and Todd, 1974), pp. 145–146. The ritual place is further discussed from a liturgical perspective by Dennis McNally, S.J., *Sacred Space: An Aesthetic for the Liturgical Environment* (Bristol, Indiana: Wyndham Hall Press, 1985).

[49] For a discussion of Shaker dances see Andrews, *The Gift to be Simple*, pp. 143–157 and Harold F. Cook, *Shaker Music: A Manifestation of American Folk Culture* (Lewisburg, Pennsylvania: Bucknell University Press, 1973), pp. 164–185. As the believers moved in square or circular patterns, they often raised their hands above their heads to gather in blessings poured out from heaven and alternately dropped them to their sides to shake from their finger tips the entanglements of sin. Cf. Caroline B. Piercy, *op. cit.*, p. 164.

[50] White and Taylor, *op. cit.*, p. 231.

[51] Cf. Andrews, *The People Called Shakers*, pp. 161–171, and Andrews, *Visions of the Heavenly Sphere*, pp. 21–28. Also note the article, "Zion Patefacta," in *The Shaker Quarterly* 2:1 (Spring 1962), pp. 8–9.

[52] Rogation Days were periods of prayer set aside for the entreaty [*rogatio*, in Latin] of God's favor, especially in blessing spring crops. Observed on April 25 and on three days prior to the feast of the Ascension, the faithful would have traditionally accompanied the priests as they walked through the fields of the parish, singing the Litany of the Saints. The ritual has still deeper roots in the ancient Roman observance of the *Robigalia*, a pagan procession also aimed at protecting spring plants from blight.

[53] Andrews, *The People Called Shakers*, pp. 160–161. Yi-Fu Tuan observes that "in Britain the custom of 'beating the bounds' required the parish priest to walk around his parish and strike certain markers with a stick." Cf. "Sacred Space: Explorations of an Idea," in Karl W. Butzer,

ed., *Dimensions of Human Geography* (University of Chicago Department of Geography Research Paper 186, 1978), pp. 85–86. The custom of walking around one's property once each year so as to reestablish the right to its possession also continued in parts of this country through the nineteenth century.

[54] Concerning the rituals of "The Midnight Cry" and "The Cleansing Gift," see Andrews, *Visions of the Heavenly Sphere*, pp. 20–21, and Caroline Piercy, *op. cit.*, pp. 154–156.

[55] June Sprigg, *op. cit.*, pp. 63–78, offers a provocative analysis of Shaker perspectives on space, observing that the nineteenth-century Shaker sensibility reacted strongly to the contemporary Victorian penchant for cluttered space, massive and heavy with things. By contrast, the believers emphasized a spacious and spare simplicity that would anticipate the unadorned functionalism of twentieth-century Bauhaus design. The Shakers were preeminently a space-saving and space-conscious people.

[56] White and Taylor, *op. cit.*, p. 232.

MYTHIC LANDSCAPES
Liminal Places in the Evangelical Revival

[1] Sawdust and "the sawdust trail" serve as a provocative, almost sacramental symbol of the revival. They speak to the experience of being "sawn down," of being reduced to dust—akin to the sackcloth and ashes symbolism of the Old Testament. The smell of sawdust further evokes memories of hard work, of deliberate decision making, and the whole process of construction—of being formed and molded. Folding chairs also seem to be a ubiquitous symbol of the revival—suggesting images of transition and ready movement.

[2] The spirit of the Southern revival, especially as it appears in the region of Appalachia, is well captured in Eleanor Dickinson and Barbara Benziger's *Revival!* (New York: Harper & Row, 1974).

[3] Cf. Arnold van Gennep, *The Rites of Passage* (London: Routledge and Kegan Paul, 1960) and Victor W. Turner, *The Ritual Process* (Chicago: Aldine Publishing Company, 1969), pp. 94–130.

[4] Cf. Brueggemann, *The Land* (Philadelphia: Fortress Press, 1977). Both temple and anti-temple traditions can be found juxtaposed in 2 Samuel 7:4–1 and 1 Kgs 8:12–61.

[5] Cf. Alan Heimert and Perry Miller, eds., *The Great Awakening* (Indianapolis: Bobbs-Merrill Company, 1967), pp. 147–148, and William G. McLoughlin, *Revivals, Awakenings, and Reform* (University of Chicago Press, 1978), pp. 60–66, 83–96.

[6] The store front offered an interesting juxtaposition of commerce

and spirituality. It was not accidental in that place that a prevalent metaphor for deepening the spiritual life was a concern to "do business with God."

[7] Carroll Smith-Rosenberg, in her essay on "Women and Religious Revivals: Anti-Ritualism, Liminality, and the Emergence of the American Bourgeoisie," argues that "geographic rootlessness" was a major characteristic of the revival convert in the nineteenth-century American revival experience. See Leonard I. Sweet, ed., *The Evangelical Tradition in America* (Macon, Georgia: Mercer University Press, 1984), pp. 218ff.

[8] Accounts of all these conversion experiences can be found in Hugh T. Kerr and John Mulder's *Conversions: The Christian Experience* (Grand Rapids: William B. Eerdmans, 1983).

[9] William James, *The Varieties of Religious Experience* (New York: Collier Books, 1961), p. 180. (Italics added.)

[10] The furnace room was, as we knew, the business end of the church—full of brooms, mops, containers of wax, hammers and screwdrivers. All this was extremely evocative for us. Researchers in Christian Education concerned with the formation of ideal learning environments might well attend to the multivalent power of such a setting.

[11] Robert L. Cohn, in his essay on "Liminality in the Wilderness," relates this phenomenon to the experience of Israel in the Sinai Desert, midway as they were between Egypt and the promised land. See *The Shape of Sacred Space: Four Biblical Studies* (Chico, California: Scholars Press, 1981). Cf. Victor Turner, *Dramas, Fields, and Metaphors* (Ithaca: Cornell University Press, 1974), pp. 231–271.

[12] Cf. William McLoughlin, *op. cit.;* Timothy Smith, *Revivalism and Social Reform* (New York: Harper & Row, 1965); and Donald Dayton, *Discovering an Evangelical Heritage* (New York: Harper & Row, 1976).

7 Precarity and Permanence: Dorothy Day and the Catholic Worker Sense of Place

[1] Dorothy Day, *Loaves and Fishes* (San Francisco: Harper & Row, 1963), p. 67. (Italics added.)

[2] *The Catholic Worker,* I:1 (May 1933), p. 4. [Hereafter referred to as *C.W.*]

[3] *C.W.,* XVIII:10 (May 1952), p. 2, as quoted in *By Little and By Little: The Selected Writings of Dorothy Day,* edited by Robert Ellsberg (New York: Alfred A. Knopf, 1983), p. 107.

[4] Emmanuel Mounier, *The Character of Man* (New York: Harper and Brothers, 1956), pp. 70–71.

[5] *C.W.,* XXI:9 (April 1955), p. 1.

[6] *C.W.,* VII:8 (May 1940), p. 8.

[7] *C.W.*, XIII:10 (December 1946), p. 4. Dorothy Day wrote of "Poverty and Precarity" in an article by that title in *The Catholic Worker*, XVIII:10 (May 1952), pp. 2, 6. Precarity is a theme that can be traced through much of her writing. Cf. *Loaves and Fishes*, pp. 82–83.

[8] The history of the Catholic Worker has been well told in Mel Piehl's *Breaking Bread: The Catholic Worker and the Origin of Catholic Radicalism in America* (Philadelphia: Temple University Press, 1982) and William D. Miller's *A Harsh and Dreadful Love* (New York: Liveright, 1973). See also Miller's *Dorothy Day: A Biography* (San Francisco: Harper and Row, 1982).

[9] Dorothy Day, *The Eleventh Virgin* (New York: Boni, 1924), p. 297. Quoted in Mel Piehl, *Breaking Bread*, p. 15. In another part of her novel, Dorothy's character remarks on her childhood, "It made me mad that we were always moving around from one place to another so that we never had any friends." *The Eleventh Virgin*, p. 304.

[10] Dorothy Day, *The Long Loneliness: An Autobiography* (New York: Harper & Row, 1952), p. 135.

[11] Maurin's distinctive form of presenting his ideas in "Easy Essays" found expression in his book entitled *The Green Revolution* (New York: Academy Guild Press, 1949). His thought is explored by Marc H. Ellis in his book, *Peter Maurin: Prophet in the Twentieth Century* (New York: Paulist Press, 1981).

[12] Dorothy Day, *Loaves and Fishes*, p. 93.

[13] Maurin's philosophical and economic thought had been formed from personalist, anarchist, and distributist ideas encountered on the continent. His interest in anarchist thought, with its distrust of all centralized bureaucracies, came by way of Tolstoy and Peter Kropotkin. English distributism, with its criticism of capitalism and stress on the spiritual value of work, made its impact on his thinking through the writings of sculptor Eric Gill, similar as they were to the work of Charles Péguy, the French poet. Cf. Mary C. Segers, "Equality and Christian Anarchism: The Political and Social Ideas of the Catholic Worker Movement," *Review of Politics* 40:2 (April 1978), pp. 196–230. The views of Péguy and Gill on a Christian conception of manual labor can be found in Péguy's *Basic Verities: Prose and Poetry* (New York: Pantheon Books, 1943) and *A Holy Tradition of Working: Passages from the Writings of Eric Gill*, ed. Brian Keeble (West Stockbridge, Massachusetts: Lindisfarne Press, 1983).

[14] The theme of the wandering, homeless Jesus is discussed by A. Voobus, in his *History of Asceticism in the Syrian Orient* (Louvain: Corpus Scriptorum Christianorum Orientalium, 1958, 1960), vol. I, pp.

84–87, and vol. II, pp. 269–271. Such ideas were mediated to *The Catholic Worker* through the writings of Thomas Merton, among others. A Christmas meditation by Merton was quoted as saying, "Into this world, this demented inn, in which there is absolutely no room for Him at all, Christ has come uninvited. But because He cannot be at home in it, because He is out of place in it, His place is with those others for whom there is no room. His place is with those who do not belong, who are rejected by power because they are regarded as weak. . . . With those for whom there is no room, Christ is present in the world." Quoted in *The Dorothy Day Book: A Selection from Her Writings and Readings*, edited by Margaret Quigley and Michael Garvey (Springfield, Illinois: Templegate, 1982), p. 46. Dorothy Day frequently wrote of St. Francis and his conception of voluntary poverty. Cf. *Loaves and Fishes*, pp. 78–89.

[15] Agnes De La Gorce, *Saint Benedict Joseph Labre*, quoted in a review article in *C.W.* XVIII:10 (May 1952), p. 4.

[16] *C.W.*, VII:9 (June 1940), p. 7.

[17] *C.W.*, VII:8 (May 1940), p. 5.

[18] The phrase is actually Jean-Pierre de Caussade's, another French spiritual writer by whom Dorothy Day was influenced, but the sentiment is characteristic of Therese. Cf. Little, pp. xxxv and 76.

[19] *C.W.*, XVII:7 (January 1951), p. 2. Dorothy Day's own book on the Little Flower is entitled *Therese* (Notre Dame: Fides Press, 1960). Robert Ellsberg's edition of Day's writings, *By Little and By Little*, gathered material around the theme of "the Little Way." Cf. pp. xxxiv, 105, 274.

[20] *C.W.*, XII:10 (December 1945), p. 2.

[21] Dorothy Day, *Loaves and Fishes*, p. 67.

[22] *Ibid.*, p. 14.

[23] *C.W.*, VII:8 (May 1940), p. 8.

[24] *C.W.*, I:1 (May 1933), p. 4.

[25] William D. Miller, *Dorothy Day: A Biography*, p. 194.

[26] *C.W.*, I:8 (February 1934), p. 4.

[27] Wendell Berry, *Standing by Words* (San Francisco: North Point Press, 1983), p. 103.

[28] Peter Maurin, *The Green Revolution*, p. 3.

[29] Walter Brueggemann, in his study of *The Prophetic Imagination* (Philadelphia: Fortress Press, 1978), develops this argument very persuasively as he compares the biblical themes of royal consciousness and prophetic insight.

[30] Stephen, for example, in his speech in Acts 7 would argue that the hope of Israel is not to be found at Sinai, nor in Canaan, nor even in

the temple of Solomon, but in Christ alone—found among the poor disciples in their midst. Cf. W. D. Davies, *The Gospel and the Land: Early Christianity and Jewish Territorial Doctrine* (Berkeley, California: University of California Press, 1974), pp. 270–272.

[31] *Ibid.*, p. 367.

[32] Dorothy Day, "Conscience and Civil Defense," *The New Republic*, August 22, 1955, p. 6. Cf. Nancy L. Roberts, *Dorothy Day and the Catholic Worker* (Albany: State University of New York Press, 1984), pp. 149–153.

[33] *Commonweal* LXII:15 (July 15, 1955), p. 364.

[34] William D. Miller discusses the ambiguity of this event in his biography, *Dorothy Day*, pp. 441–442. The history of the Koinonia Community is related in Dallas Lee's *The Cotton Patch Evidence* (New York: Harper & Row, 1971).

[35] Mounier's treatise on Christian property, *De la propriete capitaliste a la propriete humaine*, reprinted in *Oeuvres de Mounier* (Paris: Editions du Seuil, 1961), I, pp. 421–477, is well summarized in Eileen Cantin, C.S.J., *Mounier: A Personalist View of History* (New York: Paulist Press, 1973), pp. 23–25. Maurin had early been influenced by the editor of the French journal *L'Esprit* and had urged the translation into English of his book, *A Personalist Manifesto* (London: Longmans, Green, and Co., 1938).

[36] Mel Piehl, *Breaking Bread*, p. 84. Piehl quotes a friend of Dorothy's as having said, "The Eucharist is the center of liturgical worship for her. All liturgy is first of all concerned with bringing us the body and blood of Christ."

[37] Dorothy Day, *From Union Station to Rome*, pp. 11–12.

[38] T. S. Eliot, in "Burnt Norton," had spoken of being "surrounded / By a grace of sense, a white light still and moving" as he described one's encounter with the holy. T. S. Eliot, *The Complete Poems and Plays* (New York: Harcourt, Brace, and World, Inc., 1971), p. 119. Dom Virgil Michel would write in *The Catholic Worker*, "The activity of the senses is essential to the liturgical experience. The liturgy operates by an appeal to the senses, as we have seen. It is through the external gateways of the soul, the sense organs, that the soul itself is reached in the liturgy." *C.W.*, XXII:3 (October 1955), p. 5.

[39] William D. Miller, *Dorothy Day*, p. 288.

[40] *C.W.*, XXVIII:6 (January 1962), p. 7.

[41] Quoted in William D. Miller, *Dorothy Day*, p. 299. Remembering her youth in Chicago, she once said, "I collected odors in my memory, the one beauty in those drab streets. The odor of geranium leaves, tomato plants, marigolds; the smell of lumber, of tar, of roasting coffee; the smell of good bread and rolls and coffee cake coming from the small

German bakers. Here was enough beauty to satisfy me." Quoted in Mel Piehl, *Breaking Bread*, p. 7.

[42] Dorothy Day, *The Long Loneliness*, p. 51.

[43] Virgil Michel, O.S.B., "The Social Nature of Communion," in *The Social Problem*, Book Four, The Mystical Body and Social Justice (Collegeville, Minnesota: St. John's Abbey, 1938). The conception of the Church as the Mystical Body of Christ, reaching beyond the older juridical conceptions of ecclesiology, had been of great importance in nurturing the liturgical movement. Cf. Ernest B. Koenker, *The Liturgical Renaissance in the Roman Catholic Church* (University of Chicago Press, 1954), pp. 34–38.

[44] Paul B. Marx, O.S.B., discusses Dom Virgil's understanding of the Eucharist and social justice in his book *Virgil Michel and the Liturgical Movement* (Collegeville, Minnesota: Liturgical Press, 1957), pp. 176–218. Cf. Michel's own study of *The Liturgy of the Church* (New York: Macmillan Company, 1938), pp. 1–13.

[45] *C.W.*, XX:8 (March 1954), p. 3.

[46] Quoted in William D. Miller, *A Harsh and Dreadful Love*, p. 10. As early as 1933 Dorothy Day had written, "We feel that it is very necessary to connect the liturgical movement with the social justice movement." Cf. Mel Piehl, *Breaking Bread*, p. 85.

[47] Cf. Michael Harrington, "Existential Saint," *New York Times Book Review*, June 13, 1982, p. 24.

[48] Robert Steed, "Permanence and Precarity," *C.W.*, XXIV:7 (February 1958), p. 2.

[49] *Ibid.*

8 The Ephemeral Character of Place: Problems in Articulating an American Sense of Sacred Space

[1] Robert Orsi, "Everyday Miracles: the Study of Lived Religion," in David D. Hall, ed., *Lived Religion in America* (Princeton: Princeton University Press, 1997), pp. 3–6.

[2] Edward D. McDonald, ed., *Phoenix: The Posthumous Papers of D. H. Lawrence* (New York: Viking Press, 1968), pp. 141–147.

[3] Quoted in John Conron, *The American Landscape* (New York: Oxford University Press, 1973), p. xviii.

[4] Sidney Mead, in *The Lively Experiment: The Shaping of Christianity in America* (New York: Harper & Row, 1963), p. 6, argues that "it is not too much to say that in America space has played the part that time has played in the older cultures of the world."

[5] See Douglas Burton-Christie, "A Sense of Place," *The Way* (January 1999), pp. 59–72, for a fine bibliographic essay surveying recent

approaches to the study of sacred place, from cultural geography and anthropology to poetry and philosophy. Steven Feld and Keith H. Basso have edited a similarly helpful volume, *Senses of Place* (Santa Fe: School of American Research Press, 1996). Colleen McDannell demonstrates the application of material culture studies to American spirituality in her book, *Material Christianity: Religion and Popular Culture in America* (New Haven: Yale University Press, 1995).

[6] Jack Turner, *The Abstract Wild* (Tucson: University of Arizona Press, 1997), p. 11.

[7] Robert B. Riley, "Attachment to the Ordinary Landscape," in Setha M. Low and Irwin Altman, eds., *Place Attachment* (New York: Plenum Press, 1992), pp. 20–21. Proust's *Remembrance of Things Past* (1934) offered insight into the emotional ties involved in the experience of place, observing how the smallest things can trigger the memory of deep significance.

[8] Aldo Leopold, *A Sand County Almanac* (New York: Oxford University Press, 1949), p. 149.

[9] Deborah Tall, *From Where We Stand: Recovery of a Sense of Place* (New York: Alfred A. Knopf, 1993), p. 90. As geographer David Sopher, quoted on page 97, quips, "To be rooted is the property of vegetables."

[10] Wilbur Zelinsky, *The Cultural Geography of the United States* (Englewood Cliffs, New Jersey: Prentice-Hall, 1967), p. 53. Frances FitzGerald, in her book *Cities on a Hill* (New York: Simon & Schuster, 1986), shows how the American passion for "starting over" has remained operative in contemporary life.

[11] *The Geographical History of America* (New York: Random House, 1936), pp. 17–18.

[12] Richard L. Rubenstein, "The Cave, the Rock, and the Tent: The Meaning of Place in Contemporary America," *Morality and Eros* (New York: McGraw-Hill, 1970), pp. 164–182. See also W. Janzen, "Geography of Faith: A Christian Perspective on the Meaning of Places," *Studies in Religion / Science Religieuses* 3:2 (1973), pp. 166–182.

[13] Wayne Fields, "Locating America," in Milica Banjanin et al., *The Idea of Place* (St. Louis: Washington University, University College Occasional Papers), 2 (Winter 1982–83), pp. 18–20.

[14] David Sopher, "The Landscape of Home," in D. W. Meinig, ed., *The Interpretation of Ordinary Landscapes* (New York: Oxford University Press, 1979), p. 135. Some have seen the glory of America to lie in the fact that periodically it could all be pulled down. Emerson was critical of a Massachusetts state survey that proposed the building of stone houses. American houses, he thought, should be built so as to be moved easily or abandoned. Cited in David Lowenthal, "The Place of the Past

in the American Landscape," in *Geographies of the Mind,* ed. David Lowenthal and Martyn J. Boden, pp. 94–95.

[15] David Sopher, p. 136. See also Rowland A. Sherrill, *Road-Book America: Contemporary Culture and the New Picaresque* (Champaign: University of Illinois Press, 2000).

[16] Edward Everett Hale, *The Man Without a Country* (Westwood, New Jersey: Fleming H. Revell Co., 1959), pp. 51–55.

[17] Vincent Scully, *The Earth, the Temple, and the Gods: Greek Sacred Architecture* (New Haven: Yale University Press, 1962), p. 2.

[18] David Ley, "Modernism, Post-Modernism, and the Struggle for Place," in John A. Agnew and James S. Duncan, eds., *The Power of Place: Bringing Together Geographical and Sociological Imaginations* (Boston: Unwin Hyman, 1989), pp. 52–53. See also Michael Dear, "The Postmodern Challenge: Reconstructing Human Geography," *Transactions of the Institute of British Geographers,* n.s., 13 (1988), pp. 262–274.

[19] See Tony Hiss, *The Experience of Place* (New York: Alfred A. Knopf, 1990). Robert A. Orsi has edited a collection of essays focused on ethnic shrines and altared spaces in urban neighborhoods, entitled *Gods of the City: Religion and the American Urban Landscape* (Bloomington: Indiana University Press, 1999).

[20] Patrick McCormick argued this in a paper, "Sacred Space in America: Balancing the Sanctuary and the Commons," at the annual meeting of the College Theology Society, Saint Louis University, Saint Louis, Missouri, May 26, 1998. See Paul A. Jargowsky, *Poverty and Place: Ghettos, Barrios, and the American City* (New York: Russell Sage Foundation, 1997).

[21] Yi-Fu Tuan, *Space and Place: The Perspective of Experience* (Minneapolis: University of Minnesota Press, 1977), p. 6. "What begins as undifferentiated space becomes place as we get to know it better and endow it with value," he argues. See also Edward S. Casey, "How to Get from Space to Place in a Fairly Short Stretch of Time," in Steven Feld and Keith H. Basso, eds., *Senses of Place,* pp. 13–52.

[22] Charles Kuralt, *On the Road with Charles Kuralt* (New York: Putnam, 1985), pp. 160–163. See also John A. Jakle, *The American Small Town: Twentieth-Century Place Images* (Hamden, Conn.: Archon Books, 1982), and Bill Bryson, *The Lost Continent: Travels in Small-Town America* (New York: Harper & Row, 1989).

[23] See, for example, Carolyn Walker Bynum's *Holy Feast and Holy Fast: The Religious Significance of Food to Medieval Women* (Berkeley: University of California Press, 1987) and Margaret Miles's *Practicing Christianity: Critical Perspectives for an Embodied Spirituality* (New York: Crossroad, 1988).

[24] Harold W. Turner, *From Temple to Meeting House: The Phenomenology and Theology of Places of Worship* (The Hague: Mouton Publishers, 1979), p. 6.

[25] Bernard McGinn, *The Foundations of Mysticism*, vol. 1 of *The Presence of God: A History of Western Christian Mysticism* (New York: Crossroad, 1991), p. 6.

[26] Karl Rahner, ed., *Encyclopedia of Theology: The Concise Sacramentum Mundi* (New York: Seabury Press, 1975), p. 1625.

[27] *Confessions of St. Augustine*, X.viii.5.

[28] Quoted in Roderick Nash, *Wilderness and the American Mind* (New Haven: Yale University Press, 1967), pp. 19–20.

[29] Quoted in Wendell Berry, *A Continuous Harmony: Essays Cultural and Agricultural* (New York: Harcourt Brace Jovanovich, 1975), p. 8.

[30] Werner Jaeger, *The Theology of the Early Greek Philosophers* (Oxford: Clarendon Press, 1947), p. 99.

[31] See Ira G. Zepp, *The New Religious Image of Urban America: The Shopping Mall as Ceremonial Center* (Westminster, Maryland: Christian Classics, Inc., 1986).

[32] Eudora Welty, *The Eye of the Story: Selected Essays and Reviews* (New York: Random House, 1977), p. 123.

[33] Nikos Kazantzakis, *The Greek Passion* (New York: Simon & Schuster, 1954), p. 229.

[34] Ralph Waldo Emerson, *Essays: First and Second Series* (New York: Harper & Row, 1926), p. 59.

[35] On Celtic pilgrimage, see Esther De Waal, *The Celtic Way of Prayer* (London: Hodder & Stoughton, 1996).

[36] See Jonathan Sumption, *Pilgrimage: An Image of Mediaeval Religion* (Totowa, New Jersey: Rowman & Littlefield, 1975), pp. 299–300.

[37] John Kirtland Wright, "Terrae Incognitae: The Place of the Imagination in Geography," in his book *Human Nature in Geography* (Cambridge: Harvard University Press, 1966), p. 72.

9 Edwards and the Spider as Symbol: Reflections on Spirituality as an Academic Discipline

[1] Recent books on the nature and method of spirituality as a discipline include Philip Sheldrake's *Spirituality and History* (New York: Crossroad, 1992) and *Spirituality and Theology* (Maryknoll, New York: Orbis Books, 1998), as well as Bradley Hanson, ed., *Modern Christian Spirituality: Methodological and Historical Essays* (Atlanta: Scholars Press, 1990), and Kenneth J. Collins, ed., *Exploring Christian Spirituality* (Grand Rapids: Baker Books, 2000). Scholarly journals devoted to the disci-

pline include *Spiritus: A Journal of Christian Spirituality* (published by the Johns Hopkins University Press; formerly the *Christian Spirituality Bulletin*) and *Studies in Spirituality,* published in the Netherlands.

² On the relevance of Performance Theory to these questions, see Victor Turner, *From Ritual to Theatre* (New York: Performing Arts Journal Publications, 1982); Erving Goffman's work on "frame analysis" in Charles Lemert and Ann Branaman, eds., *The Goffman Reader* (Malden, Miss.: Blackwell Publishers, 1997); and David George, "On Ambiguity: Towards a Post-Modern Performance Theory," *Theatre Research International* 14:1 (1989), pp. 71–85.

³ See Sandra Schneiders, "Spirituality in the Academy," *Theological Studies* 50:4 (December 1989), p. 691.

⁴ On the importance of metaphor in the study of spirituality, see Belden Lane, "Language, Metaphor, and Pastoral Theology," *Theology Today* 43:4 (January 1987), pp. 169–177.

⁵ Paul Ricoeur, *The Symbolism of Evil* (Boston: Beacon Press, 1967), pp. 15, 161. Tillich argued that "a symbol, as opposed to a sign, *participates* in the truth to which it points." See his *Theology of Culture* (London: Oxford University Press, 1959), pp. 54–55. James W. Heisig, in his article, "Symbolism," in *The Encyclopedia of Religion,* ed. Mircea Eliade (New York: Macmillan, 1986), vol. 14, p. 204, says, "The nature of the symbolic process consists in the fact that one thing, usually concrete and particular, stands for something else, usually abstract and generalized, and becomes a focal point for thoughts and emotions associated with that referent, or a trigger for a set of habits associated with it." Cf. David Tracy, *The Analogical Imagination* (New York: Crossroad, 1981), pp. 205–206, 281–287.

⁶ Maura Campbell, "Symbol and Reality: Water, Life, Death and Christian Baptism," *Dialogue and Alliance* 4:1 (Spring 1990), p. 49. The term *myth,* as used in this paper, refers to a sacred story so basic to a community's identity that its truth is assumed without question. A *symbol* is a shorthand form used in signifying the myth, participating in its power. *Ritual* is the means by which the myth is mimed or gestured as representative practice.

⁷ See Bernard McGinn, "Ocean and Desert as Symbols of Mystical Absorption in the Christian Tradition, *Journal of Religion* 74:2 (April 1994), pp. 155–181; and Andrew Louth, *The Wilderness of God* (Nashville: Abingdon Press, 1997). Conrad Cherry plots the development of an American expression of this impulse in his study of nature symbolism from Jonathan Edwards to Horace Bushnell, *Nature and the Religious Imagination* (Philadelphia: Fortress Press, 1980).

⁸ For Augustine's Exposition of the Psalms, see *Sancti Aurelii Augustine, Enarrationes in Psalmos*, in *Corpus Christianorum, Series Latina* (Turnholti: Typographi Brepols Editores Pontificee, 1956), vols. 38–40. Bushnell's essay "Of the Animal Infestations" is found in *Horace Bushnell: Sermons*, ed. Conrad Cherry (New York: Paulist Press, 1985), pp. 175–188.

⁹ Henry C. McCook, *American Spiders and Their Spinning Work: A Natural History of the Orbweaving Spiders of the United States* (Philadelphia: Academy of Natural Sciences, 1889–1893), 3 vols. McCook also penned an article, "Jonathan Edwards as a Naturalist," for the *Presbyterian and Reformed Review* (July 1890), pp. 393–402. For a brief history of spider research and spiders in folklore, myth, and literature, see Paul Hillyard, *The Book of the Spider* (New York: Random House, 1994).

¹⁰ Augustine of Hippo, *Enarrationes in Psalmos*, Psalm 89, par. 9, line 3 (*Corpus Christianorum*, vol. 39, p. 1248); and Psalm 122, par. 6, line 32–33 (*Corpus Christianorum*, vol. 40, p. 1819).

¹¹ In medieval bestiaries, "the hideous spider" was often presented as the antithesis of the pious and graceful "praying mantis." See Louis Charbonneau-Lassay, *The Bestiary of Christ*, trans. D. M. Dooling (New York: Arkana, 1992), pp. 356–361. See also the entry on "Spider" in J. E. Cirlot, *A Dictionary of Symbols* (New York: Philosophical Library, 1971), p. 304.

¹² Edwards's fascination with nature symbolism—making use, for example, of the image of fruit trees and grafting to describe the corporate character of human nature—is examined in David Weddle, "Jonathan Edwards on Men and Trees, and the Problem of Solidarity," *Harvard Theological Review* 67:2 (1974), pp. 155–175. Clyde Holbrook emphasizes the centrality of nature imagery for Edwards, showing how the Connecticut River Valley served as stimulus to his imagination, in *Jonathan Edwards, the Valley and Nature* (Lewisburg, Pennsylvania: Bucknell University Press, 1987), pp. 15–32.

¹³ Besides these two, there are several brief references in the manuscript notebooks that made up Edwards's *Images of Divine Things* (compiled between 1728 and 1757). There, for example, he speaks of spiders as "poisonous and hurtful animals . . . [who] incline for the most part to hide themselves or lurk in secret places. Herein they are types of devils and the lusts of men." See *The Works of Jonathan Edwards*, vol. 11, *Typological Writings*, ed. Wallace E. Anderson (New Haven: Yale University Press, 1993), p. 97.

¹⁴ "The Spider Letter," October 31, 1723, in *The Works of Jonathan Edwards*, vol. 6: Scientific and Philosophical Writings, ed. Wallace E.

Anderson (New Haven: Yale University Press, 1980), p. 167. This letter drew upon a slightly earlier essay by young Edwards, "On Insects." His stress on the spider's "pleasure" in web spinning is thoroughly Calvinist. The first question of the Westminster Catechism insisted that "the chief end of man" [and woman] is "to glorify God and enjoy him forever."

15 See John Calvin, *Institutes of the Christian Religion*, trans. Ford Lewis Battles (Philadelphia: Westminster Press, 1960), I.vi. 2, p. 72. Cf. p. 61 n. Edwards writes of this "sixth sense" received by the Christian as a "true distinguishing sign" of conversion in his sermon "A Divine and Supernatural Light" (1734), and his *Treatise Concerning the Religious Affections* (1746) in *The Works of Jonathan Edwards*, vol. 2, ed. John E. Smith (New Haven: Yale University Press, 1959), pp. 205–207 and 271–275.

16 Preached at Enfield, July 8, 1741; in *The Works of President Edwards* (New York: S. Converse, 1829), vol. 7, pp. 163–177. The sermon was first preached earlier that summer in Northampton.

17 Perry Miller suggests that with the 1741 Enfield sermon, "Edwards's preaching was America's sudden leap into modernity." *Jonathan Edwards* (Amherst: University of Massachusetts Press, 1981), p. 147. Cf. J. A. Leo Lemay, "Rhetorical Strategies in 'Sinners in the Hands of an Angry God' and 'Narrative of the Late Massacres in Lancaster County,'" in Barbara Oberg and Harry Stout, eds. *Benjamin Franklin, Jonathan Edwards, and the Representation of American Culture* (New York: Oxford University Press, 1993), pp. 186–192.

18 Ernst Cassirer, in his *Philosophy of Symbolic Forms* (Berlin, 1923–29), defined the human species as *homo symbolicus*, incurably given to symbol making. Anthropologist Clifford Geertz defines culture itself as "an historically transmitted pattern of meanings embodied in symbols, a system of inherited conceptions expressed in symbolic forms by means of which men [and women] communicate, perpetuate and develop their knowledge about and attitudes toward life." *The Interpretation of Cultures* (New York: Basic Books, 1973), p. 89. While he seeks to locate symbols within their specific historical contexts, Claude Levi-Strauss looks for a universal structure of the mind that undergirds the symbol-making process. See his *Structural Anthropology* (New York: Basic Books, 1963–76). Mircea Eliade's attention to the pre- and post-verbal character of archetypes, rituals, myths, and symbols in the study of religion remains profoundly important for the study of spirituality. See *Myths, Rites, Symbols: A Mircea Eliade Reader*, ed. Wendell C. Beane and William G. Doty (New York: Harper, 1975), 2 vols.

[19] See Henry Nash Smith, *Virgin Land* (Cambridge: Harvard University Press, 1950); Leo Marx, *The Machine and the Garden* (London: Oxford University Press, 1964); Alan Trachtenberg, *Brooklyn Bridge: Fact and Symbol* (New York: Oxford University Press, 1965). Cf. Cecil F. Tate, *The Search for a Method in American Studies* (Minneapolis: University of Minnesota Press, 1973).

[20] See Giles Gunn, "American Studies as Cultural Criticism," in *The Culture of Criticism and the Criticism of Culture* (New York: Oxford University Press, 1987), pp. 147–172. For a critique of the myth and symbol school, see Bruce Kuklick, "Myth and Symbol in American Studies," *American Quarterly* 24 (October 1972), pp. 435–450.

[21] See George Lipsitz, "Listening to Learn and Learning to Listen: Popular Culture, Cultural Theory, and American Studies," *American Quarterly* 42:4 (December 1990), pp. 615–636.

Recent studies that incorporate a cultural studies approach to aspects of American spirituality include two works by Ann Taves, *The Household of Faith: Roman Catholic Devotions in Mid 19th-Century America* (Notre Dame: University of Notre Dame Press, 1986) and *Fits, Trances, & Visions: Experiencing Religion and Explaining Experience from Wesley to James* (Princeton: Princeton University Press, 1999), as well as books by Ann Braude, including *Radical Spirits: Spiritualism and Women's Rights in 19th-Century America* (Boston: Beacon Press, 1989); James T. Fisher, *The Catholic Counterculture in America, 1933–1962* (University of North Carolina Press, 1989); Jenny Franchot, *Roads to Rome* (Berkeley: University of California Press, 1994); Patrick Allitt, *Catholic Converts: British and American Intellectuals Turn to Rome* (Ithaca: Cornell University Press, 1997); and Leigh Eric Schmidt, "The Easter Parade: Piety, Fashion, and Display," *Religion and American Culture* 4:2 (Summer 1994), pp. 135–164.

William L. Portier offers a critique of cultural studies as applied to the study of spirituality, fearing that its tendency to cultural reductionism may too easily leave God out of the analysis. See his article, "A Church Polarized: Fault Lines in the History of American Catholicism," *U.S. Catholic Historian* 15 (1996), pp. 141–154.

[22] See Patricia J. Tracy, *Jonathan Edwards, Pastor: Religion and Society in Eighteenth-Century Northampton* (New York: Hill & Wang, 1980), p. 129.

[23] "Sinners in the Hands of an Angry God," *The Works of President Edwards*, vol. 7, p. 170. Tracy, p. 94. The captivity narrative of Mrs. Mary Rowlandson, one of the most widely read works of this genre in eighteenth-century New England, recounted the experience of a Puritan woman in western Massachusetts who had been captured by Quabaug

Indians in 1675 and taken up the Connecticut River Valley. See *The Narrative of the Captivity of Mrs. Mary Rowlandson* (Boston: Houghton Mifflin, 1930), p. 14 n. 17.

[24] See Edwards's notes on Sarah Pierpont, penned in the front of his Greek grammar, in *Jonathan Edwards: Representative Selections* (New York: Hill & Wang, 1962), p. 56.

[25] Roland Barthes, *Mythologies* (London: Jonathan Cape, 1972).

[26] See Rowan Williams, *Teresa of Avila* (Harrisburg, Pennsylvania: Morehouse Publ., 1991).

[27] A. R. Ammons, "Identity," in *The Selected Poems* (New York: W. W. Norton, 1986), pp. 27–28.

10 The Imagined Landscape: A Tension between Place and Placelessness in Christian Spirituality

[1] Robert C. Gregg, trans., *Athanasius: The Life of Antony and the Letter to Marcellinus* (New York: Paulist Press, 1980), p. 68.

[2] Letter 14 to Gregory Nazianzus. Quoted in Roger D. Sorrell, *St. Francis of Assisi and Nature* (New York: Oxford University Press, 1988), p. 19.

[3] *Works*, II, pp. 461, 464. Cf. Clarence Glacken, *Traces on the Rhodian Shore: Nature and Culture in Western Thought* (Berkeley: University of California Press, 1967), p. 214.

[4] *De gestis pontificum Angliae*, IV. PL 179. 1612–13. Cf. Jean Leclerq, *The Love of Learning and the Desire for God: A Study of Monastic Culture* (New York: Fordham University Press, 1961), p. 165.

[5] Simon Schama, *Landscape and Memory* (New York: Alfred A. Knopf, 1995), p. 61.

[6] See Michael Taussig, *Mimesis and Alterity: A Particular History of the Senses* (New York: Routledge, 1993). Taussig reminds us of Frazer's contention in *The Golden Bough*, "that things which have once been in contact with each other continue to act on each other at a distance after the physical contact has been severed." Quoted on pp. 52–53.

[7] Michael Pollan, *Second Nature: A Gardener's Education* (New York: Dell Books, 1995).

[8] Cotton Mather, *Magnalia Christi Americana, or The Ecclesiastical History of New-England* (New York: Russell & Russell, 1967; reproduced from the edition of 1852), vol. 1, pp. 91–99. See also Frederick W. Turner, *Beyond Geography: The Western Spirit Against the Wilderness* (New York: Viking Press, 1983), p. viii.

[9] Daniel L. Smith, *The Religion of the Landless: The Social Context of the Babylonian Exile* (Bloomington, Indiana: Meyer-Stone Books, 1989).

[10] Theodore Hiebert, *The Yahwist's Landscape: Nature and Religion in Early Israel* (New York: Oxford University Press, 1996), p. 153.

[11] These could be examined on an individual level, using the insights of Edward T. Hall's work on proxemics, or on a broader, sociogeographical level, after the manner of Whitney Cross's study of nineteenth-century revivalism in western New York. See Edward T. Hall, *The Hidden Dimension* (New York: Harper, 1965), and Whitney R. Cross, *The Burned Over District* (Garden City, New York: Doubleday, 1966).

[12] For examples of attention to spatial questions in biblical studies, see Robert L. Cohn, *The Shape of Sacred Space: Four Biblical Studies* (Chico, California: Scholars Press, 1981), and Elizabeth S. Malbon, *Narrative Space and Mythic Meaning in Mark* (San Francisco: Harper & Row, 1986). The Annales School of historical interpretation, expressed in the work of historians like Fernand Braudel, has focused on geographical and economic and social questions more than earlier historians have been prone to do.

[13] Helmut Koster, "Topos," *Theological Dictionary of the New Testament,* ed. Gerhard Friedrich (Grand Rapids: Eerdmans, 1972), VIII, p. 199.

[14] On the Greek words for place as used by Aristotle and Plato, see E. V. Walter's *Placeways: A Theory of the Human Environment* (Chapel Hill: University of North Carolina Press, 1988), pp. 6–22, 115–131.

[15] A. Marmorstein, *The Old Rabbinic Doctrine of God* (London: Oxford University Press, 1927), pp. 92–93, 109–114.

[16] See J. Abelson, *The Immanence of God in Rabbinical Literature* (New York: Hermon Press, 1969). Jürgen Moltmann discusses the Jewish Kabbalistic notion of God's withdrawing himself from the fullness of space (*zimsum*) in order to make room for creation, relating this to the Christian theology of creation. See his *God in Creation* (Minneapolis: Fortress Press, 1993), pp. 86–93.

[17] Walter Kaufmann, ed., *The Basic Writings of Nietzsche* (New York: Modern Library, 1968), p. 277.

[18] Calvin, *Institutes,* I.xiv.20 and II.vi.1. See also Belden Lane, "Spirituality as the Performance of Desire: Calvin's Metaphor of the World as Theatre of God's Glory," *Spiritus: A Journal of Christian Spirituality* 1:1 (Spring 2001).

[19] See J. B. Harley and David Woodward, eds., *The History of Cartography* (Chicago: University of Chicago Press, 1987), vol. 1, pp. 291, 310.

[20] Quoted in George H. Williams, "Christian Attitudes Toward Nature," *Christian Scholars' Review* 2:2 (Spring 1972), p. 118. See also Clarence Glacken, *Traces on the Rhodian Shore,* pp. 203–205, 239.

[21] *On the Divine Images*, I.16. *Christian Spirituality: Origins to the Twelfth Century*, eds., Bernard McGinn, John Meyendorff, and Jean Leclercq (New York: Crossroad, 1989), p. 384.

[22] Pierre Teilhard de Chardin, *Hymn of the Universe* (New York: Harper & Row, 1961), p. 70. See Ursula King, *Spirit of Fire: The Life and Vision of Teilhard de Chardin* (Maryknoll, New York: Orbis Books, 1996).

[23] *Against the Heresies*, IV. 19.2. See Paul Santmire, *The Travail of Nature* (Philadelphia: Fortress Press, 1985), pp. 31–44.

[24] *Sermons*, 241.2. See Santmire, p. 66.

[25] John Y. Fenton, ed., *Theology and Body* (Philadelphia: Westminster Press, 1974), p. 130.

[26] Quoted in Ram Dass and Paul Gorman, *How Can I Help?* (New York: Alfred A. Knopf, 1985), p. 61.

[27] Matthew Fox, ed., *Meditations with Meister Eckhart* (Santa Fe, New Mexico: Bear & Co., 1983), p. 14.

[28] *The City of God*, 22.24, and *Of True Religion*, 41.77. See Peter Huff, "From Dragons to Worms: Animals and the Subversion of Hierarchy in Augustine's Theology," *Melita Theologica* 48:2 (1992), pp. 27–43.

[29] See Dieter T. Hessel and Rosemary Radford Ruether, eds., *Christianity and Ecology: Seeking the Well-Being of Earth and Humans* (Cambridge: Harvard University Press, 2000), and Leonardo Boff, *Cry of the Earth, Cry of the Poor* (Maryknoll, New York: Orbis Books, 1998).

[30] See Verna Harrison, "The Relationship between Apophatic and Kataphatic Theology," *Pro Ecclesia* 4:3 (Summer 1995), pp. 318–332, and Harvey D. Egan, "Christian Apophatic and Kataphatic Mysticisms," *Theological Studies* 39:3 (September 1978), pp. 399–426.

[31] See Mary Gerhart, "The Word Image Opposition: The Apophatic/Cataphatic and the Iconic/Aniconic Tensions in Spirituality," in Ann W. Astell, ed., *Divine Representations: Postmodernism & Spirituality* (New York: Paulist Press, 1994), pp. 63–79.

[32] The use of the five senses and reconstruction of place are prominent motifs in the *Spiritual Exercises* of Ignatius Loyola. Cf. First Week, Fifth Exercise; Second Week, Fifth Contemplation.

[33] Samuel Terrien, *The Elusive Presence: The Heart of Biblical Theology* (San Francisco: Harper & Row, 1978). Cf. Walter Brueggemann, *The Prophetic Imagination* (Philadelphia: Fortress Press, 1978).

[34] See W. D. Davies, *The Gospel and the Land: Early Christianity and Jewish Territorial Doctrine* (Berkeley: University of California Press, 1974).

[35] Recent studies of apophatic spirituality include Denys Turner, *The Darkness of God: Negativity in Christian Mysticism* (Cambridge: Cambridge University Press, 1995), and Michael Sells, *Mystical Languages of Unsaying* (Chicago: University of Chicago Press, 1994).

[36] Gregory of Nyssa, *The Life of Moses*, II.43–46 and III.152–167; Pseudo-Dionysius, *The Mystical Theology*, I.3; *The Cloud of Unknowing*, 71–73; and John of the Cross, *The Ascent of Mount Carmel*, I.V.6. See Belden C. Lane, *The Solace of Fierce Landscapes: Exploring Desert and Mountain Spirituality* (New York: Oxford University Press, 1998), pp. 100–114.

[37] Thomas Merton joined a love for the apophatic tradition with a fascination for mountain and desert experience. See John F. Teahan, "A Dark and Empty Way: Thomas Merton and the Apophatic Tradition," *Journal of Religion* 58 (1978), pp. 263–287.

[38] Marc Augé, *Non-Places: Introduction to an Anthropology of Supermodernity* (London: Verso, 1995), pp. 96, 104.

[39] Terrence W. Tilley, "Dying Children and Sacred Space," Second Annual Lecture in Catholic Studies at Saint Michael's College, given on April 11, 1989 (published by Saint Michael's College, Toronto, Canada), p. 11.

[40] *Ibid.*, p. 14.

[41] Gregory of Nyssa, *On Pilgrimages*. See *Nicene and Post-Nicene Fathers*, series II, vol. 5, p. 383. See also Doris Donnelly, "Pilgrims and Tourists: Conflicting Metaphors for the Christian Journey to God," *Spirituality Today* 44:1 (Spring 1992), pp. 20–36.

[42] See Thomas Merton, *A Search for Solitude: Pursuing the Monk's True Life*, ed. Lawrence S. Cunningham, vol. 3 of *The Journals of Thomas Merton* (San Francisco: Harper, 1995), pp. 181–182.

[43] Richard Nelson, *The Island Within* (San Francisco: North Point Press, 1989), pp. xii, 45.